Public Sector Reform in Developing Countries

Public Sector Reform in Developing Countries

Capacity Challenges to Improve Services

Edited by

Yusuf Bangura

and

George A. Larbi

© UNRISD 2006

All rights reserved. No reproduction, copy or transmission of this publication may be made without written permission.

No paragraph of this publication may be reproduced, copied or transmitted save with written permission or in accordance with the provisions of the Copyright, Designs and Patents Act 1988, or under the terms of any licence permitting limited copying issued by the Copyright Licensing Agency, 90 Tottenham Court Road, London W1T 4LP.

Any person who does any unauthorized act in relation to this publication may be liable to criminal prosecution and civil claims for damages.

The authors have asserted their rights to be identified as the authors of this work in accordance with the Copyright, Designs and Patents Act 1988.

First published 2006 by
PALGRAVE MACMILLAN
Houndmills, Basingstoke, Hampshire RG21 6XS and
175 Fifth Avenue, New York, N.Y. 10010
Companies and representatives throughout the world

PALGRAVE MACMILLAN is the global academic imprint of the Palgrave Macmillan division of St. Martin's Press, LLC and of Palgrave Macmillan Ltd. Macmillan® is a registered trademark in the United States, United Kingdom and other countries. Palgrave is a registered trademark in the European Union and other countries.

ISBN-13: 978–1–4039–8771–6   hardback
ISBN-10: 1–4039–8771–8   hardback

This book is printed on paper suitable for recycling and made from fully managed and sustained forest sources.

A catalogue record for this book is available from the British Library.

Library of Congress Cataloging-in-Publication Data
Public sector reform in developing countries : capacity challenges to improve services /
    edited by Yusuf Bangura and George A. Larbi.
      p. cm.
    ISBN 1–4039–8771–8 (cloth)
    1. Public administration–Developing countries. 2. Decentralization in government–Developing countries. 3. Fiscal policy–Developing countries. 4. Central-local government relations–Developing countries. 5. Infrastructure (Economics)–Developing countries–Management. I. Bangura, Yusuf, 1950- II. Larbi, George A.

JF60.P865 2006
352.3′67′091724–dc22   2005044510

10 9 8 7 6 5 4 3 2 1
15 14 13 12 11 10 09 08 07 06

Printed and bound in Great Britain by
Antony Rowe Ltd, Chippenham and Eastbourne

Contents

List of Tables, Boxes and Figures

Tables

Boxes

Figure

Preface

The public sectors of many developing countries have experienced profound crises in recent decades. They have lost a great deal of their capacity to deliver services and pursue development programmes more generally. In countries afflicted by war, economic vulnerability and polarization have undermined the coherence and societal reach of state institutions. Public sector reform has been an important objective in recent years as governments and multilateral development agencies recognize the central role of the state in adjustment, poverty reduction and service provision. It is now widely believed that state effectiveness in policy design and intervention accounts for many of the gains associated with global economic restructuring and protection of vulnerable members of society. However, if there is general agreement on the need for public sector reform, there is much disagreement about its content and direction. Most developing countries pursuing public sector reforms are highly indebted. This exposes them to a brand of market-driven reform favoured by creditors and donors.

This book examines the potential and limits of managerial, fiscal and decentralization reforms. Fiscal reforms are the most consistently pursued and tend to influence reforms in the other domains. They are primarily concerned with downsizing, privatization and tax reform. Managerial reforms have been informed by New Public Management approaches, which seek to promote competition or market dynamics in the organization of the public sector. They challenge conventional practices in public administration in which the purchasing, provisioning and policy dimensions of service provision are vested in a unified bureaucracy driven by the values of public service. They posit that public officials are largely motivated by self-interest and will inflate expenditures or oversupply public goods for personal gain because of their monopolistic position in the state sector. Managerial reforms advocate instead decentralized management or executive agencies, performance management schemes and contracting out of services. Decentralization reforms involve the devolution of responsibilities to lower jurisdictions for services such as education, health, sanitation and water to improve the accountability of government providers and to ensure that services meet the needs of the population.

A major paradox of these reforms is that they are being implemented in countries perceived to have the least capacity to do so. There is a very serious problem of reform overload as governments are forced to undertake too many reforms that pay little attention to existing institutions and practices. Most countries are still grappling with the problem of how to create a professional civil service with good record-keeping, financial controls, incentives and sanctions, and that is less beholden to patronage networks. It may well be that countries will need to complete the process of constructing effective public administration systems before applying most of the reforms in New Public Management. In addition, there are major issues of governance relating to how power is exercised and office-holders are held accountable in democratic settings that are yet to be resolved in many countries with elaborate reforms. As the contributors to this book point out, the accountability-yielding powers of managerial reforms are questionable. Markets for the delivery of services are imperfect, implementation of reforms is uneven and there are dangers of regulatory capture by powerful groups or individuals.

This book highlights cases where selective use of some of the reforms has delivered positive results. However, an important conclusion is that while reforms have been ambitious and wide-ranging on paper, they have proved ineffective in improving services. Public sector reforms in poor countries need to be grounded in a policy framework that privileges the developmental role of the state if the goal of improved delivery of services, especially as they affect the poor, is to be achieved.

Thandika Mkandawire
UNRISD Director

Notes on the Contributors

Yusuf Bangura is a Research Co-ordinator at the United Nations Research Institute for Social Development, where he has co-ordinated projects on structural adjustment and livelihood strategies, public sector reform and crisis states, ethnic inequalities and public sector governance, racism and public policy, technocratic policy-making, and democracy and social policy. He has published widely on these issues, including on the politics of international economic relations.

Richard Batley is professor of development administration in the International Development Department of the School of Public Policy, the University of Birmingham. His research interests are in governance, service delivery and urban policy in India, Latin America and Africa. He has led a number of major research programmes, including the Role of Government in Adjusting Economies and the Non-state Providers of Public Services, all funded by the Department For International Development in the United Kingdom. He has also published widely on public sector reform issues. His most recent book is *The Changing Role of Government – the Reform of Public Services in Developing Countries* (Palgrave, 2004) (co-authored with George A. Larbi).

George A. Larbi is senior lecturer in public sector management and governance in the International Development Department of the School of Public Policy, the University of Birmingham. His teaching, research and consultancy interests are in governance, new approaches to public management, service delivery, civil service reform, capacity-building and institutional development. He has experience in Africa, the UK and Kazakhstan. He has published widely on public sector reform issues, and co-authored (with R. Batley) *The Changing Role of Government – the Reform of Public Services in Developing Countries* (Palgrave, 2004).

Willy McCourt is a senior lecturer in human resource management (HRM) at the Institute for Development and Management at the University of Manchester. He has published on HRM and on governance and public management in developing countries, his most recent book (with Derek Eldridge) being *Global Human Resource Management: Managing People in Developing and Transitional Countries* (Edward Elgar, 2005). He has carried out consultancy and research assignments in Africa and Asia on behalf of the Department for International Development in the UK, Danish

International Development Agency, the European Union, the United Nations and the World Bank.

Andrew Nickson is reader in public management and Latin American development at the International Development Department at the University of Birmingham, where he is Director of Post-Graduate Studies. He has extensive worldwide experience of teaching, research and consultancy on public administration reform, decentralization, and regulation of privatized public utilities. From 1992 to 1998 he directed a EU training programme for senior public administrators in Latin America and, from 1999 to 2000, he was seconded to the post of Director of a EU project for state reform in Paraguay. His recent research has focused on private sector participation in urban water supply.

Dele Olowu is Principal Governance Adviser, at the African Development Bank, Tunis, Tunisia (since June 2004). A former professor in the departments of local government and public administration at Obafemi Awolowo University, Ile-Ife, Nigeria (1991–96), he was Adviser at the United Nations Economic Commission for Africa, Addis Ababa, Ethiopia (1995–8) and taught at the Institute of Social Studies, The Hague, Netherlands (1998–2004). He has written extensively on public management issues. His previous publications include: *The Failure of the Centralized State* (Westview Press, 1990); *Better Governance and Public Policy* (ed. with S. Sako, Kumarian, 2002) and *Local Governance in Africa: The Challenges of Democratic Decentralization* (Lynne Rienner, 2004).

Paul Smoke is associate professor and Director of International Programmes at the Robert F. Wagner Graduate School of Public Service at New York University. His research and policy interests focus on public finance, decentralization and urban development, particularly in Asia and Africa. He has also worked extensively with international organizations, including various bilateral and UN agencies and the World Bank. He has authored or edited several books and published in numerous journals, including *World Development, Public Administration and Development, International Journal of Public Administration* and *Public Budgeting and Finance.*

Ole Therkildsen is a Senior Research Fellow at the Danish Institute for International Studies, Copenhagen. His research is mainly on East and Southern Africa. He has published on public sector reform, decentralization, service provision and taxation. Extended residence in East Africa, starting in 1970, and advisory and consultancy work have provided firsthand experience with public sector reform on the ground. He co-edited *Service Provision under Stress in East Africa: the State, NGOs and People's Organisations in Kenya, Tanzania and Uganda* (James Currey, 1996).

Abbreviations and Acronyms

ACBF	African Capacity Building Foundation
AGETIPS	Agences d'Execution des Travaux d'Interêt Public
AGs	Cuerpo de Administradores Gubernamentales
ANC	African National Congress
CONALEP	Colegio Nacional de Educacíon Profesional Técnica
CR	compulsory redundancy
CSA	Civil Servants' Association
CVs	Comisiones Vecinales
DAS	Departamento de Aguas y Saneamiento
DCE	district chief executive
DDC	district development committee
DDF	district development fund
DfID	Department for International Development
DoC	Drivers of Change
EPOS	Empresa Provincial de Obras Sanitarias
ERP	economic restructuring programme
ERSEP	Ente Regulador de Servicios Publicos
ESAF	Enhanced Structural Adjustment Facility
EU	European Union
FMI	Financial Management Initiative
GBS	general budget support
GDP	gross domestic product
GG	good governance
GNP	gross national product
HDI	Human Development Index
HIPC	heavily indebted poor countries
IAT	Instituto para la Adminstración Tributaria
ICAS	Instituto Centroamericano de Salud
IMF	International Monetary Fund
INMETRO	National Institute of Measurements and Technical Norms
LDC	least developed countries
MARE	Ministério da Administração Federal e Reforma do Estado
MDG	millennium development goals
MOF	Ministry of Finance
MPOG	Ministry of Planning, Budget and Management
MTM	market-type mechanism
NGO	non-governmental organization
NPM	New Public Management

OECD	Organization for Economic Co-operation and Development
OPA	Old Public Administration
OSN	Obras Sanitarias de la Nacíon
PIP	Public Investment Programme
PNDA	Programa Nacional de Desarrollo Administrativo
PPS	public-private partnership
PRP	performance-related pay
PSC	Public Service Commission
PSM	Public Sector Management
ROM	Results-Oriented Management
SAL	structural adjustment loan
SECAL	sectoral adjustment loan
SECODAM	Secretaría de Contraloría y Desarrollo Administrativo
SOE	state-owned enterprise
SUNAT	Superintendencia Nacional de Adminstración Tributaria [Peruvian National Tax Authority]
SWAP	sector-wide approach
UK	United Kingdom
UNDP	United Nations Development Programme
UWS	urban water supply
VR	voluntary redundancy

Introduction: Globalization and Public Sector Reform

Yusuf Bangura and George A. Larbi

Introduction and overview

The public sectors of most countries expanded a great deal between 1945 and 1980 despite differences in their economic systems, levels of development and ideologies. As economies grew and societies became highly differentiated, the state's conventional tasks of regulation, allocation and redistribution became more complex. Public sector growth was also a function of the types of societies various governments sought to promote. For instance, commitments to the welfare state and macro-economic stability in OECD countries encouraged acceptance of the state as a central institution for redistributing wealth, protecting the vulnerable and stimulating aggregate demand. Similarly, state-led development strategy was the dominant approach in developing countries. Governments also established parastatals on a wide range of activities because the private sector was perceived to be either too slow to respond to incentives or showed little or no interest in investing in preferred sectors. At the same time a number of enterprises were nationalized, partly or fully. Social services were also expanded as a part of efforts to develop national elites and promote citizenship or solidarity in newly independent states.

Issues of efficiency, representation, participation and accountability, though important, were not central to the growth of the state in most countries, except where democratic forms of rules and markets were already well established. The state was seen essentially as an institution that would foster unity or solidarity, promote national development and macro-economic stability, regulate foreign actors, protect domestic markets and, in some cases, redistribute wealth. This vision of the state came under considerable attack during the 1980s and 1990s in practically every region of the world in the context of fiscal and economic crisis. An alternative vision, embraced in varying degrees among countries, has sought to create a market-friendly, outward-looking, efficient, decentralized, customer-oriented, managerial and democratic state. This vision is underpinned by the

1

New Public Management (NPM) model and informed by a 'good governance agenda', which emerged in the late 1980s. The core elements in the
vision are sometimes contradictory as different social forces drive them in
different national contexts and with varying levels of capabilities. There are
tensions between, on the one hand, concerns for efficiency, market sound-
ness, deregulation, competition and stabilization, and issues of accountability, representation, participation and equity on the other.

The argument and structure of the book

This book reviews and assesses the initiatives, trends and challenges in
public sector reform in the 1990s in developing countries. Two major initiatives have been central to the process of state restructuring: public sector
management reform; and the distribution of governmental power among
competing interests in society. Public sector management reform deals with
issues of fiscal stability, organizational restructuring, managerial efficiency,
capacity-building and public accountability; whereas reforms relating to
the distribution of power are concerned with the promotion of plurality in
the central institutions of government and dispersal of power to lower
authorities. The latter is often referred to as decentralization. Both reforms
are being applied in varying degrees across regions and countries. Despite
the strong pressures for reform, there are fundamental differences
between visions and realities or between theory and practice. The content
and depth of the reforms vary considerably between countries, including
countries within the same region or with similar levels of development.
Organizational cultures and social segmentation, systems of government,
legal constraints, power relations and international donor pressures affect
choice of reform instruments and explain why some reforms have been
more difficult to implement than others.

This book makes four key arguments. First, public sector reforms are
likely to be unsustainable or ineffective if political actors and citizens have
not worked out a framework for sharing and managing governmental
power that will yield a minimum level of consensus about public policies.
The pursuit of reforms under unstable or highly contested political systems
may turn such reforms into technocratic or top-down exercises. This may
invite opposition, non-compliance, indifference or high implementation
slippage. A related – and the second – point is the need to understand the
rationale or missions of states in the period when they were seen as legitimate actors in shaping development. Much recent research, including in
economics, has demonstrated the folly of basing public policies on
assumed perfect competitive markets that will lead to optimal outcomes for
most citizens, sectors and countries. Societies have to contend with both
market and state failure; and the level of government intervention to
correct market failure or promote development cannot be determined *a*

priori. The rush for reforms, especially when driven from outside, has often wreaked havoc in vital institutions that societies had created either to foster national unity, defend disadvantaged groups and regions or support national investments. Reforms that ignore the core developmental missions of states may not only yield poor results but also undermine political settlements and make it difficult to reconstruct failing states, institutions and economies.

Third, reforms should pay special attention to the basic needs of employees. The trend in most crisis-ridden states where downsizing has not led to payment of 'living wages' exposes public servants to multiple survival strategies which may be detrimental to state capacity and administrative efficiency. A number of countries have also faced serious problems of upgrading the technical skills and physical infrastructure of their bureaucracies. Finally, reforms always create winners and losers. Governments and affected groups may need to work out ways of resolving trade-offs and compensatory issues in transparent ways before embarking on reforms that may prove to be unsustainable.

The book is divided into three parts. The first, which contains four chapters, deals with public sector management reforms; the second, comprising two chapters, examines fiscal and employment reforms; and the third, which consists of three chapters, discusses decentralization reforms. The concluding chapter teases out lessons from the experience of implementing public sector reforms in developing countries. The first section of this introductory chapter examines the global issues that are driving public sector reforms. These are discussed under the following headings: financial globalization and fiscal deficits; and adjustment programmes of multilateral agencies and democratization. Section two provides a brief summary of the various components of public sector reforms: fiscal stability and downsizing; managerial efficiency; capacity-building; and public accountability. Sections three, four and five discuss the nine chapters of the book in the context of wider debates on public sector reforms. The concluding section offers suggestions about how to ensure that public sector reforms are accountable to society and sensitive to the political realities of adjusting states, especially those with weak institutions.

Global pressures for public sector reform

Financial globalization and fiscal deficits

Among the forces that are reorienting visions about how national public sectors should be organized, four are of special significance. The first is the spread of global markets, especially those relating to financial integration and liberalization. At the end of 1995, the world's financial markets stood at US$33.5 trillion, of which the equity markets accounted for US$13 trillion and the bond markets US$20 trillion. About three-fifths of the bonds were issued by governments in OECD countries, with two-fifths to cover budget deficits (Warburton, 1999). Bond issues were seen as an alternative to central bank financing (monetization) of deficits, which was believed to be inflationary. Net capital flows to developing countries also expanded greatly from US$8.1 billion in 1970 to about US$200 billion in 1996 (IMF, 1998a). It is reckoned that developing country governments accounted for about 2 per cent of the bonds issued in the international capital markets in 1995.

About 30 big banks and investment institutions dominate the management of the funds that flow through these markets. Within countries, there has been a major process of integration of different financial institutions, such as investment, deposit and retail banks; insurance companies; estate agencies; and pension funds. This has promoted a process of securitization: the transformation of different types of financial assets into bonds. The liberalization of capital controls in the 1980s in many OECD countries has in turn transformed the integration that has taken place in national financial markets into a global phenomenon. Today, a bond may be issued, say, in Jakarta by a public authority, funded in Amsterdam, serviced in London and held as a pension fund in New York.

This process of intermediation has implications for the organization of public sectors and the behaviour of those entrusted to run them. While the choices available to savers and borrowers have increased as a result of financial globalization, the links between the two sets of actors have become progressively weakened (Warburton, 1999). Savers or investors often do not have adequate information about borrowers, especially new borrowers in foreign lands. The potential for fraud, default or poor management is thus high. These outcomes can be disastrous for savers, many of whom now include ordinary pension fund contributors or the public. This may explain in part current concerns in international financial circles for public sector transparency, protection of property rights, sound finance and deregulation. The growth of international finance has the potential to create a standardized form of public sector in countries that are well integrated into the global economy.

The second type of pressure that is changing conventional ideas about the public sector is the fiscal deficits experienced by most states in the 1970s and 1980s. Whereas the average budget balances per GDP for OECD countries between 1960 and 1969 was about 0 per cent, with Japan, Germany and Sweden recording positive balances, in the 1970–79 period average balances turned negative. Deficits were particularly high during the 1975–78 oil price-induced recession: −4.6 per cent in 1975, −4.2 per cent in 1976, −3.4 per cent in 1977 and −3.4 per cent in 1978. A deficit of about 3–4 per cent was common for much of the 1980s, with figures averaging 5–6 per cent of GDP between 1983 and 1986. Deficits of more than 10 per cent of GDP were the norm in Italy, Portugal, Ireland, Greece and Belgium.

Budget deficits were also a problem in developing countries. In Africa, average deficits between 1975 and 1978 were 6.5 per cent of GDP; and about 4 per cent of GDP in the 1980s. In this region, there were many countries with deficits of more than 10 per cent for some years: Liberia, Mauritius, Malawi, Togo, Ghana, Zaire and Zambia, for instance. In Latin America and the Caribbean, the average deficit for 1975–78 was much lower than that for Africa and OECD countries: 2.7 per cent of GDP. Average deficits, however, increased in the region during the 1980s to 5.8 per cent of GDP; and they rose to about 8 per cent of GDP between 1980 and 1986, with Brazil, Belize, Bolivia, Jamaica, Mexico, Nicaragua and Surinam sometimes recording deficits of above 10 and 20 per cent. Deficits in Asian countries averaged 4 per cent between 1975 and 1989. Bangladesh, Burma, Indonesia, Korea, Malaysia and Singapore had deficits of less than 3 per cent (IMF, 1988).

What constitutes a fiscal crisis depends ultimately on how deficits are financed, and whether an economy is growing enough to support deficits that are financed through monetary expansion or borrowing from the central bank. However, Western policy-makers and development analysts in the 1970s and 1980s associated high inflation rates, slow or negative growth, imbalances in external accounts and low domestic investments in most OECD and developing countries with the marked deterioration of government finances. The need to control budget deficits became a major issue in debates about how to get economies out of inflation and recession and promote the private sector. Issues of downsizing, marketization and privatization gained prominence as methods for controlling the fiscal deficits and restructuring the public sector.

Structural adjustment and democratization

The third pressure for reform was ideological. If globalization and the fiscal crisis provided the structural contexts for reform, it was the multilateral institutions, especially the IMF and the World Bank, that offered the arguments, policies and, in many cases, guidance for reforms leading to wide adoption of market approaches in the public sectors of developing countries. However, during the 1980s, the stabilization and adjustment programmes of these institutions focused on market efficiency, not on state reform. The social costs of adjustment, as well as the less than impressive record of implementation of reform and low growth figures in many crisis economies, led to a strong pro-active interest in state reform in the 1990s. The concepts of governance and good governance entered the development debate in the late 1980s and early 1990s in recognition of the need for reforms that address the crisis of governance in the state and to factor in the non-state actors in the development process. The 1997 World Development Report, for instance, affirmed that 'the state is central to economic and social development, not as a direct provider of growth but as a partner, catalyst, and facilitator' (World Bank, 1997: 1); and that 'the deter-mining factor behind ... contrasting developments [among regions] is the effectiveness of the state' (ibid.). In the view of the World Bank, matching the role of the state to its capabilities can create effective states; and, where capabilities are weak, by reinvigorating public institutions.

In the field of public sector reform, the World Bank has focused its support on civil service reform, including pay and employment reform; capacity-building; privatization; decentralization; and the introduction of market mechanisms (e.g. user fees) in public services. The IMF, on the other hand, has concentrated on aggregate fiscal balances, transparent budgetary practices, expenditure controls and tax administration. The key ideas of the Bank and Fund were themselves influenced by insights from new institu-tional economics and principal–agent theory. Of importance here is the view that the public sector is over-bloated and underperforms because state officials pursue their own narrow self-interests rather than the public inter-est; and that it is difficult to extract accountability and good performance from public servants because of the monopoly characteristics of public ser-vices, imperfect information about the abilities and interests of public employees, and the huge transaction costs that would be involved in efforts to write and monitor complete contracts. It is believed that subject-ing the state to greater competition may allow governments and society to overcome these problems.

The fourth pressure for reform came largely from society and is related to the wave of democratization that swept across much of the developing and transitional countries in the 1980s and 1990s. This was closely linked to the emergence and advancement of 'good governance' as a necessary con-dition for development. External donors were instrumental in pushing for democratization as part of good governance. This was reflected in the calls for better forms of representative and accountable government, and dissat-isfaction with the quantity, quality and cost of public service. However, such pressures were not always consistent as other foreign policy and com-mercial interests dictated application of the principles of democratization in specific countries. The Bretton Woods institutions – especially the World Bank – tended, however, to adopt an instrumental view of democracy. It was useful in efforts to curb corruption, change non-performing govern-ments and advance liberalization and pro-property rights policies. Populist forms of democratization that threatened market reforms were viewed with disfavour.

There were efforts by social groups and organizations to adapt to the changes involved in public sector reform and ensure that public and indi-vidual interests were protected. Where reforms were perceived to lead to better services and offered prospects for participation in governance and development, they tended to be welcomed or not strongly opposed. Where they threatened livelihoods and undermined participation and accountability they were resisted or not fully embraced. Perceptions of gains and losses vary a great deal among groups in the public sector and within society generally (Batley and Larbi, 2004). Such ambiguity has allowed external agencies and governments to retain control of the public sector reform agenda even if they have not always received the desired results.

An overview of the core elements in public sector reform

Public sector reforms cover a range of initiatives that seek to achieve four main objectives: fiscal stability; public sector efficiency; state capacity; and public accountability. Reforms dealing with fiscal stability apply to all states, although policies for achieving results may vary across countries. In general, fiscal reforms are the most consistently pursued and far-reaching of public management reforms, with direct implications for the well-being of public sector employees, state capacity and service delivery. They deal with issues of downsizing, privatization and tax reform. Reforms that seek to promote public sector efficiency focus on organizational restructuring and introduction of market or quasi-market principles in the delivery of public services. They address three main issues: decentralized management and the creation of executive agencies out of monolithic bureaucracies; performance management schemes; and contracting out services to the non-state sector. Most of these reforms come under the umbrella of NPM.

The most comprehensive and radical reforms in the field of efficiency promotion and organizational restructuring are in English-speaking OECD countries (e.g. Australia, New Zealand and the United Kingdom). However, aspects of these reforms are being applied in many developing and transition economies, through either coercive or voluntary policy transfer. The former applies mainly to countries that are heavily dependent on donors for the financing of government activities. As these reforms deal with institutional issues, there is often a wide gap between expressed goals and concrete outcomes, even in OECD countries (Ridley, 1996; Pollitt and Boukaert, 2000). Pre-reform administrative styles or methods of work, bureaucratic rivalry, institutional inertia, weak capacity and, in some cases, market failures act as serious constraints on implementation.

Capacity-building reforms tend to be restricted largely to the developing world, especially the 'least developed countries', most of which are in Africa. They became more prominent from the mid-1990s after the failures in implementing structural reforms in the 1980s and early 1990s exposed serious capacity weaknesses. They address issues relating to the technical capacities of civil servants in policy analysis and monitoring; strengthening of training institutions; improvement of human resource and financial management systems; public investments; and pay and incentive reforms. In more recent years reforms have reinforced a focus on service delivery and improvement in accountability between providers and citizens (World

Bank, 2003). Among the instruments that have emerged for the attainment of these goals are Citizens' Charters, Ombudsmen and service delivery or user surveys.

Promotion of plurality in central institutions of government and dispersal, or decentralization of power to lower authorities, are also key reform themes. Decentralization itself is an attempt to broaden the plurality of politics and prevent the concentration of power in a few hands, ethnic groups or regions. Much of the political decentralization that has taken place in developing countries has been carried out as part of wider programmes of public sector reforms. Of the four broad areas of reform, the international financial institutions attach primary importance to fiscal stability, followed, in descending order, by managerial efficiency reforms, capacity-building reforms and public accountability.

Managerial reform

Reforms dealing with managerial efficiency focus largely on the core, non-enterprise sector of the public service: central administrative, economic and social service ministries; the police; prisons and local government. Issues of managerial efficiency have also emerged in public enterprises that governments have been unwilling or unable to privatize. In general, privatization is believed to be an inappropriate instrument of reform in the core civil service sector. However, in the last 10–15 years, efforts have been made to subject this core public sector to market pressures or restructuring. As problems of administrative efficiency, accountability and corruption become entrenched in many countries, governments have sought to reform their civil service in order to be competitive in the world market as well as respond better to public demands for improved services.

Chapter 1 by George A. Larbi provides an overview of the NPM and its application in developing countries. Larbi discusses NPM in developing countries, using three of its core elements: decentralized management; performance management schemes; and contracting out public services to the private sector. The basic claim of NPM, based on public choice theory, is that traditional public administration, characterized by excessive regulations and hierarchical chains of command and division of labour, cannot work in a rapidly changing and information-based environment.

Among NPM reforms, decentralized management has been one of the key trends in developing countries and has taken different forms. These include breaking up large bureaucracies into multiple, semi-autonomous or executive agencies and corporatization of public enterprises. These have been complemented by devolution of budgets and financial controls and separation of production and provisioning functions. In the 1980s and early 1990s, decentralized management reforms in developing countries were largely found in the health sector and revenue-generating departments and units, such as customs and excise and internal revenue or tax offices. From the mid-1990s corporatization (i.e. incorporation of public organizations) became a common instrument as a way of restructuring public enterprises that could not be privatized. Larbi concludes by discussing the limitations of NPM, the capacity challenges of implementation of reforms in developing countries and the need to strengthen the capacity of the state to play its role in regulating, enabling and monitoring markets.

In recent years, however, developing countries have started to embrace more extensive forms of decentralized management reforms. Bilateral donors and multilateral agencies have been the main drivers for these reforms. Chapter 2 by Ole Therkildsen reviews some of these experiences in Tanzania, Uganda and Zimbabwe. Managerial reforms, which come under the rubric of 'Organization and Efficiency Reviews', were initiated in Tanzania in the mid-1990s. The aim was to separate the core policy-making and regulatory functions of ministries from those dealing with implementation. The latter was to be handled by executive agencies, not the ministries. The result has been a 25 per cent reduction in the number of ministerial departments. Activities that were unsuited for privatization or provisioning were transferred to 47 agencies, which would be concerned with delivery. The government's reform programme stated unambiguously that the aim of the exercise was 'to reduce the role of the public sector and make it efficient'.

A similar process is underway in Uganda. Therkildsen highlights three major restructuring exercises in the 1990s. The last, which started in 1998, deals with 'Results-Oriented Management' and 'Output-Oriented Budgeting'. It seeks to divest all service delivery functions from the central government. This has necessitated a major restructuring of local governments and reorganization of central ministries. Twelve out of 22 ministries have lost about 50 per cent of their functions. It is anticipated that at the end of the restructuring exercise there will be 17 ministries, various commissions and tertiary institutions, and 107 autonomous and semi-autonomous agencies, which will be self-accounting and with powers to hire and fire. Services that cannot be privatized or devolved would be corporatized; and ministries would be concerned only with policy-making, co-ordination, national standard-setting, monitoring and support for local governments; 54,000 civil servants are expected to lose their jobs at the end of the exercise (Therkildsen, 1999).

Chapter 3 by Andrew Nickson discusses the potential and limits of managerial reforms in Latin America. One of his case studies focuses on the reform of the tax administration system in Peru. By 1990, a bout of hyperinflation and serious macro-economic mismanagement had reduced Peru's tax revenue to 4.9 per cent of GNP. The tax office was riddled with corruption and staffs were badly paid. Under strong external pressure, the government of Alberto Fujimori introduced radical reform and created a new tax authority, SUNAT, independent of the Ministry of Economy and

Finance and accountable only to the presidency. Two-thirds of the staff were dismissed and replaced by recent graduates on short-term contracts. SUNAT also introduced a new, simplified tax system and a strictly level playing field for the treatment of taxpayers. This produced swift results: by 1993, the tax ratio had risen to 13 per cent of GDP. SUNAT became an elite corps of the civil service. Since then, however, some of the old problems have resurfaced. As the macro-economic situation improved, some of the pressure was reduced and SUNAT started to acquire traditional features of public administration – with evidence of favouritism to certain taxpayers. The government repeatedly changed the head of SUNAT, which weakened managerial cohesion. In 1997, plans for a wider reform of public administration were abandoned.

An important feature of New Public Management reforms is the development of performance contracts, which have been used extensively in public enterprise reforms as part of efforts to improve productivity and service delivery. Despite their well-known problems in the state enterprise sector, there have been efforts to promote performance contracts in the core public sector itself as managerial reforms take root in developed and developing countries. Therkildsen reports that South Africa's new public service regulations of 1998 emulated the New Zealand model by calling for the establishment of performance contracts between ministers and their chief executives and performance management mechanisms for all employees. In Tanzania, a 'Performance Improvement Component' scheme constitutes a central aspect of the managerial reforms: ministries are expected to make annual plans with budget ceilings and set clear targets, including performance indicators. In Uganda, concrete and measurable performance targets are to be set for all ministries, departments, units and officers under its 'Results-Oriented Management' scheme. A performance management system, involving top civil servants only, was introduced in Zimbabwe in 1994. Ministers and the President's Office were to review the work plans of chief executives, which were expected to specify outputs and targets. The scheme was, however, abandoned in 1996 because of problems of implementation.

Related to the issue of performance contracts is the policy of contracting out of public service provisioning to the private sector. Contracting out is often regarded as the most advanced form of marketization in managerial reforms especially where privatization has been ruled out. Because of its emphasis on market competition, the World Bank (1995) rates it best in its survey of three types of contracts in developing and transition economies, the others being performance contracts and regulatory contracts. Contracting out policies are believed to stimulate competition on the supply side and offer governments greater choice in the provision of public services.

As Larbi reveals, municipal services in a number of countries are now being contracted out as part of wider efficiency-enhancing public sector reforms. This has led to an explosion of service-oriented non-governmental organizations, especially in countries where the private sector is weak to respond to the new reforms. But there are also cases of strong private sector participation in contracting out schemes: road maintenance in Brazil; non-clinical health services in Zimbabwe; port management in Malaysia; plantations in Sri Lanka; airports in the Philippines; sugar companies in Guyana and Kenya; and hotels in Egypt and Bulgaria, for instance.

How have managerial reforms fared to date? Have they brought about changes in the way government bureaucracies operate? Have markets developed sufficiently enough to change the way agencies do business in the public sector? Has efficiency improved? Is the public better served by these reforms? Given the relatively short period in which countries have embraced the new approaches in public sector reforms, empirical studies on the subject are limited and good surveys are only beginning to emerge. Most of the good case studies on decentralized management and quasi-markets focus on the UK and, to some extent, New Zealand experiences (Ferlie et al., 1996; Lane, J.-E., 1997). Data on performance contracts and contracting out are more extensive, and some cover developing countries.

Chapter 4 by Richard Batley and George Larbi reports on the performance of specific reforms meant to redefine the role government in a number of developing countries in Africa, Asia and Latin America. These include the decentralization of service delivery management; the application of charges to users of services; privatizing and contracting out the delivery and management of public services; and the development of enabling and regulatory roles by public agencies. They argue that governments in poor developing countries may be ill equipped to adopt unfamiliar approaches to public service provision, where the conditions on which new management practices are premised may not be present. Whilst they find a broad trend of the widespread adoption by governments of the language of management reform, there has been generally much weaker implementation especially in the case of the health and water sectors. However, where these reforms are effectively implemented, there is evidence that they have a positive impact on the efficiency and responsiveness of services.

Bately and Larbi highlight a number of factors that explain the poor performance of the new managerial approaches in developing countries. These range from the difficult circumstances of reform to the challenge that they represent to vested interests, which often oppose or sabotage reforms, and to the power of citizens and policy-makers to direct providers. There are also questions about the organizational and professional capacity to implement them and about the institutional or governance conditions on which they depend. As Larbi in Chapter 1 and Batley and Larbi in Chapter 4 point out, outcomes in managerial reforms have been ambiguous in developing countries. In Ghana's health sector, for instance, devolved units lack real authority to hire and fire or to manage their own budgets independently of central authority. Centralization is linked to the wider structural adjustment programme itself, which demands strict fiscal control and centralized supervision to contain costs.

Capacity problems have also emerged in the decentralized management reforms. Decentralized management requires good monitoring, inspection and information systems, sound budgetary control systems, development of reliable performance indicators and measurements, and capacity to manage relations between central ministries and the multitude of decentralized agencies, including extraction of harmonization and accountability from the new institutions. In most poor developing countries these capacities are weak or non-existent. Batley and Larbi reinforce these observations.

The implementation of performance management schemes has also experienced some problems. In Zimbabwe the system was discontinued because ministers were worried that top civil servants would use it to create 'personal empires', 'regional cliques' and 'ethnic enclaves' (Therkildsen, Chapter 2). Studies have also shown that managers can manipulate information on performance management indicators: targets may be set low; governments can also fail to set clear objectives and priorities or, indeed, be fully committed to the contracts. Patronage methods of employment in the public service may act as important constraints (World Bank, 1995; Shirley and Xu, 1997). Serious capacity issues ranging from non-competitive markets to problems of patronage and poor regulatory and monitoring institutions also affect contracting out policies.

Fiscal reform

Managerial reforms are linked to concerted efforts by governments and multilateral financial institutions to reduce the size and cost of the state and restructure the various components of its spending activities. Policies have focused on the expenditure and revenue sides of the fiscal problem. In addition, privatization has been used as an instrument to support the goals of fiscal stability and state contraction. Governments have also adopted wide-ranging reforms related to pay and employment as part of efforts to promote fiscal discipline and competitiveness. Part II of this book discusses these issues in detail.

Chapter 5 by Yusuf Bangura examines the ways in which governments have pursued fiscal reforms, their effects on fiscal stability and state contraction or growth, as well as their social implications. Governments have made some changes on the revenue side, but most have concentrated their budget stability strategies on cutting public expenditure. During the 1960s, in most countries, public expenditure as a percentage of GDP was maintained at around 20 per cent. But by the 1980s, the figures had risen rapidly. Most developing regions were averaging around 25 per cent, while the industrialized countries were averaging considerably more. There were differences in patterns of expenditure. By and large, developing countries were devoting their funds to capital expenditure, public sector wages and government administration and spending relatively little on education and health. The industrialized countries, on the other hand, were devoting more of their expenditure to social security transfers and social services – with a particular emphasis on health. Public expenditure cuts reflected these differences. However, developing countries were more successful at cutting expenditure than industrialized ones. Developing country governments did not face powerful popular resistance to cuts compared to industrialized countries. Governments in developing countries also had their resolve stiffened by the IMF and the World Bank, which recommended public expenditure reviews and cash budgets as strategies to reduce chronic budget deficits.

The social sector has been negatively affected by public expenditure cuts. For a group of 21 countries in Africa, social expenditure between 1980 and 1990 fell from 4.6 to 2.7 per cent of GDP. The World Bank also cut some of its social spending in the 1980s. A comparison of 1972–82 and 1982–88 shows that its education expenditure (in 1990 dollars) fell from US$0.5 per person to US$0.3 (World Bank, 1994). Following widespread criticism, the Bank subsequently reviewed its policies. Now it requires borrowing countries not only to reduce expenditures, but also to restructure them, with more emphasis on basic education and primary health care. Recent improvements recorded for 32 low-income countries by the IMF – an average increase of real per capita expenditure of 2.8 per cent between 1985 and 1996 – seem small when set against overall needs.

Privatization is an important component of fiscal reform. It is partly a way of raising funds and partly a method of reducing or ending subsidies to loss-making enterprises. Between 1990 and 1996, developing and transition countries divested US$155 billion of their assets to the private sector. Governments in Latin America led the way, accounting for more than half of these sales, which they used largely to finance their deficits. Sales in Africa were much slower. The transition countries of Eastern Europe were more active but did not raise much revenue, since governments effectively gave away many enterprises via voucher schemes or sold them at lower prices to a privileged elite.

As Bangura reports in Chapter 5, there are institutional and social problems associated with privatization. Although there is a sound case for privatizing many manufacturing enterprises, the case is less strong for public sector utilities. These are frequently monopolies that, after privatization, may be tempted to raise prices, with disastrous consequences for the poor. A strong regulatory system may help to mitigate the adverse consequences of privatization. But even industrialized countries have had problems regulating private utilities. Because of their relatively weak institutions, developing countries have found it even more difficult to regulate private entrepreneurs that buy public utilities. In Argentina, for instance, regulators have proved less powerful than the utility companies, and have effectively been colonized by the interests they were designed to control. Andrew Nickson pursues the issue of privatization with a focus on the water sector and effects on the poor, within the context of municipal-level government in Chapter 9.

Another negative social outcome of privatization is unemployment. Public enterprises in developing countries usually account for a high proportion of formal sector employment – 22 per cent in Africa. Prior to sale, governments frequently lay off workers as a way of making the company more attractive to buyers, and afterwards the privatized companies continue the process as way of cutting costs. Privatization has also altered the social landscape because the process has frequently been distorted in favour of powerful groups. In transition economies, privatization has often benefited managers and workers in the most viable enterprises. In developing countries, privatization can benefit individuals from more powerful ethnic groups as the cases of Malaysia, Nigeria, Zambia and Mozambique suggest.

The provision of adequate remuneration to public sector employees is central to the development of effective public sectors. Willy McCourt addresses this issue in Chapter 6. Modern bureaucracies are founded on the premise that individuals who work in them will serve the public good as opposed to catering to personal or sectional interests. This presupposes a basic income that will allow public servants to carry out their duties without succumbing to extraneous pressures. However, the real incomes of public servants in low-income countries have fallen sharply over the years. Data by Schiavo-Campo (1998) suggest that pay declined somewhat as a proportion of GDP per capita in developing countries as a whole between the early 1980s and early 1990s. The average central government wage bill as a percentage of GDP per capita is estimated to have fallen in Africa from 6.1 per cent in the early 1980s to 4.8 per cent in the early 1990s; in Latin America from 2.7 per cent to 2.3 per cent; and in OECD countries from 1.7 per cent to 1.6 per cent. The data for Asia show an increase from 2.9 per cent to 3.8 per cent over the same period. The IMF reports that real wages declined in nine out of a panel of eighteen ESAF countries during its loan disbursement period, although a few countries like Uganda and Bolivia showed significant increases (IMF, 1998c). The complex ways in which many public servants have responded to the pay crisis – diverting time and resources to private ends and the floating of sideline activities in the informal economy – have further eroded the administrative capacities of these states.

McCourt highlights five principal problems governments have identified with respect to pay: inadequate pay across the board; opaque remuneration systems; unclear links between pay and responsibilities; ambiguous links between pay and performance; and insufficient attention to retain employees with scarce skills. Reform-oriented governments have addressed these problems in different ways: from across-the-board pay increases to consolidation of remuneration, job evaluation, promotion of performance-related pay and pay decompression. The move from opaque to consolidated systems of remuneration involves calculation of real market values for such benefits as housing, transport, health and education grants and adding them to the nominal wage to arrive at a consolidated package for employees. One exercise in this direction in Uganda transformed a previous compression ratio between the highest and lowest paid staff of 1:6.8 to 1:100. The policies of linking pay to responsibilities and pay to performance are somewhat similar to the managerial reforms considered in previous sections. Except in Malaysia where such schemes are believed to be fully operational, not many countries have embraced performance-related pay reforms in their core public sector. The problems are similar to those discussed under managerial reforms: capacity deficiencies, problems of fairness, nepotism and difficulties in quantifying the real performance of civil servants. It is reported that even in Malaysia, the civil service union and some senior officials are very hostile to the scheme.

Pay decompression has been a central policy of governments and donor agencies. Pursuit of relatively egalitarian pay policies at independence in some countries and the economic crisis of the 1970s and 1980s led to a massive compression of wages between top- and bottom-scaled civil servants in most crisis states. In Zambia, for instance, there was a distinct process of wage compression in the 1970s and 1980s: from 17:1 to 3.7:1. However, there has been a trend in the 1980s towards a policy of decompression in many countries. In Ghana, for instance, the ratio changed from 2.2:1 in 1984 to 10:1 in 1991; and in 1993, the government of Tanzania pursued a policy of raising the compression ratio from 5.74:1 to 12:1.

The World Bank and other agencies have tried to link the policy of wage decompression to retrenchment in order to encourage governments to pay living wages to the small number of public employees who will remain in the service, as well as offer attractive salaries to senior officials. This policy has only been vigorously pursued in a few countries – Uganda, Bolivia and, to some extent, Ghana in the 1980s, for instance. In these countries, governments have made a strong commitment to get out of the low wage–corruption–low morale – a low performance trap that has bedevilled their public services. They have done this by carrying out massive retrenchments. Other countries have been ambivalent in pursuing this policy because of the problems of unemployment and severance costs, as well as resistance from potentially affected groups. Governments that opt for massive retrenchment of employees are faced with very large compensation packages, which they must offer to staff to obtain compliance. It has been estimated that redundancy benefits accounted for no less than 2 per cent of government expenditure during the first five years of Ghana's voluntary retirement scheme. There is also a manpower substitution problem even when staff have agreed to retire from the service: they get re-employed as consultants. McCourt has observed this development in South Africa, Sri Lanka and Malaysia.

Even in countries that have made big strides in restoring living wages in their public services, the problem of paying competitive wages that will retain or attract the best staff remains. It is interesting to note that one of the attributes of countries such as those in East Asia that are reputed to have strong, developmental states has been payment of competitive salaries to their public servants to enable them supervise the process of industrialization and development. In Singapore, for instance, civil servants are believed to enjoy even superior salaries to their counterparts in the private sector. Salaries are still much too low in most crisis-ridden and adjusting countries and hardly compare with what they were in real terms in the early 1970s. An additional problem is that the wage share of recurrent expenditures has increased significantly in many countries. This is the case in seven out of eight countries in East and Southern Africa examined in Chapter 2 by Therkildsen. Such increases may, of course, affect resources for other service delivery inputs. Thus, low-income countries face two serious problems in pay and recurrent costs reforms: wages are outrageously low to motivate staff, and even where increases have occurred they have not been enough to meet basic living costs; yet the increases that have occurred seem to have been at the expense of other vital recurrent inputs. How to improve public sector pay and the quantity of other inputs that are essential for efficient service delivery is a challenge that crisis states need to confront in their reform programmes.

Decentralization reform

Governance reforms are among the key contextual factors shaping public sector reforms since the early 1990s, especially in poor developing countries. In practice they reinforce the case for institutional and organizational reforms in the public sector. They, *inter alia*, emphasize political legitimacy, accountability and responsiveness to citizens, but also a competent and efficient public sector, as well as a strong participatory civil society. Governance also makes the issues of representation and accountability at national and local levels important in public sector reform.

The last three chapters of this book address three important problems of governance: decentralization; capacity issues arising from reform of organizational arrangements in public services; and service delivery. There have been two main arguments for decentralization. The first focuses on public sector efficiency. It is argued that an optimal level of service provision is likely to be attained if power is devolved to local authorities, which are closer to the people and, therefore, likely to respond better to their preferences. Local governments are assumed to fare better than central governments on matters relating to allocation of public resources than on issues of redistribution and stabilization. The issues related to this argument are reviewed in Chapter 7 by Paul Smoke. The second argument treats decentralization as a conflict-resolution mechanism, especially in multi-ethnic societies. If ethnic groups are geographically separated from each other, competition for central resources and power may be lessened by granting local autonomy to groups. Chapter 8 by Bamidele Olowu addresses these issues.

The two arguments for decentralization, though interconnected, may sometimes lead to different dynamics and types of local governments. For instance, if the goal of decentralization is efficiency in service delivery, the optimal size and boundaries of local governments may not correspond to preferred ethnic political boundaries. This is because optimality must take into account issues of economies of scale, for services such as electricity generation and water supply, and inter-jurisdictional externalities (both positive and negative) for activities such as road construction and taxes. The optimal size of a local government under such conditions may well be larger than one that may be created as a response to ethnic conflict or democratization.

What is the record of decentralization in developing countries? Olowu provides an overview of decentralization reforms in Africa. He develops a framework for assessing the extent to which central power has been devolved to lower authorities in Uganda, Côte d'Ivoire, Nigeria, Ghana and Ethiopia. These five countries are among the countries in Africa that are believed to have made progress in decentralization. Olowu divides the trends in decentralization in Africa into four phases. The first, which coincided with decolonization, is generally regarded as the golden age of decentralization. Departing colonial authorities introduced elected local councils, well-defined local tax systems, and devolved powers for local authorities in minimal infrastructure services, cooperatives and community development.

Local governments lost their powers during the second phase of decentralization, which coincided with the early period of independence. Concerns for nation-building and the prevalence of one-party and military governments made it difficult for governments to devolve real power to local or district authorities. From this period until the 1990s, the most common form of decentralization was deconcentration – the delegation of powers to lower organs within the same administrative or ministerial system. The third phase of decentralization is linked to the adoption of structural adjustment programmes in the 1980s and the creation of district development agencies or funds under central government supervision or control. The democratization wave of the 1990s is associated with the fourth wave of decentralization.

Olowu develops seven indicators to assess decentralization in the five countries: allocation of responsibilities for services between central and local governments; decentralization of financing arrangements; decentralization of decision-making powers; management of the personnel of decentralized services; enforcement of local government accountability; involvement of non-state actors in the delivery of services; and political competition at local levels. Based on this framework, Uganda and Côte d'Ivoire score higher aggregate points on decentralization than Ethiopia, Nigeria and Ghana. However, Olowu reports that few countries have pursued political competition and democratic decentralization at the same time. Many governments prefer democratic decentralization within the context of a *de facto* one-party state. Experiences in Uganda, Ethiopia, Côte d'Ivoire and, until recently, Ghana vividly illustrate this point in his five cases.

Chapter 7 by Paul Smoke discusses the fiscal aspects of decentralization. This deals with the potential and problems of granting greater fiscal roles to local governments. Local governments have traditionally played a very small fiscal role in developing countries. In the 1980s, whereas local governments in OECD countries accounted for 11 per cent of total public employment, in developing countries they accounted for an average of only 4.5 per cent, ranging from 2.5 per cent in Africa to 8 per cent in Asia. A similar pattern emerges in public expenditures: data for the 1980s and 1990s suggest that local governments accounted for 32 per cent of total government spending in OECD countries as opposed to only 15 per cent in developing countries.

It is difficult to make generalizations about fiscal decentralization. There are serious data problems especially for low-income countries. Even when fiscal data are available, huge differences among countries in the way they are classified make comparisons difficult. There are also differences between unitary and federal governments in the devolution of decision-making and tax powers. The structure and characteristics of decentralized institutions vary a lot among countries, as is highlighted in the case studies of Kenya, Ethiopia and Uganda. Decentralized levels of government may also vary according to their degree of autonomy in raising revenue and taking decisions on expenditures.

Smoke assesses the desirability of fiscal decentralization on the basis of five popular claims: its stimulus to development; its macro-economic effects; its distributional impacts; its contribution to social service delivery; and its improvement of accountability to local citizens. Although most of the recent empirical evidence suggests a negative correlation between fiscal decentralization and growth, Smoke points out that the issue is far from resolved. He also points out that although inter-jurisdictional tax competition may occur among local governments and central ministries, it is not likely to be a serious problem. Absolute levels of most local taxes are fairly low and of little significance when compared to what firms pay to central governments. He concludes that the relationship between decentralization and development could be synergistic under the right conditions. He finds the empirical evidence on the negative effects of fiscal decentralization and macro-economic policies to be mixed and anecdotal. Fiscal decentralization in most developing countries is nowhere near the level of power and influence enjoyed by Brazil's state governments, whose fiscal behaviour negatively affected the central government's stabilization programmes in the 1990s.

Smoke reports that empirical studies on the distributional effects of decentralization and on the links between decentralization and service delivery are scant, and the evidence on participation and accountability is mixed. He concludes his chapter by highlighting core elements that he believes are conducive to a good fiscal decentralization programme: an adequate enabling environment; assignment of appropriate functions to local governments; assignment of appropriate revenues to local governments; developing an appropriate inter-governmental transfer system; and developing adequate local access to investment capital.

Chapter 9 by Andrew Nickson discusses the extent and ways in which the privatization of water has addressed the needs of the urban poor in the municipality of Córdoba, Argentina, as well the implications for capacity-building within the municipal government itself. The return to civil rule in the 1980s provided a strong impetus for decentralization, especially municipal-level autonomy, in much of Latin America. The municipality of Córboda is governed by a directly elected mayor and legislature. Under new constitutional arrangements, the municipality is granted a wide range of responsibilities, most of which are shared with the provincial government. The history of local government reveals, however, a political culture of clientelism in which short-term party interests determine the dynamics of provincial and local government. Nickson highlights the rather unusual arrangement in which responsibility for sanitation services was transferred to the municipality but water delivery remained the responsibility of the provincial government. His research suggests that the provincial government was unable to initiate and prepare its own documents during the negotiations on the contract, and reacted largely to the proposal offered by the concessionaire. The specific needs of the poor were not incorporated in the contract. Since the municipality was not formally involved in the negotiations, its capacity to monitor and evaluate the efficiency and effectiveness of the service was limited. The situation is further complicated when provincial and municipal governments are run by different political parties. Although there were marked improvements in the supply of water, 14 per cent of city dwellers did not receive water from the piped network operated by the concessionaire. Nickson uses the experiences of Córboda to highlight a number issues that will help promote effective public–private partnerships at local government levels.

Conclusion

This Introduction has provided a survey of the complex public sector reforms that governments and multilateral agencies have tried to pursue in the 1990s, the problems such reforms have encountered in various countries and regions, as well as their social and institutional effects. There are tremendous global pressures to change the character and functions of states. Neoliberal reformers have attacked the state's post-war nationalistic, hierarchical, redistributive and interventionist character. They seek to transform the state and its institutions into a market-oriented, lean, managerial, decentralized and customer-friendly institution. Some countries have made much progress in this transformation, but the majority of states, especially those in developing countries, have problems implementing the reforms because of capacity and institutional constraints. There is a wide gap between reform visions and realities. It is true that most countries have implemented at least some aspects of the reforms during the 1990s, but results in many cases have not been positive. The biggest efforts in reforms have been in downsizing and fiscal stability.

There is evidence that the sizes of central governments measured in terms of government expenditure per GDP and public employees per total employment outlays have shown signs of shrinkage in the late 1990s in some regions despite their stable, and in some cases growing, levels in the 1980s; and that fiscal imbalances are less than they were for most reform governments in the late 1990s. It is not clear, however, whether this trend will be sustained in most countries. Low-income, highly indebted and primary commodity-producing countries have had difficulties maintaining stable fiscal balances. There are also welfare, employment, ethnic and other social factors associated with downsizing and marketization, which are likely to affect the sustainability of the reforms.

The gradual, though sometimes ambiguous, acceptance by the World Bank of New Public Management reforms and the role of bilateral donors with experience of such reforms in their own countries have led to the export of managerial reforms in low-income countries. Whether these reforms will be effective in making civil servants deliver good services to the public is open to question because of the weak institutions and capacities of crisis states. Capacity-building reforms that would improve the pay and technical skills of public servants as well as facilitate proper management of recurrent costs, though extremely important and a precondition for serious reform, have not received the sustained attention they deserve.

We conclude with suggestions about how to ensure that reforms are socially accountable and sensitive to political realities in developing countries. Many of the principles that guide the reforms assume that there is a standardized or ideal form of government – that there is a global process of convergence in which countries will move from Old Public Administration

(OPA) to New Public Management (NPM). But as Nickson (Chapter 3) and Batley and Larbi (Chapter 4) point out, many of the poorest countries have yet to achieve the OPA stage. They lack a professional civil service and rely a lot on patronage and informal networks. In these circumstances, trying to transform existing bureaucracies along NPM lines may create little more than an empty managerial shell. Countries need to complete the process of building effective OPAs before embarking on NPM.

Reforms of the public sector cannot simply be managerial or technocratic exercises. They need to be firmly rooted in what citizens see as the mission of their state. The state's mission will undoubtedly vary according to local circumstances and levels of development. At its core the mission is not managerial, it is social. As Therkildsen (Chapter 2) notes, public sector reforms may appear technical, but they are always 'highly political and conflictual' as they 'go to the heart of who governs'. People want to move towards societies that are prosperous, equitable and harmonious. The basis for any reform must thus be broad political consensus. This consensus must be anchored on the ground rules of democracy and plural or equitable forms of representation that many countries are still struggling to construct.

References

Batley, R. A. and G. A. Larbi (2004) *The Changing Role of Government: The Reform of Public Services in Developing Countries*, Basingstoke: Palgrave.

Ferlie, E., L. Ashburner, L. Fitzgerald and A. Pettigrew (1996) *The New Public Management in Action*, Oxford: Oxford University Press.

IMF, *International Finance Statistics Yearbook* (1988) Washington, DC: International Monetary Fund.

IMF (1988a) *World Economic Outlook* (October), Washington DC: International Monetary Fund.

IMF (1988b) *Global Development Finance: Analysis and Summary Tables*, Washington, DC: World Bank.

IMF (1988c) *Fiscal Reforms in Low-Income Countries Experience under IMF-Supported Programs*, by a team led by G. T. Abed, Occasional Paper No. 160, Washington, DC: International Monetary Fund.

Lane, J-E. (1997) *Public Sector Reform: Rationale, Trends and Problems*, London: Sage.

Pollitt, C. and G. Boukaert (2000) *Poblic Management Reform: A Comparative Analysis*, Oxford: Oxford University Press.

Ridley, F. (1996) 'The New Poblic Management in Europe: Comparative Perspectives', *Public Policy and Administration*, Vol. 11, No. 1: 16–29.

Schiavo-Campo, S. (1998) 'Government Employment and Pay: The Global and Regional Evidence', *Public Administration and Development*, Vol. 18.

Shirley, M. and C. L. Xu (1997) 'Information, Incentives, and Commitment: An Empirical Analysis of Contracts between Government and State Enterprises', World Bank Working Papers (www.worldbank.org).

Therkildsen, O. (1999) *Efficiency, Accountability and Implementation: Public Sector Reform in East and Southern Africa*. UNRISD Programme Paper: Democracy, Governance and Human Rights. No. 3.

Warburton, P. (1999) *Debt and Delusion: Central Follies that Threaten Economic Disaster*, London: Penguin.

World Bank (1994) *The World Bank's Role in Human Resource Development in Sub-Saharan Africa: Education, Training, and Technical Assistance*; by Ronald Ridker. A World Bank Operations Evaluation Study, Washington, DC.

World Bank (1995) *Bureaucrats in Business: The Economics and Politics of Government Ownership*. A World Bank Policy Research Report, Oxford: Oxford University Press.

World Bank (1997) *World Development Report: The State in a Changing World*, Oxford: Oxford University Press.

World Bank (2003) *World Development Report: Making Services Work for Poor People*, Oxford: Oxford University Press.

Part I
Managerial Reform

1
Applying the New Public Management in Developing Countries

George A. Larbi

Introduction

The past two and half decades have seen waves of public sector manage-ment reforms sweeping through, first developed countries, then developing countries and transitional countries. These reforms have sought to redefine the role and institutional character of the state and of the public sector to be more market-oriented and private sector-oriented, initially in English-speaking developed countries (notably Australia, New Zealand the UK) from the late 1970s through the 1980s. In recent years a number of transi-tional and developing countries have adopted similar reforms, often under the influence of international financial institutions and external donors. This has been a product of a number of factors, including the economic and fiscal crises of the state which called into serious question the post-war consensus on the active role of the state in the economy. In developed economies the crisis in the Keynesian welfare state led to the search for alternative ways of organizing and managing public services and redefining the role of the state to give more prominence to markets and competition, and to the private and voluntary sectors. In a similar vein, the economic and fiscal crises that engulfed most developing countries in the 1970s and 1980s led to a rethinking of state-led development, which had increased the size, functions, power and the cost of the state and its bureaucracy.

A survey by the Organization for Economic Co-operation and Development (OECD) in the early 1990s concluded that new management techniques and practices involving market-type mechanisms associated with the private for-profit sector were being used to bring about changes in the management of public services in countries that have widely varying governance, economic and institutional environments (OECD, 1993a). These practices and techniques have conventionally been labelled the New Public Management (NPM) or the new managerialism (Hood, 1991; Pollitt,

1993; Ferlie et al., 1996; Lane, 2000; Christensen and Lægreid, 2002; Flynn, 2002a).

The components of NPM have evolved over the years and there is no consensus among writers on the subject of its content. However, its core feature is the attempt to introduce or simulate, within those sections of the public service that are not privatized, the performance incentives and the disciplines that exist in a market environment (Moore et al., 1994: 13). The assumption is that there are benefits in terms of efficiency and effectiveness in exposing public sector activities to market pressures and in using markets to serve public purposes, and that government can learn from the private sector despite contextual differences (Metcalfe and Richards, 1990: 155; Dent and Barry, 2004).

Some observers have argued that there are convergent trends (Kickert and Jørgensen, 1995: 501) or 'diffusion of reforms' (Halligan, 1997) as increasing numbers of countries around the world are also embracing elements of the NPM approach. A noticeable trend in public sector reforms in developing countries has been that a wider range of administrative functions and the delivery of public services are being subjected to the NPM approach, even if in rhetoric (Batley, 1999; Larbi, 1999; McCourt, 2002; Batley and Larbi, 2004).

This chapter will provide an overview of the concept of NPM, its application and limitations, especially in the context of developing countries. The chapter first outlines the key components of New Public Management, then goes on to discuss selected NPM practices, highlighting issues of institutional constraints and capacity in their application. Finally, the chapter outlines the limitations of the NPM approach, leading to a revival of interest in a capable state.

Conceptualizing the New Public Management

New Public Management has become convenient shorthand term for a set of broadly similar administrative doctrines, which dominated the public administration reform agenda of most OECD countries from the late 1970s (Hood, 1991). NPM is seen as a body of managerial thought (Ferlie et al., 1996: 9), or as an ideological thought-system based on ideas generated in the private sector and imported into the public sector (Hood, 1991; Pollitt, 1993). It captures most of the structural, organizational and managerial changes that have taken place in the public services of OECD countries.

A review of the literature suggests that NPM is not a homogeneous whole, but rather has several overlapping elements representing trends in public sector management reforms in OECD countries. As a menu of reforms aimed at transforming public administration, its components and features have been identified by a number of writers (cf. Hood 1991; Ferlie et al., 1996; Lane, 2000). The doctrinal components of NPM have been expanded and have evolved since Christopher Hood first used the term in 1991. For example, the core ideas of the United Kingdom's (UK) Citizens' Charter initiative, launched in 1993, added a consumerist dimension to public management (Talbot, 1994). Moreover, different writers have stressed different aspects of NPM. For example, Hood's original conception of NPM did not explicitly feature the issue of consumers' rights. The UK's Citizens' Charter initiative brought the issue of consumers to prominence and has since become a key feature of public sector reforms in a number of developed and developing countries. Osborne and Gaebler's *Reinventing Government* (1992) also contains some important differences in emphasis from the ideologically-driven NPM. For example, they assert their belief in government and that privatization is not the only, or often the most appropriate, solution, and that in some cases, bureaucracies work better (e.g. in social security) (ibid.). Beyond these differences, there is a common core of NPM tenets.

Following Hood (1991), Table 1.1 draws together what may be regarded as the key tenets of NPM. These ideas may be categorized into two broad strands. On the one hand are ideas and themes that emphasize managerial improvement and organizational restructuring or 'managerialism' in the public sector. This cluster of ideas emphasizes management decentralization within public services. On the other are ideas and themes that emphasize markets and competition. It should be pointed out, however, that these categories overlap in practice. They should, therefore, be seen as a continuum ranging from more 'managerialism' at one end (e.g. decentralization and hands-on professional management) to more 'marketization' and competition at the other (e.g. contracting out).

As Hood (1991) has noted, the two broad orientations of NPM are explained by their historical roots. Managerialism in the public sector is rooted in the tradition of the Scientific Management and Human Relations schools (Hood, 1991: 6–7; Pollitt, 1993; Ferlie et al., 1996: 11). This neo-Taylorist movement was driven by the search for efficiency and, according to Hood:

> generated a set of administrative doctrines based on the ideas of *professional management* expertise as portable ... *paramount* over technical expertise, requiring high *discretionary power* to achieve results ... and *central* and *indispensable* to better organizational performance, through the development of appropriate cultures ... and the active measurement and adjustment of organizational outputs. (1991: 6)

The second strand of NPM derives from the 'new institutional economics' movement, which has its theoretical foundation in public choice, transaction cost and principal–agent theories. These generated public sector reform themes based on ideas of market, competition, contracting, transparency

Table 1.1   Key components of new public management

Emphasis	NPM component	Meaning	Typical justification
Managerialism	Hands-on professional management in the public sector	Active, visible, discretionary control of organizations from named persons at the top, 'free to manage'	Accountability requires the clear assignment of responsibility for action, not diffusion of power
Managerialism	Explicit standards and measures of performance	Definition of goals, targets, indicators of success, preferably expressed in quantitative terms and to which managers would be required to work	Accountability requires clear statement of goals; efficiency requires a 'hard look at objectives'
Managerialism	Capping or hard budgets	Make budgets more transparent in accounting terms with costs attributed to outputs rather than inputs – output-oriented budgeting	Making managers more aware not merely of the current costs of operations, but also the cost of capital employed (e.g. by means of accrual accounting)
Managerialism	Greater emphasis on output controls	Resource allocation and rewards linked to measured performance; break-up of centralized bureaucracy-wide personnel management; performance agreements	Need to stress results rather than procedures
Managerialism	Emphasis on greater discipline and parsimony in resource use	Cut direct costs, raise labour discipline, resist union demands, limit 'compliance costs' to business, downsize	Need to check resource demands of the public sector and do 'more with less'
Managerialism	New forms of corporate governance	Move to board of directors model; shift power to the strategic apex of the organization	Empowerment of management, reduces influence of elected representatives and trade unions

Table 1.1   Continued

Emphasis	NPM component	Meaning	Typical justification
Managerialism	Shift to *disaggregation* of units in the public sector	Break up formerly 'monolithic' traditional bureaucracies into corporatized units or separate agencies operating on decentralized 'on-line' budgets and relating with one another and with the centre on an 'arm's-length' basis	Need to create 'manageable' units, separate policy core from operation units
Managerialism	Decentralizing management authority	Replace traditional 'tall hierarchies' with flatter structures formed and reformed around specific processes (e.g. issuing licences) rather than traditional functions (e.g. personnel, finance)	Need more quickly responding and flexible structures closer to point of service delivery; freedom to manage
Managerialism	Organizational development and learning; explicit attempt to secure cultural change	Radical decentralization with performance judged by results; explicit attempts to manage cultural change combining top-down and bottom-up processes, use of mission statements and more assertive and strategic human resource function	Need for excellence in government
Managerialism/ markets and competition	Purchaser/provider split	Clear separation (organizational and financial) between defining the need and paying for public services, and actually providing those services	Concern for a much smaller public service; gain efficiency advantages of the use of contract or franchise arrangements inside as well as outside the public sector

Table 1.1   Continued

Emphasis	NPM component	Meaning	Typical justification
Markets and competition	Shift to greater competition in the public sector – market and quasi-market type mechanisms	Move to contracting and public tendering procedures to stimulate competition between service-providing agencies	Rivalry as the key to promote cost savings, efficiency, user-responsiveness and better standards
Markets and competition	Stress on private sector styles of management practice	Move away from military style 'public service ethic', greater flexibility in hiring and rewards; greater use of public relations techniques	Need to use 'proven' private sector management tools in the public sector
Markets and competition	Customer orientation; emphasis on quality	Make public services more responsive to the wishes of their users	Increasing customer 'voice' and accountability in service provision
Markets and competition	Changing employment relations	Put increasing number of public service staff on contracts that are term-limited (not permanent), performance-related and locally rather than nationally determined	Need to improve performance while reducing the burden of large public sector wage bill; making employment more competitive

Source: Adapted from Hood (1991); see also Larbi (1999).

and emphasis on incentive structures (cf. Williamson, 1975 and 1985) as a way of giving more 'choice' and 'voice' to service users and promoting efficiency in public service delivery.

NPM shifts the emphasis from traditional public administration to public management. It is based on the belief that the traditional model of organization and delivery of public services, characterized by monopoly of government agencies, rigid bureaucratic hierarchy, centralization, direct control, excessive internal regulation and self-sufficiency, is inherently inefficient, ineffective, costly and unresponsive (Walsh, 1995; Dixon et al., 1998). Public services were provider-dominated, especially in the case of professionalized provision (e.g. education and health care) where powerful, autonomous professions defended vested interests and could not be held to account. Besides, the oversized public sector was seen as hindering economic development and growth (Flynn, 2002a). The above diagnoses pre-supposed the solution. NPM was presented as providing a future for smaller, fast-moving service delivery organizations that would be kept lean by the pressures of competition and that would need to be user-responsive and outcome-oriented in order to survive. These organizations would be expected to develop flatter internal structures (i.e. fewer layers) and devolve operational authority to front-line managers. With a downsized staff, many on performance-related rolling contracts, a good number of services would be contracted out instead of assuming that in-house provision is best. Professional dominance and demarcation in staffing would be minimized to allow for the substitution of more cost-effective mixes of staff.

In short, NPM advocates argue that the dividing line between public and private sectors will be blurred and that the same good management practices will be found in both sectors. As Turner and Hulme (1997: 232) have pointed out, the proponents of the NPM paradigm have been successful in marketing its key features and 'persuading potential patients of its curative powers', sometimes backing up their claims with empirical evidence of substantial savings in public expenditure and improved services. As noted earlier, for developing countries the NPM prescriptions have tended to be applied through powerful international donor agencies and financial institutions. What has been the experience of NPM in practice? The next section explores this question, using selected NPM practices that represent the *managerialist* and *marketization* approaches to reform. These include management decentralization, performance management and contracting out.

New Public Management: selected applications

Decentralizing management: executive agencies and corporatization

Decentralizing the management of public services is one of the core strands of NPM derived from 'managerialism'. The trend towards decentralized management in public services is part of the effort to 'debureaucratize' the public services (Ingraham, 1996: 255) as well as 'de-layer' the hierarchies within them. The key concern here is 'whether managers are free to manage their units in order to achieve the most efficient output' (Mellon, 1993: 26; see also Hood, 1991: 5–6). This aspect of NPM has taken several forms; the key ones are outlined here.

Unbundling monolithic bureaucracies: executive agencies

There are several forms of management decentralization, but this section focuses mainly on executive agencies. The first and the key trend is that parts of traditionally huge and monolithic public bureaucracies, such as ministries and departments, have been transformed into more autonomous organizations (best known as 'agencies' after the UK's Next Steps Agencies) within the public sector. This is based on the belief that such autonomous organizations can be more entrepreneurial and enhance efficiency, effectiveness and responsive in public services (Pollitt et al., 2001; Pollitt and Talbot; 2004; Thynne, 2004). This involves a split between a strategic policy core and large operational arms of government with increased autonomy. Agencies are then required to conduct their relations with each other and with the parent departments/ministries on a contractual basis rather than through the traditional hierarchy. In practice, executive agencies have meant structural changes in the organization of government. They have greater managerial flexibility in decision-making, especially in the allocation and use of human and financial resources in return for greater accountability for results, at least in principle. As Jervis and Richards have argued, the executive agency idea was born out of:

> the desire to remove the framework of governance for public services from the arena of contested democratic politics. Placing public services at arm's length from politicians was intended to give managers sufficient space to get on with management, within the broad framework laid for the public service. (1995: 10–11)

Among OECD countries, the UK, Australia and New Zealand have been the key pioneers in this type of reform in the public sector, though there is variation in what constitutes an agency and the degree of autonomy allowed in practice (Pollitt and Talbot, 2004; Thynne, 2004; Verhoest et al., 2004). About 57 per cent of civil servants worked in 126 executive agencies in the UK by 2001 (James, 2003: 67). In New Zealand activities that are considered economic or commercial were separated from administrative or regulatory ones in large, multi-purpose ministries to form public enterprises. These agencies are headed by managers on fixed-term contracts with considerable autonomy, including the right to hire and fire (World Bank, 1997: 87).

The executive agency idea has caught on in a number of developing and transitional countries and has influenced the restructuring of both line and sector ministries and departments. Apart from Tanzania and Jamaica (see Boxes 1.1 and 1.2), other countries that have adopted the agency reforms include Ghana, Uganda, Latvia, South Korea and Thailand, to name just a few. Latvia has created about 150 agencies, whilst Jamaica has eight (covering activities such as estate management, information services, registrar general – births, deaths, marriages, etc.; management training and registrar of companies) (Talbot and Caufield, 2002; see also Pollitt and Talbot, 2004; and Pollitt et al., 2004). A number of countries also hived off their Customs and Excise and other revenue agencies from the Ministry of Finance to form semi-autonomous agencies. These include countries in Africa (e.g. Ghana, Kenya, Malawi, South Africa and Uganda), Asia (e.g. Singapore and

Malaysia) and Latin America (e.g. Bolivia, Mexico, Peru and Venezuela) (see Taliercio Jr, 2004). In Ghana, the operational arm of the Ministry of Health was hived off into an executive agency – the Ghana National Health Service – whilst the Community Water and Sanitation Agency was created in 1998 out of the then Ghana Water Company. Singapore has transformed operational parts of ministries, departments and statutory boards into semi-autonomous agencies (e.g. public works, internal revenue, ports, broadcasting, etc.), with greater operational flexibility in finance and human resources. Malaysia has introduced similar organizational restructuring under the Malaysia Incorporated Policy (Haque, 2002).

A common trend in health sector reforms in a number of developing countries is the decentralization of service provision to autonomous hospitals, as in Sri Lanka and Ghana (Mills et al., 2001). The introduction of autonomous hospitals is usually accompanied by the creation of independent hospital management boards. The principal reasons for targeting large hospitals for reform are that they consume a high proportion of the national health budget and are often the inefficient parts of the public

---

Box 1.1   Executive agencies in Tanzania

Tanzania's 'Organization and Efficiency Reviews', initiated in the mid-1990s, aimed at separating core policy-making and regulatory functions of ministries from those of implementation, with the latter handled by executive agencies. The result has been a 25 per cent reduction in the number of ministries and the creation of twelve agencies since 1997. The list of potential agency candidates has increased to about 50. A recent independent evaluation of the performance of these agencies suggests significant improvements in the services provided by these agencies, including better road maintenance by the Tanzania Roads Authority; higher quality airport services; faster business registration and improved counter services; and more efficient and effective National Statistics Office.

Source: Adapted from Kirasu (2002) and Talbott and Caufield (2002).

Box 1.2   Jamaica – the Office of the Registrar-General

In Jamaica the Office of the Registrar-General was one of the eight government units given agency status. It was able to use its own funds to finance the establishment of several regional offices. This improved access for local population and also generated greater revenues by cutting out middlemen who had used the Office's former inaccessibility to create a shadow economy in birth, death and marriage certificates.

Source: Talbot and Caufield (2002).

health system. Reforms were, *inter alia*, meant to improve efficiency by separating the purchaser (Ministry of Health) role from the provider (the hospital) role, thereby freeing the provider from the traditional bureaucratic and hierarchical structures, as well as to improve responsiveness to users' needs and preferences through market-based incentives (e.g. user fees) (Bennett et al., 1995).

The development of executive agencies has been accompanied by delegation of authority to senior management in public agencies – giving top management 'freedom to manage' with clear responsibility and accountability – and reducing the management role of the centre. Another complementary reform to the creation of executive agencies is the delegation of budgets and financial control, as well as some aspects of human resources management to agencies. This usually goes with the setting of explicit targets for agencies and other autonomous bodies.

Deepening autonomy: corporatization of public organizations

Another form of management decentralization is corporatization resulting largely from the restructuring of state or public enterprises and boards in several countries. Corporatization transforms public organizations into legal entities with responsibility and authority according to the company law, and thus can sue and be sued. This transformation is often accompanied by commercialization of the operations of the public organizations and also removes borrowing restrictions that are normally placed on public enterprises. Corporatization is aimed at deepening the autonomy of the public organizations by freeing them from political controls and interference and by giving them more commercial freedom (Thynne, 1998; Batley and Larbi, 2004).

In utility services such as urban drinking water and electricity, and in financial services (e.g. state-owned banks and insurance), corporatization has transformed the former state enterprises into more autonomous entities, short of privatization (e.g. in Ghana, Tanzania and Uganda). A study of reforms in agricultural marketing also found evidence of corporatization and commercialization of state boards and enterprises in Ghana and Zimbabwe. In the case of Ghana, the Cocoa Marketing Board (Cocobod) was restructured in the 1980s and 1990s by breaking it up into several corporatized subsidiary companies, including the Produce Buying Company and the Cocoa Marketing Company. In Zimbabwe the dairy, cotton and grain marketing boards were among those that were liberalized and corporatized in the 1990s, in the wake of adjustment-driven reforms (Hubbard, 2003). In these cases, the reformed entities were allowed to operate under the company law with independent boards. Where this arrangement has been allowed to work, it has minimized political interference in operational matters and significantly improved operational performance (e.g. in the cases in Cocoa Marketing Company in Ghana and

Dairy Board Zimbabwe limited). Malaysia has also corporatized a number of public organizations, including social security, banking, postal services, etc. (Haque, 2002). Corporatization is expected to deliver considerable operational autonomy and flexibility similar to the organizational and management structures found in private companies, but with emphasis on results or outcomes.

The benefits expected and the objectives of management decentralization may vary from one organizational context to another. However, the economic and administrative cases for management decentralization rest on bringing service delivery closer to consumers, improving the central government's responsiveness to public demands, improving the efficiency and quality of public services, and empowering lower units to feel more involved and in control. It is also meant to reduce overload and congestion at the centre and speed up operational decision-making and implementation by minimizing the bottlenecks associated with over-centralization of powers and functions in the hierarchy of a public service organization or ministry. Thus management decentralization seeks to increase the operational autonomy of line managers and agencies, leaving only broad policy guidelines to be worked out at the centre.

Emerging issues in decentralizing management

The application of management decentralization as an element of NPM in varying contexts and in different forms suggests that there are some institutional constraints with implications for the capacity of central agencies to manage the process. Drawing on the experience of the UK, Walsh (1995) has pointed out some of the initial constraints on the management of reforms in the public services, with particular reference to financial devolution under the Financial Management Initiative (FMI). These observations are even more pertinent and acute in the context of developing countries and merit attention. These include the following:

- resistance from different levels of the civil service to the FMI and the Treasury's reluctance to reduce centralized control;
- concern about the erosion of the traditional concept of the civil service as a unified body, and resistance from people who would like to preserve the traditional approaches; increased discretion of the line manager was seen as a challenge to the traditional dominance of the policy stream within the civil service;
- inadequacy of available technical systems, e.g., accounting information systems; the FMI was 'constrained by the relative failure of performance indicators which were subject to manipulation by managers' (Walsh, 1995: 170);
- the FMI left the structure of control relatively unchanged, reflecting the difficulty of making fundamental changes in existing structures.

The UK's experience with management devolution shows that unless devolved management and control involve a substantial change in power structure, devolution of control by itself will only have limited impact. As Walsh (1995) points out, there is the risk that autonomy would be subverted or eroded by ministers and top bureaucrats at the centre: 'These limitations are always likely to occur when the devolution of control takes place within organizational frameworks that are still strongly hierarchical' (Walsh, 1995: 178). Financial devolution within a framework of central control will tend to encourage local managers to remain oriented to the senior controllers of the organization, rather than outward to users. Highlighting a key institutional constraint in decentralizing management in the form of executive agencies, Walsh adds that:

> Departmental arrangements have not always changed to represent the quasi-contractual relationship between the minister and the head of the agency. Formal organizational change has not been matched by deeper change in the institutional character of the service. (ibid.: 188; emphasis added)

He goes on to argue that:

> The development of executive agencies in central government has, so far, had limited effect because it has not been accompanied by significant changes in the financial regime that operates within the civil service. The service is still dominated by an institutional framework that assumes central control, uniformity, and traditional concepts of financial control.... . but the experience of other agencies and other countries suggests that without attention to fundamental institutional issues traditional approaches will tend to reassert themselves. (ibid.: 191)

A study of reforms in Zimbabwe's health sector also notes that the governance and institutional contexts posed severe constraints in decentralizing management (Russell et al., 1997). These included unreformed institutions, such as centralized public service commission regulations and treasury expenditure controls – all of which prevent managers of decentralized units from having control over operational inputs. Similar observations have been made concerning health sector reforms in Sri Lanka (Russell and Attanayake, 1997) and Ghana (Larbi, 1998). Even in the case of autonomous agencies and corporatized organizations, continued political interference and controls and lack of financial independence have, in some cases, undermined operational autonomy and performance (e.g. the Cotton Company and the Cold Storage Commission in Zimbabwe and the Ghana Water Company) (Batley and Larbi, 2004). In general, there is reluctance in most central control agencies in developing countries to devolve budgets and financial control partly for fears about financial accountability and partly because of the stringent regime of expenditure controls that were associated with the introduction of structural adjustment programmes. In addition, a culture of centralization often prevails even when formal decentralization has taken place.

The implications of decentralized management for capacity

Again, Walsh (1995) makes some points on the capacity implications of management decentralization, which are also relevant to developing countries, including the capacity to:

- develop monitoring and inspection procedures to check whether managers and decentralized units are achieving their targets and working within defined strategies, as well as setting and monitoring performance;
- develop an information system that would provide appropriate intelligence for managers at all levels, to develop a budgetary control system for administrative costs, and to develop performance indicators and measurements;
- manage relations between departments and a network of non-departmental bodies and agencies through which services are delivered. The capacity to manage programme expenditure efficiently and effectively depends on capacity to manage the inter-organizational networks through which services are delivered;
- co-ordinate the activities of devolved units to ensure harmonization and improve accountability.

These capacity issues apply to developing countries with even greater significance (Larbi, 1998) because capacity weaknesses tend to be more acute. Management decentralization requires not only relaxing controls over inputs but also setting up monitoring systems for outputs and outcomes. The experience of developing countries suggests that the introduction of executive agencies requires the existence of a credible system for monitoring before relaxing controls over finance and inputs. Where these controls are weak, or undeveloped and arbitrary, behaviour cannot be checked; introducing greater managerial flexibility may only increase arbitrary and corrupt behaviour (World Bank, 1997: 20). Planning, budgeting and management systems within decentralized units are often weak, while financial and human resources at these levels are often lacking.

Performance management in the public sector

Performance management is one of the central themes of NPM. It is underpinned by principal–agent theory, which doubts that managers and organizations (agents) will voluntarily make changes to improve performance in the interests of the public or policy makers (principals) unless there are incentives or sanctions for them to do so through contractual arrangement. Performance management attempts to link increased managerial freedom with increased emphasis on output controls. What this means in practice is a shift from inputs and processes to outputs in control and accountability mechanisms, requiring public organizations, managers and employees to work to performance targets and output objectives. Performance management links the organization and the individual by developing a purposeful result-oriented direction, which drives both the setting of organizational objectives and defining individual tasks (Agere and Jorm, 2000; Flynn, 2002b).

The trend in performance management has taken several forms and activities, including performance measurement, performance targets, performance auditing, performance appraisal and performance contracting, but only a few of these can be discussed here.

A number of developing countries have introduced performance management schemes as part of public sector reforms, at both individual and organizational levels. At the individual level, performance evaluations and incentive systems have been introduced in a number of countries, including Ghana, and several countries in eastern and southern Africa (see Therkildsen, this volume) and Malaysia and Singapore (in south-east Asia). Several countries have also introduced performance-based, limited-term contracts for selected public service positions, including for chief directors (permanent secretaries) and chief executives of semi-autonomous agencies (e.g. Ghana and Kenya). Most developing countries have also replaced the annual confidential reports on employees with a relatively 'objective' system of performance appraisals, which involves spelling out and agreeing performance criteria for each member of staff and allowing for a development plan to be put in place for recognition and/or promotion.

At the organizational level, governments have also adopted performance management systems. Uganda's Results-Oriented Management (ROM; see Box 1.3 below) is a typical example. Similar schemes have been introduced in Tanzania with performance-based budgeting in ministries (see Therkildsen, this volume). Another key trend in performance management is the increasing resort to performance contracting[1] as an instrument to restructure state-owned enterprises (SOEs), especially large, strategic ones that are politically difficult to privatize. As part of the performance orientation in government, the common purposes of performance contracting are to clarify the objectives of service organizations and their relationship with government, and to facilitate performance evaluation based on results instead of conformity with bureaucratic rules and regulations (Islam, 1993; Mayne and Zapico-Goñi, 1997; Shirley and Xu, 1997).

Managing the interface between government and SOEs tend to be problematic in developing countries, a reflection of the difficulty of balancing control and autonomy.[2] Excessive controls and frequent political interventions and policy instability are some of the institutional problems of SOEs cited in the literature (World Bank, 1995; Fernandes, 1986; cf. Shirley, 1989). In line with the new institutionalist perspective in public sector management reforms, as reflected in agency and public choice theories, and in the policy prescriptions based on them, performance contracting between governments and SOEs have widely been introduced as an instrument for restructuring SOEs and for managing the government–SOE interface.

Though contractual relationships have been implicit between government and SOE management, the current trend is to make such contracts more explicit by formally spelling out the obligations of management and government in written performance contracts. The World Bank has been instrumental in the introduction of performance contracting in a number of developing countries (World Bank, 1995). Between 1978 and 1988, eleven African countries adopted performance contracting under World Bank programmes (Shirley, 1989) – all, except Ghana, in francophone Africa. A study by the World Bank also identified 385 such contracts in 28 countries, 136 of them in Africa. These were across sectors ranging from agriculture and extractive industries to transport, telecommunications and utilities (World Bank, 1995).

Issues in the application of performance management systems

Performance management schemes have had some positive impacts on service delivery despite some difficulties of operationalising the concept in practice. Experience, however, suggests that top civil servants in developing countries do not usually have control over operational resources and have limited managerial freedom due to central control over employment and expenditure. This, together with the unpredictability of budgets and weak information systems, undermine the operation of performance management systems (see Uganda's case in Box 1.3; see also Therkildsen, this volume). Selling the new system to staff, overcoming resistance to change, and developing appropriate capacity to implement and manage the new system are some of the key challenges (Agere and Jorm, 2000).

In the specific case of performance contracting, implementation has also been problematic, mainly because a number of critical institutional preconditions are often absent to make the system work as expected (Mallon, 1994; World Bank, 1995; Shirley and Xu, 1997). These preconditions, drawn from the cited studies, include:

- the need for governments (as principals) to state explicitly their objectives, prioritize them and translate into performance improvement targets;
- the need for principals or governments to have a 'hard budget' in place in order to minimize or even eliminate *ad hoc* subsidies and financial bail-outs of agencies;

Box 1.3   Results-oriented management (ROM) in Uganda

The second phase of Uganda's Public Sector Reform Programme (1998–2002), introduced a system of Results-oriented Management (ROM) in the public service. The ROM process cascades down through all levels of the Public Service and involves the following:

- establishing the mission and key objectives of each ministry or district;
- determining priorities, formulating strategies and allocating resources to achieve the objectives;
- identifying objectives, outputs and targets for all levels of the organization to support achievement of the key objectives;
- establishing a linkage between input/budgets and outputs/performance to ensure best use of resources and value for money;
- developing performance indicators and information systems to enable politicians and managers to monitor performance;
- publishing performance standards, targets and results.

At the individual staff level, a new staff appraisal scheme based on individual targets was introduced to support the implementation of ROM. ROM was expected to align organizational-level objectives with individual staff performance. For each ministry and district, a ROM focal point officer and ROM coordinator have been appointed respectively to act as change agents.

The implementation of ROM requires a cultural change in public organizations and individual staff. Understanding and accepting the system is crucial, but institutionalizing ROM is proving difficult. This is mainly due to weak capacities in the ministries and districts, which lack skilled and motivated staff. In addition, delays and shortfalls in actual disbursement have made implementation of planned activities difficult. Embedding ROM in the Public Service is one of the objectives of the third phase of Uganda's PSRP (2002–2007).

- the need for principals to signal credibly their commitment to the contract, e.g. by prompt payment of bills (in the case of utilities) and not reneging on other commitments;
- the delegation of meaningful autonomy to senior managers. This has been problematic in some cases, partly because of the reluctance of central controlling agencies to relinquish their controls over finance and personnel, and partly due to political interference. However, if managers are to be held accountable for results, they must be free from blatant political patronage and from pervasive external interference in operational matters;
- reliable and functional managerial information systems in place to enable management by results. The availability and quality of informa-

tion and how this is managed is a key capacity issue in applying performance contracts;

- the monitoring of performance contracts. There is, therefore, the need for effective and competent monitoring agency with skilled personnel. Monitoring also requires independent auditing by qualified managerial experts and accountants;
- a system of rewarding or penalizing managers according to their performance needs to be in place and must be seen to be working.

The studies cited above suggest that most of the conditions fail to materialize in the context of developing countries. For example, where the appointment of managers is based on patronage rather than merit, it may be difficult to penalize poor performance, which may be excused or tolerated rather than sanctioned. In reviewing the experience of Bolivia in performance contracting, Mallon (1994) notes that the vulnerability of the system to politicization was a major problem for implementation. Also, the autonomy of the technical staff that monitored performance contracting was compromised due to their inability to resist interfering.

Studies by Ayee (1994) and Larbi (2001) on performance contracting in Ghana also suggest that one of the main constraints was government reneging on its commitments. In India, Islam (1993) has noted that extensive control by multiple agencies is one of the constraints on capacity to implement performance contracting in public enterprises. In some cases the assumptions under which targets are set can quickly change in an unstable situation and undermine achievements.

The review of performance management schemes suggests their successful introduction and implementation require certain preconditions. There are capacity issues ranging from autonomy of managers and predictability of resources, through to an effective management information system and effective monitoring system.

Contracting out service delivery

As part of the efforts to reconfigure state–market relationships in order to give more prominence to markets and the private sector, contracting out the provision of public services is increasingly advocated in developing countries. Contracting out refers to the outsourcing or buying in of goods and services from external sources instead of providing such services in-house. The responsibility of the public organization is to specify what is wanted and let the private or voluntary sector provide it. This and other forms of private sector participation methods are being used in those public services that cannot be privatized for strategic, political or other reasons (see Savas, 2000 and Batley and Larbi, 2004 for examples). Contracting out thus puts competitive market forces directly at the service of government.

Box 1.4   Contracting out urban infrastructure

A number of African countries contracted out urban infrastructure development. The case of Agences d'Exécution des Travaux d'Intérêt Public (AGETIPS), non-profit, non-governmental agencies, is widely cited as very successful. Operating in francophone African counties, AGETIPS enter into contractual arrangements with governments to implement infrastructure projects. With increased managerial autonomy, transparent procedures and protection from political interferences, these organizations have, *inter alia*, regularly obtained unit prices of 5 to 40 per cent lower than those obtained by the administration through official bidding and have been able to complete projects on schedule with relatively minimal cost overruns.

Source: World Bank, 1994.

Though contracting out or outsourcing of public service delivery is not new, what is new is the extension of the practice to cover activities that have traditionally been carried out by in-house arrangements. Where outputs are easily specified but direct competition is impossible, competition managed through various forms of contracts such as service contracts, management contracts, leases, and long-term concessions can yield efficiency gains (see Box 1.4).

In the health sector, a number of countries have contracted out one or more non-clinical services such as cleaning, laundry, catering, security and maintenance (e.g. Zimbabwe, Bombay, India, and Thailand) and outpatient and in-patient hospital care (e.g. South Africa) (Bennett et al., 1995; Mills et al., 2001). In the infrastructure sector, Brazil contracted out road maintenance to private contractors and this led to 25 per cent savings over the use of government employees (World Bank, 1997; see also Box 1.4). Also management of ports in Malaysia, plantations in Sri Lanka, airports in the Philippines and hotels in Egypt and Bulgaria have been contracted out (see Savas, 2000). Under its private sector participation programme, Tanzania has contracted out cleaning services in government ministries and there are plans to scale up contracting out to other services in the public sector. Ghana, Zimbabwe and other countries have also contracted out municipal services such as waste collection and street cleaning (Batley 1996; Awortwi, 2004). In the urban drinking sector, some states in Nigeria have introduced concession contracts and other forms of private sector participation in the water sector (Jawara, 2004). Argentina, Bolivia and other Latin American countries have also introduced concession and lease contracts in the water sector (see Nickson and Franceys, 2003; Nickson, this volume).

Thus there is a noticeable trend of increasing the role of non-state providers in the delivery of public services. Whilst there have been some obvious benefits, there are also implementation problems and risks, which are discussed next.

Institutional constraints and capacity issues in contracting out

The extension of contracting out in the public sector raises a number of issues with implication for service delivery. First, introducing contracting out assumes that the capacity exists within the private sector to take on the provision of contracted out services. This is not always the case in some developing countries, or in the case of all services. In the health sector, for example, the private sector may be ill-equipped to take over the provision of non-clinical services, as was the case in hospital laundry in Ghana. It is also the case that the capacity to manage and monitor contracts with a large variety of providers is usually lacking in government organizations (Batley and Larbi, 2004).

Second, the prevalence of patronage systems, corruption and other institutional weaknesses undermine the successful introduction of contracting out policies. In such circumstances contracting out may be economically inefficient and wasteful, if there are no mechanisms to mitigate the constraints. In general, an effective use of market mechanisms must be accompanied by effective regulatory and monitoring capacity (Batley and Larbi, 2004). The institutional context of a country, therefore, needs to be taken into consideration in extending contracting out to new areas.

Third, there is no guarantee that the private sector under competitive contracting will perform better than the public sector. The evidence on the efficiency of contracting out is mixed (Batley, 1996) and has been challenged by recent studies (cf. Boyne, 1997). In some cases the outcome for the service user or the taxpayer is worse (cf. Awortwi, 2004). Indeed, the World Bank advises that: 'Contracting out, setting up performance-based agencies, and ensuring formal accountability for results are not viable options for many services in countries with weak capacities' (1997: 91). This is particularly acute in services like health and education whose providers interact daily with the people they serve, are geographically dispersed, have substantial discretion, and produce outputs that are difficult to monitor and are not subject to competitive pressure. For such services the risk of market failure is high. Incentives for hard work, regular monitoring and supervision, greater clarity of purpose and task may boost incentives to improve performance in these areas (ibid.).

Fourth, there are some services that could be at great risk if contracted out, either because they are essential to the core business of the organization or because they are of strategic importance. The protection of privacy could be at risk (as in social security and tax systems) or there could be a risk of loss of control and over-dependence on the outside agency (OECD, 1993b).

While the above are constraints on capacity to contract out and manage contracts, there are more explicit capacity issues that have to be considered.

First, on the managerial capacity implications of contracting out, one would agree with Metcalfe and Richards that no matter what area of activity is contracted out, the transfer of responsibility for supply of services does not absolve government from managerial responsibility (1990: 167). Government would still retain the responsibility for planning and financing, and deciding what should be provided and at what cost, as well as laying down the 'rules of the game'. In general, greater use of contracting out must be accompanied by effective regulatory and monitoring capacity. For most poor developing countries this is not always easy to achieve and is even more daunting in the case of social services, such as health and education. Regulating and monitoring a large number of small-scale providers is usually beyond government capacity in poor and weak states.

The second capacity issue is that in contracting out, the government becomes a customer. Like all rational customers government would have the responsibility for evaluating the product, deciding whether it meets stated standards and determining how to ensure satisfactory contract performance, i.e. government should have the capacity to manage contracts. Third, another management responsibility with implications for capacity is the availability and analysis of comparative data about public and private performance to assist evaluation, which could then form the basis for a review of the policy of contracting out a particular activity.

It is apparent from the above that contracting out imposes managerial responsibilities on the government or its administrative agencies for planning, financing, monitoring, regulating and evaluating contracts. These roles may not require a large workforce operating on civil service terms and conditions of employment, which in-house provision would require. However, they certainly do require more high-level and highly trained management and technical personnel than developing countries can often afford. As contracting out becomes more widespread in public sector organizations in developing countries, the difficulty of managing a network of contracts and subcontracts becomes more apparent. The expected improvement of performance in contracting out will depend, first, on the appropriate choice of form of contract, and then on effective management of contractual relationships. At the same time the implications of contracting out for the cost (price) of public services, for access to these services and for public reaction to possible price increases may be cause for concern in politically sensitive services, such as health and water.

Limitations of the NPM: emphasizing capable states

This chapter has discussed the application of selected NPM practices to developing countries, highlighting not just their benefits but also issues of institutional constraints and capacity in their application. Apart from the above, the optimism of NPM advocates is countered by critics who argue that NPM has produced some disagreeable consequences and that it does not offer a 'magic bullet' or toolkit for the problems in the public sector (Dent and Barry, 2004). In fact, the evidence of superior efficiency claimed by NPM advocates has been questioned in recent years on methodological ground and that equity might suffer even if efficiency is achieved (Boyne, 1997; Boyne et al., 2003). A recent evaluation of NPM-type reforms in three services in Britain – education, health and housing – suggests that reforms in health and housing appear to be associated with higher efficiency, whilst there was increased responsiveness to users in housing and education (Boyne et al., 2003). However, equity declined in all three cases. A study of contracting and other forms private provision of public services in six developing countries also concludes that: 'The presumption that involving the private sector makes for higher levels of performance is given only partial support' by the evidence (Batley, 1996: 748).

Le Grand and Barlett (1993) have pointed out that quality in service provision may fall as minimalist, economizing managerial standards, increasingly replaces aspirational professional standards. With too much emphasis on cost reduction, NPM may encourage the pursuit of efficiency in flawed policies with short-term gains, undermining the capacity of the state to take a long-term perspective on services such as education, technology, health and the environment. These are issues that need to be considered in seeking to apply NPM to poor developing countries.

In lamenting the collapse of the welfare state, critics of NPM also point to increasing inequality, as market-type mechanisms produce 'market niche-seeking' behaviour by public service providers (e.g. 'good' secondary schools biasing their entry procedures towards the children of parents of higher socio-economic groups). Thus the cultural and organizational change in social provision, expressed in the concepts of markets and individualism, may arguably create conditions of social exclusion even in economically advanced countries (Mackintosh, 1998). Such reforms may, therefore, harm most of those in need of state provision and welfare safety-nets: the poor and the vulnerable groups. These concerns are even more pertinent in the context of developing countries where poverty and problems of access to services are even deeper and could undermine efforts to reduce poverty and realize the Millennium Development Goals (MDGs). We need to understand more the effect of NPM reforms on service delivery, particularly for the poor and vulnerable groups.

The egalitarian critique of NPM (Dunleavy and Hood, 1994) also notes that it may promote self-interest and corruption as policy-makers and senior bureaucrats opt for privatization and contracting out because of increased opportunities for rent-seeking and other forms of corruption. Critics also argue that NPM has led to falling ethical standards in public life with increasing incidence of greed, favouritism or conflicting interests. For developing countries, where patronage systems are more prevalent and accountability mechanisms are weak, the adoption of NPM may lead to more abuses and arbitrary use of discretion (e.g. in contracting) (cf. Schick, 1998; Awortwi, 2004).

NPM promises improved accountability by: clearly defining who is responsible for what; emphasizing accountability for performance or result; developing comprehensive monitoring, reporting and evaluation mechanisms; and increasing voice and exit mechanisms to make service providers more responsive to users. However, there are risks and complaints about loss of public and traditional channels of local accountability as functions are fragmented among numerous agencies and many are privatized or contracted out to profit-seeking commercial firms (Dunleavy and Hood, 1994; Bogdanor, cited in Ferlie et al., 1996). Fragmentation makes accountability and monitoring more difficult. For poor developing countries, alternative systems of accountability are yet to develop and embed themselves in the public sector. Reducing rules and controls have potentially increased the risk of mistakes, abuse and corruption.

Context does matter in the application of NPM reforms. Specific NPM approaches may work better in some contexts than others. The public service sector covers a wide variety of activities, some of which have high technological content and results can easily be measured (e.g. telecommunications) and others low; some are person-centred (e.g. health and education) and some not; some competitive, some very hard to remould into a competitive format. It is important to bear these differences in mind, because they increase or decrease the chances of NPM being a 'good fit' in developing countries. Countries also do differ in their capacity to adopt particular NPM techniques. As noted in the previous sections, the different NPM components have their own capacity implications and preconditions. Also the legal, political and administrative systems of different countries will have an influence on the way NPM works in practice. This challenges the globalization and convergence thesis in NPM discussions as it overrides the distinct political and cultural characteristics of states. Even within its OECD heartland there is only convergence at the level of rhetoric and similar pressures for change, but convergence of practice or implementation and results play out differently according to the political and legal arrangements. Thus the mixture of strategies, priorities and methods adopted by governments vary widely (Pollitt, 2002; Pollitt and Boukaert, 2000; see also Ridley, 1996).

Given the different and difficult circumstances of reforms in poor developing economies and the potential risks mentioned above, it is doubtful whether a universalistic approach to NPM is a tenable option. The radical reforms of some of the NPM pioneers (e.g. the UK and New Zealand) may not be a universally appropriate model for developing countries to emulate (Schick, 1998; Batley and Larbi, 2004).

The above criticisms of NPM, concerns about social cohesion, equity and stability, and the poor results of reforms in developing countries in the 1980s, have revived interest in the active role of the state in development and service delivery in the past decade. The debate is now about how to revitalize the state to enable it perform its role effectively. As the former UK Secretary of State for International Development, Clare Short, noted, the main focus of development policy, the elimination of poverty, could only be achieved 'through strong and effective states', and that 'the era of complete enmity to the public sector in general and to State provision in particular is coming to an end' (cited in Minogue et al., 1997). Given the focus on poverty alleviation in the context of the MDGs, the role of the state and its working in partnership with non-state actors have increasingly become important.

Refocusing on the 'effective state' was given prominence in the 1997 World Development Report (WDR), which marks a significant shift in thinking about the state and its role in development: the need to factor the state back into development. Subsequent WDRs have reinforced the need for synergy between the state and non-state actors (e.g. for service delivery). The rethinking in the Bank suggests that in reforming the public sector the NPM way does not lend itself to clear, unambiguous solutions; the NPM model is not a panacea for the problems in the public sector.

The enthusiasm for neo-liberal policies and NPM practices that characterized most of the 1980s and early 1990s has been tempered in recent years and, in some cases, the more extreme forms of the NPM approach have been rejected. For example, user charges in basic education have been reversed in most countries in Africa and are no longer a policy option of the World Bank in basic education and health. There is recognition that imposing one template of reform on all, irrespective of context, is unwise and may even precipitate conflict and undermine stability. The way forward is to make the state work better, not to dismantle it. The Bank suggests two strategies. The first is to match the state's role to its capability; the earlier mistake was that the state tried to do too much with few resources and limited capacity. The second approach is to strengthen the capability of the state by reinvigorating public administration institutions so that they can perform their enabling, regulating, monitoring and co-ordinating roles. This will entail creating effective rules and restraints, encouraging greater competition in service provision, applying measures to monitor performance gains and achieving a more responsive mix of central and local governance by steering policies in the direction of greater decentralization (World Bank, 1997). The Bank is moving to make institutional reform and capacity-building in the public sector the core of its work (World Bank, 2003a). *The World Development Report 2004* put emphasis on service delivery for the poor. The current phase of public sector reforms in most developing countries puts emphasis on service delivery, but there is a need to strengthen the link between public sector reform and improvement in service delivery in the design of reforms.

In conclusion, NPM-type reforms may hold some potential for developing countries, but there is a need to recognize that countries differ widely in terms of their institutional conditions and their capacity to implement public sector management reforms based on NPM principles and practices. There is a need also for more process and contingent approaches, which will sequence and phase in reforms to meet existing capacity for implementation. It is now accepted that context does matter in the design of reforms. While the New Public Management approach may not be a panacea for the problems of public sector management in developing countries, careful and selective adaptation of some elements to selected sectors and activities may be beneficial. Implementation needs to be sensitive to operational reality and what is feasible in the economic, social and political contexts of countries. We need to understand better the internal factors and institutional conditions that drive reforms in order to match reform need and suitability to particular contexts.

Notes

1. Different terms are used in different countries for performance contracting. In India the term 'memorandum of understanding' is used (Trevedi, 1990); in Senegal the term 'contract plan' is used; while in Pakistan 'signalling system' is used (Islam, 1993). Bolivia (Mallon, 1994) and Ghana (Ayee, 1994; Larbi, 1998) use the term 'performance contract' or 'agreement'.
2. For a detailed discussion of the problematic relationship between government and public enterprises, see Fernandes (1986).

References

Agere, S. and Jorm, N. (2000) *Designing Performance Appraisals: Assessing Needs and Designing Performance Management Systems in the Public Sector*, London: Commonwealth Secretariat.

Awortwi, N. (2004) 'Getting the Fundamentals Wrong: Woes of Public–Private Partnerships in Solid Waste Collection in Three Ghanaian Cities', *Public Administration and Development*, 24(3): 213–24.

Ayee, J. R. A. (1994) 'Corporate Plans and Performance Contracts as Devices for Improving the Performance of State Enterprises', *African Journal of Public Administration and Management*, III: 77–91.

Barnum, H. and J. Kutzin (1993) *Public Hospitals in Developing Countries: Resource Use, Cost, Financing*, Baltimore, MD: Johns Hopkins University Press.

Batley, R. (1996) 'Public and Private Relationships and Performance in Service Provision', *Urban Studies*, 33(4–5): 723–51.

Batley R. A. (1999) 'New Public Management in Developing Countries: Implications for Policy and Organizational Reform', *Journal of International Development*, 11: 761–5.

Batley, R. A. and G. A. Larbi (2004) *The Changing Role of Government: The Reform of Public Services in Developing Countries*, Basingstoke and New York: Palgrave Macmillan.

Bennett, S., S. Russel and A. Mills (1995) *Institutional and Economic Perspectives on Government Capacity to Assume New Roles in the Health Sector: A Review of Experience*, The Role of Government in Adjusting Economies Paper 4, School of Public Policy, University of Birmingham.

Borins, S. (1997) 'What the New Public Management is Achieving: A Survey of Commonwealth Experience', *Advances in International Comparative Management*, Supplement 3: 49–70.

Boyne, G. A. (1997) *Public Choice Theory and Public Management: A Critique of the Evidence of Service Contracting in US Local Government*, the Second International Research Symposium on Public Services Management, 11 September, Aston University, Birmingham.

Boyne, G. A., C. Farrel, J. Law, M. Powell, M. R. Walker (2003) *Evaluating Public Management Reforms*, Open University Press: Buckingham.

Christensen, T. and P. Lægreid (eds.) (2002) *New Public Management: The Transformation of Ideas and Practice*. Aldershot: Ashgate.

Clarke, J. and J. Newman (1997) *The Managerial State: Power, Politics and Ideology in the Remaking of Social Welfare*, London: Sage.

Dent, M. and J. Barry (2004) 'New Public Management and the Professions in the UK: Reconfiguring Control?', in M. Dent, J. Chandler, and J. Barry, *Questioning the New Public Management*. Aldershot: Ashgate, pp. 7–20.

Dixon, J., A. Kouzmin and N. Korac-Kakabadse (1998) 'Managerialism – Something Old, Something Borrowed, Little New: Economic Prescriptions versus Effective Organizational Change in Public Agencies', *International Journal of Public Sector Management*, 11(2/3): 164–87.

Downs, A. (1967) *Inside Bureaucracy*. Boston, MA: Little, Brown.

Dunleavy, P. and C. Hood (1994) 'From Old Public Administration to New Management', *Public Money and Management*, 14(3): 9–16.

Ferlie, E., A. Pettigrew, L. Ashburner and L. Fitzgerald (1996) *The New Public Management in Action*, Oxford: Oxford University Press.

Fernandes, P. (1986) *Managing Relations between Government and Public Enterprises: A Handbook for Administrators and Managers*, Management Development Series No. 25. Geneva: International Labour Organization.

Flynn, N. (2002a) 'Explaining the New Public Management: The Importance of Context', in K. McLaughlin, P. Osborne and E. Ferlie, *New Public Management: Current Trends and Future Prospects*, London: Routledge.

Flynn, N. (2002b) *Public Sector Management*, London: Prentice Hall.

Halligan, J. (1997) 'New Public Sector Models: Reform in Australia and New Zealand', in J. E. Lane (ed.), *Public Sector Reform: Rationale, Trends and Problems*, London: Sage, pp. 17–46.

Haque, Shamsul M. (2002) 'Structures of New Public Management in Malaysia and Singapore: Alternative Views', *Journal of Comparative Asian Development*, 1(1): 71–86.

Hood, C. (1991) 'A Public Management for all Seasons', *Public Administration*, 69(1): 3–19.

Hubbard, M. (2003) *Developing Agricultural Trade: New Roles for Government in Poor Countries*, Basingstoke and New York, Palgrave Macmillan.

Ingraham, P. W. (1996) 'The Reform Agenda for National Civil Service Systems: External Stress and Internal Strains', in H. A. G. M. Bekke, J. L. Perry and T. A. J. Toonen (eds.), *Civil Service Systems in Comparative Perspective*. Bloomington: Indiana University Press, pp. 247–67.

Islam, N. (1993) 'Public Enterprise Reform: Managerial Autonomy, Accountability and Performance Contracts', *Public Administration and Development*, 13(2): 129–52.

James, O. (2003) *The Executive Agency Revolution in Whitehall: Public Interest Versus Bureau-Shaping Perspectives*, Basingstoke: Palgrave Macmillan.

Jawara, Dawda K. (2004) 'Non-state Providers of Basic Services: Case Study – Nigeria's Water Supply Sanitation Sector', in G. Larbi et al., *Study of Non-State Providers in Nigeria*, Mimeo, University of Birmingham.

Jervis, P. and S. Richards (1995) 'Strategic Management in a Re-invented Government: Rowing 1, Steering 0', Paper presented at the Strategic Management Society's 15th Annual Conference on Strategic Discovery: Opening New Worlds, 15–18 October, Mexico City.

Kickert, W. J. M. and T. Beck Jørgensen (1995) 'Introduction: Managerial Reform Trends in Western Europe', *International Review of Administrative Sciences*, 61(4): 499–510.

Lane, J. E. (2000) *New Public Management*. London: Routledge.

Larbi, G. A. (1998) 'Institutional Constraints and Capacity Issues in Decentralising Management in Public Services: The Case of Health in Ghana', *Journal of International Development*, 10(3): 377–86.

Larbi, G. A. (1999) *New Public Management Approach and Crisis States*, Discussion Paper 112, Geneva: United Nations Research Institute for Social Development.

Larbi, G. A. (2001) 'Performance Contracting in Practice: Experience and lessons from the Water Sector in Ghana', *Public Management Review*, 3(3): 305–24.

Le Grand, J. and W. Barlett (1993) *Quasi-Markets and Social Policy*. London: Macmillan.

Mackintosh, M. (1998) 'Public Management for Social Exclusion', in M. Minogue, C. Polidano and D. Hulme (eds.), *Beyond New Public Management: Changing Ideas and Practices in Governance*, Cheltenham: Edward Elgar.

Mallon, R. D. (1994) 'State-owned Enterprise Reform through Performance Contracts: The Bolivian Experiment', *World Development*, 22(6): 925–34.

Mayne, J. and E. Zapico-Goñi (1997) *Monitoring Performance in the Public Sector: Future Directions from International Experience*, London: Transaction Publishers.

McCourt, W. (2002) 'New Public Management in Developing Countries', in K. McLauglin, S. P. Osborne, and E. Ferlie (eds.), *New Public Management: Current Trends and Future Prospects*, London and New York: Routledge, pp. 227–42.

Mellon, E. (1993) 'Executive Agencies: Leading Change from the Outside', *Public Money and Management*, 13(2): 25–31.

Metcalfe, L. and S. Richards (1990) *Improving Public Management*, 2nd edition, London: Sage.

Mills, A. (1995) 'Improving the Efficiency of Public Sector Health Services in Developing Countries: Bureaucratic vs. Market Approaches', PHP Departmental Publication No. 17, London: London School of Hygiene and Tropical Medicine.

Mills, A., S. Bennett, and S. Russel (2001) *The Challenge of Health Sector Reform: What Must Governments Do?* Basingstoke and New York: Palgrave.

Minogue, M., C. Polidano and D. Hulme (1997) 'Reorganizing the State: Towards More Inclusive Governance', *Insight*, 23: 1–2.

Moore, M., S. Stewart and A. Hoddock (1994) *Institution Building as a Development Assistance Method: A Review of Literature and Ideas*, Report to the Swedish International Development Agency (Sida), Stockholm.

Nellis, J. (1989) *Public Enterprise Reform in Adjustment Lending*, Washington, DC: World Bank Working Paper, Country Economics Department.

Nickson, R. A. and R. Franceys (2003) *Tapping the Market: The Challenge of Institutional Reform in Urban Water Supply Sector*, Basingstoke and New York: Palgrave Macmillan.

OECD (1993a) *Public Management Development Survey 1993*, Paris: OECD.

OECD (1993b) *Managing with Market-type Mechanisms*, Paris: OECD.

Osborne, D. and T. Gaebler (1992) *Reinventing Government: How the Entrepreneurial Spirit is Transforming the Public Sector*, Reading, MA: Addison-Wesley.

Pollitt, C. (1993) *Managerialism and the Public Services: The Anglo-American Experience*, 2nd edition, Oxford: Blackwell.

Pollitt, C. (2002) 'New Public Management in International Perspective: An Analysis of Impacts and Effects', in K. McLauglin, P. Osborne and E. Ferlie, *New Public Management: Current Trends and Future Prospects*, London: Routledge, pp. 274–92.

Pollitt, C., Bathgate, K., Caufield, J., Smullen, A. and Talbot, C. (2001) 'Agency Fever? Analysis of an International Policy Fashion', *Journal of Comparative Policy Analysis*, 3(3): 271–90.

Pollitt C. and G. Boukaert (2000) *Public Management Reform: A Comparative Analysis*, Oxford: Oxford University Press.

Pollitt, C. and C. Talbot (eds.) (2004) *Unbundled Government: A Critical Analysis of the Global Trend to Agencies, Quangos and Contractualism*, London: Routledge.

Pollitt, C., C. Talbot, J. Caufield and A. Smullen (2004) *Agencies: How Governments Do Things through Semi-autonomous Agencies*, Basingstoke: Palgrave.

Ridley, F. (1996) 'The New Public Management in Europe: Comparative Perspectives', *Public Policy and Administration*, 11(1): 16–29.

Russell S. and N. Attanayake (1997) *Sri Lanka – Reforming the Health Sector: Does Government Have the Capacity?* The Role of Government in Adjusting Economies Paper 14, Birmingham: Development Administration Group, University of Birmingham.

Russell, S., P. Kwaramba, C. Hongoro and S. Chikandi (1997) *Zimbabwe – Reforming the Health Sector: Does Government Have the Capacity?* The Role of Government in Adjusting Economies Paper 20, Birmingham: Development Administration Group, Birmingham University of Birmingham.

Savas, E. S. (2000) *Privatisation and Public–Private Partnerships*, London and New York: Chatham House.

Shick, A. (1998) 'Why Most Developing Countries Should Not Try New Zealand's Reforms', *World Bank Research Observer*, 13(1): 123–31.

Shirley, M. (1989) *The Reform of State-owned Enterprises: Lessons from the World Bank Lending*, Washington, DC: The World Bank.

Shirley, M. and C. L. Xu (1997) *Information, Incentives, and Commitment: An Empirical Analysis of Contracts between Government and State Enterprises* (Working Papers available on-line at http://www.worldbank.org/pub/decweb/workingpapers), Washington, DC: World Bank.

Stark, A. (2002) 'What is the New Public Management?' *Journal of Public Administration Research and Theory* 12(1): 137–51.

Talbot, C. (1994) *Reinventing Public Management: A Survey of Public Sector Managers' Reactions to Change*, Corby, Northants: The Institute of Management.

Talbot, C. and J. Caufield (2002) 'Hard Agencies in Soft States? A Study of Agency Creation Programmes in Jamaica, Latvia and Tanzania', A report for the Department for International Department (DFID), London.

Taliercio Jr, R. (2004) 'The Design, Performance and Sustainability of Semi-autonomous Revenue Authorities in Africa and Latin America', in C. Pollitt and C. Talbot (eds.), *Unbundled Government: A Critical Analysis of the Global Trend to Agencies, Quangos and Contractualism*. London: Routledge, pp. 264–82.

Therkildsen, O. (1999) *Efficiency, Accountability and Implementation: Public Sector Reform in East and Southern Africa*, Programme Paper 3: Democracy, Governance and Human Rights, Geneva: UNRISD.

Thynne, I. (1998) 'Government Companies as Instruments of State Action', *Public Administration and Development*, 18(3): 217–28.

Thynne, I. (2004) 'State Organizations as Agencies: An Identifiable and Meaningful Focus of Research?', *Public Administration and Development*, 24(2): 91–9.

Treuedi, P. (1990) *Memorandum of Understanding: An Approach to Improving Public Enterprise Performance* New Delhi: Internatioanl Management Publishers.

Turner, M. and D. Hulme (1997) *Governance, Administration and Development: Making the State Work*, Basingstoke and London: Macmillan.

Verhoest, K., G. B. Peters, G. Bouckaert and B. Verschuere (2004) 'The Study of Organizational Autonomy: A Conceptual Review', *Public Administration and Development*, 24(2): 101–18.

Walsh, K. (1995) *Public Services and Market Mechanisms: Competition, Contracting and the New Public Management*, London: Macmillan.

Williamson, E. O. (1975) *Markets and Hierarchies*, New York: Free Press.

Williamson, E. O. (1985) *The Economic Institutions of Capitalism*, New York: Free Press.

World Bank (1994) *World Development Report 1994: Infrastructure for Development*, New York: Oxford University Press.

World Bank (1995) *Bureaucrats in Business: The Economics of Government Ownership*, New York: Oxford University Press.

World Bank (1997) *The World Development Report 1997: The State in a Changing World*, New York: Oxford University Press.

World Bank (2003a) *Reforming Public Institutions and Strengthening Governance*, Washington, DC: World Bank.

World Bank, (2003b) *World Development Report 2004: Making Services Work for Poor People*, New York: Oxford University Press.

2
Elusive Public Sector Reforms in East and Southern Africa[1]

Ole Therkildsen

Introduction

Few independent observers are prepared to defend the *status quo* of public sector arrangements in sub-Saharan Africa. As Mkandawire and Soludo (1999: 135) write, the 'need to reform African administrative structures to ensure efficiency and reduce the likelihood of corruption are obvious'; so is the need to increase democratic accountability. Such concerns are linked to debates about the proper role of the state and the market in countries where the prospects for significant economic growth are uncertain and state institutions are weak; where there are significant gaps between demand and supply of public services; where inequities in access to the services actually delivered are considerable; and where the legitimacy of many states are questioned (Mutahaba et al., 1993; Bangura, 1999; Batley and Larbi, 2004).

Three main questions derived from these debates are addressed in this chapter: Has the size of the state changed and its activities become more focused? Has public sector accountability improved? Is there political support for the reform initiatives? Kenya, Malawi, Mozambique, South Africa, Tanzania, Uganda, Zambia and Zimbabwe are included in the analyses. The period from the mid-1980s to around 2000 is covered.

As shown in the following, the answers to these questions are elusive and vary considerably across countries. On the one hand, official government and donor documents, consultancy reports and academic writings are full of visions and ideas about how to improve the public sector. On the other hand, seemingly well-designed reform measures are often undermined by political conflicts and poor implementation – or no implementation at all.

The analyses presented here are based on a literature review and on interviews with politicians and civil servants directly engaged in the reform work in the region. Available information does not, however, cover all countries and relevant issues equally well. Moreover, comparisons across countries and time are affected by problems of methodology and data, which this chapter shares with other writings on the subject. Analyses of more specific measures, such as reform of public enterprises, local government reform, sector and tax reforms, pay reform and changes in public expenditure management are not explicitly dealt with.

The chapter is divided into six sections. The first presents the general context of public sector reform in the region. Then each of the above questions is addressed in turn, followed by conclusions.

Reform context

The eight countries included in this analysis are very different with respect to political, economic, administrative, social and cultural history. They also differ in the size of the public sector, domestic resource base, donor dependency and level of service delivery. Four countries – Malawi, Mozambique, Tanzania and Uganda – are among the poorest in the world. Except for South Africa, all are heavily indebted, in particular Zambia. Six of the eight countries (except South Africa and Zimbabwe) had been approved for HIPC relief by the end of 2003 (Addison et al., 2004: 7). During the past decade, democratization has affected political life in all the countries. However, prolonged civil war has afflicted Mozambique, South Africa and Uganda in the recent past. Moreover, several countries in the region are still engaged in armed conflicts or threatened by internal unrest. But even considering these difficult circumstances, most independent observers agree that public sectors organizations in the region do not perform well. For many citizens the provision of law and order, education, health care, road maintenance, agricultural extension and other services has deteriorated. For the African public sectors to reach the Millennium Development Goals (MDGs) by 2015 is, therefore, an enormous challenge.

The roots of the public sector problems in Africa are contested. Some point to the importance of the marginalization of the continent in the global capitalist economy. Contrary to neo-liberal claims, economic liberalization in Africa combined with the continued protection and subsidization in the North (especially of agricultural products) may undermine the economic growth of poor countries (Leys, 1994; Wade, 2004). These countries are also susceptible to extreme large-scale external shocks, such as volatile and declining terms of trade (Nissanke and Ferrarini, 2004). This contributes significantly to the extreme resource scarcity of public sector operations and to their poor performance. Others single out poor macroeconomic policies as a major cause of fiscal instability, deteriorating economic growth and increased inflation that contribute to declining state capacity. In addition, the problems of the public sector in Africa are increasingly regarded as institutional and caused by inappropriate governance arrangements. They cause varying degrees of well-known 'bureaupathologies' (Caiden, 1991: 27): inefficiency, centralization, fragmentation, poor leadership, lack of capacity, patrimonialism, rent-seeking, corruption, as well as poor accountability and legitimacy (Mukandala, 1992; Kiggundu, 1998; van de Walle, 2001). Some regard these problems as specifically related to 'African' culture and ethnically segmented societies (Haque, 1996; Chabal and Daloz, 1999). Others challenge such generalizations (Therkildsen, 2005).

Contested and changing views of the state and its role in development underlie these diagnoses. Donors, the World Bank and the IMF in particular have been especially influential in defining the 'problems' of the African public sector and the required remedies. Around the time of independence, in the 1950s and 1960s, the World Bank emphasized the state as a planner. In the 1970s, it focused on the state as the facilitator of development. This was replaced, in the 1980s, by the view of the state as a main problem. By the 1990s the view had changed once again: the state was now seen as an enabler of development (Marquette, 2003: 17). With the introduction of poverty-oriented debt relief (and the emphasis on Poverty Reduction Strategy Papers (PRSP) and MDGs) the donor view of the state is changing once again: the state is important and must play a more active role if the new poverty targets are to be achieved. Further changes lurk on the horizon. The emerging concerns about terrorism and its possible links to failed states may bring security issues onto the reform agenda (Fukuyama, 2002).

The focus in this chapter is on the last two decades. During this period many reform initiatives have been driven by fiscal stability targets with the New Public Management (NPM) approach providing the conceptual basis for several reform measures as far as efficiency and accountability initiatives are concerned. NPM focuses strongly on performance ('value for money', 'economy, effectiveness and efficiency') and transparency (Jann, 1997: 96; Larbi, 1999; see also Larbi this volume). Specific NPM initiatives include the introduction of private sector styles of management practice; marketization and the introduction of competition in service provision; explicit standards and measures of performance; greater transparency; pay reform; and emphasis on outputs (Hood, 1991). A number of measures that run counter to NPM are, however, also used. These include: strengthening public expenditure and revenue management through increased central level control over budgeting within specified budget frameworks; improving central financial controls and audits; and sharpening staff classification, establishment and recruitment procedures and the central control over these (Polidano, 1999).

Whatever the particular circumstances of individual countries may be, the official language of reform reflects apparently similar efficiency and accountability concerns in all countries in the region. Indeed, it reflects an internationalization of that language. In South Africa, for example, the government aims to make the public sector 'needs based, designed to meet the needs of all citizens-customers ... mission-driven and results-oriented ... focusing on ... results and outputs ... based on a facilitative ... state to mobilise the potential of civil society ... thereby empowering the citizens to share the responsibilities of governance' (Presidential Review Commission, 1998: chapter 3.1.3). The Ugandan vision statement (a fashionable word in many official reform documents) emphasizes 'improved service delivery', 'smaller', 'more efficient and effective', 'performance-based', 'responsive', 'fully accountable for outputs' and 'transparent' (Ministry of Public Service, 1993). In the current Public Service Reform Programme the focus is on 'least cost ... quality ... and appropriateness' of services, and on a public sector that facilitates the 'growth of a wealth creating private sector' (Mitaka and Katuramu, 2002: 82).

There are several reasons for such similarities in stated visions. No doubt the language serves to 'sell' reforms by seeking to convince domestic and external audiences that change is taking place, is desirable, or – failing that – is necessary or inevitable. Furthermore, many key decision-makers regard the problems facing the public sectors in the region as similar (see, for example, the articles in Kiragu and Mambo, 2002). A final reason is that most reform activities in the region are funded by donors (South Africa and, recently, Zimbabwe, being the exceptions). Thus, Africa has hosted the majority of World Bank projects with a civil service reform component since 1980 (Mukherjee and Manning, 2003: table 2). Compared to similar World Bank reform projects elsewhere, the African ones have been the most intensive in terms of number and breadth (Berg, 1999: 2–4). Bilateral donors are also increasingly active. In poor, aid-dependent African countries donors should, therefore, be regarded as key actors in the policy and implementation processes.

This does not imply that public sector reforms are simply imposed by donors. There is often co-operation with domestic members of pro-reform political and bureaucratic elites. And there are conflicts with reluctant or anti-reformer elites about the content, speed and depth of reforms. Interest groups outside the political and administrative establishment often play a less prominent role in the reform processes, with labour unions being a clear exception in some countries in the region.

A final feature of the change processes in the region should be mentioned. A gradual shift in the functional responsibilities between the public and the private and voluntary sectors is taking place. It is mainly pushed by capacity declines of the former and pulled by increasing domestic and foreign financing of the latter (Semboja and Therkildsen, 1995). Moreover, while reform-driven retrenchments have largely reduced employment at the lower levels of the public sector, professional and managerial staff are drained away from the upper levels by more attractive employment conditions in the private sector, among NGOs and donors, or in the international labour market. Brain drain is an increasingly serious problem

(Commission for Africa, 2005). Moreover, staff either abandon public employment entirely or straddle by combining a job in the public sector with private endeavours. In addition, the HIV/AIDS pandemic is increasingly taking its toll (de Waal, 2003). These changes erode public sector efficiency and accountability, although their impacts differ widely across countries in the region.

Thus, despite similarities in public sector problems, reform language and objectives, and despite significant donor influence on the reforms in most countries in the region, there are significant differences in the scope, content, speed and impact of the actual reform work on the ground. The following empirical analyses of reform experiences in the region clearly illustrate this.

Has the size and activities of the state changed since the mid-1980s?

Improved efficiency is the overriding aim of present public sector reforms in most African countries, as it is the holy grail of reform efforts in the North (Wright, 1997: 11). Reduction and refocusing of state activities are said to be needed, because the state is over-extended.

Arguments for such views are inspired by public (rational) choice theory, which emphasizes government rather than market failure. It focuses on rent-seeking in the public sector and on the need to contain the self-serving private interests of politicians and bureaucrats. Principal–agent theory provides additional arguments for reform by identifying the problems of multilayered bureaucratic hierarchies, multiple principals with conflicting objectives, long-term and unspecified contracts between principal and agent, and monopolistic agents that are difficult to motivate and control. Finally, an institutional economics perspective is influential. The economic characteristics of goods and services, such as the excludability and rivalry in consumption, and the monopoly, scale-economy and externalities in production are used to identify those goods and services that are most relevant for state involvement (see also Batley and Larbi, 2004: chapter 3).

The influences of these theoretical arguments have changed over the years concurrent with changing World Bank views. Thus, just a decade ago the World Bank (1994: 99) argued that the 'public sector lies at the core of the stagnation and decline in growth in Africa'. It has 'taken on too much' in providing essential services such as primary schools, with too few resources and little capability, and it has failed as a result. The capability of the state – its ability to promote and undertake collective action efficiently – is over-extended. Consequently, governments should concentrate their efforts less on direct intervention and more on enabling others to be productive. Furthermore, increased competition in service provision, both within the private sector and within the public sector itself, is required to raise efficiency. That means not just 'less government' but 'better government'. This focus on government failure dates back to the 'Berg Report' (World Bank, 1981). It overturned the conventional view of the previous twenty years during which a substantial interventionist role of the state was considered critical to overcome widespread market failures. More recently, the World Bank (1997: chapter 3 and p. 158) has taken a more balanced view of the role of the state in development. It now argues that 'without an effective state, sustainable development, both economic and social, is impossible'. It proposes the following 'core' functions: safeguarding law and order, protecting property rights, managing the macro-economy to promote and regulate the market, providing basic social services and infrastructure, and protecting the vulnerable and destitute. In short, to improve state capability and efficiency requires macro-economic stabilization and a refocusing of the role of the state on 'the fundamentals' so as to increase efficiency.

Such views are contested. The faith in market solutions has been dented by the often disastrous socio-economic consequences of liberalization in many of the post-communist transitional economies. The very uneven impact of structural adjustment programmes in sub-Saharan Africa has not helped either (Botchwey et al., 1998). Increased efficiency does not always proceed with increased effectiveness (the extent to which the objectives of a policy or programme are achieved). Proponents of the developmental state are, therefore, particularly concerned with its role in promoting development. They argue that 'the fundamentals' for African countries cover a wider range of activities than those proposed by the World Bank and the IMF. They also argue that normative and political considerations are central to such decisions. An active and effective state is critical for equitable development in the poorest countries where the private sector is weak and where poor infrastructure, social service delivery and market structures are major constraints for development (Rapley, 1996: 124–5; Mkandawire and Soludo, 1999: 126–34).

In practice, the narrower view of core state functions has formed the basis for much of the actual reform work until recently. Consequently, the refocusing of public sector functions is regarded as important to achieve capacity improvements. A variety of measures are used. These include staff reductions and changes/cuts in budgetary allocations among activities; restructuring of public organizations through the re-organization of ministries; and privatizing, decentralizing, delinking or hiving off of central government functions to local governments, other public bodies and NGOs or to the private sector.

Tables 2.1 and 2.2 present various indicators for changes over time in the size of the state and in its activities. The data are from different periods, depending on the specific country and indicator in question. Moreover, the

Table 2.1 Changes in the size of the state from the mid-1980s to around 2000 (compounded per cent change per year)

	Government employment		Military employment		Real government consumption per capita	
	Mid-1980s–mid-1990s	Mid-1990s–around 2000	Mid-1980s–mid-1990s	Mid-1990s–around 2000	Mid-1980s–mid-1990s	Mid-1990s–around 2000
Kenya	1.4	0.4	4.2	0.0	-2.3	1.9
Malawi	2.0	2.8	-0.4	0.0	0.0	1.4
Mozambique	-0.8	1.2	-3.8	15.9	-0.6	13.8
South Africa	0.0	-3.9	-1.6	-7.5	0.3	3.1
Tanzania	-1.2	-6.1	-1.1	-5.6	-2.8	-9.7
Uganda	-3.0	3.0	5.5	8.3	5.6	8.7
Zambia	2.2	0.9	2.8	0.0	-6.1	-2.5
Zimbabwe	0.4	1.5	-0.3	-2.0	-4.0	0.4

Notes: Data for the period mid-1980s to mid-1990s from Therkildsen (1999a: appendix 2 and 3), which also indicates the exact periods to which the changes refer. Malawi data, from Valentine (2003). Data for the period mid-1990s to around 2000 are from IISS (2003), the IMF (latest issue of country 'Statistical Appendix'), the World Bank Africa database and the World Bank (2003). The exact periods varies across countries and indicators. Data for Malawi, Mozambique and Tanzania are from Valentine (1999, 2001, 2002 and 2003).

Table 2.2 Changes in budget allocations (compounded per cent change per year)

	Government wages and salaries Expenditures		Military spending (real per capita)		Government education spending (real per capita)		Government health spending (real per capita)	
	Wage bill (% of recurrent expenditures; mid-1980s–mid-1990s)	Real wages/salaries 1992–2001	Mid-1980s–mid-1990s	Mid-1990s–2000	Mid-1980s–Mid-1990s	Mid-1990s–around 2000	Mid-1980s–mid-1990s	Mid-1990s–around 2000
Kenya	-0.4	-5.8	-7.1	2.5	1.2	-0.9	2.0	0.0
Malawi	1.1	2.1	-6.1	-37.7	-1.1	5.7	1.4	-1.7
Mozambique	2.3	18.7	-15.4	5.0	n.i	4.1	n.i	15.5
South Africa	2.7	n.i.	-4.4	-6.8	0.8	n.i	0.8	-2.0
Tanzania	1.0	8.1	-2.0	2.0	3.3	24.0	5.7	n.i
Uganda	7.0	21.1	4.4	-10.1	4.0	10.9	8.5	38.4
Zambia	9.1	n.i	-2.6	-23.5	-3.1	-12.0	-5.7	-0.9
Zimbabwe	1.7	1.3	-2.9	-5.6	-0.9	-35.0	-0.3	-16.4

Notes: Data for the period mid-1980s to the mid-1990s from Therkildsen (1999a: appendix 2 and 3), which also indicates the exact periods for which the changes refer. Data for the period mid-1990s to around 2000 are from IISS (1999, 2003), the World Bank Africa data base, World Bank (2003), and WHO (2004). The health spending figures for the period after the mid-1990s are based on international dollar rates. The exact periods varies across countries and indicators.

time periods chosen (before and after the mid-1990s) reflect the fact that it was around this time that reforms in many countries moved from a focus on reductions and cost-containment to a focus on service performance. The recent emphasis on poverty alleviation, from around 2000, has not yet been captured by the statistics presented here. Moreover, the statistics are not always consistent across countries or between time periods. The quality and scope of data are still deficient despite a decade-long focus on government operations. Comparisons of trends should therefore be done with caution (Therkildsen, 1999a: appendix 1).

With respect to changes in the size of the state, three indicators are used here. Table 2.1 shows that until the mid-1990s the size of the state – measured in terms of government employment – shrank in Mozambique, Tanzania and Uganda. The size remained fairly stable or increased in the remaining six countries during that period. Nevertheless, government employment measured in relation to population declined in all countries. Measured as general government consumption per capita, the size of the state has also declined significantly in all countries except Uganda (and remained fairly stable in Malawi, Mozambique and South Africa). After the mid-1990s, more countries are recording upwards trends in government and military employment as well as in per capita real government consumption. This reflects that the earlier strong focus on retrenchment has been replaced with new concerns about service delivery and (military) security. In particular, Mozambique and Uganda, two countries that experienced civil conflicts in the past, have increased the size of their military employment significantly in recent years.

Concurrent with such changes there has been some refocusing of government expenditures (Table 2.2). A shift in recurrent expenditures towards wages took place in all countries until the mid-1990s. Efficiency may have suffered as a result, because relatively fewer funds are available for non-wage recurrent expenditures. Except in Mozambique and Uganda[2] (and possibly South Africa and Tanzania), pay reform may not have raised real take-home pay for civil servants significantly, although past declines may have stopped in some countries (although not in Kenya, where declines have been substantial). The reason is that although nominal wage increases often result from consolidation of allowances into wages, these are taxed. Real take-home pay may, therefore, decrease as a result. Only in South Africa do civil servants generally get something approaching a 'living wage'.

Real per capita government spending on education and health (where such information is available) has generally increased from the mid-1980s to around 2000, although not in Zambia and Zimbabwe (where declines have been dramatic). Military expenditures have generally fallen except, lately, in Kenya, Mozambique and Tanzania. Obviously, the sustainability of these resource allocation trends is difficult to assess, and little is known about refocusing in other sectors than those mentioned above. Moreover, increased resource allocation does not automatically translate into improved service outcomes because of reallocations at organizational level, including corruption (Reinikka and Svenson, 2002), and because households, not the state, typically account for a substantial share of spending on social services. However, the HIPC debt relief has affected social spending positively since 2001 in countries that reached the decision point (Malawi, Mozambique, Zambia, Tanzania and Uganda). The MDG initiatives – and the increasing aid allocation to Africa that started around 2000 – will also improve funding of the public sector.

Attempts to refocus government activities through restructuring have also led to mixed results. Restructuring of ministries is a general feature of reform in the region. It has often led to reductions in the number of ministries and to attempts at refocusing ministerial roles on policy-making, regulation and monitoring. At the same time, establishment of executive agencies (e.g. for taxation, health, roads, water) is strongly pushed. There is now a growing concern, however, that many of the new agencies risk becoming second-generation parastatals that drain government budgets without providing effective services (Kassami et al., 2002). Contracting out is emerging in various sectors in South Africa, Zambia and Zimbabwe, but apparently only on a limited scale. Various degrees of devolution of ministerial implementation functions to local government are also typical. Uganda has moved decisively in that direction, while trends are more mixed in the other countries, and Kenya maintains the status quo (Ndegwa, 2002). Co-ordination of central and local government restructuring is generally poor, as is the co-ordination of sectoral reform work.

Has public sector accountability improved?

Improved accountability in the conduct of public affairs is another reform objective in many countries inside and outside Africa (Wright, 1997; Olowu, 1998: 619–20). The accountability of the state to society is about those with authority being answerable for their actions to the citizens, whether directly or indirectly. It is one of the defining features of a democracy. Thus a polity is democratic to the extent that 'institutionalised mechanisms [exist] through which the mass of the population exercise control over the political elite in an organised fashion' (Moore, 1998: 86). Day and Klein (1987: 26–7), furthermore, make an important distinction between political and managerial accountability. The latter refers to making those with delegated authority answerable for carrying out agreed tasks according to agreed criteria of performance.

The desired basic accountability mechanisms are as follows. Political representatives are elected. These, in turn, elect political heads of administrations that are supposed to control and steer public organizations via hierarchy, rules and procedures right down to the bottom of the bureaucracy. But in practice this does not work well. Administrative systems are not tightly controlled, rule-based hierarchies, but complicated and more or less closely integrated networks. Nor are states any longer externally and internally sovereign. Moreover, the basic accountability mechanism assumes that politicians make decisions up-front, and that bureaucrats loyally implement them. In practice it is often difficult or impossible to separate policy-making and implementation. Many important policy decisions are actually made by officials and other stakeholders during implementation. It is, furthermore, unrealistic to assume that policy decisions are made in agreement and with full operational knowledge about means–ends links. To the contrary, there are frequent political conflicts about ends, and uncertainty about means. Finally, the accountability problem is complicated by deficiencies in the political process itself. Civil servants may have legitimate reasons to override decisions of their opportunistic, self-serving, or irresponsible political masters.

There is plenty of empirical evidence to show that even in consolidated democratic states there are major deficits in accountability (Hill and Gillespie, 1996; Jann, 1997; DeLeon, 1997). Such problems of accountability are generally deeper in the countries considered here (Caiden, 1991: 280–1; Dia, 1993: 13; Mkandawire and Soludo, 1999: 135; Olowu, 1999). Moreover, the exercise of citizens' influence over state revenues and expenditures is an important component of effective democracy (Moore, 1998: 85). But in aid-dependent countries, of which there are several in the region, donors provide a substantial share of government funding and are *de facto* an integrated part of both the policy-making and the budgetary processes. Typically, therefore, donors require that recipient governments are accountable to them for the use of aid funds. This further weakens already fragile domestic accountability mechanisms. In aid-dependent countries the issue of accountability, therefore, includes the role of donors.

Various political and economic reform initiatives of the 1990s and the recent PRSP approaches address some of the accountability problems discussed above. The focus in this analysis is, however, on performance management inspired by NPM concepts. It points to new ways of addressing age-old problems of accountability.[3]

Performance management

Unfortunately, independent research on the accountability implications of NPM-inspired reform measures in African countries is very limited. The approach taken in the following is, therefore, to assess key assumptions of NPM against conditions in a poor, aid-dependent country so as to answer the initial question: has public sector accountability improved?

Accountability is assumed to be enhanced by performance management. The basic idea is that public sector managers undertake to meet explicit targets or carry out specific activities. In return, government commits itself to provide various resource inputs and to give more authority to public managers over operations, including budgeting, purchasing and personnel. Thus, making targets transparent makes it easier to establish the basis for managerial accountability and to achieve outputs without which the notion of accountability becomes irrelevant (Hill and Gillespie, 1996: 167). This requires that political visions are translated into clear and explicit managerial targets combined with increased managerial autonomy and incentives to perform. Political accountability is thereby enhanced in two ways. Explicit targets help managers – in dialogue with politicians – to match them with political priorities. And by monitoring the extent to which targets are met, politicians can, in turn, hold managers accountable for their performance or lack of it. Finally, performance targets and the monitoring of them can make service provision more transparent to customers.

According to this line of argument, increased transparency and explicit performance targets are further steps towards better democratic control and accountability of bureaucracy. It is a point that often gets lost in the rhetoric about 'value for money' so closely associated with recent NPM-inspired reforms (Jann, 1997: 87). Several countries are in the process of establishing performance management arrangements.

In *South Africa*, for example, new public service regulations came into effect in early 1998. They form the basis for establishing performance contracts between ministers and their chief executives. Performance management mechanisms *per se* will also be effected for all employees. Moreover, the White Paper on Transformation of the Public Service from 1995 requires national and provincial departments to redirect resources to areas and groups previously neglected, to set service standards, to define outputs, targets and performance indicators, and to benchmark them against comparable international standards (Singh et al., 1998: 17 and 32). This is combined with moves towards larger managerial autonomy for departments (PRC, 1998: chapter 4.5). However, implementation proceeds cautiously and recent analyses indicate that 'the culture of accountability to citizens' will, at best, take a long time to emerge (Ramaite, 2002).

In *Tanzania*, a Performance Improvement Component is now the central plank of the reform programme in the future (Government of Tanzania, 1998: chapter 4). Each ministry will make an annual plan within its total budget ceiling so that output-based budgets can be matched to objectives and targets, performance indicators can be established, and activities planned accordingly. If a ministry meets its performance targets, the Ministry of Finance will promote that ministry from the cash budgeting system to a more predictable resource base. A significant degree of autonomy in the allocation of funds will also be given. Performance management systems have been installed in most ministries and performance agreements have been signed with several of them. Experiences so far have shown, as Mollel and Yambesi (2002: 78) conclude, that the 'road to performance improvement is long and rough, but not impossible'. Rugumyemheto (2004) provides a more optimistic assessment.

In *Uganda*, the implementation of Results-Oriented Management (ROM) is a major reform objective. Specific and measurable performance targets are to be established for each ministry, department, unit and individual officers. ROM will also be introduced in local governments. Moreover, there are plans to introduce annual performance contracts with the more than 100 proposed autonomous and semi-autonomous bodies (Ministry of Public Service, 1998: 40). The system will be linked to the budget process and will form the basis for making annual plans based on agreement with the Ministry of Finance. A service delivery survey was made in 1992 with World Bank assistance to provide a base line against which to measure the reform progress and allow policy-makers 'to assess reform inputs and outcomes in terms of the highest net marginal benefits to the public' (Langseth, 1996: 61). Progress on ROM has been limited, however, except for a wave of facilitation and training workshops. ROM and Output-Oriented Budgeting re-emerged on the reform agenda in 1996, following the further devolution of functions to local governments. However, ministries argue strongly that they cannot deliver because they are under-staffed, and they request extra staff whenever shortfalls in performance arise (Okutho, 1998: 15–17). Nevertheless, the increasing uses of performance indicators at sector level – and the tying of donor inputs to performance targets – have emerged as central features of the public policy debate including the dialogue with donors (Adam and Gunning, 2002).

In *Zimbabwe*, a performance management system was introduced in 1994. It included top civil servants only, but was supposed to be extended to the entire service. The system required that heads of ministries prepare work plans specifying outputs and targets and a review by the respective minister and the Office of the President and the Cabinet (Moyo et al., 1998). Although the system was supposed to be a key element in the country's Civil Service Reform Programme, it was abandoned prematurely in 1996, 'as it was realised that a lot more ground work needed to be carried out first'. Furthermore, many top civil servants were against the system. They wanted power to hire and fire their junior staff if their own tenure in office was to depend on the performance of their ministries and/or departments. This was resisted due to dangers of creating 'personal empires', 'regional cliques', and even 'ethnic enclaves'. In the end, therefore, the *status quo* prevailed. Control of the civil service is still held by the Public Service Commission and 'only the most mundane of administrative activities' related to recruitment, training and staff promotion are decentralised to ministries (Makumbe, 1997: 10–11). The performance management system appears now to be implemented extremely cautiously (Zondo, 2002).

As indicated by the experiences from Uganda and Zimbabwe, there are major problems in applying these performance management principles. This is not surprising given the controversial track record of such principles elsewhere (Pollitt, 1995). A major reason is that the political and managerial implications of performance-based contract arrangements are complex and controversial. They are based on assumptions that are not generally met under prevailing conditions.

Thus, meaningful contracts cannot be established without predictability of resources. But in countries that have operated a cash budget system – such as Malawi, Tanzania, Uganda and Zambia – resource allocations depend on the actual revenues collected during the preceding period. Revenues are heavily dependent on rainfall and/or donor funding, both of which are erratic. Indeed, aid flows are even more volatile than tax revenues.

The measurability of performance is problematic too, in both sectors with soft and varied outputs and especially in the absence of a common and broadly accepted framework for defining what 'good' performance means. As a result, information about actions, including statistical data, becomes less meaningful to the actors (citizens, politicians or managers) in the accountability arena. It may also affect bureaucrats in unexpected ways. Montgomery (1986: 411–12) argues that without strong countervailing political forces and strong constitutional or institutional restraints for ensuring accountability, officials – although formally being free to take risks – seldom do so, because they are uncertain about which public priorities and values they are expected to advance by such action. The framework may develop through the political process and through a dialogue with users, but if such processes are weak, it is unlikely that greater transparency and more information will increase accountability. The only thing that has been made more visible 'is ambiguity' (Day and Klein, 1987: 243).

Accountability is further weakened by uncertainties about causal links between means and ends. When this is the case, a performance contract cannot specify the service delivery outcomes of specified amounts of inputs with precision in advance. Equally important, such contracts will not work as intended if there is insufficient political will to enforce compliance. An analysis of experiences with performance contracts in state-owned enterprises concluded that they 'rarely improve incentives and may do more harm than good' because the political costs of enforcement are often considerable (World Bank, 1995: 7). This is precisely the problem. The assumption in NPM is that transparency promotes political accountability, because politicians will be better informed about what is actually delivered, and they will act on such information. The opposite may also happen, as Wright (1997: 11) notes with respect to Western Europe: politicians conveniently hide behind managerial discretion and autonomy.

Where such problems prevail, performance-based arrangements linked to increased management authority may not improve accountability. Indeed, they may contribute to further corruption, because regulatory and monitoring mechanisms often are weak (Szeftel, 1998). This has been a concern in many Western countries where such mechanisms are generally stronger. It would therefore appear that the applicability of performance management is rather limited in the region. General use – as seems to be the aim in South Africa, Tanzania, and Uganda – is questionable. Performance contracts and empowerment measures cannot replace political accountability. The cart cannot push the horse.

Is there political support for the reforms?

Reform is basically about inducing changes in relations of power between state and society, between politicians and bureaucrats, and between government organizations (Caiden, 1991: 66). Implementation of reforms, therefore, involves varying degrees of enforcement of change against resistance. This resistance tends to take place during implementation rather than during the policy-making phase, and makes it important to understand the politics of reform implementation (leaving aside the substantial implementation issues related to reform funding, management, and coordination and monitoring). Three important actors in the reform process – interest groups, state elites and donors – are discussed below.

Interest groups

The stakes of interest groups in public sector reforms tend to be ambiguous and conflictual. Even when they have clear interests in specific reform measures, their power to influence them does not depend only on their economic and other interests, but also on their capacity to organize, which is often low. Moreover, the institutional mechanisms through which interests are translated into political demands are often weak or non-existent (Haggard and Kaufmann, 1992). Batley (1999: 11) confirms the weak fingerprints of interest groups in reform implementation, particularly of the poor, whom he calls the 'silent stakeholders of reform'. Such observations are, however, only partly confirmed in the case studies presented here.

First of all, there have been several instances of organized demands for public sector reform in the region. The influence of unions in South Africa is an example. Here the Congress of South African Trade Unions, through its close relations with the ANC, has some influence on the framework for the reform of the public sector. Corporatist institutions have also been set up. They allow business and unions to influence economic, social and labour policies, although they leave out the voices of the unemployed and the poor (Nattrass and Seekings, 1998).

More generally, popular protests (or the fear of them) combined with the ruling elites' concern about electoral support, do influence the reforms in significant ways. During the transition to multi-party rule in Malawi, for example, significant changes in pay and education policy took place in the wake of public protests. In Tanzania the run-up to the year 2000 presidential, national and local elections influenced pay policy decisions and the speed and scope of local government reform (Therkildsen, 1999b). But the political pressures are contradictory. On the one hand, the standard argument that salaries of government employees must be raised to contain corruption may not find wide political support with a public that regards civil servants as already well paid. Indeed, using the average incomes of the population at large as the yardstick, the civil service in Africa is the relatively best paid in the world (Schiavo-Campo, 1998). On the other hand, the importance of the 110,000-member strong teachers' union in Tanzania is reflected in the unexpected pay raise for teachers in 1997 decided against the technical recommendations to the Cabinet. This was a politically motivated move intended to attract support for the ruling party from the largest group of civil servants. Through direct contacts to the president, this union has also succeeded in halting present government plans to transfer all primary school teachers from central to local government service as part of the efforts to devolve personnel management to urban and rural councils.

It is also noteworthy that in 1990 a Ministry of Health proposal to introduce user charges in health services in Uganda was stopped due to widespread public opposition. This did not prevent the local authorities from raising revenues in this way, and a nation-wide system was eventually introduced in 1992, when the World Bank made it a condition for new loans to the health sector. But Uganda also provides an interesting example of how public opinion may support reform measures. Thus, the 'absence of popular uproar' against the massive retrenchments in the 1990s is partly explained by the lack of public sympathy for civil servants and the negative image of its perceived laxity and poor service delivery (Brown et al., 1995: 33).

In Zimbabwe, student unrest in 1992 against raising the private costs of university education, and a wave of riots in 1993 in low-income suburbs in Harare to protest against price increases on bread and flour, contributed to weakening the government's commitment to reform (Botchwey et al., 1998: 109). Moreover, the adverse effects of the economic reform programmes on real wages in the public sector have resulted in multiple strikes. Health sector personnel, for example, went on strike in 1988, 1989, 1994 and twice in 1996 (Bennett et al., 1999: 9). There were new strikes in 1998. The 1996 strikes involved most of the civil service. According to Makumbe (1997: 11–16), they were caused not only by dissatisfaction with pay increases and proposed new salary scales. They were also a protest against the blatant display of wealth among top government leaders, generally deteriorating living standards, dwindling funds to the public services, and a lack of machinery for union negotiation with government about terms and conditions in government service. Despite the deepening economic crisis in Zimbabwe, civil servants have benefited from several pay raises, while expenditures on health and education has declined; see Table 2.2. This is a clear pointer to the political importance of civil servants, which is the focus of the next section.

State elites

Although specific circumstances are important, most reform initiatives in the region tend to be designed and implemented in a top-down fashion by political and bureaucratic elites (the role of donors are dealt with below). There are several reasons for this. Such elites have substantial power over the policy agenda because of their unique position in both the policy process and in important political institutions, including the state itself. This position is amplified by the weaknesses of the institutional framework for dialogue and negotiations with various interest groups about reform issues. Moreover, state elites engage in crucial mediating roles between international and domestic stakeholders of reform, and donors are important actors, as shown in the next section.

It is, however, striking that the role of political elites often seems rather inconspicuous and limited, while that of the technocrats is significant. This is perhaps not surprising because of the strong emphasis on fiscal stability and use of budgetary instruments to change the size and functions of the public sector. This focus has generally strengthened the power of the Ministry of Finance (MOF). Botchwey et al. (1998: 81–82) observed, for example, that despite the initial pro-reform posture of the ruling party in Malawi, it was the MOF that pushed through the reforms of the mid-1990s (with funds from the IMF). As hardship set in, this quickly led to a sense of 'hopelessness ... and imposition' in the top levels of government, as they struggled with the political implications. The bureaucracy, for its part, 'remained half-hearted at best and mostly cynical about the reforms and about the role of the rising number of well-paid external advisors'. The MOF left the rest of the ministries 'marginalized and resentful'. In South Africa, the MOF designed the Macro-Economic Strategy for Growth, Employment and Redistribution, which is central to the current reform efforts. In Zambia, the MOF has become the *de facto* lead agency for reform, instead of the formally designed Management Development Division in the Cabinet Office. The same trend is obvious in Uganda and emerging in Tanzania.

While the influence of bureaucratic elites is easy to verify, it is more difficult to find clear cases of active political elites in reforms apart from two countries. In South Africa, the transformation of the public sector inherited from the apartheid regime is clearly politically led. Support for the longer-term reform aspects is likely to be more conflictual, as pointed out by the Presidential Review Commission (1998). In Uganda there has also been substantial support for reforms from the political leadership with the president in the lead (Okutho, 1998). He sacked, for example, ten principal secretaries in July 1996, some of them allegedly because of their poor performance in reform activities. Since then the president's attention has moved from reform issues to the conflict in the north, the ongoing controversies about constitutional reform and the implications of the moves to increased political competition. However, the parliament has become more influential in reform issues. It has, for example, been very active in drafting the legislation for the local government reform. In addition parliamentary committees now oversee (as yet feebly) the implementation of many public sector reform activities.

In all countries, even where reforms seem to be pushed most decisively by political-administrative elites, there are many conflicts. For one of the many reform paradoxes is that it is often the very elites, whose past decisions and present privileges and rent-seeking possibilities are now challenged by reform initiatives, that are also deeply involved in reform implementation. Reform commitment is therefore often contingent for personal or ideological reasons. It also depends on larger political considerations as well as on results on the ground.

Thus, even in Uganda, where reforms are most decisively implemented, Botchwey et al. (1998: 91) note that the 'most significant, even if unorganised, source of opposition to ... reforms are mid-to-senior level civil servants' who have lost their rent-seeking opportunities. Oyugi (1990: 69) argues that 'the "class" orientation of the bureaucracy ... stands in the way of any change effort that is not in their interest ... Invariably, the bureaucracy would ignore everything but the salary increases!' da Silva and Solimano (1999: 47–8) claim that self-interest is an acute problem in war economies like that of Mozambique, where 'the commitment to reforms by ruling elites is a function of the perception of what would happen to their individual utility, not to social welfare'.

Such conflicts are not limited to countries with unchanged political leadership. Even where this has changed significantly, many top civil servants remain. In Malawi, for example, there were profound disagreements between politicians and the majority of top civil servants inherited from the one-party era about their respective roles and about what their loyalty and professionalism should mean in a career civil service (Adamolekun et al., 1997: 216–17). Similarly, in Zimbabwe, '[a]lthough the [reform] programme was conceived by politicians, communication broke down during its implementation' according to senior civil servants (Moyo et al., 1998: 5). In South Africa, the Constitution forces the government to retain many senior civil servants from the old regime, many of whom are demotivated and, in some cases, hostile to the reform (PRC, 1998: section 2.1.3).

Public sector reforms also give rise to inter-organizational conflicts. The control over local-level activities is a prominent arena. This is especially the case where substantial local government reforms are underway. In Uganda, for example, where the formal devolution of power is considerable, 'practically all ministries ... put up ... silent or quasi-active resistance to letting go of many of the decentralized functions' (MPS, 1998: 60). In some countries, sector ministries may seek to retain or increase their control by proposing service boards to be in charge of specialised services such as health, water and roads, as mentioned earlier. Health service boards, delinked from local governments, are, for example, part of health sector reforms in Tanzania, Zambia and Zimbabwe. Another contentious issue concerns the extent to which central government transfers of funds to local authorities should be earmarked to specific purposes (making the authorities agents of central government), or be provided as block grants (allowing the authorities to allocate funds on the basis of local priorities). Often donors are key stakeholders in this issue, since they provide substantial recurrent and investment costs to health, education and water in many countries in the region.

General interpretations of the various conflicts are therefore difficult to make. Elite resistance to reforms is not based on self-interest alone, nor is it fixed once and for all. Thus the Ugandan leadership changed its views on reform towards the positive while that of Zimbabwe changed towards the negative during the course of implementation (Botchwey et al., 1998: 88–90 and 109–10). But perhaps the most problematic assumption in much of the literature is that reforms are often regarded as intrinsically good, and resistance to them therefore motivated by suspect motives of self-interest.

This view is difficult to defend in light of the limited success of the public sector reforms so far in improving service delivery. Reforms are often politically unattractive, because of their frequent association with cutbacks in service provision, retrenchment (the public sector being the single largest employer in the formal sector) and the introduction of user charges (Radoki, 1999: 12). Indeed, the strong emphasis on cutbacks in the reforms until recently is a main cause of resistance among officials, as Mkandawire and Soludo (1999: 135) argue. The observations by Adamolekun et al. (1997: 220) that 'no champion for reform has emerged at the political level' in Malawi, and by Makumbe (1997: 7) that there is a 'lack of political commitment to the [civil service reform] programme by senior policy-makers' in Zimbabwe, are valid for other countries in the region as well. In fact, lack of clear political commitment to public sector reform was identified as a major problem by top civil servants engaged in this work in the region (Therkildsen, 1998: 5).

Donors

Despite much talk about partnership and 'common interests', the reality is that the prominent roles of donors in many countries *de facto* make them part of the policy-making and implementation processes, while their accountability to recipient citizens, bureaucrats and politicians is limited.

For the external influences on public sector reforms in most African countries are substantial (Haggard and Kaufmann, 1992). They are transmitted through trade links with international markets (exclusion, economic crises and external shocks), through leverage (conditionality and aid dependency) and through social and political networks (shared ideological and professional views).

Economic crisis has been a key factor in bringing public sector reforms and the need for additional external funding on the agenda (see Bangura and Larbi's Introduction to this volume). Typically, such reforms are closely linked to the structural adjustment programmes negotiated with the World Bank and the IMF. These institutions often make access to funding conditional on changes in the public sector and on the provision of substantial technical inputs. Obviously, such influences are pronounced in the poor, aid-dependent countries where multilateral and bilateral donors typically are major stakeholders in the reforms (as is the case in all countries in the region except South Africa). Thus in a recent IMF study, Abed et al. (1998: 27) note that 'civil service reforms constituted an important element of fiscal reform, with the World Bank mostly taking the lead'. Ellis (1999: 4) simply states that 'reforms are externally driven'. Also Batley (1997: 22) sees donor imposition as a major driving force in many reforms. In a comparative study of the changing role of governments in adjusting economies, he found that developing countries with the least capacity to resist external demands for change and to carry them through, tend to be engaged in (or at least plan) the most far-reaching reforms.

These general observations are supported by country evidence. Botchwey et al. (1998: 81) found that in Malawi 'too many initiatives were being initiated by different donors ... nobody seems in charge ... donors often push agendas of their own ... Given the government's limited technical capacity and the pressures on such capacity ... the entire policy agenda has tended to be dominated unduly by the Fund.' Adamolekun et al. (1997: 218) add that 'capacity overload' resulted from the numerous donor interventions in Malawi. For example, in 1996, seven donors were involved in civil service reform-oriented activities in the MOF alone (IMF, UNDP, DfID, EU, CIDA and the World Bank). Although commenting on economic reforms, da Silva and Solimano (1999: 42) note that 'reform in Mozambique was mainly triggered by an exceptional conjunction of external political factors and did not come from a strong commitment for reform'. In Tanzania, more than a dozen major reform initiatives are presently being implemented with donor assistance, although the political support for reform is fragile (Therkildsen, 1999b). In Zimbabwe, the government adopted the Civil Service Reform Programme in reaction to the 'dictates' of some of the structural adjustment conditionalities (Makumbe, 1997: 5). This is confirmed by the IMF's own analyses, which found that the fiscal measures demanded by the fund required 'an astonishing contraction' of non-debt payments, and 'a massive underestimation' of its social costs (Botchwey et al., 1998: 102–10).

However, there is also another important dimension to the government–donor relationship: that of collusion. In Tanzania, for example, resource-starved ministries sometimes make specific reform proposals in order to attract donor funding, while institutional changes are often a condition for donor support. Both parties, therefore, have a joint interest in reforms, although their motivations may differ (Therkildsen, 1999b). Similarly, Wuyts (1996: 742) describes how sector ministries in Mozambique collude with donors to protect their specific sectoral programmes, because availability or promises of donor funds strengthen a sector's bargaining power with the central authorities. Senior civil servants from Zimbabwe report that some ministries accept donor financing for reform purposes 'regardless of the priority of the project, but simply because the donor wished to provide the funding' (Moyo et al., 1998: 15).

It is also well known that lack of coordination between donor-funded activities often gives recipient organizations some leeway *vis-à-vis* donors. The same donor may even have conflicting interests, which may provide recipients with room for manoeuvre. Wuyts (1996: 743) illustrates this by showing how the World Bank helped to impose local counterpart fund requirements on ministries in Mozambique, and then sought to circumvent these conditions to protect its loan-financed programmes, when the MOF tried to reduce such programmes in favour of grant-supported activities. The PRSP process, where it has taken some root, is, however, evolving as a useful mechanism for better coordination, although it is still a very technocratic exercise with recipient country politicians looking on from the sideline.

Finally, the effects of donor imposition are sometimes difficult to distinguish from the effects of the adaptation of ideas from elsewhere. Indirect and diffuse pressures are exerted on domestic reform agents through increasingly global professional, political and social networks. Ingraham (1996: 248) argues that such pressures constrain the possibilities for innovation and home-grown responses to public sector problems. As noted earlier, ideas about reform are, indeed, remarkably similar despite diversities in national contexts and domestic influences. South Africa, for example, receives limited aid for public sector reforms, but has assiduously followed the Washington Consensus with respect to structural adjustment. Similarly, many proposals concerning the transformation of its public sector are inspired by the NPM model and not imposed by donors. The recent proposals for reform in Tanzania made by the reform agency of the government also illustrate a considerable inspiration of such measures (Government of Tanzania, 1998). No doubt key international institutions, such as the OECD and the World Bank, try to influence the scope and content of reforms through a 'mass propaganda type of diffusion' (Hood,

1996: 273). Economies of scale encourage such organizations (and the bilaterals) to search for and promote 'best practices' models, and public sector reforms are no exception.

It is, therefore, obvious that donors are as often part of the problem of the public sector in many countries in the region as they are part of the solution (Birdsall, 2004). Reform of the public sectors in donor-dependent countries must go hand in hand with aid reforms.

Elusive reforms

Three main questions are addressed in this chapter: Has the size of the state changed and its activities become more focused? Has public sector accountability improved? Is there political support for the reform initiatives?

The analyses show that public sector reform efforts in east and southern Africa have produced rather mixed results over the last twenty years. However, the goalposts have changed over time. While cost-cutting and containment of the state were high on the formal reform agenda in most countries from the mid-1980s and until recently, the emphasis now is also on improved public sector performance with respect to poverty alleviation and the MDGs. The fight against terrorism may result in additional demands. Thus, the reform agendas in the region do not just reflect national and local concerns. They also reflect international priorities, approaches and pressures.

To assume that the public sector changes analysed here are driven just by simple notions of efficiency, effectiveness and accountability is therefore problematic. The analyses show that reforms are highly political and generate (often) legitimate conflicts among domestic interests (especially trade unions and state elites) and donors. Moreover, reforms are shaped by the national and local contexts in which they are implemented. Consequently, the future of public sector reforms and their outcomes will depend on the politics of reform to a considerable degree. This has several implications.

First, fiscally-driven reductions of state employment and functions have gone too far, as various observers now agree, although they otherwise have sharply different opinions about public sector reforms. Thus, the IMF study by Lienert and Modi (1997: 10) states that present reforms have been 'overemphasizing downward quantitative adjustments'. The World Bank (1997: 24) finds that governments mired in debt tended to go too far in removing themselves from 'vital functions' in infrastructure, health and education to meet interest obligations (an overshoot often pushed by donors, it should be added). Mkandawire and Soludo (1999: 136) conclude that 'the emphasis should be on reconstruction rather than retrenchment' (although this analysis shows that retrenchments have been relatively modest except in Uganda and Tanzania). A better focus on and understanding of the developmental role of the state in very resource-poor countries is, therefore, needed. Increased spending on service delivery is a necessary, although not a sufficient, condition for service improvements. But as long as fiscal stability remains the overriding reform concern in practice, and with limited progress on economic growth, trade negotiations and revenue collection, significant efficiency gains are very difficult to achieve.

Second, much more attention should be given to the political dynamics of reform. Unfortunately, the basic premise in much of the literature is that reform of the public sector is intrinsically desirable, and resistance to change therefore motivated by suspect motives of self-interest among state elites. But domestic resistance against reform is not just based on entrenched self-interests, nor is it fixed once and for all, as proponents of the overextended state seem to assume. Ambivalence, if not resistance, is understandable in the light of the mixed improvements of reforms for service levels for citizens, and for real take-home pay increases for civil servants in the region.

Third, donors influence the political dynamics of reform too, although they do not suffer the consequences of their action when things go wrong. Donors should not become more directly involved in the politics of reform. Instead, they should take the domestic political dimension of their support (or withdrawal) from domestic reform processes seriously. This would also help to bring the limited domestic political (and technical) capacity to implement them to the fore. Conditionality, as is now increasingly acknowledged, is not the answer to resistance to reform. The track record of donors in reform work suggests that they do not have privileged knowledge about how to redress efficiency, accountability and service delivery problems in the region. An aid reform is urgently needed.

This points, finally, to a blind spot in present reform work: the lack of attention to and understanding of the 'ground level' of the public sector. The problems of the lower levels of the political-administrative machinery, and their relations with urban, village and community-based groups, are particularly relevant from a broader efficiency, accountability and service delivery perspective. The co-production and co-financing at this level, mediated through social relations, have been the backbone of numerous developmental initiatives in many countries in the region over the years, as Semboja and Therkildsen (1995) and White and Robinson (1998) show. Yet present reforms not only tend to be top-down in design and implementation, they also tend to focus on the upper levels of central and local government. That is to start at the wrong end of the stick. A better understanding of the interactions between government agencies and citizens at the service delivery points is necessary in order to improve future reform work.

Meanwhile, it is clear that poor African countries will not meet the Millennium Goals by 2015. They simply have the longest way to go to reach them. Unfortunately, the MDGs were set globally without much regard for each country's actual public sector capacity and other specific conditions. This neglects one of the key lessons about public sector reforms in Africa (and elsewhere): the design and implementation of reforms must be based on and reflect actual political, economic and social conditions on the ground. Not only may the MDGs create undue pessimism about the development progress that has occurred in many countries in the region; they may also put harmful pressure on the public sectors in African countries to try to meet unrealistic MDGs. A much more context and country specific approach to poverty alleviation is clearly needed. The MDGs should not be viewed as realistic targets but as reminders of increasing global inequality and injustice that urgently need to be addressed.

Notes

1. This is a shorter, revised and updated version of Therkildsen (1999a).
2. Nevertheless, more than twice the total Ugandan wage bill for core ministries is spent on consultancies according to the 'Background to the Budget, 2004/2005' Ministry of Finance, (p. 39).
3. Another major initiative to improve accountability concerns the empowerment of the public and the citizens *vis-à-vis* service providers and the public sector. It includes measures to strengthen community-based organizations, increase choice of service providers, Citizen's Charters, ethical codes of conduct for public servants, user surveys, etc. (see Therkildsen, 1999a for analyses).

References

Abed, G. T. et al. (1998) 'Fiscal Reforms in Low-income Countries: Experience under IMF-Supported Programs', *Occasional paper*, No. 160, Washington: IMF.

Adam, C. S. and J. W. Gunning (2002) 'Redesigning the Aid Contract: Donors' Use of Performance Indicators in Uganda', *World Development*, Vol. 30, No. 12: 2045–56.

Adamolekun, L., N. Kulemeka and M. Laleye (1997) 'Political Transition, Economic Liberalization and Civil Service Reform in Malawi', *Public Administration and Development*, Vol. 17: 209–22.

Addison, T., H. Hansen and F. Tarp (eds.) (2004) *Debt Relief for Poor Countries*, Basingstoke: Palgrave.

Bangura, Y. (1999) *Public Sector Restructuring: The Institutional and Social Effects of Fiscal, Managerial and Capacity Building Reforms*, UNRISD, Occasional Paper No. 3. Geneva 2000: The Next Step in Social Development.

Batley, R. (1997) 'A Research Framework for Analysing Capacity to Undertake the "New Roles" of Government', in *The Changing Role of Government in Adjusting Economies*, Paper No. 23, University of Birmingham, September.

Batley, R. (1999) 'An Overview of Findings', Paper No. 2, Workshop on the Changing Role of Government in Adjusting Economies. School of Public Policy, The University of Birmingham, 28–30 March.

Batley, R. and G. Larbi (2004) *The Changing Role of Government: The Reform of Public Services in Developing Countries*, Basingstoke: Palgrave Macmillan.

Bekke, H. A. G. M., J. L. Perry and T. A. J. Toonen, (eds.) (1996) *Civil Service Systems in a Comparative Perspective*, Bloomington: Indiana University Press.

Bennett, S., S. Russell and A. Mills (1999) 'Health Sector – Summary Paper', No. 3. Workshop on the Changing Role of Government in Adjusting Economies, School of Public Policy, University of Birmingham, 28–30 March.

Berg, E. (1999) 'Aid Failure: The Case of Public Sector Reform', Revision of October Aid Conference paper, University of Copenhagen. April.

Birdsall, N. (2004) 'Seven Deadly Sins: Reflections on Donor Failings', *Working Paper* No. 50, Washington: Center for Global Development.

Botchwey, K., P. Collier, J. W. Gunning and K. Hamada (1998) 'Report of the Group of Independent Persons Appointed to Conduct an Evaluation of Certain Aspects of the Enhanced Structural Adjustment Facility', Washington: IMF.

Brown, K., K. Kiragu and S. Villadsen (1995) 'Uganda Civil Service Reform Case Study', Report for the UK Overseas Development Administration and Danida, April.

Caiden, G. (1991) *Administrative Reform Comes of Age*, Amsterdam: Elsevier.

Chabal, P. and J. Daloz (1999) *Africa Works: Disorder as Political Instrument*, London: James Currey.

Commission for Africa (2005) *Our Common Interest*, March, London.

Day, P. and R. Klein (1987) *Accountabilities: Five Public Services*, London: Tavistock Publications.

DeLeon, L. (1997) 'Administrative Reform and Democratic Accountability', in W. Kickert (ed.), *Public Management and Administrative Reform in Western Europe*, Cheltenham: Edward Elgar.

Dia, M. (1993) 'A Governance Approach to Civil Service Reform in Sub-Saharan Africa', *World Bank Technical Paper* No. 225.

Duffield, M. (2002) 'Reprising Durable Disorder: Network War and the Securisation of Aid', in *Global Governance in the 21st Century: Alternative Perspectives on World Order*, eds. B. Hettne and B. Oden, Stockholm: Expert Group on Development Issues. SIDA, p. 2.

Ellis, F. (1999) 'An Overview of Policy Implications', Workshop on the changing role of government in adjusting economies, University of Birmingham, 28–30 March.

Fukuyama, F (2004) *State Building: Governance and World Order in the Twenty-first Century*, London: Profile Books.

Government of Tanzania (1996) 'Vision, Strategy and Action Plan, 1996–1999', Civil Service Reform Programme, Civil Service Department, President's Office, March.

Government of Tanzania (1998) 'Strategy and Action Plan, 1998–2003', (Draft), Public Sector Reform Programme, Dar-es-Salaam: Civil Service Department, President's Office, December.

Haggard, S. and R. Kaufmann (1992) 'Institutions and Economic Adjustments', in S. Haggard and R. Kaufmann (eds.), *The Politics of Economic Adjustment*, Princeton, NJ: Princeton University Press.

Haque, M. S. (1996) 'The Contextless Nature of Public Administration in Third World Countries', *International Review of Administrative Sciences*, Vol. 62: 315–29.

Hill, M. and D. Gillespie (1996) 'Social Control of Civil Service Systems', in H. A. G. M. Bekke et al., *Civil Service System in a Comparative Perspective*, Bloomington: Indiana University Press.

Hood, C. (1991) 'A Public Management for all Seasons', *Public Administration*, Vol. 69, No. 1: 3–19.

Hood, C. (1996) 'Exploring Variations in Public Management Reform of the 1980s', in H. A. G. M. Bekke et al. (eds.), *Civil Service System in a Comparative Perspective*, Bloomington: Indiana University Press.

Ingraham, P. W. (1996) 'The Reform Agenda for National Civil Service Systems: External Stress and Internal Strain', in H. A. G. M. Bekke et al., *Civil Service System in a Comparative Perspective*, Bloomington: Indiana University Press.

International Institute of Strategic Studies (IISS) (1999, 2003) *The Military Balance*, Oxford: Oxford University Press.

Jann, W. (1997) 'Public Management Reform in Germany: A Revolution without a Theory?' in W. Kickert (ed.), Public Management and Administrative Reform in Western Europe, Cheltenham: Edward Elgar.

Kassami, C., F. Mugasha and B. van Arkadie (2002) 'Final Report of the Committee to Advise the President on more effective Public Administration Budgeting', Kampala, Mimeo.

Kickert, W. (ed.) (1997) *Public Management and Administrative Reform in Western Europe*, Cheltenham: Edward Elgar.

Kiggundu, M. N. (1998) 'Civil Service Reforms: Limping into the Twenty-First Century', in M. Minogue, C. Polidano and D. Hulme (eds.), *Beyond the New Public Management, Changing Ideas and Practices in Governance*, Cheltenham: Edward Elgar.

Kiragu, K. and H. L. Mambo (2002) *Public Service Reform Comes of Age in Africa*, Dar-es-Salaam: Mkuki na Nyota Publishers.

Langseth, P. (1996) 'The Civil Service Reform Programme', in P. Langseth and J. Mugaju (eds.), *Post-conflict Uganda: Towards an Eeffective Civil Service*, Kampala: Fountain Publishers.

Larbi, G. A. (1999) 'The New Public Management Approach and Crisis States', *UNRISD Discussion Paper*, No. 112.

Leys, C. (1994) 'Confronting the African Tragedy', New Left Review, No. 204: 33–47.

Lienert, I. and J. Modi (1997) 'A Decade of Civil Service Reform in Sub-Saharan Africa', *IMF Working Paper*, December.

Makumbe, J. M. (1997) 'The Zimbabwe Civil Service Reform Programme: A Critical Perspective', *The Changing Role of Government in Adjusting Economies*. Paper No. 16. Development Administration Group, University of Birmingham.

Marquette, H. (2003) *Corruption, Politics and Development: The Role of the World Bank*, Basingstoke: Palgrave Macmillan.

Ministry of Public Service (1993) 'Uganda Civil Service Reform: Visions, Objectives, Strategy and Plan', Kampala, May.

Ministry of Public Service (1998) 'Re-structuring of Government Ministries/Departments', Final report, Kampala, March.

Mitaka, J. and D. Katuramu (2002) 'Uganda: Pursuing a Results-oriented Management Culture', in K. Kiragu and H. L. Mambo, *Public Service Reform Comes of Age in Africa*, Dar-es-Salaam: Mkuki na Nyota Publishers.

Mkandawire, T. and C. C. Soludo (1999) *Our Continent, Our Future: African Perspectives on Structural Adjustment*, Trenton: Africa World Press.

Mollel, R. H. and G. D. Yambesi (2002) 'Tanzania: Focus on Performance Improvement and Incentives', In K. Kiragu and H. L. Mambo, *Public Service Reform Comes of Age in Africa*, Dar-es-Salaam: Mkuki na Nyota Publishers.

Montgomery, J. D. (1986) 'Bureaucratic Politics in Southern Africa', *Public Administration Review*, Vol. 46, No. 5: 407–13.

Moore, M. (1998) 'Death without Taxes: Democracy, State Capacity and Aid Dependence in the Fourth World', in M. Robinson and G. White (eds.), *The Democrahc Developmental State: Politics and Institutional Design*, Oxford: Oxford University Press.

Moyo, J. G. et al. (1998) 'Civil Service Reform in Zimbabwe', Paper presented to the Eastern and Southern Africa consultative workshop on Civil Service Reform, Arusha, 4–6 March.

Mukandala, R. S. (1992) 'To be or not to be: The Paradoxes of African Bureaucracies', *International Review of Administrative Sciences*, Vol. 58, No. 4: 555–76.

Mukherjee, H. (2003) 'Recent Lending for Civil Service Reform: Discernible Trends', Mimeo, Washington: World Bank.

Mutahaba, G., Baguma, R. and M. Halfani (1993) *Vitalizing African Public Administration for Recovery and Development*, West Hartford: Kumarian Press.

Nattrass, N. and J. Seekings (1998) 'Democratic institutions and development in post-apartheid South Africa', in G. White and M. Robinson, 'Civil Society and Social Provision: The Role of Civil Organization', in M. Minogne et al., *Beyond the New Public Management*, Cheltenham: Edward Elgar.

Ndegwa, S. N. (2002) 'Decentralization in Africa: A Stocktaking Survey', *African Region Working Paper Series*, No. 40, Washington: World Bank.

Nissanke, M. and B. Ferrarini (2004) 'Debt Dynamics and Contingency Financing: Theoretical Reappraisal of the HIPC Initiative', in T. Addison, H. Hansen and F. Tarp *Debt Relief for Poor Countries*, (eds.), Basingstoke: Palgrave Macmillan.

Okutho, G. (1998) 'Public Service Reform in Africa: The Experience of Uganda', Paper presented to the Eastern and Southern Africa consultative workshop on Civil Service Reform, Arusha, 4–6 March.

Olowu, B. (1998) 'Strategies for Improving Administrative Efficiency in the Democratizing States of Africa', *International Review of Administrative Sciences*, Vol. 64: 611–23.

Olowu, B. (1999) 'Redesigning African Civil Service Reforms', *Journal of Modern African Studies*, Vol. 37, No. 1: 1–23.

Oyugi, W. (1990) 'Civil Bureaucracy in East Africa: A Critical Analysis of Role Performance since Independence', in O. P. Dwiwedi and K. M. Henderson (eds.), *Public Administration in World Perspective*, Ames: Iowa University Press.

Polidano, C. (1999) 'The New Public Management in Developing Countries', Paper presented at the 3rd International Research Symposium on Public Management, Birmingham: Aston Business School, 25–26 March.

Pollitt, C. (1995) 'Justification by Works or by Faith? Evaluating New Public Management', *Evaluation*, Vol. 1, No. 2: 133–54.

Presidential Review Commission (1998) *Developing a Culture of Good Governance*, Report of the Presidential Review Commission on the reform and transformation of the public service in South Africa, 27 February.

Radoki, C. (1999) 'Water and Health Care Provision: The Views of Users', Workshop on the Changing Role of Government in Adjusting Economies, School of Public Policy, University of Birmingham, 28–30 March.

Ramaite, M. R. (2002) 'South Africa: Accelerating the Transformation Process', in K. Kiragu and H. L. Mambo, *Public Service Reform Comes of Age in Africa*, Dar-es-Salaam: Mkuki na Nyota Publishers.

Rapley, J. (1996) *Understanding Development: Theory and Practice in the Third World*, London: UCL Press.

Reinikka, R. and J. Svensson (2002) 'Local Capture and the Political Economy of School Financing', *World Bank Discussion Paper 2227*, Washington DC: World Bank.

Robinson, M. and G. White (eds.) (1998) *The Democratic Developmental State: Politics and Institutional Design*, Oxford: Oxford University Press.

Rugumyemheto, J. (2004) 'Innovative Approaches to Reforming Public Services in Tanzania', *Public Administration and Development*, Vol. 24: 437–46.

Schiavo-Campo, S. (1998) 'Government Employment and Pay: The Global and the Regional Evidence', *Public Administration and Development*, Vol. 18, No. 5: 457–78.

Semboja, J. and O. Therkildsen (1995) *Service Provision under Stress in East Africa: The State, NGOs and People's Organizations in Kenya, Tanzania and Uganda*, London: James Currey.

da Silva, L. A. P. and A. Solimano (1999) 'The Transition and the Political Economy of African Socialist Countries at War (Angola and Mozambique)', in J. A. Paulson (ed.), *African Economies in Transition. Volume 2: The Reform Experience*, Oxford: University of Oxford.

Singh, M., D. Du Toit and T. Masilela (1998) 'Public Service Reform in South Africa', Paper presented to the Eastern and Southern Africa consultative workshop on Civil Service Reform; Arusha, 4–6 March.

Szeftel, M. (1998) 'Misunderstanding African Politics: Corruption and the Governance Agenda', *Review of African Political Economy*, No. 76: 221–40.

Therkildsen, O. (1998) 'Consultative Workshop on Civil Service Reforms in Eastern and Southern Africa: Means, Ends and Lessons', Report prepared for the Ministry of Foreign Affairs, Denmark. Danida, March.

Therkildsen, O. (1999a) *Efficiency, Accountability and Implementation: Public Sector Reform in East and Southern Africa*, Programme Paper: Democracy, Governance and Human Rights. No. 3, Geneva: UNRISD.

Therkildsen, O. (1999b) 'Public Sector Reform in a Poor, Aid-dependent Country, Tanzania', *Public Administration and Development*, Vol. 20, No. 1: 61–71.

Therkildsen, O. (2005) 'Understanding Public Management through Neopatrimonialism: A Paradigm for all African seasons?' In U. Engel and G. R. Olsen (eds.), *The African exception*, Abingdon: Ashgate.

Valentine, T. R. (1999) 'Pay Reform Implementation Study: Operationalising the Medium-term Public Service Pay Policy', Final report prepared for the Public Service Reform Programme, Tanzania, June.

Valentine, T. R. (2001) 'Towards a Medium-term Pay Reform Strategy for the Mozambique Public Service: Final Report', Report prepared for the Technical Unit for Public Sector Reforms. October.

Valentine, T. R. (2002) 'Revisiting and Revising Tanzania's Medium-term Pay Reform Strategy', Final report; prepared for the Civil Service Department. April.

Valentine, T. R. (2003) 'Towards a Medium-term Pay Policy for the Malawi Civil Service: Final Report', Prepared for the Department of Human Resource Management and Development, Ministry of Finance, June.

de Waal, A. (2003) 'How will HIV/AIDS Transform African Governance?' *African Affairs*, Vol. 102, No. 406: 1–23.

van de Walle, N. (2001) *African Economics and the Politics of Permanent Crisis, 1979–1999*, Cambridge: Cambridge University Press.

Wade, R. (2004) 'Is Globalization Reducing Poverty and Inequality?' *World Development*, Vol. 32, No. 4: 567–89.

White, G. and M. Robinson (1998) 'Civil Society and Social Provision: The Role of Civic Organizations', in M. Minogue et al. (eds.), *Beyond the New Public Management: Changing Idelas and Practices in Governance*, Cheltenham: Edward Elgar.

World Bank (1981) *Accelerated Development in sub-Saharan Africa*. Washington: World Bank.

World Bank (1994) *Adjustment in Africa: Reforms, Results, and the Road Ahead*, Oxford: Oxford University Press.

World Bank (1995) *Bureaucrats in Business: The Economics and Politics of Government Ownership*, Washington: World Bank.

World Bank (1997) *World Development Report, 1997: The State in a Changing World*, Oxford: Oxford University Press.

World Bank (2003) *African Development Indicators 2003*, Oxford: Oxford University Press.

World Health Organization (2004) *The World Health Report*, Geneva: WHO.

Wright, V. (1997) 'The Paradoxes of Administrative Reforms', in W. Kickert (ed.), *Public Management and Administrative Reform in Western Europe*, Cheltenham: Edward Elgar.

Wuyts, M. (1996) 'Foreign Aid, Structural Adjustment, and Public Management: The Mozambican Experience', *Development and Change*, Vol. 27, No. 4: 717–50.

Zondo, Margaret A. R. (2002) 'Zimbabwe: Building on Effective Leadership and Participation', in K. Kiragu and H. L. Mambo, *Public Service Reform Comes of Age in Africa*, Dar-es-Salaam: Mkuki na Nyota Publishers.

3
Public Sector Management Reform in Latin America

Andrew Nickson

Introduction

Beginning in the 1980s many Latin American countries have launched major state reform initiatives. These were driven primarily by the forces of globalization which placed tighter budgetary constraints on governments and made economic performance increasingly contingent on the ability to deal successfully with intensified international competition. These economic changes were accompanied, in many cases, by processes of political democratization that generated new pressures for reshaping state structures. The first phase of these state reform initiatives, carried out under strict conditionality with the IMF and World Bank, focused on three strategies designed to achieve macro-economic fiscal balance: downsizing of central government staffing levels; privatization of state enterprises; and decentralization of service provision.

These 'first-generation' reforms were successful in reducing the fiscal deficit, but were carried out without a clear vision of the desired role of the state, except for the simplistic view that it should be 'smaller'. For this reason, they were unsuccessful in addressing the challenge of improving overall economic performance in the global economy. During the 1990s many Latin American countries embarked on a 'second-generation' of state reforms. This emphasizes a greater concern for what has been dubbed the 'four Es': the effectiveness of public sector intervention in terms of coverage and quality of service; the economic efficiency of service delivery; improved equity of service delivery through a more targeted approach to current and capital expenditure in the social sectors (especially health and education); and the creation of an enabling environment for private sector development.

Yet despite this new concern for issues of effectiveness, efficiency, equity and enabling in the public sector, the system of public administration that is responsible for attaining such objectives remains a neglected area of concern for state reformers. A major international symposium on state reform in Latin America in 1993 had virtually nothing to say on the issue of public administration reform (Bradford, 1994). This is surprising because over the past two decades major reforms have been undertaken in the public administration of many OECD countries with the aim of improving performance on the 'four Es' (Hood, 1991). These reforms, referred to collectively as the 'New Public Management' (NPM), are increasingly been applied in low- and middle-income countries, raising questions about the universal applicability of such 'policy transfer'. This chapter examines the application of NPM in Latin America. The main characteristics of the public administration system in Latin America are described. The limited experience of NPM initiatives in Latin America is then reviewed by reference to a country profile and two case studies. The progress towards creating a professional civil service is discussed. The chapter concludes with an assessment of the impact of NPM in Latin America.

Before proceeding, it is necessary to point out a salient feature of the historiography of public administration reform in Latin America – its highly prescriptive and normative nature. As a consequence, much of the writing on the subject suffers from four drawbacks. First, there is an overemphasis on legal reforms as a panacea to administrative problems. Second, there is a tendency to exaggerate the extent of the stated reforms that are underway or about to get underway. Third, relatively little attention is devoted to any analysis of the actual manner in which the public administration system functions in practice. Fourth, insufficient consideration is granted to the importance of change management as part of the overall reform process.

The public administration system in Latin America and NPM

A key feature of the public administration system of Latin America that distinguishes it from its counterparts in the rest of the world is the centralist tradition of *caudillismo* (political bossism). This pork-barrel political culture thrives on the absence of job stability and the constant rotation of an underpaid and overstaffed bureaucracy. Public sector employment is not viewed as an input required in order to produce outputs for citizens in the form of service provision. On the contrary, it is viewed as an output in its own right – a just reward for favours rendered or to be rendered. Largely because of clientelism, personnel systems remain weak and highly fragmented throughout the region. Recruitment and promotion are still primarily based on patronage rather than merit. Only Chile has something approaching a genuine public administration career system. But even here, as in the rest of the region, the career path is truncated at the level of the departmental head because more senior posts are confidence posts (*cargos de confianza*), whose holders change frequently in response to changes at the political level.

As a result, the absence of a genuine career system is a striking feature of the public administration in Latin America that distinguishes it from its counterparts in many parts of the world. Familial and political ties retain a major influence over the selection of all grades of staff. Posts are rarely advertised, and attempts to introduce recruitment by competitive examination have often been thwarted by the recruitment of 'temporary' staff who are subsequently transferred onto the permanent register. Even when recruitment is ostensibly by open competition, clientelist considerations often continue to play a role in the final decision. The subtle manipulation of merit-based practices in order to disguise clientelism is also rife. Promotion criteria are usually rigidly defined and are based primarily on length of service and educational qualifications rather than on job performance. Although elementary forms of staff appraisal have been introduced, patron–client relationships usually inhibit any meaningful performance assessment.

The absence of a permanent career-based cadre of senior administrators has given rise to a number of negative features within the public administration system that pose difficulties for the introduction and sustainability of NPM initiatives. It leads to problems of administrative discontinuity and loss of institutional memory at times of political change, as well as encouraging 'short-termism' and a 'crisis management' approach to decision-making. The legal provisions for transparent and accountable personnel systems are rarely enforced because of the widespread prevalence of clientelism. As a result, the regulatory and enabling skills required by NPM initiatives are often lacking. The lack of a professional ethic means that trust within the bureaucracy is not based on an overall code of conduct but on personal, patron–client relationships where trust is fluid and limited. Accountability to civil society is weak and information is withheld from the public. Because the core allegiance of public administrators is to patron–client networks rather than to professional bodies, they are reluctant to encourage the participation of citizens in the public policy-making process. This often contributes to resource misallocation.

Efficient mechanisms to evaluate the performance of the public sector are often lacking. Programmes are evaluated in accordance with mere procedural compliance, e.g. the amount of the budget that is spent, rather than the efficiency of the expenditure. In the absence of a professional ethic, there is little sense of a shared responsibility between line ministries and the Ministry of Finance over auditing. Control mechanisms emphasize accounting but not accountability, and especially not individual responsibility for outcomes.

In addition to the absence of a career-based civil service, two other features of the administrative traditions of Latin America pose difficulties for the introduction of NPM initiatives. The first of these is the presidential system of government that prevails throughout the region. While state reforms are complex and difficult to achieve in any country, it is argued that they may be somewhat easier in those parts of the developing world where parliamentary systems – that usually provide greater coherence between the executive and legislative branches of government – exist. This harmony is critical to delivering the legislative changes needed for fundamental organizational, financial and personnel management reforms. It is perhaps not surprising that the most successful and profound NPM reforms among OECD countries have taken place in the United Kingdom, New Zealand and Australia. The demonstration effect of these successes is considerably easier to replicate in those Anglophone countries that share a parliamentary system. Such policy transfer may be more problematic in Latin America where presidential systems, often characterized by extreme lack of coherence between the executive and legislative branches, are the norm.

The second feature that poses obstacles to the introduction of NPM reforms is the rigid interpretation of the Luso-Hispanic tradition of administrative law that infuses the public administration system throughout the region. This tradition is based on the principles of legitimated procedures that focus more on inputs than results. This emphasis on the means rather than the goals of public administration places limits on the devolution of authority and restricts accountability procedures. This is most noticeable with regard to the way in which the Comptroller-General's office, a kind of national audit office, functions in Latin America. Its overriding objective is to ensure the legality of revenue generation and expenditure. Hence public sector performance is evaluated in terms of budgetary conformity, financial propriety and legality. This form of financial supervision is essentially punitive rather than supportive in nature. The Comptroller-General's office provides little guidance on management practices, carries out no comparative analysis of expenditure by different government ministries and thus offers little information on managerial efficiency and effectiveness in the public sector.

This strong tradition of administrative law in Latin America poses particular obstacles to the introduction of contractual arrangements within the public sector that are a major feature of the NPM. Such contractual arrangements – executive agencies, competitive tendering and market testing – have been introduced in the context of the relatively loose legal constraints of the common law tradition in Anglo-Saxon countries. Even in these countries there is growing recognition that a contract culture cannot be imposed simply by law and that, as important, is the establishment of trust between the parties (Coulson, 1997). In Latin America, where administrative law has been applied in a more rigid manner even than in its Iberian birthplace, precisely because of the lack of confidence in government, the introduction of a contract culture based on trust is problematic. Latin America may well be a region where 'the full realization of NPM requires far-reaching changes in the legal and institutional framework' (Ormond and Löffler, 1998: 12).

An overview of the extent of NPM implementation in Latin America

Due in part to the structural features outlined above, the introduction of NPM-type initiatives into the public administration system of Latin America has been very limited to date. As a result of the widespread privatization of water, electricity and telecom corporations that took place during the so-called 'first-generation' reforms, there is now considerable experience in the establishment of regulatory institutions, but these suffer from problems of lack of managerial autonomy and regulatory capture.

Despite the noticeable advances towards greater decentralization of functions to municipal government (Nickson, 1995), central government remains highly concentrated throughout Latin America. The deconcentration of managerial responsibility within line ministries for personnel and financial management, both functionally and geographically, remains surprisingly limited. Although decentralized salary payment through the commercial banking system has become widespread, the level of pay negotiation, as well as hiring and firing, remain highly centralised. The devolution of budgetary authority to line managers with central ministries is still rare. Overall, the balance between control and flexibility remains extremely tilted towards the former.

The devolution of managerial authority through the establishment of executive agencies and associated performance contracts is an important mechanism for increasing accountability by promoting a results- and evaluation-oriented system of management within the public sector. But despite rhetoric to the contrary, the actual experience of such reforms is extremely limited to date in Latin America. Nowhere have senior management posts been awarded on a contract basis linked to performance evaluation. A major reason is the absence of any tradition of a transparent mechanism for the appointment and performance evaluation of senior public administrators. Without these structures in place, the appointment of agency chief executives on a contract basis yet subject to political patronage could actually increase the existing level of corruption.

The application of market-type mechanisms (MTMs) in the public sector has also been very limited. In the case of contracting out, where the public sector purchases a service from the private sector that was traditionally produced in-house, the letter rather than the spirit of NPM is applied. Prior to the emergence of the NPM paradigm, this arrangement was already widespread at the central government level (e.g. in catering, cleaning and printing) and at the municipal level (e.g. refuse collection). But efficiency gains continue to be limited by the lack of transparency in the awarding of such contracts and weak monitoring of their implementation. The practice of 'market testing', whereby in-house operations are also allowed to submit a bid, is virtually unknown. The awarding of these contracts has tended to be shrouded in secrecy, the contract details themselves have been kept confidential, and little attention has been paid to the introduction of performance targets or to the implementation of penalty clauses. For this reason, citizens have not necessarily perceived 'contracting out' as a mechanism for improvement in the quality of service provision.

Latin American countries are beginning to finance public services through user charges. The aim of user charging is not simply to achieve cost recovery but also to make public services more effective, efficient and equitable. This is achieved through the transparency of costs and benefits of individual services to users and providers alike. In turn, this imposes discipline on user demand for services and also fosters cost-consciousness and customer orientation of the supplier. User fees have been introduced slowly in the Venezuelan hospitals in response to the financial crisis of the health sector. Changes to the legal framework, involving the establishment of not-for-profit medical foundations, were necessary in order to enable the retention of revenue from user charges. The introduction of user fees in the education sector has been much more limited. This is most noticeable in higher education, where traditional financing arrangements continue to underpin a large and regressive transfer of income to the top three deciles of the population.

Measures to improve citizen accountability, such as citizens' charters, codes of conduct and the publication of target achievement performance indicators remain extremely limited. They are usually the result of initiatives by individual reformers (mayors, state governors, and ministers). Such initiatives are rarely institutionalised and frequent changes in political leadership deprive them of sustainability.

A country profile and three case studies

In most Latin American countries, NPM initiatives have been introduced in a haphazard and piecemeal fashion. The exception is Brazil, where the central government made a concerted attempt to introduce public sector reform within a consistent NPM paradigm. We now examine that experience. This is followed by three case studies of NPM-type initiatives that have attracted international attention – the reform of the national tax authority of Peru, the introduction of Internet technology for tax administration in Brazil, and the use of a voucher system for the prevention of sexually transmitted diseases in Nicaragua.

The New Public Management in Brazil

When President Fernando Henrique Cardoso took office in 1995 the Brazilian public administration system was widely recognized to be in

crisis, itself a reflection of a wider fiscal and political crisis of the state
(Bresser Pereira, 1997: 5). This crisis had been brought to a head by the
extreme bureaucratic rigidities introduced by the 1988 Constitution. The
problem of high payroll expenses in the public sector was not due to excessive government employment, but due to excessively high pay, pensions
and perks. Compared with equally qualified workers in the private sector,
salaries of public employees were 30–50 per cent higher for federal administration and judicial and legislative workers, and 20–35 per cent higher for
employees in federal and state enterprises. Compared with their private
sector counterparts, pension levels of civil servants were 25–50 per cent
higher depending on their salary level, gender and occupation. Compared
with equally qualified private sector workers, job stability or permanency of
tenure was between 15–30 per cent greater for government workers (Foguel
et al., 2002).

The Cardoso government announced an ambitious plan for public
administration reform, the *Plano Diretor da Reforma do Aparelho do Estado*
(White Paper on the Reform of the State Apparatus), and this was approved
in September 1995. A new Ministry of Federal Administration and State
Reform, *Ministério da Administração Federal e Reforma do Estado* (MARE) was
created to spearhead the reform process. The content of the proposed
reforms reflected the views of Carlos Bresser Pereira, the new head of
MARE. A former professor of public administration, he had been strongly
influenced by the British experience of NPM and was a leading exponent of
its virtues in Latin America.

The plan divided public sector institutions into four categories. First,
there were the core institutions of government with the strategic function
of defining public policy at the federal, state and municipal levels. Second,
there were operational activities in sectors that were defined as exclusively
of the state. These would function through the establishment of executive
agencies. Third, there were the operational activities in sectors that were
defined as not exclusively of the state (e.g. hospitals, universities,
museums and research centres). These would function through social
(public non-state) organizations (i.e. not-for-profit foundations). Finally,
there were market-based activities that would be privatized. The strategic
core would make use of a new instrument – the management contract – in
order to define the objectives of the executive agencies and social organizations, determine their respective performance indicators, and guarantee
the necessary human, material and financial resources for them to carry
out the agreed objectives. Managers of executive agencies and social organizations would be granted financial independence to manage their own
budgets, to hire and fire staff and to determine salary levels. They could
also purchase inputs according to general procurement principles instead
of having to follow restrictive and detailed laws as in the past.
Underpinning the reform plan was a strong commitment to viewing the

citizen as a direct client of the state, rather than merely as a taxpayer, as had been the case in the past.

Despite the initial high hopes, little has been achieved to date with regard to implementing the Brazilian reform agenda. Out of the 31 public foundations and 100 other state agencies that were eligible for conversion into executive agencies, action was taken in only one case – The National Institute of Measurements and Technical Norms (INMETRO). The negotiations on restructuring this institution began in January 1996 and required the drawing up and approval of its internal work plan and the signing of a management contract with the supervisory ministry. Following a long delay, INMETRO was officially declared to be an executive agency on 30 July 1998.

The second period of office of President Cardoso (1999–2003) introduced major political changes that effectively shelved the ambitious objectives stated in the 1995 White Paper on the Reform of the State Apparatus. The fledgling Ministry of Federal Administration and State Reform (MARE) was abolished in 1999 and its functions absorbed by the Ministry of Planning, Budget and Management (MPOG). Although the contract that INMETRO had signed stated that its leadership could be removed only in the event of non-compliance with its performance targets, the head of the organization was removed by the incoming minister of the supervisory ministry. His replacement was an outsider who had not been involved in the negotiations to convert INMETRO into an executive agency. Despite the assurances to the contrary that had been written into the contract, MPOG removed the financial autonomy of INMETRO, which was henceforth subjected to the same budgetary restrictions as the rest of the federal government. The extinction of MARE also put an end to the autonomy of INMETRO in the management of its human resources. The tendering of goods and services was the only area in which INMETRO was allowed to retain some autonomy (Tristão, 1999: 7–8). Plans to convert other public foundations and social organizations into executive agencies were frozen as a result. All of these initiatives were dependent upon soft loan finance from the Inter-American Development Bank (Elena, 1998: 8–9).

The extremely slow progress in implementing NPM initiatives occurred because they were dependent on a reform of the administrative articles of the 1988 Constitution. Only this would enable the flexibilization of job tenure, the end of the one single legal contract (*regime jurídico único*) for all public sector posts, including the so-called autonomous agencies and foundations, and the ending of *isonomia salarial* (salary equality) as a constitutional precept. So far, the units selected to become executive agencies are constituent parts of ministries and thus have the same legal and managerial rigidities as the ministries to which they belong. At present public sector employees may not be dismissed for lack of efficient performance or because of over-staffing or redundancy. A related reform of the articles of the 1988 Constitution concerning social security is another prerequisite for administrative reform. First, this would enable retirement to be based on both age and length of service, thereby enabling an extension of the retirement age from the current 50 to around 60. Second, the reform would make the value of retirement benefits proportional to individual contributions, and not equal to 100 per cent of final salary, as mandated by the 1988 Constitution. Political setbacks suffered by the Cardoso government with regard to these constitutional amendments regarding public sector job tenure and social security have effectively frozen NPM reforms in Brazil. Resistance has come from two sources. First, it came from the medium and lower levels of the public administration, mediated through their respective trade unions. Second, it came from patrimonial politicians who feared that they would lose control over patron–client support mechanisms.

The Peruvian National Tax Authority (SUNAT)

The experience of SUNAT, the tax authority of Peru, provides a striking example of the possibilities and problems of introducing NPM-type reforms in Latin America. By the first half of 1990, a bout of hyperinflation and serious macro-economic mismanagement had reduced the Peruvian tax ratio to 4.9 per cent of GDP. The 3,000 staff members of the tax department were poorly paid and corruption was rife within the organization. Under strong external pressure, the incoming government of President Fujimori introduced a radical reform in the tax administration in an effort to comply with harsh fiscal targets imposed as a condition for IMF assistance. From mid-1991 a new tax authority, *Superintendencia Nacional de Administración Tributaria* (SUNAT), was created. No longer dependent on the Ministry of Economy and Finance, it was accountable directly to the presidency. This high degree of financial and managerial autonomy insulated it from clientelism and corruption. A top-class managerial team was recruited on merit and the bulk (2,034) of the 3,025 staff was dismissed. They were replaced by recent graduates who were selected on the basis of open competition. A specialized training institute, the *Instituto para la Administración Tributaria* (IAT) was established to train these new recruits. All staff members were placed on short-term contracts, subject to six-monthly performance evaluation. Two consecutive failure ratings led to instant dismissal.

The new SUNAT leadership simplified the tax system, reducing the number of taxes from 60 to nine. A strict 'level playing field' was introduced in the treatment of taxpayers, in sharp contrast to the previous tradition of rampant favouritism in exchange for backhanders. In response, the tax ratio rose rapidly to 13 per cent by 1993. The financial independence of SUNAT was guaranteed by a ruling that enabled it to retain 2 per cent of tax proceeds for its own personnel and capital expenditure needs. By 1992, staff numbers had returned to the 1990 figure of 3,025, but the staff profile had changed dramatically. Average monthly salaries had risen from $150 in 1990 to $1,200 in 1993. A strong *esprit de corps* developed among SUNAT staff members, who were soon regarded as an elite corps within the wider civil service.

However, as the national tax effort and overall macro-economic situation improved, the external pressure from the IMF diminished. From 1996 the traditional features of the public administration began to re-emerge inside SUNAT. The government repeatedly changed the head of SUNAT, leading to a loss in managerial cohesion. Plans for a wider reform of the public administration were abandoned in 1997. As its 'mystique' began to wear off and internal staff controls were loosened, an uneven playing field re-emerged within SUNAT, with growing evidence of political favouritism in the treatment of taxpayers (Durand and Thorp, 1999).

The growing problems encountered by SUNAT highlights a missing ingredient that differentiates this experience from the classic parameters of NPM. For although the organization was granted a high degree of managerial and financial autonomy, this was never formalized through a legally binding management contract. On the contrary, the degree of autonomy remained conditional on the goodwill of the president. When that goodwill was withdrawn, SUNAT became vulnerable once again to the traditional pressures of clientelism found in the rest of the public administration. The SUNAT experience suggests that a combination of economic crisis and external pressure is the key enabling factor for the introduction of NPM initiatives in the public administration of Latin America. But it also suggests that, in the absence of management contracts, such reforms may not be sustainable once these conditions no longer apply.

Voucher system for the prevention of sexually transmitted diseases, Nicaragua

The use of vouchers as a mechanism for the provision of merit goods in targeted social programmes is an increasingly common form of market-type mechanism (MTM) associated with the NPM. Under this arrangement, individuals receive entitlements to a good or service that they may 'cash in' at some specified set of providers, who in turn redeem them for cash from a public funding agency. Vouchers usually take the form of pieces of paper authorising a named person to receive a specified service from a list of designated providers. Contracts between the funding agency and the provider are drawn up so as to guarantee quality and accountability. One of the first trials of a voucher system for health services in low-income countries – specifically for the prevention of sexually transmitted diseases – began in Nicaragua in 1996.

Female sex workers in Nicaragua suffer from high rates of sexually transmitted diseases (STDs) as well as frequent unwanted pregnancies and back street abortions. In spite of these problems and in spite of their key role in the chain of venereal disease transmission, these women do not generally make regular use of health services. This is because of fear of stigmatization, insufficient awareness of the risks to their health or simply because they cannot afford to go to a clinic that they perceive to be of adequate quality. The project, managed by the *Instituto Centroamericano de Salud* (ICAS), addressed this problem by targeting the 1,200 female sex workers in Managua. The project increased the use of health services by sex workers by distributing vouchers giving them the right to a free gynaecological consultation every month at a clinic chosen by them from a list of approved public and private providers. To be included on the list, the clinic had to offer the gynaecological services at a price below a set limit and in a manner that treated the women with dignity.

Six rounds of voucher distribution were made from June 1996 to February 1999. In that time over 6,000 vouchers were distributed of which 39 per cent were redeemed. Redemption rates in the last two rounds of voucher distribution were both 44 per cent, the highest so far. The incidence rate of STDs in women using vouchers more than once dropped by 65 per cent over the period under review. A total of 17 different service providers were contracted as part of the project. Although the economic benefits to them were not particularly significant, the main advantage that the clinics perceived from participating in the project was the improvement in the technical quality of their services brought about by the contracts. This was a consequence of the quality specifications imposed by ICAS, and the competition created among providers for voucher income.

The project demonstrated that a voucher system can produce efficiency gains and stimulate improvements in the quality of health services, partly through the use of competitive tendering and partly through the use of monitored contracts with strict quality specifications and sanctions for failure to comply. It also proved an extremely effective mechanism for improving the customer orientation of the health services. The project also challenged the assumption that it would be too expensive to contract out basic health services to private providers. The unit cost of private consultations purchased through the voucher system ($6.27) was lower than in the public sector ($7.65) (Sandiford et al., 1999).

The search for a professional civil service

The very limited impact of NPM initiatives to date in Latin America can be linked to the absence of a key factor required for their success – namely, a professional civil service. Civil service reform is among the most crucial ingredients for sustainable improvement in the capacity of the state to discharge its two principal policy formulation functions in the post-adjustment era. The first is to create the enabling environment for the efficient functioning of the private sector, and the second is to create the regulatory environment for the efficient delivery of basic public services. Yet of all public sector activities, civil service reform is the area where success has been hardest to achieve in Latin America (Rowat, 1999; Shepherd, 1999).

Many attempts have been made to introduce a professional civil service in Latin America, but few have taken root. The most serious experiment was in Argentina, where the *Cuerpo de Administradores Gubernamentales* (AGs), an elite corps of senior administrators was created in 1986. Entrants were chosen on the basis of competitive examination and interview, but were confirmed only after successfully completing an intensive training programme. Between 1988 and 1995, a total of 198 AGs were recruited in four separate batches. They were deployed in a range of federal, state and municipal institutions. After 1995, political interference by the government of President Menem led to growing problems. The criteria for selection of the institutions to which AGs were seconded became subject to political favouritism rather than career planning. No more batches were recruited after 1995. This lack of 'new blood' contributed to the development of a powerful sense of corporate identity among the remaining AGs, which made them virtually immune from external scrutiny. A committee selected by the Association of AGs itself carries out performance evaluation and no AG has been dismissed from the service since its inception.

In Mexico, the Ministry of Foreign Affairs, the Ministry of Education, the Electoral Commission, the National Institute of Statistics and Geography, and the Agricultural Professional Service are the only parts of the public administration that have a quasi-career service. These are small and separate initiatives, covering no more than 30,000 administrators out of a total federal government payroll of 1.5 million (Pardo, 1996). Furthermore, horizontal mobility, a fundamental feature of an integrated civil service system, is lacking among these administrators who were selected on merit. Most of the 120,000 middle-level positions within the public administration remain discretionary posts where selection is not by merit (Méndez, 1997: 7).

In 1996 the Mexican government of President Zedillo announced the *Programa Nacional de Desarrollo Administrativo* (PNDA), the latest in a long line of plans to modernize the public administration, to be spearheaded by a new Ministry of Administrative Development, *Secretaría de Contraloría y Desarrollo Administrativo* (SECODAM). The core proposals included the introduction of a selection process for entry into the public administration, in-service training programmes, a strengthening of the civic and ethical values of public administrators, and a more effective implementation of existing laws controlling their behaviour. A key element of the announced reforms was the introduction of service standards and performance indicators, and associated monitoring systems. SECODAM also started to rate public sector institutions according to their degree of customer-friendliness. These NPM-type reforms have had some success, as in the states of Nuevo León (Roel, 1996), Tamaulipas and Chihuahua. A much-vaunted initiative took place in 1998 when the Federal Institute for Technical Education, *Colegio Nacional de Educación Profesional Técnica* (CONALEP) was granted 'executive agency' status. But a few months later, its activities were decentralised to the 31 states of the nation.

The long-term success of the SECODAM initiatives was conditional upon the implementation of associated plans within the PNDA to introduce a professional civil service among the 120,000 middle- to upper-ranking posts in the public administrations. These are currently confidence posts, *cargos de confianza*, where appointment is primarily based on political criteria. The draft bill envisaged a three-band job classification system with seven points in each band. Entry to the service would be by examination, and open to candidates from within and from outside the public sector. It was originally envisaged that the necessary legislation would be approved in 1997 and introduced from 1999. But the plans hit an impasse when they were opposed by trade unions representing lower-level workers in the public administration. The unions argued in favour of having one single system covering lower- and middle-level posts, which would be effectively controlled by the union.

In several countries, national institutes of public administration were set up during the 1980s, most notably in Argentina (*Instituto Nacional de Administración Pública*, INAP), Brazil (*Escola Nacional d'Administração Pública*, ENAP) and Mexico (*Instituto Nacional de Administración Pública*, INAP). All three were modelled on the French system of the *Ecole Nationale d'Administration* (ENA). But rarely was any attempt made to integrate the training of elite civil servants with subsequent career planning, itself an essential ingredient of the French model. In the late 1990s, a senior French civil servant carried out an internal review of the experience of transplanting the French model of public administration training in Latin America and concluded that it had been a dismal failure. In all three countries, the national institutes of public administration had become infected with the very ills of the public administration system – clientelism, inflexibility of job tenure, organizational rigidities and constant changes of leadership – that they were designed to eradicate (Chaudury et al., 1994).

Conclusion

In marked contrast to the improvement in macro-economic management within the region, and with the noticeable exception of Chile, the overall performance of the public administration system in Latin America has shown little improvement in recent years. The debate and practice of state reform in Latin America has focused on policy design (fiscal balance, privatization and decentralization) to the neglect of the problems of policy implementation. Yet the pressures of globalization and fiscal stringency continue to make reforms imperative in this area in order to 'get more from less'. The ideas of NPM can usefully be adapted and applied to make the Latin American public administration more responsive and efficient. The need for such measures has been publicly recognized by the leading professional association for public administration in the region (CLAD, 1998). There are few studies from Latin America that argue against the merits of the core separation of 'principal' and 'agent' that is a central feature of NPM (Tendler and Freedheim, 1994).

Nevertheless, only a very limited number of NPM-type reforms have been introduced during the 1990s. This reflects a major policy transfer problem that has been identified with NPM in other parts of the world, namely that the timing, design and content of the reforms have been primarily driven by external donor agencies. By contrast, local 'ownership' of the reform process has been rhetorical and instrumental in nature, and designed primarily to access foreign loans. This has meant that the pace of reform has been slow and very patchy to date. Personnel policy remains geared towards downsizing, with little attention paid to raising staff productivity. Policy towards loss-making state enterprises is still focused on privatization rather than delegating managerial and financial autonomy within the framework of executive agencies and performance contracts.

This chapter has argued strongly that only a professional civil service can provide the 'grease' (informal networks based on a shared professional culture and common ethical standards) that oils the wheels of NPM-type administrative reforms. These networks are crucial for the emergence of the more flexible and deconcentrated administrative structures advocated by the NPM paradigm. They facilitate the co-ordination between different levels of government which is essential for effective programmes of decentralization and administrative deconcentration. They provide the institutional memory that ensures a smooth transfer of power from one political party to another at the municipal, state and national levels of government. They promote the co-operation between the three branches of government – the executive, the legislature and the judiciary – that is necessary to carry through the major legal reforms to make NPM reforms possible. These issues are not problematic where senior administrators share a common culture and professional ethic, as do those in OECD countries experimenting with NPM initiatives. But in Latin America the primacy of the political allegiance of senior administrators to their organizational heads, the lack of job tenure and the lack of horizontal mobility all conspire to militate against the essential ingredients of co-ordination, flexibility and inter-organizational trust that are required to implement NPM-type reforms.

The successful transfer of the NPM paradigm to Latin America is, therefore, problematic, given the absence of those structural features – a professional civil service and strong systems of accountability and transparency to civil society – that have to a large extent insulated the governance system of high-income countries from the inherent dangers associated with greater managerial autonomy in the public sector. Foremost among these dangers is the question of corruption. According to the World Bank, Latin America is the region of the world characterized by the greatest degree of inequality in income distribution and, according to rankings by Transparency International, Latin American countries are among the most corrupt in the world. The network of familial and clientelist relations that infest the organizational culture of the public administration system of the region as well as the weak mechanisms of accountability and transparency to civil society are major causes of this widespread corruption and the persistence of high levels of inequality. Consequently, there is a real danger that, under pressure from multilateral lending institutions, a too rapid application of key operational mechanisms of NPM such as executive agencies and contracting out, could actually worsen rather than improve existing levels of inequality and corruption in the region.

In summary, the countries that have pioneered NPM counted on the existence of a classic system of public administration that had been drawn up along Weberian lines many years ago. The greater flexibility and managerial autonomy implicit in NPM was introduced within the framework of long-standing ethical codes of conduct and networks of mutual trust based on a sense of shared professionalism that already existed among senior and middle-ranking civil servants. In sharp contrast, NPM is being introduced in Latin America in a context where a 'classic' system of public administration has never existed and where governments are still wrestling with the task of constructing it.

As one perceptive critic has remarked: 'Latin America is caught in the middle of a paradigm shift from the old, or "classic" public administration to the New Public Management, without ever having fully implemented the old public administration' (Méndez, 1997). This chapter has argued strongly that only those countries that have built up a professional civil service, the cornerstone of the Old Public Administration (OPA), are in a position to move towards the New Public Management. This is because the OPA provides the foundation on which NPM may be built. Where that foundation does not exist, as in Latin America, there is a real danger that the NPM edifice will crumble into the sand.

References

Arellano Gault, D. (1999) 'Innovation and Institutionalisation: Challenges for the New Public Management in Mexico (The administrative modernization program in Mexico City, 1995–1997)', Paper presented at 4th International Conference of CLAD on State Reform and Public Administration reform. Mexico City, 19–22 October.

Barrera Restrepo, E. (1999) 'New Public Management en América Latina: Una evalu-ación en Colombia', Paper presented at 4th International Conference of CLAD on State reform and public administration reform. Mexico City, 19–22 October.

Bradford, C. I. (ed.) (1994) *Redefining the State in Latin America*. Paris: OECD.

Bresser Pereira, Luiz Carlos (1997) 'Managerial Reform in Brazil's Public Administration', Paper presented to the annual congress of the International Political Science Association (IPSA), Seoul, Korea, August.

CLAD (1998) *A New Public Management for Latin America*, Venezuela: Centro Latinoamericano de Administración para el Desarrollo.

Chaudury, S. A. et al. (eds.) (1994) *Civil Service Reform in Latin America and the Caribbean*, Technical Paper No. 259 Washington, DC.: World Bank.

Corrêa Leite, Jaci (1999) 'Innovative Use of the Internet in Public Management: The Brazilian Pioneer Experience', Paper presented at the 3rd Conference of the International Public Management Association, Aston University, Birmingham, 25–27 March.

Coulson, A. (1997) *Trust and Contracts in Public Sector Management*, Birmingham: University of Birmingham, School of Public Policy.

Durand, F. and Thorp, R. (1999) 'La reforma tributaria: análisis del experimento SUNAT', in J. Crabtree and J. Thomas (eds.), *El Perú de Fujimori*, Lima: Universidad del Pacífico and Instituro de Estudios Peruanos, pp. 379–408.

Elena, Jorge C. (1998) 'Public Sector Reform in Brazil', Paper presented at British Council Seminar, London, 23 November.

Foguel, M. et al. (2002) 'Improving Public Sector Efficiency in Brazil', in I. S. Gill and C. E. Montenegro (eds.), *Crafting Labour Policy: Techniques and Lessons from Latin America*, Washington, DC: World Bank.

Hood, C. (1991) 'A Public Management for all Seasons', *Public Administration*, Vol. 69, No. 1 (Spring): 3–19.

Méndez, J. (1997) 'Administrative Modernization and Political Transition in Developing Countries: The Case of Mexico', Paper presented at the Round Table, International Institute of Administrative Sciences (IIAS), Quebec, 14–17 July.

Nickson, R. A. (1995) *Local Government in Latin America*, Boulder, CO: Lynne Rienner.

Ormond, D. and Löffler, E. (1998) 'New Public Management: What to Take and What to Leave', Paper presented at the 3rd International Conference of CLAD on State Reform and Public Administration Reform, Madrid, 14–17 October.

Pardo, M. (1996) 'La profesionalización del servicio público en México: una tarea pendiente', *Revista de IAPEM* (Instituto de Administración Pública del Estado de México), no. 31 (julio–septiembre), pp. 61–78.

Roel, S. (1996) *Estrategias para un gobierno competitivo: Cómo lograr administración pública de calidad – una nueva paradigma*, México, DF: Castillo.

Rowat, M. (1999) 'The Emerging Role of the State in Latin America', *Public Management*, Vol. 1, No. 2 (June): 261–87.

Sandiford, P., Salvetto, M. and Segura, Z. (1999) 'Clinics for Sex Workers in Nicaragua', in M. Harper (ed.), *Public Services through Private Enterprises: Microprivatization for Improved Delivery*, Delhi: Vistaar Publications.

Shepherd, G. (1999) 'El desafío de la reforma administrativa en América Latina', *Reforma y Democracia* (Caracas), No. 13 (February): 99–116.

Tendler, J. and Freedheim, S. (1994) 'Trust in a Rent-seeking World: Health and Government Transformed in Northeast Brazil', *World Development*, Vol. 22: 1771–91.

Tristão, G. (1999) 'A flexibilização como estratégia de reforma: avaliando a experiência das Agências Executivas', Paper presented at the 4th International Conference of CLAD on State Reform and Public Administration Reform, Mexico City, 19–22 October.

4
Capacity to Deliver? Management, Institutions and Public Services in Developing Countries

Richard Batley and George A. Larbi

Introduction

Over the last two decades there has been worldwide emphasis on reducing the role of government and on reforming public management by adopting aspects of private sector practice. The research on which this chapter is based was concerned with the fact that similar management practices were being introduced in developing and transitional countries, often in association with economic adjustment. There has been considerable research on the difficult process of adjustment but little systematic comparison of the process and outcomes of public management reform for improved service delivery in these countries. Most of what exists raises abstract questions about the relevance of new managerial approaches or is specific to particular countries or sectors (see Manning, 2001 for a survey).

The research investigated the application of such reforms in Africa, Asia and Latin America. Underlying the enquiry is the question whether approaches generated from a diagnosis of the 'over-interventionist' state in, say, Britain or New Zealand are appropriate responses in states where the levels of public management capacity, market development, resources, political inclusiveness, legal effectiveness, political and economic stability are quite different (Minogue, 1998). Our core argument is that governments may be ill-equipped to adopt unfamiliar approaches to public service provision, where the conditions on which new management practices are premised may not be present. This argument is rooted in the particular context and history of developing countries. At the time of the independence of most countries following the Second World War, the 'modern' (Weberian) public administration was at its height in Western countries (e.g. Britain, Germany and the USA) and could cope with expansion of the state by consolidating into public sector organizations, existing providers of services like urban water. For developing countries (with the possible exception of India), the 'modern' bureaucracy never had time to evolve by the time of independence. But the state took on and expanded its 'modern' public sector roles wholesale at independence. This was not the result of an historical evolution driven by 'internal' forces consistent with the social and political realities of the new states. Thus, whilst in developed Western countries, New Public Management emerged in the 1980s to address the weaknesses of established bureaucracies, in developing countries the 'modern' state and its associated bureaucratic apparatus never fully developed. In a sense there was no proper 'old' public administration (except in principle) for a 'new' public management to reform it. The state apparatus in most cases is still characterized by patrimonial, clientelistic and rent-seeking features. The priority may be to reform the state itself to enable it perform its basic roles.

This chapter examines performance in the implementation of management reforms and then seeks explanations for reform effectiveness or ineffectiveness in four spheres:

1 The circumstances of reform and in particular the depths of the economic and political crisis that engendered the case for change.
2 The political significance of reforms.
3 The principal–agency characteristics of service sectors.
4 The managerial capacity and institutional conditions of systems of governance.

The analysis leads to recommendations that service reform needs to take these factors into account in developing a more variegated approach that recognizes the characteristics of service sectors and country contexts. It is worth noting here that a similar call to tailor reform approaches to the nature of the service task, to its political salience and to the skills and motivation of staff has recently been made in the context of developed countries (Pollitt, 2004).

The research approach

The analysis which follows is based on research in four core countries – Ghana, Zimbabwe, India and Sri Lanka – and in several reference countries where more limited research was undertaken – Bolivia, Argentina, Venezuela, South Africa, Kenya and Thailand.[1] The research project examined experiences in these countries of reform in four service sectors: urban water supply; curative health; business promotion; and agricultural marketing services.

The core countries were chosen because of their different public sector traditions and experience of economic and state reform. Ghana and Sri Lanka came earlier to adjustment than Zimbabwe and India, whereas the latter have had more stable, traditional public administrations. The East

Asian and Latin American cases were selected because of their relatively deeper involvement in the 'destatization' of their economies, and because of their different administrative traditions and relatively higher levels of market development.

The four service sectors – curative health, urban drinking water, agricultural marketing and business development – were selected for a number of reasons: (1) their impact on the livelihoods of the poor; (2) the different conditions that they offer for the exercise of control by 'principals' (citizens and policy-makers) over service delivery 'agents'; and (3) the different 'technical' cases for government intervention that they present given the likelihood and form of possible market failures: while none of them are pure 'public goods', the sectors can be seen as being on a roughly declining scale from a stronger (health) to a weaker (business development) case for direct government involvement.

The research examined the application in these countries and sectors of the sorts of reform that carry the label of the 'new public management' (Hood, 1991, 1995; Ferlie et al., 1996) and that may be crystallized into three core central tendencies as follows:

- *Organizational restructuring* in order to shift emphasis from centralized administration to decentralized management through the creation of autonomous and semi-autonomous agencies and the devolution of resources and operational decisions to frontline managers.
- *Use of market-type mechanisms* such as charging for services, privatization and contracting out, whilst regulating providers and making services responsive to users/customers.
- *Performance assessment based on outputs* – an attempt to shift the methods of doing business in the public sector away from complying with procedural rules towards 'getting results'.

Table 4.1 indicates the specific types of reform that were identified in the four service sectors. These were the decentralization of service delivery management; the application of charges to users of services; privatizing and contracting out the delivery and management of public services; and the development of enabling and regulatory roles by public agencies. For Ghana and Sri Lanka these were 'second-generation reforms' which followed the earlier thrust during the 1980s to reduce state intervention in the management of the economy. For the later reformers, India and Zimbabwe, first- and second-generation reforms were slower and became conflated.

Performance of specific reforms

For each of the main reform types that were examined, Table 4.2 summarizes the experience of implementation and the positive and negative effects

Table 4.1 Reform types analysed by sector

Reform type	Health care	Urban water supply	Business promotion services	Agricultural marketing
Decentralizing management within public sector	Autonomous hospitals Strengthening deconcentrated units	Corporatization of utilities	Autonomous agencies	Corporatization of marketing boards
Charging users	Charging users for a wide variety of services	Increase in existing tariffs	Charging for technical services	Charging for some support services
Contracting out	Contracting ancillary and clinical services	Franchise and concession		Contracting of services
Other private sector participation	Church/NGO provision	NGO and informal provision	Divestiture of state textiles manufacture	Liberalization of markets
Enabling private sector	Tax-breaks, loans, grants and subsidies	Attempts to encourage private sector participation	Marketing, advice and promotion	Market information services
Regulating service providers	Regulation of hospitals, professions and pharmaceuticals	Environmental and economic regulation; tariff regulation; contracting	Regulatory control and quality certification	Quality assurance

Table 4.2 Summary of performance of organizational reforms

Organizational reform type	Implementation of reform	Positive effects or gains	Negative effects or risks
Decentralized management	Widespread formal adoption in all sectors in all countries, but patchy implementation in most cases	Gains in technical efficiency and service quality Autonomy is more easily guarded where there are clear user accountability and own sources of finance	Autonomy can easily be lost, especially in politically sensitive services
User fees	Widespread introduction of user fees in health services in Africa Recognition of need for water tariffs to reflect true costs Delivery of business services normally on a fee basis	Most applicable where the service is optional and consumption measurable Gains in allocative efficiency	Difficulty of application in non-measurable, politically sensitive services Severe problems of equity in charging for health care. Exemption systems normally fail
Contracting out	Widespread application of short-term contracts in water, agriculture and health care Limited application of long-term contracts and concessions	Gains in technical efficiency	Failures in designing, managing and monitoring long-term and more complex contracts
Regulation	Widespread formal existence of regulatory frameworks especially in health and water	Gains in clearer separation of regulatory and supply roles in water	Poor implementation of regulatory roles, especially in the health sector Interference by politicians and professional interests

Table 4.2 Continued

Organizational reform type	Implementation of reform	Positive effects or gains	Negative effects or risks
Enabling of independent providers	General shift to enabling roles in agricultural and business development	Some effective market support in business sector, especially where the agency has autonomy from government	Weak application and impact of enabling functions in water, agriculture and health
			Government support services often not trusted by private sector

of change. The table picks out the factors that are common between the service sectors, while the text also identifies some of the main differences.

Decentralizing management

The research found some evidence of varying degrees of decentralization of service delivery responsibility *within the public sector* of all four countries. In the health sector, there has been significant deconcentration of provision and management responsibilities, as well as delegation of budgets to field units at sub-national levels in both Ghana and Zimbabwe. However, in India and Sri Lanka, resistance by central health bureaucrats had delayed delegation of health management responsibilities to lower levels of government. Among the four countries, only Ghana had introduced and implemented a policy of hospital autonomy and also created an executive agency, the Ghana Health Service, out of the Ministry of Health, thus separating the policy arm of the ministry from the operational arms.

It is difficult to make a direct link between reforms and improvement in performance. Sri Lanka had better health status indicators among the four case study countries, but this was due more to other factors, such as its focus on primary health care and female literacy, than to organizational reforms. Sri Lanka reduced the infant mortality rate by almost half (15.35 per 1,000 births) compared to Ghana (72.02 per 1,000 births) and Zimbabwe (56.2 per 1,000 births). In Ghana and Zimbabwe decentralization brought greater share of resources to lower units and frontline health managers, but improvement in health outcomes has been very slow. Improvement in performance is partly hampered by weak management systems (e.g. budgeting, planning and human resource management systems).

Like health, performance was mixed in agricultural trade. In almost all the countries examined, governments continued to provide subsidies to loss-making marketing boards and other parastatals. In the case of Zimbabwe, losses of the grain marketing board reached about 5 per cent of GDP in 1993 due largely to overpricing of grains purchased from farmers (Hubbard, 2003). However, there were examples of good performance. For example, corporatization and commercialization of Cocobod in Ghana and Dairy Board of Zimbabwe (DBZ) led to significant improvement. In the case of DBZ, it became increasingly profitable from 1994 when it was commercialized and freed from statutory responsibilities and political control; its profit increased from $Z32 million in 1994 to over $Z70 million in 1997 when it was privatized (Hubbard, 2003). The performance of other organizations such as Sri Lanka's Paddy Marketing Board, Ghana's Food Distribution Corporation and Zimbabwe's Grain Marketing Board, was less impressive. The explanations for poor performance included lack of financial independence, political interference, corruption and weak leadership.

In the case of the water sector performance was generally poor on a number of indicators. Apart from Zimbabwe (Bulawayo), which showed improvement in operational efficiency, effectiveness and equity, the performance of the other three core countries showed little or no improvement over the reform period. For example, the unaccounted for water rate was 25 per cent for Zimbabwe, whilst for the other three countries the figure ranged between 40 and 60 per cent (see Nickson and Franceys, 2003).

Despite the limited real reform, our findings show that, where it does occur, managerial autonomy (in control over financial and human resources and policy implementation) is associated with improved performance. Management autonomy not only supports efficiency, but also enables the development of a strategic approach freer from political intervention. However, this is more difficult to sustain in the more politically sensitive services such as health and water that attract frequent political interventions to control prices and access. In Kenya, Sri Lanka and India, political sensitivity extended also to the marketing of staple grains, leading to agitation by farmers and consumers and pressure on politicians to rescind reforms and reassert price controls. Managerial autonomy is more likely to be safeguarded where agencies have a degree of self-sufficiency in their sources of finance and where there is a routinized form of accountability both to government and to service users or local voters. The autonomy of managers is best defended where it is transparently subject to formal rules of accountability rather than to haphazard interventions by political leaders and public protest.

User fees and charges

The rationale for the introduction of charging has varied across sectors and countries. The objectives usually included equity, increasing allocative efficiency and accountability to clients (World Bank, 1993; 2003). However, in practice charging has often been introduced simply in order to raise revenue or to recover cost and repay credit. It was most easily introduced in the case of sectors with low equity concerns (such as business services), where the service was optional to the client, and where the service being offered (for example, domestic tap water) was measurable and a private rather than a public good. However, user fees were widespread in the health sector in sub-Saharan Africa in the 1980s and 1990s in the context of structural adjustment programmes.

In the case of health, although exemption systems were set up in Ghana and Zimbabwe, they often failed to protect the poor. To illustrate, in Ghana's Volta Region, a survey showed that less than one in a thousand contacts granted exemptions, and, even so, 71 per cent of exemptions granted were to health sector staff (Nyonator and Kutzin, 1999). Zimbabwe had an exemption system based on an income threshold ($Z400), but in practice only 20 per cent of the eligible poor were granted exemption (Russell et al., 1997). In both countries the introduction of user fees led to a decline in hospital attendance, and in some cases delays in going to hospital. Thus, though user fees can be used as an instrument to promote equity, its effectiveness depends on the capacity of governments to design effective and functioning exemption systems for the poor and vulnerable groups, or to ensure that subsidies are specifically targeted on the poor.

The performance of the water sector in regard to equity is no better. The poor tend to pay more for water because of limited direct access to public supplies. In India, a survey of 35 urban centres in Pune and Mahastra states showed that ordinary consumers paid between US$0.47 and US$1.90/m^3 compared to only US$0.06–US$0.07/m^3 for metered water tariff (Rakodi, 1998). Some countries have sought to address the equity issue through life-line provision for the quantity of water required for basic needs, but this applies only to households connected networks.

In agricultural marketing, safety nets for the poor are required when food supplies are entrusted to the market, in order to ensure that all can buy staple food. There is a shift towards market-based food security by state withdrawal from the purchase and distribution of food and the introduction of income-based relief in the form of cash or vouchers: food stamps in Sri Lanka, cash payment for drought relief for some states in India, and income-based safety programmes during drought in Namibia and Botswana (Hubbard, 2003).

The impact of charging on efficiency and effectiveness was difficult to assess because of data availability and reliability problems. In health, Ghana was able to recover, on average, 8.5 per cent of its recurrent health budget from user fees and Zimbabwe only 2.4 per cent between 1985 and 1994. In the case of Ghana, the bulk of user fee revenue came from drug user fees under the drug revolving fund. One positive impact was the adequate and regular supply of essential drugs to health facilities and an end to shortages of medical supplies that characterized the pre-user fee period. Where user fees were scaled or cascaded down the health system such that primary health care was either free (e.g. Zimbabwe) or attracted only minimal charges relative to the higher levels, it encouraged more efficient use of the secondary and tertiary hospitals.

For urban drinking water, Zimbabwe and some of our reference countries (Argentina and Bolivia) performed better at raising a substantial proportion of their revenue through tariffs. It is only recently that the Ghana Water Company has been able to recover its operational and maintenance cost from tariffs. Part of the explanation for poor performance of tariffs is that it is subject to political decision making processes as was the case in Ghana in the 1990s and also in Sri Lanka.

In general, charging for goods and services has an equitable effect for services only where merit good or equity concerns can be covered by effective exemption or scaled charging systems, and where charges are administered systematically. Charging for health and other social services present much greater difficulties of defining and identifying those who are eligible and of monitoring the abuse of charges by agencies (Mills et al., 2001; Kessler, 2003).

Contracting out direct service provision

Contractual arrangements for service delivery are not new in any of the countries or sectors under study, so making and managing contracts do not involve completely new roles for governments. What is new is that many governments are moving further along this road, partly by their own choice but also often under pressure of donors and due to their own incapacity to maintain in-house services. The moves are towards more contracting out (if not full privatization, as in some agricultural services), deeper and longer-term contracts, and the replacement of loose by more formal agreements with private providers (e.g. agreements between governments and mission hospitals in Ghana and other African countries).

However, short-term and simpler contracts remain much more common than more elaborate forms. Most contracts are for purchases of specific supplies or public works, though a longer-term relationship is often maintained with selected contractors through repeat orders. Also common are service and management contracts, where particular inputs or particular aspects of the service (for example, maintenance, cleaning or catering in health) are supplied to the public sector over a period of roughly one to five years. What remain uncommon are longer-term arrangements, such as lease, franchise and concession, where all or part of the service are financed or managed or both financed and managed. Where these do apply (e.g. our reference countries in Latin America), it is mainly in the water sector or where there are other large-scale capital works (Nickson and Franceys, 2003). However, there is more discussion about moving public services into private management than action, at least in the poorer countries that were the focus of this study.

Governments have usually chosen more easily specifiable activities for contracting – generic support services (for example, transport, maintenance and security) and services involving large capital works (water supplies, flour mills). More qualitative services (such as clinical health services) and less discrete activities (managing professional services) were rarely contracted out and, if they were, often presented problems of management. In the health sector only Zimbabwe had contracted out clinical health services among our four core countries during the study period.

The evidence of this research is that there are advantages to be gained from contracting out all or part of services. There are gains to governments or taxpayers in off-loading risk and costs to the private sector, and gains in managerial control of work forces that were previously employed directly and are now on contract through companies. In cases where contracts work effectively (Table 4.3), there was evidence of gains in managerial efficiency by comparison with direct public provision. There were also widespread

Table 4.3 Contract types and examples studied

Contract type	Business support	Agricultural marketing	Water supply	Health care
Works/supplis 'spot' contracts (one-off)		Maize export and transportation – Kenya	Transport and tankers – India	Construction, equipment maintenance, drug supply – general
Service and management contracts (< 5 years)		Grain storage – India and Sri Lanka	Sewerage treatment and pumping plants – India. Water utility – Chile	Cleaning, catering, security – India, Sri Lanka, Thailand Diagnostic services – India, Thailand Clinical services – South Africa
Lease (10–12 years)			Water utilities – Ghana (proposal)	
Build-operate-transfer (BOT) (20–30 years)		Wheat mill – Sri Lanka	Water supply – Malaysia	
Concession (20–30 years)			Water utility – Argentina	
Joint venture (indefinite)	Export promotion agency – Zimbabwe		Water utility – Colombia	Church and mining company facilities – Ghana, Zimbabwe

reported gains in service performance to customers. However, there are some caveats. First, particularly in the health sector, there was sometimes a cost/quality trade-off, meaning that driving down costs through contracts was in some cases at the expense of the quality of the service (for example, catering) (Mills et al., 2001). Second, contracts work only where they are effectively designed and managed; there were many cases not listed in the table where contracts have been proposed but not implemented or have failed. Third, where contracts succeed in raising performance, this may be due not so much to competition or to the greater efficiency of the private sector as to the contractual process itself. Contracts have the benefit of requiring a clearer specification of expectations and providing a basis for monitoring of performance (Mills et al., 2002). In spite of the benefits of contracting, there are also practical difficulties associated with insufficient monitoring mechanisms when contracts are designed, leading to poor quality work in some cases.

Regulatory and enabling roles

Regulation is a fundamental role of government but has historically tended to over-extend, with the effect of suffocating markets without achieving the purposes of public policy. The forms of regulation that were examined in this research are those that have become more important after 'market-unfriendly' regulation had been swept away. They are based on the view that, without appropriate state intervention, sometimes markets would fail to deliver services efficiently. The state needs to regulate markets in order to make them more effective.

The cases of regulation that were examined involved setting and applying conditions for the allocation of monopoly rights in the case of urban water, and ensuring the quality and quantity of health care services where clients would otherwise be under-served or uninformed. The enabling policies that were examined went a step further; these anticipate and seek to avoid market failure by acting to reinforce the capacity of actors – consumers and producers – to enter and operate in the market. Among all the sectors, business support services were the clearest case of enabling action (Jackson, 2002).

Both regulatory and enabling roles are a considerable challenge to the capacity of any government. They require capacity to understand and exercise critical judgement about market conditions, obtain necessary information and act independently of political and self-interested pressures. It is not surprising that, in the study countries, there were many deficiencies in performance. More surprising is that there were also some relatively successful cases.

The study of urban water reform showed that there could be gains from the introduction of an independent regulator, even where the organizational and institutional conditions are not perfect. The clearest case is where the regulator is outside the apparatus of government and the company is privately managed. Such conditions have so far been met primarily in middle- and upper-income countries rather than the poorest that were the main focus of this research. In most of the countries studied regulatory roles were embryonic or poorly performed. But the case of Ghana showed that, even where the water supply company was still publicly owned, an independent regulator has had the effect of improving water standards and adjusting tariffs to reflect real costs (Nickson and Franceys, 2003).

Health care regulation was poorly undertaken in all countries studied, except Thailand. Until recently, regulation has been neglected by government and by external funding agencies. Standards of professional care and of drug control have frequently not been set; and where standards have been set, they have rarely been applied through inspections; and governments and professional councils rarely have an adequate basis of information on private firms and practitioners. Underlying the poor performance of almost all the professional councils were absent or ineffectual supervision and monitoring by ministries of health. (Mills et al., 2001).

Enabling services to businesses included agencies intended to 'facilitate' firms by providing consultancy, advice, training, research and development, and others intended to 'promote' investment, marketing and exports. A number of agencies performed well in Zimbabwe, India and Sri Lanka. They maintained a portfolio of services that were in demand by private firms, had staff and financial resources adequate to deliver them, and had relationships with government and the private sector that gave them credibility without compromising their autonomy. The best performers, such as (until recently) the Zimbabwe export and investment promotion agencies, had a direct measure of their relevance to industry in the fact that their services were financially rewarded in direct proportion to the service given (Jackson, 2002).

Explanations of performance

The broad picture is of the widespread adoption by governments of the language of management reform, but generally much weaker implementation especially in the case of the health and water sectors. Where decentralized management, contracting out and the regulation and support of independent service delivery agencies are effectively implemented, there is evidence that they have a positive impact on the efficiency and responsiveness of services. User charging can also benefit the poor where it removes inequitable subsidies, where charges can be carefully calibrated to consumption and ability to pay, or where exemptions from payment can be managed. However, these reforms have rarely been effectively implemented. The following sections trace the explanations for weak reform policies and implementation to a series of linked factors: the background circumstances under which reforms have been undertaken, the political stakes associated with reforms, the respective power of 'principals' and 'agents' in the reform process, and the managerial and institutional constraints on the capacity for implementation.

The circumstances of reform

The period from the late 1980s until the present has been one of attempts at extraordinarily radical public sector reform. They challenged the previous great period of radical reform in the 1950s and 1960s in South Asia and Africa (or the 1930s to 1950s in Europe and Latin America), which had established the responsibility of the state for social services and economic development. Developing countries shared in a practically worldwide convention in favour of direct public ownership or state management as the preferred model of intervention. Post-colonial governments added redistributive and nation-building intentions whose interventionism was often enhanced by commitments to reversing colonial inequalities, to state socialism and national planning.

The established model of direct state intervention in the provision of goods and services has presented barriers to change, which have had particular force in the poorer developing countries. Although the statist model was even less fiscally sustainable than in the West and although it never achieved the same level of inclusiveness of benefits, it was more deeply ingrained in their power structures. In the poorer countries with weaker market systems, power and privilege existed in the function of state action, and the relief of poverty depended on access to state redistributed wealth. To challenge the statist model was therefore to challenge the foundations of the state and its legitimacy (Sandbrook, 1993).

The primary impulse to public sector reform in developing countries has been the economic crisis that characterized the 1980s and which, for many, has since persisted. Radically new approaches to public management had to be developed in even more difficult circumstances than those experienced by reformers in more advanced countries. Particularly in Africa, Latin America and Eastern Europe, economic adjustment and public sector reform were often delayed until the point that the fiscal crisis was deep and public resources exhausted. They have, therefore, often taken place in the context of already rapidly declining public services, a spiral of decline from which it is difficult to recover. The reforms themselves have usually generated a first impact of increased stress and poverty for those sections of the population that had access to services and employment (Moser et al., 1993; Stiglitz, 2002).

Moreover, the public administration that was expected to carry out the reforms was itself demoralized by the decline in real salaries, threats to job security and severe cuts in numbers – up to 40 per cent, for example, in

Ghana. 'Government agencies were expected to co-operate in diminishing or dismantling their own power' (Hirschmann, 1993: 114). The climate of change has, therefore, often been one of suspicion and resistance, unmatched by support from any clear constituency for change. The international reform ideology changed only later to recognize the importance of capable states to effective service delivery and to functioning markets (World Bank, 1997, 2003).

Political stakes in the reform of public management

The first wave of reforms in the 1980s and early 1990s, under pressure of economic crisis and structural adjustment, was focused on macro-economic stabilization. Several factors made for their relatively quick implementation: the immediacy of the financial crisis, the availability of ready-made models of neo-liberal economic reform and the 'stroke-of-the pen' nature of many of the policy changes (for example, devaluation). The more recent organizational reforms in basic service delivery, particularly in health, education, water and sanitation present a much harder reform task. They embody more institutional elements, implying the change or redefinition of the 'rules of the game' conditioning relations between politicians, citizens, consumers and officials. They also have less clear-cut goals, offer uncertain benefits, involve multiple actors, challenge existing provider groups and require long-term commitment on the part of government. (Nelson, 2000; Grindle, 2004).

Many reforms in public service delivery are likely to remain within the 'bureaucratic arena', engaging neither public support nor opposition. Grindle and Thomas (1991) distinguish reforms that become matters of wide public mobilization from those that generate responses largely within the bureaucracy. They argue that the political stakes are higher in the first case; determined political support is needed to drive them through. In the second case, the political stakes are lower; the crucial issues are within the competence and compliance of the bureaucracy.

The factors that Grindle and Thomas identify as determining whether reforms become openly political or are managed internally are summarized in Table 4.4. These include the distribution of the concrete costs and benefits of reforms between government and sections of the public, and also factors to do with the 'visibility' of reforms, their administrative complexity, whether public support is required for their implementation, and the duration of the process of implementation. So, reforms such as the introduction of user fees are likely to become matters of open public debate – the benefits are most obviously to the public purse, the costs are to consumers, and their impact is immediate and visible. Decision-makers, therefore, confront high political stakes in pushing such reforms.

According to this framework, many of the management reforms listed in Table 4.4, for example management decentralization, are likely to generate

Table 4.4   The public and bureaucratic arenas of response and resistance to reform

Characteristic of reform	Features of reforms in the public arena, requiring political support and stability	Features of reforms in the bureaucratic arena, requiring bureaucratic compliance
Dispersal of the costs	Costs have wide impact among the population	Costs focus on government institutions
Dispersal of the benefits	Benefits are focused on government	Benefits are not immediately felt by bureaucracy and only in long term by public
Technical and administrative complexity	Reforms have low administrative content and can be done quickly	Reforms are administratively complex
Level of public participation	Reforms require wide public involvement and are 'visible'	Reforms require limited public involvement and are 'invisible'
Duration and visibility of reform process	Reforms can be achieved quickly and are visible	Reforms require sustained effort with few immediate visible returns
Examples	User fees Privatization and contracting out of services	Decentralized management

Source: Adapted from Grindle and Thomas (1991).

less public reaction. They are a matter of detailed working out and interaction within the government system, requiring a high degree of sustained technical competence and commitment. They may have great significance for the population, but only in the longer term and not in direct and immediate costs or benefits. The arena of reform is, instead, likely to be within the bureaucracy where the interests and behaviour of officials and professionals are affected. Grindle and Thomas argue that, in these cases, the political stakes are relatively low: the risk to government is only of failure to achieve bureaucratic compliance rather than of loss of public support.

Our research suggests a modification of Grindle and Thomas's argument in two main respects. First, as the previous section indicated, there is not such a clear distinction between the bureaucratic and public arenas. In weaker political economies, particularly the African cases in this study, the bureaucratic arena is itself highly politicized and interconnected with societal interests; it is where power, employment and patronage are concentrated. So, reforms that in more advanced countries have had relatively low political salience, in poorer and weaker government systems may be highly politicized. Second, where (as this section goes on to suggest) policy reform is led by external agencies (donors) rather than by government, citizens have less reason to be engaged, the public arena is weakened and policy-making becomes more exclusive and closed. So, management reforms may be both highly politically salient and yet covert, contained within the rela-tionship between donors, politicians and officials without the participation of citizens.

Principals and agents in public service reform

To consider the relationship between these actors in the different service sectors and countries, our research adopted a broad principal–agency framework. The principal–agent model (Stiglitz, 1987; Walsh, 1995; Lane, 2000) examines organizational relationships as a tension between the 'prin-cipal' who demands a service and the 'agent' who provides it. The model assumes that actors are motivated by rational self-interest. The question, then, is how principals can manage the self-interest of those empowered to act on their behalf, their agents, so that it is aligned with the purposes that they (the principals) wish to achieve. The problem arises not just from conflicts of interest but also from the privileged access of the agents to information – the problem of asymmetrical information. The agents who have been employed to provide a service will tend to use their superior knowledge to divert benefits in their own direction.

In a democratic polity, the ultimate principals are the citizens, or con-sumers of specific services. In principal–agent theory, they are 'principals' in the sense that politicians, as agents, seek their mandate from and act as the representatives of the public. In their turn, appointed officials are, in theory, the agents of political leaders in executing policy. Each has a measure of autonomy and each has interests to advance. The likelihood of the principal effectively controlling the agent depends on (1) how much information the principal has about the performance of the agent, and (2) how far the principal can structure the relationship so as to control the agent.

Our research revealed that, paradoxically, it was normally the supposed 'agents' of the policy process – international and key domestic officials – who were the key leaders or 'principals' of change. This was most clearly the case in the reforms directly associated with the 'conditionality' of struc-tural adjustment: privatization and deregulation of the productive sectors, increases in tariffs and fees, and cuts in staffing. These could be driven through by international agencies with the acquiescence of political leaders and the technical participation of top officials of core ministries – Offices of the President or Prime Minister and Ministries of Finance. Donors, and par-ticularly international financial organizations, have been fundamentally important actors in these stroke-of-the-pen economic reforms. Nevertheless, there were some cases where governments had been the initiators of liberalizing reforms. Among the four core countries, this was most clearly the case in Sri Lanka, which, in 1977, launched its own liberalization programme involving the privatization of state enterprises and the promotion of foreign inward investment.

Until recently, the social sectors – and also internal agricultural trade – have been freer from the attention of the international financial institutions, and therefore generally slower to reform. In the health sector, chronic fiscal crisis, and then the new poverty agenda and sector-wide approaches of donors, eventually forced reconsideration of the role of the state, particularly in Africa. However, in this sector, the technical advisers of donor and international organizations generally played the role of encouraging, financing and endorsing rather than imposing reform. Pressure was greatest where the crisis was deepest, with the effect that there were more elaborate plans for reform in Zimbabwe and Ghana, and even in Thailand after the 1997 crisis, than in South Asia. The consequence has been a large gap between radical reform design and modest outcomes, particularly in Africa.

By comparison with macro-economic and industrial reform, there was much less high-level political and core official involvement in health and water reforms. Here, line ministry officials often had the key role in managing change and were likely to let it lapse. Professional staff – engineers in water, doctors in health – are much more important in the direction of these sectors than they are in ministries of industry and agriculture, and were likely to have a continuing role whatever the reform (see also Nelson, 2000 on social reforms in Latin America). Their involvement often had the effect of blocking change. Where social reform was more successful (e.g. health care in Ghana), it had been led by a small reform team which included donors, core ministries and line ministry officials with high-level political support.

The characteristics of service sectors have an effect on the balance of the relationship between principals (citizens and policy-makers) and agents (official providers) and therefore on the drive for and the resistance to reform.[2] We found that control by citizens and clients is greater where they can organize themselves and can exercise informed choice, and by policy-makers where they can gather information and measure the performance of providers. The providers or agents are more likely to be able to assert their own control (and often resistance) where they can form professional groups or can unionize, where there are few alternative providers with the necessary capacities, and where the service is monopolistic. These considerations are listed in the top two rows of Table 4.5.

Drawing on the research in Ghana, Zimbabwe, India and Sri Lanka, Table 4.5 summarizes the balance of power between principals and agents in three service sectors. The table is schematic, ignoring the differences between country contexts, and grouping business development and agri-

Table 4.5 The capacity of control by principals and agents

Service	Capacity of control by principals			Capacity of control by agents	
	Capacity of clients to organize	Capacity of clients to exercise influence	Policy-makers' control of performance	Providers' self-organization	Agency organizational dominance
Curative health	Weak: Clients are scattered and use service in crisis	Weak: Information asymmetry limits choice, but alternative providers exist	Weak: Service effort and output difficult to assess; information asymmetry. Difficult to specify contract	Strong: Strong unionisation and medical professions' interests in direct provider organizations and ministry. Some major suppliers/contractors	Dominant: Large direct deliverers with high autonomy
Urban piped water	Strong: Service is area-based and regular, facilitating client organization	Medium: Clients have information on service, but no alternative suppliers of piped water	Strong: Service effort and output is easy to measure and monitor. Relatively easy to specify contract	Medium/strong: Strong presence of engineers in provider organizations and ministry; moderate unionization; big contractor interests	Dominant: Monopolistic with a high degree of autonomy in management, or large contractor
Business and agriculture services	Medium/Strong: Services are for specific user groups. Stronger in industry than agriculture	Strong: Users have choice about whether to use the service	Medium: Service effort and output difficult to assess; information asymmetry. Difficult to specify contract	Weak: Small organizations with a relatively weakly established professional base and low unionization	Weak: Non-monopolistic

cultural services into one category for comparative purposes. It illustrates how principals are weakest and the agents are strongest in the case of curative health services. In urban water supply, there is a greater possibility of balance between the two sides. In business and agricultural services, the agent-providers have relatively lesser possibility of dominating the principal and of limiting reform that does not suit them.

The managerial capacity and institutional conditions for reform

The new managerial approaches confront problems of implementation due not only to the difficult circumstances of reform, to the challenge that they represent to vested interests and to the power of citizens and policy-makers to direct providers. There are also questions about the organizational and professional capacity to implement them and about the institutional or governance conditions on which they depend. For the purpose of analysis we categorize the capacity issues into three:

1   factors of organizational and management capacity that are largely internal to the public service organizations;
2   inter-organizational relationships;
3   the governance and institutional conditions that are external to but also penetrate sector organizations.[3]

Table 4.6 summarizes the leading constraints on capacity for implementation of each of the main reforms against these three headings.

Our research (Batley and Larbi 2004) showed that many of the problems encountered in the implementation of the new approaches are due to weak capacity at the organizational level. In the case of user fees in health, for example, it was evident that weaknesses in capacity were partly due to the rush to implement without adequate preparation. Often the relevant public organizations did not have the basic administrative capacities to manage the implementation of user charges and exemption systems effectively. Defective billing and collecting systems (also in the water sector) and weak accounting systems were unable to generate information for frontline managers in the health sector (Mills et al., 2001).

In contracting out and regulation, poor information and inadequacy of information management systems were key weaknesses in management capacity. In the health sector, for example, failures in the financial and information systems necessary to the monitoring and payment of contractors were common, even in middle-income countries such as Mexico, South Africa and Thailand. These often included the most basic failures in filing and records (Bennett and Mills, 1998). In the case of water regulation, agencies lacked clear mandates and autonomy, and often experienced problems of access to the information needed to make judgements about price, profitability and performance (Nickson and Franceys, 2003).

Table 4.6 Key constraints on governments' capacity to perform new management roles

Factors	Decentralizd managerial autonomy	User fees	Contracting	Regulation
Internal organizational factors	Low pay and inability to attract and retain skilled staff	Weak capacity to manage exemption systems in health	Weak basic administrative and financial systems and skills	Lack of staff skills in accounting and performance assessment
	Inadequate information systems for accountability	Weak billing and collection systems	Limited experience of contract design	Weak staffing for self-regulation in health
		Weak accounting systems and corruption	Staff resistance and lack of incentive	Vested professional interests
			Poor information systems to compare bids and performance	Inadequate information on price and performance
Inter-organizational factors	Lack of clarity of authority relationships	Lack of central monitoring and guidelines	Poor definition and coordination of roles.	Blurred boundaries between government, regulators and the regulated
	Lack of operational autonomy from central control agencies	Gap between policy design and implementation agencies.	Gap between contract design and implementation agencies	Gap between policy and implementation agencies.

Table 4.6 Continued

Factors	Decentralizd managerial autonomy	User fees	Contracting	Regulation
External institutional factors	Intervention by political and bureaucratic leaders Centralized civil service rules and systems	Political intervention in charges Civil society opposition High levels of poverty limits the scope for charging	Socio-political opposition to 'privatization' Economic and financial instability affects large water contracts Limited private sector development and trust Weak legal framework Unpredictable policy Centralized civil service rules and systems Lack of culture of performance	Political and professional influence on regulator Economic and political instability Business sector distrust of government Partiality of judiciary Weak demands of civil society Neutrality of regulator not understood

A common constraint on capacity across sectors and countries was the inability to attract and retain the required calibre of staff, a problem that was more pronounced in Ghana and recently in Zimbabwe than in India and Sri Lanka. This problem is rooted in a wider macro-governance context characterized by low pay and poor conditions of service in the public sector. However, attraction and retention were less problematic in financially autonomous and commercially oriented agencies (e.g. Zimtrade in Zimbabwe and the Cocoa Board in Ghana) able to offer improved pay and better incentives to staff (Jackson, 2002).

The sector organizations that have been the direct subject of reforms are part of a network of other organizations and are embedded in a wider governance environment that may enable or disable the application of the new approaches in public management. The management capacity issues discussed above cannot therefore be dissociated from wider inter-organizational relationships and from the broader governance environment.

Our research identified a number of inter-organizational factors that constrained the implementation of some of the new management approaches. As Table 4.6 shows, the key inter-organizational problem that constrained decentralized management across the four sectors was the lack of clarity of authority relationships, which often led to tension between autonomy of decentralized units and control by central bodies. This was evident in the case of the Ghana Water Company, which was subject to multiple controls from the government, the sector ministry, the State Enterprises Commission and the regulatory commission. In the case of user fees, an example of inter-organizational failures was the lack of clear guidelines from the ministries of health to health facility managers on how revenue from user fees was to be used. In Ghana, for example, there was no dedicated unit at the centre to produce and monitor guidelines for exemptions from user fees, thus leaving facility managers to use their discretion on who would be exempted.

In the water sector, the non-payment of bills by other public organizations and governments reneging on their financial commitments were major constraints on the finances available to water providers to deliver effective services (e.g. in India and Ghana). Other common inter-organizational task network problems included weak coordination between policy and implementing bodies and between different levels of government due to lack of clear definition of reporting relationships. In the health sector, for example, we found weak or absent oversight by ministries of health of the medical councils that were supposed to maintain professional standards. For example, in Tamil Nadu (India) the medical council had no reporting responsibility to the state department of health, whilst in Sri Lanka responsibility for implementing the Nursing Homes Act was transferred to provinces without any new guidance (Mills et al., 2001).

Public sector organizations are embedded in a wider governance environment which earlier wave of reforms in the 1980s largely ignored. The second wave of reforms in the 1990s, which embodied elements of the new management approaches, at least formally recognized the need to give attention to the transformation of the 'hard to change institutions which structure political and economic life' (World Bank, 2000). However, our research showed that the fundamental constraint to reforms remained their incompatibility with the prevailing institutional conditions. Reforms intended to give managers more autonomy, to engage private providers and to enhance responsiveness to consumers are difficult where governmental accountability is not well established, the boundaries between political and administrative action are blurred, civil society is weak, there is political and economic instability, public administration is ineffective and property rights are unclear (Burki and Perry, 1998; Schick, 1998).

In the countries examined in this study, hierarchical bureaucracy had not been significantly reformed. In almost all cases, we found that unreformed centralized civil service rules and systems asserted themselves over the formal delegation of autonomy to managers, public corporations and agencies. The Asian countries – India, Sri Lanka and particularly Thailand – generally had the experience and skills to design and negotiate contracts for support services in health. Typically, however, the process of contracting was concentrated in the central civil service. Governments had standard contract forms, which ensured that contracting took place in a systematic way, but left little room for flexible adjustment to local circumstances. Standardized terms, fixed prices and slow payment of contractors led to restricted private sector interest in competing for contracts. Particularly in Sri Lanka, this led also to low incentives for hospital staff to monitor contracts over which they had no clear authority (Russell and Atanayake, 1997).

Beyond governance, there are broader institutional preconditions for the adoption and implementation of the new approaches. For example, build-own-operate and concession contracts in the water sectors of India and Sri Lanka had stalled due to the incapacity of governments to demonstrate that the legal, financial and market conditions existed to justify and secure private investment. A BOT (build-operate-transfer) arrangement to develop new water supplies for Hyderabad Water Supply Board failed on these grounds. The Board was unable to convince international bidders that the revenue and payments for their water would be forthcoming (Franceys, 1998; Franceys and Sansom, 1999). Moreover, lack of trust between government and private firms about their respective motives presented a widespread constraint on the development of long-term contracts.

The institutional conditions external to regulatory organizations but necessary to them are even more exacting, particularly in the context of developing countries. Problems included instability of the political economy, difficulties in maintaining separation from political influence, weak demands of civil society and doubts about the independence of the judiciary to adjudicate in cases of dispute. However, the key external constraint to the effective operation of regulatory and enabling agencies was the undermining of their autonomy by political and vested interests. Few agencies could assume even that their own staff would expect to operate within a 'culture of neutrality' where regulation and support services applied without favouritism. In the case of health regulation it is clear that the same professional interests usually operated in government, the private sector and the regulator, preventing any disruption of those interests. Political leaders overrode the independence of water and health regulators and sometimes directed enabling agencies. The capacity of civil organizations, consumer organizations or the private sector to act as a countervailing force to this political pressure was usually weak (Batley and Larbi, 2004).

Conclusion

This chapter has raised questions about the appropriateness of the radical and comprehensive application of new public management reform models to low-income countries such as those covered in our research. The lesson is not that such reforms cannot work in developing countries. Where they have been effectively implemented, they have often delivered services more effectively and responsively. The problem is in the achievement of the implementation and maintenance of management reforms. Among the countries studied, reform designs were ambitious and wide-ranging on paper, but actual implementation has usually been weak.

To explain this, it is necessary to consider the nature of the reforms. First, changes in forms of management may have a long-term effect in the improvement of service delivery, but most do not bring quick or visible effects and arouse little public support. On the other hand, management reforms may well arouse opposition in the bureaucracy and among professions and unionized workers; resistance from these sources has a high political salience in developing countries. Second, there is the nature of the service sectors in which reform is taking place. The characteristics of social services, such as curative health, give the 'principals' of reform (citizens and policy-makers) a weak hand by comparison with their 'agents' (service providers). Citizen-clients are weakly organized to make demands and policy-makers have a weak information base from which to exercise control over service providers.

Third, there may be weak organizational capacity to undertake and to sustain reforms. New management approaches (managerial responsibility for budgets and performance, contract-making and monitoring, pricing of services, regulation and support of market actors) require new skills and new forms of organization. Inadequate information systems and problems of staff retraining, recruitment and retention are also important obstacles.

More surprisingly, we found that it was often basic administrative failures (in, for example, record-keeping, financial control, enforcement of sanctions, and the clarity of authority relations within and between organizations) which undermined more advanced management. The 'old public administration', which is often not fully consolidated in developing countries, remains an important part of effective management.

Fourth, we analysed the institutional context of reform. Failure to implement reform was generally found to have less to do with personal and organizational capacities than with underlying conditions and institutions: political and macro-economic instability, uncertainty of legal and judicial frameworks that would ensure a rule-based environment for providers of services, centralized control of operational resources, blurred boundaries between political and administrative responsibility, weak civil society demands and weak traditions of accountability for performance. Reforms very often fail to take account of these realities. The crises that galvanize the case for change very often also bring in a wide range of powerful external agencies that come armed with their own reform agendas. The danger is that they seek to apply a full programme of reforms conceived elsewhere (with multiple rich country variations), unrelated to local conditions. Unlike developed countries where reforms can be instigated and developed in response to local pressures, policy-makers in developing countries have less opportunity to develop their own policy discourse.

The implications of the analysis for policy and practice are first that public service reform needs to take account of each country's conditions and context, based on local initiatives within a sustained long-term approach. Second, more attention needs to be given to the sequencing and phasing of reforms to existing capacity, to take into account institutional conditions and to match reform ambitions to realities. Given weak capacities, the approach to reforming public services might be based on incremental steps within a long-term strategy, starting with the reform of basic incentives that strengthen accountability and improve performance. The initial focus would be on services that are easier for principals to control, on reforms that are less politically salient and on skills that can be built up in non-critical services.

The third implication for policy is that some of the problems inherent in the transformation from traditional to new public management in low-income countries may be transitional (for example, the lack of certain skills), whilst others may be more fundamental and institutional. One task of reformers is to be able to distinguish between transitional and more fundamental capacity problems. The former may require short-term capacity development interventions (for example, appropriate training and technical assistance for the establishment of adequate management information systems and improving financial accountability). It is less clear what the latter requires: external interventions to challenge and change organizational and individual behaviours, or patience whilst countries develop their own responses? This research inclines us to the second response.

Notes

1. The research on which this chapter is based was funded by DFID between 1996 and 2000, under Contract No. CNTR 94 2117A. A fuller account is given in Batley and Larbi (2004), whilst the sector studies upon which this article draws are reported in Mills et al. (2001); Jackson (2002); Hubbard (2003); Nickson and Franceys (2003).
2. This argument is similar to that of James Q. Wilson (1989) on the influence of the measurability of organizational processes, outputs and outcomes on their style of management. But our analysis considers the resources of principals and agents not only in terms of their information, but also of their capacity to organize.
3. These categories for analysing capacity are similar to those of Hilderbrand and Grindle (1995) and are set out more fully in Batley and Larbi (2004).

References

Batley, R. A. and G. A. Larbi (2004) *The Changing Role of Government: The Reform of Public Services in Developing Countries*, Basingstoke and New York, Palgrave Macmillan.

Bennett, S. and A. Mills (1998) 'Government Capacity to Contract: Health Sector Experience and Lessons', *Public Administration and Development*, Vol. 18, No. 4: 307–26.

Burki, S. J. and G. Perry (1998) *Beyond the Washington Consensus: Institutions Matter*, World Bank Latin American and Caribbean Studies: Viewpoints, Washington DC: World Bank.

Ferlie E., L. Ashburner, L. Fitzgerald and A. Pettigrew (1996) *The New Public Management in Action*. Oxford: Oxford University Press.

Franceys, R. (1998) 'Sri Lanka: Urban Water Supply', *Role of Government in Adjusting Economies Paper 17*, Birmingham: School of Public Policy, University of Birmingham.

Franceys, R. and K. Sansom (1999) 'India: Urban Water Supply', *Role of Government in Adjusting Economies Paper 35*, Birmingham: School of Public Policy, University of Birmingham.

Grindle, M. S. (2004) *Despite the Odds: The Contentious Politics of Education Reform*, Baltimore, MD and London: Johns Hopkins University Press.

Grindle, M. S. and J. W. Thomas (1991) *Public Policy and Policy Change: The Political Economy of Reform in Developing Countries*, Baltimore and London: Johns Hopkins University Press.

Hilderbrand, M. E. and M. S. Grindle (1995) 'Building Sustainable Capacity in the Public Sector: What Can Be Done?' *Public Administration and Development*, Vol. 15, No. 5: 441–63.

Hirschmann, D. (1993) 'Institutional Development in an Era of Economic Policy Reform Concerns, Contradictions and Illustrations from Malawi', *Public Administration and Development*, Vol. 13, No. 2: 113–28.

Hood, C. (1991) 'A Public Management for All Seasons?' *Public Administration*, 69: 3–19.

Hood, C. (1995) 'Contemporary Public Management: A New Global Paradigm', *Public Policy and Administration*, Vol. 10, No. 2: 104–17.

Hubbard, M. (2003) *Managing the Liberalization of Agricultural Markets in Developing Countries*, Basingstoke and New York, Palgrave Macmillan.

Jackson, P. B. (2002) *Business Development in Asia and Africa*, Basingstoke and New York, Palgrave Macmillan.

Kessler, T. (2003) Review of the World Development Report on Making Services Work for Poor People, Citizens' Network on Essential Services (CNES), available at: http://www.servicesforall.org/html/tools/2004WDR_review_print.shtml.

Lane, J.-E. (2000) *The Public Sector: Concepts, Models and Approaches*, 3rd edition, London, Newbury Park and New Delhi: Sage.

Manning, N. (2001) 'The Legacy of the New Public Management in Developing Countries', *International Review of Administrative Sciences*, Vol. 67: 297–312.

Mills, A., S. Bennett and S, Russell (2001) *The Challenge of Health Sector Reform: What Must Governments Do?* Basingstoke and New York, Palgrave Macmillan.

Mills, A., R. Brugha, K. Hanson and B. McPake (2002) 'What Can Be Done about the Private Health Sector in Low-income Countries?' *Bulletin of the World Health Organization*, Vol. 80, No. 4: 325–30.

Minogue, M. (1998) 'Changing the State: Concepts and Practices in the Reform of the Public Sector', in M., Minogue, C. Polidano and D. Hulme (eds.), *Beyond the New Public Management: Changing Ideas and Practices in Governance*, Cheltenham: Edward Elgar, pp. 17–37.

Moser, C., A. Herbert and R. Makonnen (1993) *Urban Poverty in the Context of Structural Adjustment: Recent Evidence and Policy Responses*, Discussion Paper, Urban Development Division, Washington DC: World Bank.

Nelson, J. M. (2000) *The Politics of Social Sector Reforms*, Washington DC: Overseas Development Council, www.iadb.org/sds/doc/nelson1.pdf

Nickson, R. A. and R. Franceys (2003) *Tapping the Market: The Challenge of Institutional Reform in the Urban Water Supply Sector*, Basingstoke and New York, Palgrave Macmillan.

Nyonator, F. and J. Kutzin (1999) 'Health for Some? The Effects of User Fees in the Volta Region of Ghana', *Health Policy and Planning Policy and Planning*, Vol. 14, No. 4: 329–41.

Pollitt, C. (2004) 'Strategic Steering and Performance Management: Agencies – Beautiful Form or Weak Variable?' *Paper for the ESRC/EPSRC International Colloquium on Government and Performance*, University of Birmingham, 15–16 March.

Russell, S. and N. Atanayake (1997) 'Reforming the Health Sector in Sri Lanka: Does Government have the Capacity?' *The Role of Government in Adjusting Economies Paper 14*, School of Public Policy, University of Birmingham.

Russell, S., P. Kwaramba, C. Hongoro and S. Chikandi (1997) 'Reforming the Health Sector in Zimbabwe: Does Government have the Capacity?' *The Role of Government in Adjusting Economies Paper 14*, School of Public Policy, University of Birmingham.

Sandbrook, R. (1993) *The Politics of Africa's Economic Recovery*, Cambridge: Cambridge University Press.

Schick, A. (1998) 'Why Some Developing Countries Should Not Try New Zealand's Reforms', *World Bank Research Observer*, Vol. 13, No. 1: 121–32.

Stiglitz, J. (1987) 'Principal and Agent', in J., Eatwell, M. Milgate, and P. Nennan. (eds.), *The New Palgrave Dictionary of Economics*, London: Palgrave, pp. 241–53.

Stiglitz, J. (2002) *Globalization and its Discontents*, London: Penguin.

Walsh, K. (1995) *Public Services and Market Mechanisms: Competition, Contracting and the New Public Management*, Basingstoke and London: Macmillan.

Wilson, J. Q. (1987) *Bureaucracy: What Government Agencies Do and Why They Do It*, New York: Basic Books.

World Bank (1993) *World Development Report 1993: Investing in Health*, New York: Oxford University Press.

World Bank (1994) *World Development Report 1994: Infrastructure for Development*, New York: Oxford University Press.

World Bank (1997) *World Development Report 1997: The State in a Changing World*, Oxford University Press: New York.

World Bank (2000) *The Road to Stability and Prosperity in Southeastern Europe: A Regional Strategy Paper*, Europe and Central Asia Region, Washington, DC: World Bank.

World Bank (2003) *World Development Report 2004: Making Services Work for Poor People*, Washington, DC: World Bank.

Part II
Fiscal Reform

5
Fiscal and Capacity-Building Reform
Yusuf Bangura

Introduction

There have been concerted efforts by governments and multilateral financial institutions to reduce the size of the state and restructure the various components of its spending activities. Policies have focused on the expenditure and revenue sides of the fiscal problem. In addition, privatization has been used as an instrument to support the goals of fiscal stability and state contraction. How have governments gone about pursuing these goals? What results have they yielded? Is the state contracting or still growing in various regions of the world? Has fiscal stability been achieved? And what are the social implications of the fiscal reforms?

This chapter discusses the social and institutional effects of two key reform measures associated with fiscal stability and downsizing – public expenditure reforms and privatization. It also looks at policies oriented towards improving the capacities of states in low-income countries. Reforms dealing with fiscal stability apply to all states, although policies for achieving results may vary across countries. In general, fiscal reforms are the most consistently pursued and far-reaching of public management reforms, with direct implications for the well-being of public sector employees, state capacity and social development. They deal with issues of downsizing, privatization and tax reform. Capacity-building reforms, on the other hand, tend to be restricted largely to the developing world, especially the 'least developed countries', most of which are in Africa. They address issues relating to the technical capacities of civil servants in policy analysis and monitoring; management of recurrent expenditure costs to ensure sustainability of projects; public investments; and pay reforms.

Public expenditure reform

During the 1980s, average central government spending per GDP varied between 25 per cent in South Asia and 39 per cent in the Middle East and

131

North Africa, with Africa (27 per cent), East Asia and the Pacific (26.5 per cent), and Latin America (26.5 per cent) occupying intermediate positions. The figure for the industrialized countries was 35 per cent (World Bank, 1997a). All regions arrived at these levels of expenditures from relatively low figures of less than 20 per cent during the 1960s. Levels of state expenditure did not correlate with levels of economic development. However, there were marked differences in the expenditure patterns of developed and developing countries. On the average, the largest share (more than 45 per cent) of central government expenditure in industrialized countries was accounted for by social security transfers and social service (especially health) provisioning (IMF, 1996). In developing countries, except for Latin America, social security and welfare occupied minor roles in public expenditure profiles. Instead, the largest shares were taken up by capital expenditures (on average, more than 30 per cent), government administration (15 per cent) and wages (26 per cent). Expenditures on education (11.4 per cent on average) and health (about 5 per cent) were much lower than capital expenditures. The emphasis on capital expenditure in developing countries should be understood in the light of the strong need expressed by new states for rapid infrastructure development and growth.

Public expenditure reforms in the 1980s and 1990s have reflected these differences in expenditure patterns. In industrialized countries, the emphasis has been on the welfare and social service components of state expenditures, although the extent of adjustment has varied among countries. In these countries, expenditure reforms seek to address the problems associated with changes in demographic trends and high dependency ratios;[1] unsustainable tax burdens; informalization, tax evasion and erosion of the tax base; as well as high wage costs and rigid labour markets that may undermine national competitiveness as countries become further integrated into the global economy. Trends in welfare expenditure reforms reflect differences in welfare state systems. Countries that have opted for wide-ranging neo-liberal reforms – Britain, New Zealand, the United States, Canada and Australia – have pursued policies of labour market and wage flexibility, greater selectivity in welfare support and gradual erosion of benefits and coverage.

Scandinavian countries, on the other hand, have been concerned about how to adjust their traditionally active labour market policies, relative gender equality and high rates of labour force participation, as well as their generous benefit schemes, to problems of declining revenues and growing public dissatisfaction with high taxes. Fiscal reforms in these countries have focused on reducing unemployment benefits and marginal tax rates;[2] extending pension contribution years; tying benefits closely to contributions; privatizing some aspects of service delivery; and promoting workfare schemes as a central component of unemployment benefits. Most other European countries have traditionally supported high social transfers at the expense of social services, although there are trends in recent years to carry out more radical reforms of their welfare systems. In these countries, especially the Latin ones in Southern Europe, social expenditure policies are oriented towards protection of the male employee who is expected to shoulder the responsibilities of the family. They have also tolerated large-scale unemployment, early retirement and high pension payments, even though their sustainability has been seriously questioned (Esping-Andersen, 1996).[3]

There is controversy among scholars on the question of whether public expenditures in industrialized countries, especially expenditures relating to welfare and social services, have declined. Data for the 1980s suggest that total and central government expenditures grew, albeit marginally, from 45 per cent to 47 per cent and 30 per cent to 33 per cent of GDP respectively; and expenditure on social security and health as a percentage of GDP also rose in most countries. This has led to the conclusion that the welfare state has shown a remarkable degree of resilience and that social expenditure reforms have been modest (Esping-Andersen, 1996; Pierson, 1996; Stephens, 1996). Pierson attributes this resilience to three main issues: since the welfare state is believed to represent the current *status quo*, radical reform is difficult to implement in political systems where a coalition of parties share power; despite the costs of the welfare system, it continues to enjoy high public support; and some of the beneficiaries of welfare have proved to be well organized in protecting benefits.

Data for the 1990s and new insights on patterns of social expenditure restructuring have challenged this view of welfare state resilience. Clayton and Pontusson report that when issues of inequality, mass unemployment and wider public sector reforms are factored into the analysis, 'major changes ... in the scope and organization of public welfare provision [have occurred] ... across the OECD area ... generally' (1998: 69). In 15 OECD countries for which data are available, wage inequality between the top and bottom income groups increased among men in twelve countries and in nine among women between 1975 and 1995; the percentage of the population earning less than 40 per cent of the median income grew between 1980 and 1991 in the four countries that are often used to illustrate different models of welfare state systems: Sweden (16.4–20.6), Germany (13.1–14.1), Britain (20.0–25.7) and the USA (18.8–21.0); and the percentage of individuals receiving means-tested social assistance increased in all but three OECD countries between 1980 and 1992.

In Sweden, since some benefits, such as the supplementary pension scheme, sick pay and parental leave insurance, are tied to employment, a doubling of the unemployed population in the first half of the 1990s increased the number of people who were excluded from universalistic welfare programmes. Total social spending per poor person grew less than real GDP per capita in Sweden, Germany, Britain and the USA between

1979 and 1992; and the average annual growth of total social spending per aged and unemployed person fell sharply in the four countries between 1980 and 1993. Using current socio-economic data from the OECD's *Historical Statistics*, Clayton and Pontusson reveal a consistently downward trend in the growth rate of real government expenditure for the years 1960–73 (3.6 per cent), 1973–79 (2.8 per cent), 1979–89 (2.4 per cent) and 1989–94 (1.2 per cent). The size of the public sector labour force also fell sharply for most countries during the 1990s. In European OECD countries, it would seem that social expenditure restructuring has affected the social services much more than social security transfers. The public share of total health expenditure fell or remained the same in nine out of twelve European countries during the 1990s.

Expenditure reforms in developing countries

Public expenditure reforms in developing countries have focused largely on cutbacks in capital expenditures, the wage bill, employment and administration. The IMF and the World Bank have played major roles in influencing the size and composition of expenditures in these countries. Before the Poverty Reduction and Growth Facility, the IMF tried to achieve this through its Enhanced Structural Adjustment Facility (ESAF), which was established in 1987, and was targeted at low-income countries. Its loans carried lower interest rates and longer repayment periods than normal IMF stand-by arrangements. By 1997, about 80 countries were eligible for ESAF loans and 35 ESAF arrangements were in operation. The World Bank's work in public expenditure reform is carried out through its Structural Adjustment Loans (SALs) and Sectoral Adjustment Loans (SECALs). Between 1979 and 1994, about 250 of these loans in 86 countries addressed fiscal reforms. 51 per cent of the loans went to Africa and 23 per cent to Latin America. Other regions, including transition economies in Eastern Europe, accounted for less than 10 per cent each. However, the share in value of loans was roughly equal between Africa (30 per cent) and Latin America (29 per cent), with transition economies accounting for 16 per cent of the total (World Bank, 1997b).

For loans that are directly related to expenditure reforms, which fall under the World Bank's Public Sector Management (PSM) portfolio, the distribution has been different. Even though Africa attracted more of these loans, implying more intense reform activities, half of the value of these loans went to Latin America in 1995–97, more than 25 per cent to transition economies and only 12 per cent to Africa. The Africa share had dropped from about 20 per cent in the period 1988–92 (World Bank, 1997c; Berg, 1999). A World Bank evaluation report (1997b: 84) on fiscal management reported that 'low-income countries tended to face more binding conditions than high income countries, and conditions tended to be stronger in AFR (Africa) and ECA (Eastern Europe and Central Asia) than in

Table 5.1   Loan conditions by expenditure reform objective, 1980–94

	Number of countries on which condition was imposed
Expenditure reforms	126
Streamline budgetary processes and accounts	42
Civil service reform	42
Privatization and marketization	43
Social sector restructuring	60
Poverty alleviation	10
Participation	1
Others	

Source: Adapted from World Bank (1997b).

LAC (Latin America and the Caribbean)'. Table 5.1 highlights the distribution of loan conditions by expenditure reform goals in 1980–94. The single largest number of reform activities was in capital expenditure (52). Indeed, reforms dealing with direct expenditure reduction objectives account for more than half of the total activities (126).

What have been the outcomes of expenditure reforms in developing countries? Reductions in overall fiscal deficits became visible for most regions only during the 1993–97 period: from –6.3 per cent to –2.9 per cent for Africa; –2.9 per cent to –2.4 per cent for Asia; and –8 per cent to –3.6 per cent for the Middle East and Eastern Europe. Latin America achieved fiscal stability by 1990 (–0.2 per cent); fiscal deficits rose to –0.9 per cent in 1993 and –1.9 per cent in 1994 before declining to –1.7 per cent in 1996 and 1997 (IMF, 1998a). Both the IMF and World Bank report that adjustment has taken place largely on the revenue side of the fiscal equation[4] (IMF, 1998b). However, data for Africa from the World Bank's African Development Indicators (1998/99) suggest that public expenditure as a percentage of GDP fell consistently from 30.8 per cent in 1992 to 21.8 per cent in 1996, even though it rose to 22.3 per cent in 1997. ECLAC (1996–97) data for Latin America suggest that expenditures have been fairly stable, with periodic minor contractions and overruns during the 1990s for some countries. Only in Mexico and Honduras have expenditures fallen consistently and sharply during the review period. In Mexico, public expenditure as a percentage of GDP dropped from 31.8 per cent in 1990 to 23.6 per cent in 1997. Expenditure cuts of about 4 per cent of GDP were also recorded in the Middle East and North Africa between 1979 and 1994 (World Bank, 1997a).

Table 5.2 provides insights into government expenditure trends in various regions. The data suggest that although governments grew, albeit slowly, up to the early 1990s, it seems that for some regions, governments were beginning to shrink in the mid to late 1990s. For OECD countries, it is the rate of growth of public expenditures per GDP, rather than the absolute

Table 5.2   Are central governments shrinking? Trends in public expenditure in various regions of the world (per GDP)

	1980	1990	1993	1994	1995	1996	1997
Sub-Saharan Africa(a)	25.5	26.3	27.0	26.8	23.5	21.8	22.3
North Africa (a)	39.0	29.4	34.4	32.5	30.7	28.9	30.4
Latin America (b)			24.5	21.7		23.6	23.4	23.6
South and East Asia (c)	29.4	37.3			30.2	26.2	

Note: Sub-Saharan Africa excludes South Africa.
Source: (a) World Bank's *African Development Indicators* (1998/99);
(b) from ECLAC's *Economic Survey of Latin America and the Caribbean* (1996–97); c) from the Asian Development Bank's *Key Indicators of Developing Asia and Pacific Countries* (1997 and 1998).

level, that has been declining. It is difficult to establish whether the decline observed in other regions, such as Sub-Saharan Africa, North Africa and Asia is a sustainable trend, given the marginal changes involved. It should be noted that despite the importance given to expenditure adjustment by the Fund and the Bank, fiscal data are not always accurate, especially for developing countries. Public expenditure data produced by the key international financial institutions are often incomplete for many countries, which makes it difficult to assess the effects of reforms across regions (see Therkildsen, 1999, for a discussion of data problems). Regional averages also conceal country differences in performance, which can sometimes be significant. Fiscal adjustment on both the expenditure and revenue sides of the equation has been particularly difficult for low-income, highly indebted and primary commodity exporting countries, despite each being a recipient of more than three adjustment loan programmes and intense fiscal surveillance from the Bank and the Fund (World Bank, 1997b; IMF, 1998c).

Public expenditure reviews and cash budgets

Problems of expenditure restructuring in low-income countries encouraged development of two major reform instruments: public expenditure reviews; and cash budgeting. Public expenditure reviews examine all aspects of a loan recipient's public expenditures, including sectoral allocations, investment programmes and budget policies. They are seen as a way of checking expenditures that are likely to escape verification of public investment programmes. The number of reviews grew considerably in the 1990s. Between 1987 and 1998 more than 200 reviews were carried out in loan recipient countries. However, it has been found that most expenditure reviews are prepared by Bank staff or foreign consultants and lack national participation (IMF, 1998c); and impacts have been modest or negligible. Critics, including independent Bank-sponsored evaluation teams, maintain that reviews are often delayed and hardly match a country's budget cycle; their recommendations are unprioritised and sometimes even duplicate the failed policies of governments in several contexts (World Bank, 1998a; Berg, 1999).

Cash budgeting acts as an agent of restraint on the spending habits of ministers and bureaucrats. It aims to stop government treasuries from printing money or borrowing from the central bank to meet their obligations. Cash budgeting creates new rules and procedures on fiscal management: finance and line ministries can only spend what they have in the bank; overdrafts are disallowed. Variants of the cash budget rule include proposals for balanced budgets, which most states in the US have adopted; and numerical limits on fiscal deficits and debt, which the EU has imposed on members for monetary union and participation in the European Monetary Union. A growing number of fiscally distressed economies, including Zambia, Uganda, Tanzania, Peru, Bosnia-Herzegovina and Malawi, are currently implementing cash budgets, (Bolnick, 1997; Carlson, 1998; Chiwele et al., 1999; Stasavage and Moyo, 1999; Therkildsen 1999).

In Zambia, which is one of the most celebrated cases, a monitoring committee comprising officials from the Ministry of Finance and the central bank was created – the Joint Data Monitoring Committee – to ensure that the cash budget was effectively implemented (Bolnik, 1997). The Committee met daily to vet fiscal and monetary data and submitted weekly reports to top government officials concerned with economic policy-making. In the case of Uganda, considerable authority was given to the Ministry of Finance to determine appropriate monthly spending levels as well as the distribution of funds to line ministries. Under the Ugandan scheme, the Finance Minister was not prohibited from borrowing from the central bank and the president could intervene on spending policies.

The cash budget contributed to a reduction of budget deficits in the countries that have used it. In Zambia, for instance, during the first year of the policy, the government turned a deficit of K69 billion into a surplus of K24 billion (Bolnik, 1997). The sustainability of the policy is, however, open to serious doubt. First, governments have found it difficult to stick to the cash budget rules all year round because of their negative implications for public service provisioning. Studies on Zambia's cash budget have revealed wild fluctuations in expenditures, with cash outflows outpacing cash inflows during some months in the budget cycle. Political leaders have intervened at critical periods to request central banks to lend money to ministries in order to prevent cash problems turning into political crises. For instance, the Bank of Zambia gave the Ministry of Finance K5 billion to avert a major catastrophe in maize marketing and crop financing in the 1993–94 cropping season. The government had overestimated the capacity of the private sector to take over the parastatals' functions of crop financing and marketing. High interest rates were a severe constraint on private traders and service providers to participate in the liberalised agricultural sector. A food crisis was averted only when the government stepped in to assist the private traders and violated its own cash budget principles (Bolnik, 1997; Chiwele et al., 1999).

Second, Bolnick (1997) and Stasavage and Moyo (1999) have shown that cash budgets can distort the composition of expenditures. Faced with a cash constraint, ministries are likely to spend money on non-essentials: there may be money for foreign travel instead of rural extension work; workers may not be paid, but officials may still receive their perks and have their offices refurbished, etc. Stasavage and Moyo demonstrate that cash budgets may punish social ministries and reward offices associated with the presidency. In Zambia, the presidency had expenditure overruns equivalent to 1 per cent of total expenditures in 1994. This was roughly the same as the 12 per cent shortfall experienced by the Ministry of Health in the same period. In Uganda, expenditure overruns in the President's Office were almost equal to the combined shortfalls of the ministries of agriculture (–51 per cent) and education (–29 per cent). Third, cash budgets may make it difficult for line ministries to plan properly. It may undermine efforts to introduce performance targets for employees as well as social pacts to minimise industrial conflicts.

Social effects of expenditure reforms in low-income countries

In general, expenditure reforms had strong negative effects on the social sectors of adjusting countries in the 1980s (World Bank, 1994; Cornia et al., 1988). In Africa, for instance, government and World Bank expenditures per GDP in 21 countries for which data are available show a sharp deterioration: they fell from 4.6 per cent in 1980 to 2.6 per cent in 1985 and rose slightly to 2.7 per cent in 1990. Education's share of total government budgets even fell more sharply: from 20 per cent in 1980 to 9.8 per cent in 1985; they only recovered in the late 1980s, recording 13.6 per cent in 1990. Obsessed with fiscal and other problems of economic stabilization, the World Bank considerably reduced its lending to the education sector, introduced more intrusive rules for its loan programmes, and encouraged 'non-sector-specific' cuts on civil service wages and employment levels that further hurt labour-intensive sectors like education (World Bank, 1994).

An evaluation report in 1994 on the World Bank's role in human resource development in Africa found that the Bank's annual loans on education fell from $0.50 per person (in 1990 US dollars) for the period 1972–81 to $0.32 per person during the period 1982–88 (World Bank, 1994: 44). The World Bank's contribution as a percentage of the education budgets of a panel of 21 countries actually collapsed from 37.3 per cent in 1975 to 0.9 per cent in 1985 (p. 103). Following criticisms from international organizations, such as UNICEF, civil society groups as well as social democratic governments and political parties, the Bank rethought its expenditure reform policies in the late 1980s and early 1990s.

The Bank's focus since then has been not only to demand lower aggregate expenditures from loan recipients, but to recommend restructuring of the composition of expenditures: shifting resources in favour of non-wage activities, maintenance and social expenditures; and ensuring that primary education and health care are protected or enjoy superior funding at the expense of tertiary services. Recent IMF data suggest that some progress has been made in achieving these objectives. Despite the insistence on aggregate expenditure controls, 32 low-income countries under ESAF experienced an increase in real per capita spending on health and education by an annual average of 2.8 per cent between 1985 and 1996.[5] However, although this is an improvement on the record of the 1980s, it may not represent substantial progress when set against the very large, unmet needs for education and health services as well as the diminishing or stagnant incomes that are still a feature of many low-income countries.

Privatization

Privatization, or the transfer of state assets to the private sector, is a central component of downsizing. It contributes to fiscal stability in two main ways. First, gains can be made on the expenditure side by withdrawing subsidies to loss-making companies and imposing hard budget constraints on the economic decisions of managers. A privatized loss-making enterprise can also contribute to government revenues through taxation if its activities turn out to be profitable. Second, the revenue derived from selling state enterprises to the public can help governments close their fiscal gaps. In general, however, fiscal problems are cash flow problems, which may not be eliminated by one-off sales. Privatization may improve a country's fiscal position only if the public enterprises account for high fiscal expenditures (Hachette, 1996).

The expenditure reduction goal of privatization has been important in most countries that have implemented privatization programmes. Many state enterprises in developing and transition economies have enjoyed what Kornai has referred to as 'soft budget constraints': unlimited access to subsidies and grants; soft credit systems; and preferential treatment in tax rates (Raiser, 1996). A soft budget constraint encourages managers to believe that the state would come to their rescue if they encountered difficulties. It reduces the incentive to minimize costs. One feature of the privatization policies of countries faced with these problems has been to corporatize the enterprises and withdraw or minimise government support as a first step towards full privatization.

The revenue-raising aspect of privatization has largely been limited to Latin America and OECD countries that have implemented big privatization programmes, using methods of direct public auctions on stock markets. In sub-Saharan Africa, and North Africa and the Middle East, privatization has been very slow, involving mainly small and medium-sized enterprises. As Table 5.3 shows, privatization receipts in these two regions are the lowest in the world. The role of privatization as a revenue-generating instrument has also been limited in the transition economies because of the voucher scheme that has been used to facilitate sales. Vouchers have been distributed to the adult population, often at give-away prices (Rodinelli, 1994), to deflect public criticism of privatization and encourage popular participation in the evolving market economies.

Between 1985 and 1995 eleven European Union countries[6] netted almost $97 billion from privatization, which was about an average of 3 per cent of their GDPs. The greatest gains per GDP were made by the UK (9 per cent), Portugal (5.8 per cent) and Sweden (3.9 per cent). Privatization became a useful tool of budget deficit reduction as countries struggled to meet the Maastricht budgetary criteria for joining the European Monetary Union. Privatization receipts were seen as less politically risky than public expenditure cuts or tax increases in efforts to reduce the public debt. Cash-strapped governments often announced targets for annual privatization revenues as part of budget forecasts, underlining the direct link between privatization and fiscal policy (Parker, 1998).

The financing of fiscal deficits and attraction of foreign investment were important goals in the privatization strategies of Latin American countries. Data for Chile (1983–86), Argentina (1985–91) and Mexico (1983–90) suggest the use of privatization as a deficit-financing instrument, including financing of current expenditures. Peru and Venezuela have also relied on

Table 5.3   Privatization revenues in developing and transition societies ($million)

	1990	1991	1992	1993	1994	1995	1996	Total
Latin America and Caribbean	10,915	18,723	15,560	10,487	8,198	4,615	14,143	82,641
Transition Countries	1,262	2,551	3,626	3,988	3,956	9,741	5,466	30,591
East Asia and Pacific	376	835	5,161	7,155	5,507	5,411	2,697	27,123
South Asia	29	996	1,557	974	2,666	917	889	8,028
Sub-Saharan Africa	74	1,121	207	640	602	472	745	3,861
Middle East and North Africa	2	17	70	419	782	746	1,477	3,510

Source: World Bank (1998b).

privatization receipts to overcome severe fiscal constraints. Mexico, Chile and Argentina have used privatization receipts to reduce the stock of their domestic public debt. In Mexico, for instance, a special fund was created in 1990 to retire some of the government's domestic debt obligations using privatization revenues: $7 billion was retired in 1991 and $5 billion in the first quarter of 1992 (Devlin, 1994).

Privatization is now a global phenomenon. Between 1990 and 1996 states in developing and transition economies divested $155.654 billion of their assets to the private sector. If we add the privatization transactions of industrialized countries, which had a value of about $175 billion between 1988 and 1993, it is clear that governments are disengaging, even if unevenly, from direct ownership of business enterprises. Indeed, the number of privatization transactions multiplied more than five-fold from 696 in the period 1980–87 to 2,655 in 1988–93, with all regions showing positive change. Even though the share of public enterprises in the gross domestic products of all developing regions changed little in the 1980s, the 1990s witnessed distinct reductions for most regions. The share of public enterprises in the GDPs of industrialized countries has consistently declined since 1982.

Welfare effects of privatization

The arguments for privatization seem compelling when enterprises are located in competitive markets and governments do not have to worry about the social or welfare objectives of public enterprises. Under such conditions, a privatized company will be judged largely by the criterion of productive efficiency. Is the company able to keep supply costs as low as possible? Insights from principal–agent theory affirm that private companies are likely to be more productively efficient than public enterprises because private managers can be held accountable to only one objective – profitability – which may limit discretionary or opportunistic behaviour by managers. A private company with low profits will also experience a declining share price and be exposed to takeover threats from competitors. Furthermore, private companies may have large shareholders who are likely to be active monitors of company performance; and managers' pay in a private firm may be tied to performance, thus encouraging efficient decisions and work practices. Empirical studies comparing the two types of enterprises seem to support these theoretical insights (Vining and Boardman, 1992; Brown 1998; Parker, 1998). However, the advantages which private firms enjoy over public enterprises may be eroded if equity holdings are widely dispersed, large firms can postpone or immunize themselves from takeover bids and public enterprises can be corporatized or made to operate like private firms.

Besides, a large number of the enterprises that have been privatized since the 1990s operate in monopolistic or quasi-monopolistic markets and produce goods and services that have strong implications for welfare: electricity, telecommunications, water, post, railways and energy. In developing and transition societies, infrastructure privatization accounted for about 42 per cent of the privatization receipts between 1990 and 1996 (World Bank, 1998b). Privatization of utilities also gained momentum in EU countries during the 1990s (Parker, 1998). In dealing with these types of enterprises, public welfare may be negatively affected if governments are concerned only about cost reduction or productive efficiency. Since many of these enterprises are monopolies, the new private owners may raise prices substantially above their marginal costs and reap monopoly profits. This will affect consumers, especially poor social groups, who may be excluded from the consumption of basic goods and services. Therefore, when issues of allocative efficiency, or the setting of prices at marginal cost levels, are considered the ownership form is not significant in determining public welfare outcomes. In other words, private forms of ownership are not inherently superior to public ones.[7]

One way governments have tried to overcome the constraints of monopoly and defend public welfare in privatization programmes is by unbundling the various components of enterprises,[8] stimulate competition and establish regulations. Advances in information technologies, especially in such areas as fibre optics, cellular and satellite phones, long-distance phone calls and data transmission, have greatly increased competition in the telecommunications sector. Where effective regulations are in place, such as in Chile (World Bank, 1995; Betran and Sera, 1996) and New Zealand (Halligan, 1997), it has been shown that companies do not just make good profits; services to consumers can also improve. However, data on competitiveness in the global telecommunications industry suggest that there is no correlation between ownership type and economic performance even in this increasingly competitive sector. Brown (1998) reports that in 1995, although the US telecom industry, which is completely privately owned, charged the least fixed prices for business customers globally, the state-owned telecom company in Iceland had the lowest prices for call charges; and even though the US scored best in global multi-factor productivity, the state-owned Swiss company led in 'revenue per employee' and 'revenue per line'. Where regulations are weak, as in the Philippines telecom industry, privatization has led to very high profits for the new owners but less network expansion and poor services to consumers.[9]

Studies of the UK experience suggest questionable outcomes for a number of privatized utilities. Privatized enterprises have continued to enjoy incumbency or monopolistic advantages: even after twelve years of privatization, British Telecom (BT) controlled 90 per cent of the revenue from household calls and 83 per cent of the total telecom market in 1996; prices paid by consumers for BT services fell by only 1 per cent in four years compared to a drop of 20 per cent for businesses; the Consumer

Association in Britain found that for a sample of tickets it bought in 1996 to test whether the new rail companies were charging fair prices, it paid about 73 per cent more than the real price, and that individual tickets 'were overpriced by more than £50';[10] unmetered water bills rose by 39 per cent between 1989/90 and 1995/96 in England and Wales; the only visible gains in the privatized utilities were in the gas sector where prices fell by 20 per cent, but this was thought to be related to the sharp drop in natural gas costs (Meek, 1998). The situation in many developing countries where regulatory regimes are weak suggests that the welfare effects of privatization in many utilities may be negative, even though privatized companies may be making profits.

A recent World Bank publication on privatization in Africa notes that: 'In not one country with a privatization program has there been an effort to develop a regulatory framework as an integral component of that program ...' (World Bank, 1998d). A study by Manuel Angel Abdala (1994) arrives at a similar conclusion for Latin America even though a few countries have made progress in establishing regulatory regimes: 'Widespread privatisation has been encouraged all over the region. With a few exceptions, however, the transfer of ownership was hurried and performed under constraints imposed by economic and political objectives that tended to overlook the importance of regulating private monopolies' (Abdala, 1994: p. 45). In Brazil, the regulatory institutions were taken over or 'colonized' by the very interests they were designed to control. In Argentina, the privatized public utilities were so large and commanded so much market clout that they were more powerful than the regulatory bodies (Mairal, 1996). Chile has been the exception: a regulatory framework was established before privatization; and the close links between the regulators and the supervisory ministries were severed, which have allowed the autonomous regulatory commissions to develop arms-length relations with the privatized companies (Betran and Serra, 1996; World Bank, 1995).[11]

Unemployment effects of privatization

There are additional social problems associated with privatization: unemployment and inequality; ethnic and regional imbalance; and loss of national wealth of a strategic nature to foreign interests. Privatization is often associated with short-term retrenchment as new managers seek to restructure what are believed to be over-bloated enterprises, minimize costs and change the terms of employment from permanent tenure to one based on performance and profitability. For instance, in the celebrated case of New Zealand, the state-owned Telecom Company laid off 30 per cent of its workforce in two years before the company was sold to the public; and British Telecom lost 100,000 workers between 1989 and 1994.

The unemployment effects of privatization must be a cause for concern in developing countries, especially low-income countries and economies in transition, which are reputed to have very large public sector employment outlays. In 1990, public enterprise employment accounted for about 11 per cent of total employment in developing countries; the African average, which was the largest, was 22 per cent. And most people in East and Central Europe were employed in public enterprises under communism. However, the persistence of monopolistic market structures even under privatization has made it possible for governments and privatized companies to minimize the incidence of retrenchment in some cases. For instance, fears of massive retrenchment and salary decreases associated with Chilean privatization in the first half of the 1980s, led most governments in Latin America to extract guarantees of job stability from new owners of privatized companies during the early years of asset transfers. Petrazzini (1996) argues that companies tended to respect these guarantees because they inherited a monopoly market and did not have to be competitive to make profits. Workers' militancy may also check the pace and volume of retrenchment as has been reported in the case of Ghana, which witnessed declining levels of retrenchment and wide differentials between planned and actual retrenchments as the privatization programme progressed (World Bank, 1995). In aggregate terms, however, the 42 largest state enterprises in Ghana experienced a drop in employment from 241,000 in 1984 to 83,000 in 1991.

The situation in transition economies is even more serious because of the strong links between social welfare benefits and employment: under communism, state-owned enterprises offered their employees paid vacation, sickness benefits, health services, subsidized rent and kindergartens, loans, retirement assistance, supplementary pension and subsidised food and transport (Standing, 1996). In the absence of state provision, retrenchment may result in not only loss of income but also loss of access to social services. Countries that have been concerned about the welfare effects of privatization have tried to protect some of these benefits, even at huge costs to their economies. The voucher scheme that most countries in the region have used to facilitate privatization has ensured that managers and employees can resist outside pressures for competition if they are determined to do so. Studies on privatization in Russia confirm this point. Managers and employees, or insiders, owned 64.26 per cent of the total shares in 314 sampled companies in 1994 after privatization. Filatochev, Wright and Bleaney (1999) report that expectations that insiders would divest their shares to outside interests or foreign corporate investors have been unfounded. Both managers and workers want to keep their jobs and have colluded to restrict outside penetration of the firms. In 1995/6 the percentage of shares controlled by insiders has gone down to only 61.48. Where employees have sold their shares these have gone largely to managers who work in the companies – not to outside interests.[12]

Ethnicity and nationalism

Privatization can also affect ethnic relations and stability especially in deeply divided multi-ethnic societies. The transfer of state assets to the private sector through market instruments often creates winners and losers of a highly lopsided nature. If the privatization outcomes are perceived to reflect strong ethnic or racial biases, losers may seek to obstruct the programme or use the perceived losses as an excuse to stoke up ethnic feelings in the wider body politic. The early efforts at privatization in Nigeria in the late 1980s met with strong criticisms from northern business groups and elites who complained that public auctions of federal assets through the Nigerian Stock Exchange would result in a high number of the assets going to business groups and individuals in the south west region, who were believed to have benefited from the enterprise indigenization programmes of the 1970s. Northern state governments set up trust funds to buy up some of the assets divested by the federal government, leading to the anomalous situation where privatization was occurring at the centre, whereas governments at the sub-national level were increasing their stakes in public assets. The fears of northern businessmen were allayed when the chairman of the largest northern state enterprise, Northern Nigerian Development Corporation, was made director of the federal privatization commission and a scheme was devised to allocate some of the shares on non-competitive terms (Olukoshi, 1990).

In Malaysia, Goh and Jomo K. S. (1998) report that the government allocated 30 per cent of the shares of all privatized companies to the *Bumiputera* (indigenous Malay), whose marginalization in the economy contributed to the race riots of 1969. Prior to privatization, the government had tried to promote Malay interests largely through public sector jobs and scholarships while allowing Chinese business groups to dominate the private sector. Privatization without quotas would further have strengthened Chinese dominance of the economy, provoked hostilities from the Malay, and racialized the debate on retrenchment and restructuring in the newly privatized companies. A similar problem emerged in Tanzania during the debate on privatization in the late 1980s and early 1990s. The African elites who dominate the public sector complained that the previous *Ujama* (socialist development strategy) had made it difficult for Africans to set up private businesses as the minority Asian business community had done. Privatization would, therefore, in their view, empower Asians at the expense of the African majority (Booth, 1990). One prominent politician even tried to mobilize popular support and votes on this platform as the political system itself was being liberalized, leading to strains between the two communities. Similarly, the Kenyan government opposed the privatization of maize marketing in the 1980s because of fears that the benefits would largely accrue to the Asian business community (Mosley, 1988; Mkandawire, 1994). The rapid rate of acquisition of public assets in

Southern African countries in recent years by Afrikaners, especially in Mozambique and Zambia, may provoke a backlash and further poison race relations in that region.

Closely related to the problems of ethnicity are developing country concerns about the transfer of national assets of a strategic nature to foreigners (Mkandawire, 1994). World Bank (1998b) data suggest that foreign investors accounted for 44 per cent (or $69.782 billion) of the revenue from privatization between 1990 and 1996. More than half of this went to Latin America, followed by the transition countries of Europe and Central Asia. The least, about 0.8 per cent, went to the Middle East and North Africa. Sub-Saharan Africa and South Asia accounted for slightly over 2 per cent each. The foreign takeover of national assets may be seen as an inevitable outcome of the process of globalization or the transnationalization of states in the world economy. It may help the growth of stock markets in developing countries, provide new sources of capital to depressed economies and contribute to the performance of ailing public enterprises. However, a high proportion of the foreign capital that participates in these enterprises is of the portfolio type, which has proved to be highly volatile and disruptive of national economies. Between 1990 and 1996 such investments accounted for about 38 per cent of foreign participation in privatization transactions in developing countries; in 1996, this was about 50 per cent. Vital national infrastructure and other key economic sectors, which citizens may regard as 'national industrial champions', may be exposed to serious crises if there is a sudden flight of capital. Indeed, there was a sharp drop in portfolio investment in privatized enterprises in developing countries in 1995 – from US$5.965 billion in 1994 to US$2.959 billion in 1995 – following the Mexican financial crisis of that year.

Capacity-building reform

All reforms – fiscal, managerial or political – face capacity problems. Change is disruptive; those who stand to benefit may be weakly organized or not strategically located to defend the reforms; doubts may exist about the commitment of reforming governments; losers may fight back or withdraw support; the reform programmes may be poorly conceived; and infrastructure may not be in place to ensure a smooth transition or success. Even when reforms are broadly accepted, old bureaucratic work methods and traditional behaviours may still influence those entrusted to implement them. Capacity problems are more serious in low-income, crisis-ridden countries where state systems are either in disarray or have suffered serious erosion following long-running recessions, globalization pressures and poorly thought-out structural adjustment policies.

In 1998, 79 countries were classified as poor by the IMF and qualified for concessional assistance under the organization's ESAF facility. About 55 of these countries fall under the UNDP's 'low human development' classification in its Human Development Index: they do rather poorly in a composite index that combines GDP per capita, longevity and education. Forty-eight countries with a population of 550 million account for UNCTAD's least developed countries, which receive special focus in the organization's work on trade and development. About two-thirds of these countries are in Africa. A World Bank (1997b) review of public expenditure reforms in low-income countries found that least developed, highly indebted and primary commodity-producing countries had great difficulties meeting expenditure targets. Key features of these countries are: very low GDP per capita; poor growth records; high levels of aid dependency; intense exposure to exogenous shocks in commodities markets; high debt and capital flight; weak formal state structures; entrenched and widespread patronage networks; increasing informalization of economies and societies; and collapsing incomes for public servants. A majority of these countries are multi-ethnic and currently account for most of the civil wars, collapsed states, refugees and displaced people in the world. Many of those that have tried to transit from authoritarian to democratic rule have faced very serious setbacks.

The issue of stateness, or state capacity, is thus central to any reforms or development programmes that these countries seek to advance. The institutional reforms relating to privatization, performance contracts, decentralized management and contracting out are so complex and demanding that it is doubtful whether low-income crisis-ridden states would be able to implement them without major improvements in capacities. As many scholars have pointed out, low-income crisis states face a dilemma: they are being asked to undertake complex institutional tasks at a time when their capacity to do so is not only limited but is being undermined by programmes of downsizing (Hutchful, 1997, 1999; Mkandawire and Soludo, 1999; Olukoshi, 1999).

Three issues are central to the capacity problems of low-income countries: developing the necessary technical expertise that will enable national bureaucrats independently to formulate, implement and monitor public policies, projects and programmes; tackling the enormous problems of recurrent costs associated with state expansion and economic crisis; and paying public servants adequate remuneration that can motivate them to offer good public service and minimize their current propensity to 'moonlight' or engage in multiple survival strategies.

As we have already noted, data on expenditure suggest a decline in central government expenditures during the 1990s. By 1997, African governments were spending less than other developing regions. Data compiled by Schiavo-Campo (1998) also suggest that the central wage bill of African countries as a proportion of GDP declined from 6.1 per cent in the early 1980s to 4.8 per cent in the early 1990s – again recording the sharpest decline among developing countries. The same goes for public employment. The available data suggest that Africa had fewer people working in the public sector than other developing regions: this was 1.9 per cent of the population in Africa compared to 4.6 per cent in Latin America, 4.9 per cent in the Middle East, and 3.1 per cent in Asia and the Pacific. One can conclude, on the basis of these data, that Africa today is the most under-governed region in the world. The sharp reductions in expenditure, income, and employment have affected the incentive structures of African bureaucracies, making public service unattractive or not fully rewarding. The next two sections examine issues related to technical capacity and recurrent costs. Reforms dealing with pay issues are discussed by McCourt in chapter 6.

Technical capacity

The development of technical capacity is tied to issues of training and retraining, and the funding of universities and public administration institutes. During the 1980s, the tertiary institutions of crisis states experienced profound crisis as salaries slumped, facilities for teaching and research became scarce, infrastructures were left unrepaired, and teachers left in droves to join the private sector or tap into overseas opportunities. The problem was compounded by the reform policies of leading financial agencies involved in adjustment and institutional reform. These placed less attention on universities in low-income countries, which were believed to be inequitable and offer low rates of return, and subordinated the needs of education in general to the requirements of market-oriented adjustment based on the misguided belief that adjustment would be temporary.

A case in point was the World Bank's policy document *Education in Africa* (1988). A later independent Bank review (1994) found that Bank strategies 'seldom attempt to link and integrate educational and national development plans; it almost seems, at times, that they run parallel, but independent tracks' (p. 45). It was very critical of the tendency to make 'across-the-board recommendations without adequate country-specific justification', such as 'the near universal recommendation to reallocate within the education budget from higher to primary education and the strong tendency (in 13 of the 19 projects reviewed) to recommend increased user charges'. The report concluded that 'such recommendations are unlikely always to be correct'.[13] Bank support for higher education in Africa plunged dramatically in the 1980s even though it rose in the rest of the developing world. In the period 1969–79 higher education lending to Africa was US$0.93 per capita, higher than that for the rest of the world at US$0.78; but in 1980–87, the period when adjustment policies were being pushed relentlessly, lending to Africa dropped to US$0.51 per capita whereas that for the rest of the world rose to US$0.86 per capita (World Bank, 1994: annex table 7). The fall in lending is even more pronounced for universities: from US$0.38 per capita in 1969–79 to US$0.10 in 1980–87.

Adjustment encouraged heavy reliance on expatriate technical staff. This was for basically two reasons: the programmes were initially very unpopular among large segments of the professional classes and funding agencies wanted governments to act quickly to contain domestic resistance, alter the state's role in the economy and stimulate markets. The heavy reliance on expatriates to formulate, write and monitor adjustment programmes in crisis-ridden countries undermined national ownership of such programmes and further weakened state capacities. The World Bank has estimated that about 100,000 resident foreign advisers were employed in the public sectors of Africa in the 1980s at a yearly cost of more than US$4 billion, representing roughly 35 per cent of Official Development Assistance to the region (Jaycox, 1993).[14] This figure does not include the exponential growth of short-term foreign consultants employed by multilateral agencies and other donors to undertake short visits to countries implementing adjustment and other related programmes. In a well-publicized speech in 1993, the former vice president of the World Bank's Africa region, Edward Jaycox, denounced expatriate technical assistance as 'a systematic destructive force, which is undermining the development of capacity in Africa' (Jaycox, 1993). A similar assessment of technical assistance was made in the same year by the UNDP in an influential and highly critical publication *Rethinking Technical Co-operation* (UNDP, 1993).

As an alternative policy, the World Bank and the UNDP sought in the 1990s to reduce their dependence on resident technical experts and 'projectize' civil service reform; they also suggested compensatory schemes for top-level civil servants as well as support for training and equipment. However, despite efforts in rectifying the dependency problem in the field of technical capacity, the new emphasis on national ownership and local capacity-building and utilization has not yielded much because of the continued need for quick results in adjustment programmes. There is much discussion about rebuilding African universities and institutes and using national researchers and consultants in externally funded development programmes, but not much in the way of comprehensive strategies and actions. The Bank and other bilateral and multilateral donors seem to have taken a short-cut by launching the African Capacity Building Foundation based in Harare, Zimbabwe. The ACBF provides grants to autonomous and semi-autonomous policy-oriented research centres as well as government policy units geared to improving the analytical skills of nationals, many of whom may be called upon to assist governments in the formulation and monitoring of public policies.

By 1998 the ACBF had supported 36 projects in 29 institutions in 20 countries. Among the institutions supported were six training projects and 17 policy units. However, the funds at the disposal of the ACBF to carry out its work are meagre, which should underscore the point that policy should be oriented towards vigorously reviving national universities and public administration institutes: of a projected income of US$103.67 million over a five-year period only US$56.363 million had been received by October 1998. Participation of public sector officials in the ACBF seminars is reported to have increased from 3,524 in 1997 to 6,648 in 1998. However, the government policy units and autonomous institutes funded by the Foundation have been found to be ineffective and some institutions still rely excessively on external resource persons for their work (ACBF, 1998). The Foundation itself is wholly donor-funded and maintains very close institutional ties with the World Bank.

Managing recurrent costs

Closely linked to the issue of technical capacity is the problem of recurrent costs which has arisen in most crisis states. The policy reforms of the 1980s did not focus on this issue as the main concern was with macro-economic stability. As budgets dried up or got squeezed by stabilization programmes, the physical damage on infrastructure became glaring: roads and public utilities were in disrepair; schools lacked teachers, books, pens and other supplies; salaries were unpaid or delayed; vehicles for health and agricultural extension were without fuel or spare parts; government offices were without paper, typewriters and photocopiers, etc. Carlson (1999) reports that in the transport sector, it has been estimated that pot-holed roads in Zambia increased vehicle operating costs by 17 per cent, and in Kenya a shortfall of US$40 million in road maintenance expenditures in 1993 increased vehicle operating costs by US$140 million.

Foreign aid programmes can complicate the problems of recurrent costs, especially in crisis-ridden states that are aid-dependent. Foreign aid often involves development of new physical and social infrastructure, which can generate high levels of recurrent funding requirements for the aid recipient government. It has been estimated that annual recurrent costs in poor countries can be up to 70 per cent of the initial investment. Most donors have failed to recognize the problem. They insist that governments pay counterpart and recurrent costs even when adequate measures have not been taken to facilitate this at the inception of projects and recipients have demonstrated a poor record of compliance. In order not to harm the survival of the projects, donors are forced to create parallel structures in the bureaucracy, such as supporting local salaries, creating special project management units, and providing equipment as well as other facilities necessary for the functioning of their projects. This may distort the incentive structures of local bureaucracies.[15] Saasa and Carlson (1996) demonstrate this problem in a case study of Zambia's Educational Materials Project (ZEMP). ZEMP was largely run by a group of foreign experts as an enclave within Zambia's educational system. The government failed to mobilize the necessary resources to ensure full participation in the project: local staff were poorly paid and lacked transport facilities. The latter opted instead for the easy option of allowing the foreign experts to run the show even when it was clear to them that this was unsustainable.

The World Bank's Public Investment Programme (PIP), which aimed to protect high-priority development expenditures from spending cuts, tried to resolve this problem. But its rigid pro-forma calculations on rates of return that it tried to impose of loan recipients was a serious constraint. Ministries were urged under PIPs to develop forward budgets that would reflect accurate costs of projects, including operating and maintenance costs. As Berg (1999) stated in his review of this scheme, there were conceptual and practical problems in its implementation. At the conceptual level, it is difficult to make assumptions about staffing levels, salaries and productivity as well as levels and types of maintenance, including whether capital replacement costs should be estimated. Ministries thus sometimes return the proforma forms with many blank or uncompleted spaces.

The World Bank's own review of PIPs (1998c) suggested that poor countries did not have the capacity to make the detailed calculations required under the Bank's format. The end result was that recurrent costs were not given sufficient attention by ministries and most estimates were biased and low. At the practical level, PIPs encourage the development of a two-track budget system: ministries pile projects that have high recurrent costs in the PIP, not in the regular budget, as a way of accumulating donor funds, even though estimates of these costs and ways of financing them may not have been properly worked out. These strategies further complicated the recurrent costs problems: projects were funded by donors on the understanding that these were properly costed, only for the recurrent costs crisis to show up later. Much remains to be done in the area of recurrent costs management in crisis states if the public bureaucracies of low-income countries and the projects they support are to function properly.

Conclusion

We conclude with suggestions about how to ensure that reforms are socially accountable and sensitive to political realities in developing countries.

Sustainable reforms require effective and equitable governments. As Therkildsen (this volume) notes, public sector reforms may appear technical, but they are always 'highly political and conflictual' as they 'go to the heart of who governs'. Their actual implementation is always strongly influenced by local agendas. It is thus important to build the necessary political support base if reforms are to stand any chance of being institutionalized in the long run. The vast majority of countries that are implementing public sector reforms are also grappling with complex programmes of democratization, which seek to lay ground rules for the way their societies are governed. There are outstanding issues of governance that have not been resolved satisfactorily in the vast majority of low-income crisis societies, which raise serious questions about their capacities to implement far-reaching reforms in their state sectors.

Reform governments and agencies should try to understand and support some of the enduring missions of states. In the quest to solve chronic fiscal crises and other ills like corruption, weak accountability and poor service delivery, there has been a tendency by reformers to ignore or underplay the vital missions accorded to states in the post-war or post-independence periods. Two myths need to be exposed. First, the so-called revolution in managerial reforms or New Public Management is grounded in the belief that globalization and market competition will produce a standardized state system, which every country that wants to participate productively in the global economy will have to embrace. The global convergence of public administration systems is a strong message that comes through in the highly influential book by Osborne and Gaebler (1992).

It is difficult to see how this dream of global convergence can be realized in the field of institutional development when countries still differ in terms of how they practise capitalism and the benefits and costs they derive from it. Even the practice of so-called 'old public administration' in its Weberian ideal form was not only problematic for countries with strong public administration systems, there were also significant variations in its applica-tion in low-income countries where issues of patronage and informality were well entrenched. Imposing a standard set of reforms in countries with different institutional traditions because of an assumed global imperative may create empty managerial shells out of current poorly performing administrative systems. To satisfy donors, governments may proclaim they are implementing reforms when, in fact, nothing substantive is really hap-pening as far as institutionalisation is concerned. Old practices may con-tinue and the state may appear missionless and directionless.

The second myth that needs to be exposed is the so-called search for the right size of the state. Countries differ so much in history, social prefer-ences and developmental goals that there can never be a right state size. Efforts to look for one, as some multilateral agencies are urging govern-ments to do, are fruitless and diversionary. Three arguments have been advanced for a small state in a competitive global economy: state expan-sion crowds out private investments; state growth requires high taxes, which will undermine incentives and productivity and force individuals to evade taxes or exit highly taxed countries; and poor countries do not have the money to support big states and should learn to cut their coat according to their size, or in World Bank parlance tone down their ambi-tions and match the state's role to its capabilities or resources (World Bank, 1997a).[16]

There is no doubt that private investments and price stability may suffer if states indulge in high levels of over-expenditure and borrow heavily in domestic markets to finance deficits, but the extent to which this can actually harm economies is debatable; besides, it has been shown that state expenditures can also facilitate or crowd in private investments especially under market environments that are uncertain to private investors. It is quite possible that in industrialized countries, such as those in Scandinavia, where tax rates are really high, there may be a need to stabilize public expenditures and lower marginal tax rates to stimulate competitiveness, but this should not be seen as a general rule that should apply to all countries.

Many countries in the developing world have low corporate and income tax rates and opportunities for other types of taxes remain untapped. States in many of these countries lack the territorial and social reach of their advanced counterparts. Many of them are hardly overblown, even though they have been less than careful in the way they have spent public funds. Their limited social and territorial reach may explain why simple social and political conflicts often become unmanageable and threaten the state system itself. It is, of course, true that states should learn to balance their ambitions with their capabilities to avoid the problems of recurrent expenditure costs, fiscal crises and failed projects. But there is no hard-and-fast rule about how this should be done in a global economy that can reward some countries and at the same time harshly punish others through commodity price fluctuations, high debt burdens and capital flight.

While cost issues should be central to discussions of state endeavours, reform policies should also strongly focus on the kinds of problems different state systems have tried to solve in the post-war period: national integration or nation-building in multi-ethnic societies, such as in Africa; rapid industrialization in all developing countries, with the East Asian countries providing appropriate state-led institutional models for this purpose; social equity in former Soviet countries; and wealth redistribution and welfare in Western Europe. Costly mistakes have been made in the pursuit of these goals in different countries, but the goals themselves remain impeccable. They are at the heart of the aspirations of broad masses of people to create developmental, humanistic and harmonious societies. Important though some of their prescriptions are, it is hard to see how the new, market-based institutional reforms will lead to the realization of these social goals. The failure to pay sufficient attention to these goals in the last decade and half of market reforms may largely explain the high incidence of failed states, civil wars, political violence and stagnant development in large parts of the world today.

For reforms to be institutionalized and serve the public good, they must also allow for effective pressures to be brought to bear on public managers in service delivery. Agent–principal theorists assume that by emphasizing the role of markets in service delivery, the reforms themselves will empower users of services, who will punish bad providers and reward good ones by spending their money or public vouchers as they deem fit. The accountability-yielding powers of New Public Management have, however, been seriously questioned by a host of authors (see Ferlie et al., 1996 for a review). Quasi-markets are imperfect, application of reforms is uneven, and powerful interest groups or individuals may collude with managers to reap rent or offer low quality and reduced services. This has led to calls, including among individuals supporting NPM, for more explicit, accountability-focused reform policies. These policies include the Citizens' Charter in the UK, which is being copied by South Africa and Zimbabwe (Therkildsen, this volume); creation or strengthening of public complaints commissions, such as Ombudsmen in Malawi, South Africa, Tanzania, Zambia and Zimbabwe; and service delivery or user surveys, which are being implemented in Uganda, Nicaragua, Mali, Bolivia, Tanzania and India, for instance.

Collective and individual actions for public accountability entails deepening and defending the civil rights of citizens; promoting a free press and an independent judiciary; as well as improving the organizational capacities of groups that act on behalf of citizens in bringing pressure to bear on government officials. It also means that parliamentary parties that have emerged in democratic transitions are transformed from their current character of being narrow, elitist, electoral bodies to organizations that reflect, and can act on, broad social interests in pursuing public policies.

Notes

1. Labour force participation rates are falling due to high levels of unemployment, whereas the proportion of the aged is rising, raising the problem of unsustainable, state-financed pension schemes and other traditional welfare services.
2. The Swedish government announced big income tax cuts in its 2000 budget proposals: the US$1.2 billion taxt cuts are targeted at middle- and low-income earners. *Financial Times*, 21 September 1999.
3. It has been estimated, for instance, that 60 per cent of Italy's expenditure on welfare goes on pension payments. The European average is 45 per cent. Because of the high pension share of public expenditure, Italy finds it difficult to finance a system of unemployment benefits. Economists contend that the welfare programme rewards the old and punishes the young, by making the latter immobile, risk-averse and dependent on their parents. See J. Blitz, 'Bold Vision of Italian Pensions Reform Evaporates in Face of Opposition', *Financial Times*, 17 September 1999.
4. The IMF has been pursuing a wide range of tax reforms in developing countries: the core of these reforms focuses on simplification of the tax system, reforming and granting autonomy to the tax administration system, bringing more taxpayers into the tax system, promoting value added tax or consumption tax, and reducing states' dependence on international trade taxes.
5. Concerns have been expressed about the IMF's methodology on social spending reviews, which uses GDP deflators instead of social sector wage deflators. The

latter would be a more accurate measure of real trends in education and health expenditures since 90 per cent of education and most of health expenditures are wage-related. See exchange between N. Alexander, Director of Globalization Challenge Initiative, and S. Gupta, Chief, Expenditure Policy Division, IMF; *Financial Times*, 12 and 19 July 1999. Gupta concedes the point, but states that wage deflators are hardly available for most countries. For ten countries for which the IMF has such data, which are not revealed, he states that their expenditures on health and education increased on average by 2 per cent.

6. Austria, Denmark, Finland, France, (West) Germany, Italy, Netherlands, Portugal, Spain, Sweden and the UK.

7. A World Bank study by Galal et al. (1994) reports that in eleven out of its twelve case studies, privatization produced on average net welfare gains for consumers. Brown (1998) has challenged the methodology used for the study because of its subjective judgements in dealing with counterfactual arguments. The Galal study fails to separate gains attributed to privatization from gains due to other factors.

8. For railways, for instance, different lines will be allocated to different companies; for electricity, generation will be separated from distribution; for water, competition will be encouraged by allowing different companies to supply different regions, etc.

9. In the Philippines telecom industry, for instance, rates of return are estimated to be 25.7 per cent.

10. The new UK strategic rail authority announced in 1999 that the 25 privatized train operators showed signs of improvement in the four-month period to July 1997 compared with the same period in the previous year: more trains ran on time and cancellations were fewer: of the 77 route groups into which the rail system is divided, 41 reduced cancellations, 18 increased cancellations and 18 stayed the same. On punctuality, 40 route groups showed improved performance and 30 recorded a worse performance. *Financial Times*, 16 September 1999.

11. These examples are taken from Hutchful's study for UNRISD 'From Neo-liberalism to Neo-institutionalism: The World Bank, Aid Conditionality, and Public Sector Reform', UNRISD, Mimeo.

12. Contrast the Russian experience with that in Hungary, where voucher-mediated privatization ultimately led to the formation of corporate mutual fund banks and higher levels of outside participation in the privatized companies.

13. The World Bank evaluation report found that the Bank's recommendations in Zaire and Tanzania to increase the burden of education costs borne by parents and local communities did not take into account the fact that parents were already contributing large shares (more than 60 per cent in Zaire and 30–35 per cent in Tanzania) and that children were being withdrawn from school because of these costs. The equity argument against funding universities was also questioned on the following grounds: there are large differentials in unit costs among the three tiers of education, 'not only because of differences in student subsidies but also because of differences in student–teacher ratios and teacher salaries, which arise from differentials in educational goals, teacher qualifications, and labor market conditions, plus the relative absence of economies of scale at the tertiary level'. The inequity argument would be compelling if different social groups have unequal access to higher education, but the Bank does not provide evidence in this area. A large number of graduates, probably the majority, still come from humble backgrounds in most countries.

14. The UNDP puts the figure at 40,000 in its report *Rethinking Technical Co-operation* (1993). An independent, IMF-sponsored review of ESAF by Botchwey et al. (1998) singled out the issue of programme ownership as one of the most important problems that work against Fund programmes in low-income countries. Donor representatives are reported to have said, 'they saw ownership as acceptance by the recipient country of what donors want'; 'Ownership exists when they do what we want them to do voluntarily'.
15. An additional problem of foreign aid in low-income countries is its tendency to increase the workload of scarce bureaucrats. The President of the World Bank, James Wolfenson, stated that Tanzania prepares about 2,400 progress reports quarterly every year for all its donor partners. *Financial Times*, 30 October 1999.
16. Despite the Bank's critical stand on some aspects of New Public Management and increasing recognition of capacity issues, its approach to reform is still managerial as it does not pay sufficient attention to the goals, aspirations or missions of states in its 'role-capability' thesis for reshaping the state in a changing world.

References

Abdala, M. A. (1994) 'The Regulation of Newly Privatised Firms: An Illustration from Argentina', in W. Baer and M. Birch (eds.), *Privatisation in Latin America: New Roles for the Public and Private Sectors*, New York: Praeger.

African Capacity Building Foundation (1998) *1998 Status Report on Project Implementation*, Harare: ACBF, October.

Asian Development Bank (1997) *Key Indicators of Developing Asia and Pacific Countries*, Manila, Philippines.

Ayee, J. R. A. (1994) 'Corporate Plans and Performance Contracts as Devices for Improving the Performance of State Enterprises', *African Journal of Public Administration and Management*, No. III: 77–91.

Bangura, Y. (1998) *Democratisation, Equity and Stability: African Politics and Societies in the 1990s*. Discussion Paper 93, Geneva: UNRISD.

Bartlett, W. and J. Le Grand (1993) 'The Theory of Quasi-Markets', in J. Le Grand and W. Bartlett (eds.), *Quasi-Markets and Social Policy*, London: Macmillan.

Berg, E. (1999) 'Aid Failure: The Case of Public Sector Reform', Revision of October Aid Conference Paper, University of Copenhagen, Denmark, April.

Betran, E. and P. Sera (1996) 'Regulatory Issues in the Privatisation of Public Utilities: The Chilean Experience', in OECD, *Privatisation in Asia, Europe and Latin America*. Paris: OECD.

Bolnik, B. (1997) 'Establishing Fiscal Discipline: The Cash Budget in Zambia', in Merilee Grindle (ed.), *Getting Good Government in the Public Sectors of Developing Countries*, Cambridge, MA: Harvard University Press.

Booth, D. (1990) 'Structural Adjustment in Socio-political Context: Some Findings from a Local Study in Tanzania', Hall Papers in Developing Areas. No. 4, Hull: University of Hull, Centre of Developing Area Studies.

Boston, J. et al. (1996) *Public Management: The New Zealand Model*, Aukland: Oxford University Press.

Brown, A. (1998) 'The Economics of Privatisation: A Case Study of Australian Telecommunications', in M. Hossain and J. Malbon (eds.), *Who Benefits From Privatisation?* London and New York: Routledge.

Carlson, J. (1999) 'Swedish Aid and State Capacity in Developing Countries', Geneva: UNRISD, Mimeo.

Chiwele, D., P. Muyatwa-Sipula and H. Kalinda (1999) *Private Sector Response to Agricultural Marketing Liberalization in Zambia: A Case Study of Eastern Province Maize Markets*. Research Report No. 107, Uppsala: Nordiska Afrikainstitutet.

Clayton, R. and J. Pontusson (1998) 'Welfare-State Retrenchment Revisited: Entitlement Cuts, Public Sector Restructuring and Inegalitarian Trends in Advanced Capitalist Societies', *World Politics*, No. 51, October: 68–98.

Cornia, A., R. Jolly and F. Stewart (eds.) (1987) *Adjustment with a Human Face, Vol. 1. Protecting the Vulnerable and Promoting Growth*, Oxford: Clarendon Press.

Devlin, R. (1994) 'Privatisation and Social Welfare in Latin America', in G. Bird and A. Helwege (eds.), *Latin America's Economic Future*, London: Academic Press.

Downs, A. (1967) *Inside Bureaucracy*, Boston, MA: Little, Brown.

ECLAC (1996–97) *Economic Survey of Latin America and the Caribbean*, Santiago: ECLAC.

Esping-Andersen, G. (ed.) (1996) *Welfare States in Transition: National Adaptations in Global Economies*, London: UNRISD and Sage Publications.

Ferlie, E. A., Pettigrew, L. Ashburner and L. Fitzgerald (1996) *The New Public Management in Action*. Oxford: Oxford University Press.

Filatochev, I., M. Wright and M. Bleeney (1999) 'Privatisation, Insider Control and Managerial Retrenchment in Russia', *Economics of Transition*, Vol. 7, No. 2: 481–504.

Galal, A., L. Jones, P. Tandon and I. Vogeslang (1994) *Welfare Consequences of Selling Public Enterprises: An Empirical Analysis*, Oxford: Oxford University Press.

Goh, W. and Jomo K. S. (1998) 'Privatisation in Malaysia: A Social and Economic Paradox', in M. Hossain and J. Malbon (eds.), *Who Benefits from Privatisation?* London and New York: Routledge.

Hachette, D. (1996) 'Fiscal Aspects of Privatisation', in W. Glade (ed.), *Bigger Economies, Smaller Governments: Privatisation in Latin America*, Boulder, CO: Westview Press.

Halligan, J. (1997) 'New Public Sector Models: Reform in Australia and New Zealand', in J.-E. Lane (ed.), *Public Sector Reform: Rationale, Trends and Problems*, London: Sage Publications.

Hirschman, A. O. (1971) 'How to Divest in Latin America and Why', in A. O. Hirschman, *A Bias for Hope*, New Haven, CT: Yale University Press.

Hutchful, E. (1997) *The Institutional and Political Framework of Macro-Economic Management in Ghana*, Discussion Paper No. 82, Geneva: UNRISD.

Hutchful, E. (1999) 'From Neo-liberalism to Neo-institutionalism: The World Bank, Aid Conditionality, and Public Sector Reform', Geneva: UNRISD, Mimeo.

IMF (1988) *International Financial Statistics Yearbook*. Washington, DC: IMF.

IMF (1996) *Government Finance Statistics Yearbook*. Washington, DC: IMF.

IMF (1998a) *World Economic Outlook*, October. Washington, DC: IMF.

IMF (1998b) *Fiscal Reforms in Low-Income Countries Experience under IMF-Supported Programs*, by a staff team led by G. T. Abed. Occasional Paper, No. 160, Washington, DC: IMF.

IMF (1998c) *External Evaluation of ESAF*, Report by a Group of Independent Experts. Washington, DC: IMF.

Jaycox, E. V. K. (1993) 'Capacity Building: The Missing Link in African Development', Washington, DC: The World Bank's Regional Office, 20 May.

Kelsey, J. (1995) *Economic Fundamentalism: the New Zealand Experiment – A World Model for Structural Adjustment?* Pluto: London.

Kickert, W. J. M. (1997) 'Anglo-Saxon Public Management and European Governance: The Case of Dutch Administrative Reforms', in J.-E. Lane (ed.), *Public Sector Reform: Rational, Trends and Problems*, London: Sage Publications.

Kickert, W. J. M. and F. O. M. Verhaak (1995) 'Autonomising Executive Tasks in Dutch Central Government', *International Review of Administrative Sciences*, Vol. 61, No. 4: 531–49.

Lane, J.-E. (1997) 'Public Sector Reform in Nordic Countries', in J.-E. Lane (ed.), *Public Sector Reform: Rational, Trends and Problems*, London: Sage Publications.

Larbi, G. (1998) 'Institutional Constraints and Capacity Issues in Decentralizing Management in Public Services: The Case of Health in Ghana', *Journal of International Development*, Vol. 10, No. 3: 377–86.

Larbi, G. (1999a) 'Trade Unions, Public Sector Employees and New Public Management Reforms: Impact, Responses and Reactions to Change', Geneva: UNRISD, Mimeo.

Larbi, G. (1999b) *The New Public Management Approach and Crisis States*. Discussion Paper 113, Geneva: UNRISD.

Le Grand, J. and W. Bartlett (1993) 'Introduction', in L. Grand and J. Bartlett (eds.) *Quasi-Markets and Social Policy*, London: Macmillan.

Maganu, E. T. (1990) 'Decentralization of Health Services in Botswana', in A. Mills et al. (eds.), *Health System Decentralization: Concepts, Issues and Country Experience*, Geneva: World Health Organization.

Mairal, H. A. (1996) 'Legal and Other Issues in Privatisation: The Argentine Experience', in OECD, *Privatisation in Asia, Europe and Latin America*, Paris: OECD.

Mallon, R. D. (1994) 'State-owned Enterprise Reform Through Performance Contracts: The Bolivian Experiment', *World Development*, Vol. 22, No. 6: 925–34.

March, J. G. and J. P. Olsen (1989) *Rediscovering Institutions: The Organizational Basis of Politics*, Toronto: The Free Press.

Meek, C. (1998) 'Privatisation Doesn't Necessarily Equal Competition: The UK Experience', in M. Hossain and J. Malbon (eds.), *Who Benefits from Privatisation?* London and New York: Routledge.

Mkandawire, T. (1994) 'The Political Economy of Privatisation', in G. Cornia and G. K. Helleiner (eds.), *From Adjustment to Development in Africa: Conflict, Controversy, Convergence, or Consensus?* London: Macmillan.

Mkandawire, T. and C. Soludo (1999) *Our Continent, Our Future: African Perspectives on Structural Adjustment*, Trenton: Africa World Press.

Montoya-Aguilar, C. and P. Vaughan (1990) 'Decentralization and Local Management of the Health System in Chile', in A. Mills et al. (eds.), *Health System Decentralization: Concepts, Issues and Country Experience*, Geneva: World Health Organization.

Mosley, P. (1988) 'Privatisation, Policy-based lending and World Bank Behaviour', in P. Cook and C. Kirkpatrick, *Privatisation in Less Developed Countries*. London: Harvester Wheatsheaf.

Niskanen, W. A. (1971) *Bureaucracy and Representative Government*. Chicago: Aldine-Atherton.

Niskanen, W. A. (1973) *Bureaucracy: Servant or Master?* London: Institute of Economic Affairs.

O'Donnell, G. (1994) 'Delegative Democracy', *Journal of Democracy*, Vol. 5, No. 1: 55–68.

OECD (1995) *Governance in Transition: Public Management Reforms in OECD Countries*, Paris: OECD.

OECD (1996) *OECD Economic Surveys 1995-1996: New Zealand*, Paris: OECD.

Olukoshi, A. (1990) 'The Historic Significance of the Policy of Privatisation in Nigeria', in R. Olaniyan and C. Nwoke (eds.), *Structural Adjustment in Nigeria: The Impact of SFEM on the Economy*, Lagos: Nigerian Institute of International Affairs.

Olukoshi, A. (1999) *The Elusive Prince of Denmark: Structural Adjustment and the Crisis of Governance in Africa*, Research Report No. 104, Uppsala: Nordiska Afrikainstitutet.

Osborne, D and T. Gaebler (1992) *Reinventing Government: How the Entrepreneurial Spirit is Transforming the World*, Reading, MA: Addison-Wesley.

Parker, D. (1998) 'Privatisation in the European Union: An Overview', in D. Parker (ed.), *Privatisation in the European Union: Theory and Policy Perspectives*, London and New York: Routledge.

Paul, S. and S. Sekhar, 'A Report Card on Public Services', *Regional Development Dialogue*, Vol. 18, No. 2, Autumn: 119–32.

Petrazzin, B. A. (1996) 'The Labour Sector: A Post-Privatisation Assessment', in W. Glade (ed.), *Bigger Economies, Smaller Governments: Privatisation in Latin America*, Westview.

Pierson, P. (1996) 'The New Politics of the Welfare State', *World Politics*, No. 48, January.

Propper, C. (1994) 'Quasi-markets, Contracts and Quality in Health and Social Care: The US Experience', in J. Le Grand and W. Bartlett (eds.), *Quasi-Markets and Social Policy*, London: Macmillan.

Raiser, M. (1996) *Soft Budget Constraints and the Fate of Economic Reforms in Transition Economies and Developing Countries*, Keiler Studien, University of Kiel, No. 281.

Rodinelli, D. (1994) 'Privatisation and Economic Reform in Central Europe: Experience of the Early Transition Period', in D. Rodinelli (ed.), *Privatisation and Economic Reform in Central Europe*, Westport, CT: Quorum Books.

Saasa, O. and J. Carlson (1996) *The Aid Relationship in Zambia: A Conflict Scenario*, Uppsala: Nordiska Afrikainstitutet.

Schiavo-Campo, S. (1998) 'Government Employment and Pay: The Global and Regional Evidence', *Public Administration and Development*, Vol. 18.

Schmitter, P. C. and J. R. Grote, 'The Corporatist Sisyphus: Past, Present and Future', Conference Paper, European University Institute, Mimeo, Nota di Lavoro, Fiesola, September.

Scott, G. (1996) *Government Reform in New Zealand*, IMF Occasional Paper, No. 140, Washington, DC.

Shirley, M. and C. L. Xu (1997) *Information, Incentives, and Commitment: An Empirical Analysis of Contracts between Government and State Enterprises*, World Bank Working Papers, World Bank website.

Standing, G. (1996) 'Social Protection in Central and Eastern Europe: A Tale of Slipping Anchors and Torn Safety Nets', in G. Esping-Andersen (ed.), *Welfare States in Transition*, London: UNRISD and Sage Publications.

Stasavage, D. and D. Moyo (1999) 'Are Cash Budgets a Cure for Excess Fiscal Deficits (and at What Cost)?', Centre for the Study of African Economies. WPS/99-11, May.

Steinmo, S. (1994) *Taxation and Democracy: Swedish, British, and American Approaches to Financing the Modern State*, New Haven, CT and London: Yale University Press.

Stephens, J. (1996) 'The Scandinavian Welfare States: Achievements, Crisis, and Prospects', in G. Esping-Andersen (ed.), *Welfare States in Transition*, London: UNRISD and Sage Publications.

Therkildsen, O. (1999) *Efficiency, Accountability and Implementation: Public Sector Reform in East and Southern Africa*, UNRISD Programme Paper: Democracy, Governance and Human Rights 3, Geneva.

UNDP (1993) *Rethinking Technical Co-operation: Reforms for Capacity Building in Africa*; Regional Bureau For Africa, UNDP, coordinated by E. Berg, New York: UNDP.

Vining, A. R. and A. Boardman (1992) 'Ownership Versus Competition: Efficiency in Public Enterprise', *Public Choice*, No. 73: 205–39.

Walsh, K. (1995) *Public Services and Market Mechanisms: Competition, Contracting and the New Public Management*, Basingstoke and London: Macmillan.

Warburton, P. (1999) *Debt and Delusion: Central Bank Follies That Threaten Economic Disaster*, London: Penguin.

World Bank (1988) *Education in Sub-Saharan Africa: Policies for Adjustment, Revitalisation, and Expansion*, A World Bank Policy Study, Washington, DC: The World Bank.

World Bank (1994) *The World Bank's Role in Human Resource Development in Sub-Saharan Africa: Education, Training and Technical Assistance*. A World Bank's Operations Evaluations Study by R. G. Ridker.

World Bank (1995) *Bureaucrats in Business: The Economics and Politics of Government Ownership*. A World Bank Policy Research Report, Oxford: Oxford University Press.

World Bank (1997a) *World Development Report: The State in a Changing World*, Oxford: Oxford University Press.

World Bank (1997b) *Fiscal Management in Adjustment Lending*, Washington, DC: World Bank.

World Bank (1997c) *Annual Report*, Washington, DC: World Bank.

World Bank Operations Evaluation Department (1998a) 'The Impact of Public Expenditure Reviews: An Evaluation', November, Washington, DC.

World Bank (1998b) *Global Development Finance: Analysis and Summary Tables*, Washington, DC: World Bank.

World Bank (1998c) *The Public Expenditure Management Handbook*, Washington, DC: World Bank.

World Bank (1998d) *Privatization in Africa*, Washington, DC: World Bank.

World Bank (1998/99) *African Development Indicators*, Washington, DC: World Bank.

6
Employment and Pay Reform in Developing and Transition Societies

Willy McCourt

The significance of employment reform

What has come to be called pay and employment reform, or (somewhat misleadingly) civil service reform, is one of the most important human resource initiatives to be taken by developing country governments in recent years. Reform in this context refers to those measures that governments have taken to alter the employment and payment of their staff, typically within some larger programme of macroeconomic reform. 'Reform' is often a euphemism, since in practice the most prominent measure has been job reduction, with which reform has frequently been synonymous (Pronk, 1996).

It is easy to demonstrate the importance of reform. Between 1987 and 1996 the World Bank assisted no fewer than 68 developing and transition countries with reform programmes (Nunberg, 1997), a large figure that excludes countries that have reformed under their own steam. China, which in 1998 embarked on a reform programme designed to cut the number of its civil servants by half – or, in other words, by a projected four million people (*Economist*, 1998), is the most dramatic example. There are others, such as Malaysia and South Africa. In 1996, South Africa's Finance Minister announced the government's intention to reduce the number of civil servants by a quarter, from 1.2 million to 900,000.

The aims of reform

What is the purpose of pay and employment reform? It is surprising how seldom this question is asked. Reforms of pay and employment have often been intimately linked with wider public sector reform. In the case of developing countries, the latter comes under the heading of 'structural adjustment' and is sufficiently widely known to not require restating here (Nelson, 1990; Mosley et al., 1991; see World Bank, 1981). In the case of the so-called transition economies of Central and Eastern Europe, it is part and parcel of the transition from a socialist, planned economy to a capitalist, market economy (World Bank, 1996). The influence of public sector reform in industrialized countries, in particular what has come to be called the 'New Public Management' (Dunleavy and Hood, 1994; OECD, 1994), is also apparent. These three schools of thought have many common features, leading some to posit a growing globalization of public management (OECD, 1994). They share an emphasis on a reduced role for the state, a reduction in public expenditure and a concomitant reduction of the public payroll. (For a general discussion of public sector reforms as a whole, see Bangura, 2000.)

The Washington model of reform

Thus pay and employment reforms have typically been one component of an economic programme in which the private sector replaces the public sector as the engine of economic growth. In this context the objective of reform might be stated as '*a lean and efficient public service*'. It is easy to see how actions such as reducing the number of civil servants and eliminating ghost workers contribute to this objective.

This, in essence, is what has been labelled the 'Washington model' of employment reform (see McCourt, 2001). In this model, the reduction of the number of civil servants is supposed to be offset by an increase in the wages of those who survive, and particularly of senior and specialist staff. Evidence has been produced (World Bank, 1997) for the existence of a link between the level of wages in the public sector and the incidence of corruption, and some writers (such as Stevens, 1994b) have also argued for steps to 'decompress' public wages, so that the income differential between high- and low-paid staff, which has decreased in many countries, would increase again.

Other approaches

That is one model of reform. But governments may have other fish to fry where reform is concerned. Griffin commented on agriculture reform that 'Rather than criticizing governments for failing to attain, or offering advice on how to attain, a *non-goal*, it would be instructive if more time were devoted to analysing what governments actually do and why' (1975: 2). The same is true of pay and employment reform. To the extent that reform is internally driven, there are likely to be objectives that differ from those of the Washington model. While Singapore, for instance, has been preoccupied by the need to retain staff in the face of competition from the private sector in a tight labour market, South Africa has emphasized transforming an apartheid bureaucracy, through affirmative action, into a public workforce which represents the ethnic and gender composition of the country's population. Sri Lanka has been using constitutional reform as a device to solve the problem of Tamil insurgency by co-opting Tamil representatives into the system of governance. Uganda has attempted to free resources to meet the government's commitment to universal primary education.

Such objectives may overshadow conventional efficiency objectives. 'A rightsized and representative public service' was the stated objective of the South African government's reform programme in a project agreement with the United Kingdom. But an evaluation after 15 months of assistance found that while substantial progress had been made toward achieving representativeness, little had been made toward rightsizing (McCourt, 1998). Thus an analysis of trends in pay and employment reform must be sensitive to the actual priorities of governments, and not impose on them the priorities that others might wish them to have.

Unions and reform

It follows that there is the potential for disagreement between different reform stakeholders. One might expect that worker representatives would disagree with particular vehemence with any objective that entailed job losses. But in practice civil servants' unions have sometimes acquiesced in reform, or even been prepared to recognize national objectives that might override their members' welfare. 'Government believes we are hostile to reform,' said one union official in Sri Lanka, 'but we support reform. If reform is constructive and in the interests of the country, we support it.' Similarly, the Civil Servants' Association (CSA) in Ghana 'gave its blessing' to reform. But agreement with the aims of reform does not preclude disagreement about its conduct. Speaking on the reaction of civil servants to reforms in Uganda, an official said that '[t]he whole reform process was welcomed, but the way it was handled is now detested'. One aspect of the conduct of reform in which unions had a particular interest was, naturally, their participation. Union representatives resented their exclusion from the reform dialogue in Sri Lanka and Uganda.

Donors and reform

The main donor involved in pay and employment reform has been the World Bank. Between 1981 and 1991, 44 developing countries received assistance with civil service reform from the World Bank alone (Nunberg, 1994). The International Monetary Fund (IMF), with its remit for macroeconomic stabilization, tends not to intervene directly, though a preferred figure for civil service expenditure may appear as a 'structural benchmark' in an IMF loan. The United Nations Development Programme (UNDP) is also active in many countries. Among bilateral donors, the UK's Department for International Development (DFID) has been heavily involved, and other bilateral donors have also supported reform in line with their different development priorities.

Diverging objectives of donor agencies and recipient governments have sometimes led to difficulties. This is illustrated by the case of Sri Lanka, which has made several attempts at pay and employment reform since an Administrative Reforms Committee produced a comprehensive report in 1987. Early attempts at reform were ineffectual: a first round of reform in the late 1980s implemented a recommendation to increase civil service pay, but not the related recommendation to reduce the number of jobs. The second round of reform, in the early 1990s, had structural weaknesses and centred on a voluntary redundancy (VR) package that, although expensive, again failed to reduce the number of jobs.

The perception in Sri Lanka that donors, following the early reform failures, were pressing for a harsh package of reform measures created a focus for opposition to reform. Donors were identified with a privatization programme that was perceived to be harsh. As a result, even an innocuous measure like performance appraisal could be portrayed by staff, and resisted, as a World Bank imposition. Thus in the latest round of reform the government has only a limited package of external assistance, and no external advisers. A senior government official commented, 'We don't want our programme to be donor-driven. We have avoided a situation where donors can hold us to account'. In the donor community, however, the government was seen as dragging its feet and not being serious about reform, and its proposed major restructuring of central–local relations was seen as an expensive irrelevance. This was certainly true in the context of employment reform. But the plan was motivated mainly by a desire to confront the problem of Tamil insurrection by conceding greater autonomy to regions, and to Tamil areas in particular (McCourt, 1998c).

Thus where political commitment to a cost-driven programme was already strong, as in Ghana and Uganda, donor involvement contributed to the implementation of sharply focused programmes. But in more complex stakeholder environments, such as Sri Lanka and South Africa, donors were apt to be heavy-footed, and even to create a focus for opposition to reform.

Influences on reform

In this section I review the political, economic and social factors that have influenced the conduct and outcomes of reform.

Political factors

The success of reform has been affected by the degree of political support for it. World Bank evaluations have identified political commitment as the key factor in the success of reform (Nunberg, 1997). Clearly it is helpful to have a strong leader with a personal commitment, as recently seen in Malaysia and Uganda, but authoritarian governments have also been a negative influence on reform (Nelson, 1990). In countries where authority is more diffused, it has been necessary painstakingly to construct a reform coalition. That has been the case in South Africa and Sri Lanka, whose governments were coalitions that included trade unions. Moreover, political will has been a function of the quality of advice offered to politicians: implementation of reform in Ghana was delayed by opposition from senior civil servants, not politicians (Burton et al., 1993), and donor influence may have undermined rather than bolstered political will in some cases (World Bank, 1998).

Economic factors

The context in which pay and employment reform has taken place means that reform in this area has been fiscally driven: it is the economic agenda that has dominated discussion. The economic context has clearly had an impact on reform, though in a somewhat complex way. Prosperity may facilitate reform by allowing a government to buy off opponents (as with Malaysia's pay reforms and the UK's winding down of its coal industry), but it may also allow it to postpone still further the evil day of root-and-branch reform (as, at the time of writing, in Sri Lanka). Adversity may also have a paradoxical effect. In Ghana it dictated that overstaffing in public enterprises should be addressed, but also that government would initially fail to do so effectively because it could not afford the severance benefits to which retrenchees would be entitled (Davis, 1991).

Social factors

Social factors have also had a bearing on the progress of reform. Despite declining wages, public employment continues to be attractive in many countries. For example, there were 214,000 applications for 782 public clerical vacancies in Sri Lanka in 1997 (McCourt, 1998b). When combined with ascriptive tendencies in a society where patronage is rife, this can exert strong upward pressure on public employment, which is difficult to contain. Decentralization of recruitment authority to public enterprises as part of a World Bank-sponsored reform programme in Nepal led to a considerable increase in nepotistic appointments (McCourt, 1998c).

Pay and employment reform: What has happened? Scope of analysis

In discussions of pay and employment reform there is often confusion about its scope: Are public enterprises included or not? What about local authorities? and so on. It is helpful to present this visually, as in Figure 6.1.

In common with other writers, in this chapter I deal mainly with pay and employment reform in 'general civilian government employment'. This comprises employees of both central and local government (including provincial administrations, local authorities, and so on). It includes specialist categories of staff like teachers and health workers. But I shall also

Figure 6.1   The universe of public sector staffing

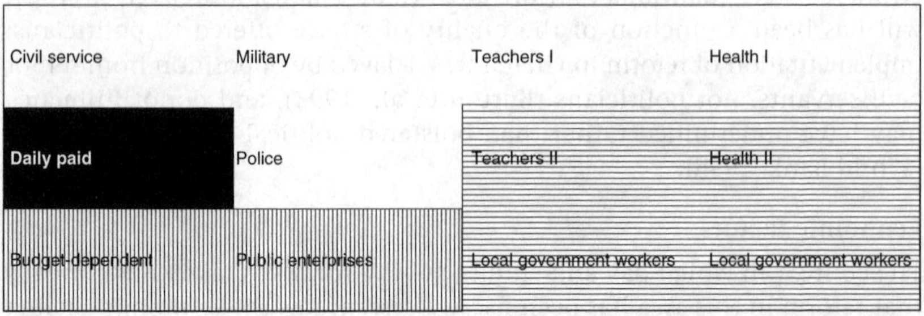

Source: Stevens (1994b).
Key: Unshaded areas indicate central government payroll. Black shaded area indicates daily paid staff. Vertical shaded areas indicate parastatals. Horizontal shaded areas indicate local government payroll. Proportions are illustrative and do not represent public employment shares of any particular country.

include some material in relation to other categories of staff. In terms of Figure 6.1, these are principally employees of state-owned enterprises and budget-dependent agencies, and members of the armed forces.

Calculating the size and cost of the civil service

'There is no more hazardous cross-country comparison than in the area of civil service employment and wages,' say Schiavo-Campo et al. (1997: 1), and their caution is echoed by Abed et al. (1998), and Lienert and Modi (1997). Schiavo-Campo et al. point to formidable methodological difficulties, which include:

- the unreliability of statistics in many countries;
- different methods for calculating the size and composition of the public service in different countries (so that, for example, teachers may or may not be included in the total of central government employees); and
- difficulties in calculating the total value of remuneration, since benefits-in-kind may or may not be included in figures for total remuneration.

Clearly it would be ideal to have better, standardized data. However, it should be recognized that this would require a massive harmonization exercise, entailing, among other things, changes in public accounting methods and improvements in the collection of basic statistics. For the foreseeable future we will be obliged to make the best of unsatisfactory data.

Government employment in the mid-1990s

Bearing the above provisos in mind, Table 6.1 lists summary statistics for relevant regions (and OECD countries, for comparative purposes), using data usually not earlier than 1994.

Table 6.1 Government employment, early 1990s

Region	GCGE as % of population	GCGE as % of total employment	Govt. manufacturing wages	Wages as % of GDP	Wages as % of govt. spending*	Avg. govt. wage: GDP per capita
Sub-Saharan Africa	2.0	6.6	2.0	6.7	35.3**	5.7
Asia	2.6	6.3	1.8	4.7	22.4	3.0
Eastern Europe and former USSR	6.9	16.0	0.6	3.8	15.1	1.3
Latin Americaand Caribbean	3.0	8.9	1.5	4.9	27.1	2.5
Middle Eastand North Africa	3.9	17.5	1.0	9.8	34.8	3.4
OECD	7.7	17.2	1.6	4.5	12.2	1.6

Sources: Schiavo-Campo et al. (1997); *World Bank (1997); **Lienert and Modi (1997).

Notes: GCGE is 'general civilian government employment', and includes all public employees except employees of state-owned enterprises and the armed forces. Country groupings are those used by the World Bank. OECD countries are generally excluded, with these exceptions: Mexico is included in Latin America and the Caribbean; South Korea is included in Asia. Asia comprises the Indian subcontinent, Southeast Asia and the Pacific. Middle East and North Africa are selected countries where the World Bank is active. All averages are unweighted.

Changes in government employment

The difficulties of making cross-country comparisons are compounded with longitudinal comparisons. The only reliable source for any earlier period is Heller and Tait (1983). It has a narrower base (of 45–50 developing countries only, excluding the Middle East and North Africa, and also Eastern Europe and the USSR), and a somewhat different method of calculation. As a result, it is possible to compare central government employment and wages only.

A further relevant source of data is the IMF's review of the fiscal reform experience of 36 developing and transition countries that undertook macroeconomic and structural adjustment using IMF structural adjustment facilities between 1985 and 1995 (Abed et al., 1998). They compare figures from the beginning of the reform programme with the latest available figures. They record an average drop of 0.44 per cent in the number of public servants and an average rise of 3.29 per cent in the size of the wage bill. Again there are difficulties with these figures: for the most part, they relate only to central government employees, and it is possible that pushing some spending off-budget means that the figures quoted overstate the actual reductions. Moreover, average figures disguise huge variations between countries. In many countries, reductions in the wage bill have coincided with reductions in the value of real wages.

The overall trend

In general, allowing for the admittedly unsatisfactory nature of the data and for wide variations between countries, there is an overall downward trend in the size and cost of the central civil service, and there is no evidence that the decline has bottomed out. Schiavo-Campo et al. report that sub-Saharan Africa makes a very large contribution to this reduction, while elsewhere the reduction is partly (in the case of Asia) or even wholly (in the case of Latin America and the Caribbean) offset by an increase in local government employment. Relative to per capita gross domestic product (GDP), central government wages have fallen, most dramatically in Africa. Wages have risen in Asia, but this is mainly attributable to India, where civil servants' wages rose after 1986.

What differences can be observed between regions that are not captured in the above statistical data? We must be cautious, since there is perhaps as much variation within as between regions. This can be illustrated by comparing developments in Uganda and its neighbour, Kenya. In Uganda, government wages rose substantially as a proportion of GDP; in Kenya, by contrast, they fell somewhat. However, some generalizations may be possible (and here I follow Schiavo-Campo et al.'s analysis). Reform in Africa has by and large been limited to job reduction – improving the quality of administration remains to be addressed. In South Asia, there is scope for considerable job reduction, accompanied by deregulation and the depoliti-

Table 6.2 Changes in central government employment, early 1980s and early 1990s

	Central government % of population		Wage bill as % of GDP		Average government wage: GDP per capita	
	Early 1980s	Early 1990s	Early 1980s	Early 1990s	Early 1980s	Early 1990s
Sub-Saharan Africa	1.8	1.1	10.8	7.9	6.1	4.8
Asia	2.6	1.1	7.5	4.9	2.9	3.8
Latin America and Caribbean	2.4	1.5	7.3	4.7	2.9	2.3
OECD	2.9	1.9	5.5	4.4	1.7	1.6
Average	2.5	1.5	7.7	5.4	3.5	3.2

Source: Schiavo-Campo et al. (1997), incorporating Heller and Tait (1983).

Notes: Data for early 1990s are limited to the Heller and Tait sample and thus differ from those shown in Table 6.1 above. In Latin America and the Caribbean, and also to some extent in Asia, reduction in central government employment was offset by growth in local government. It was particularly in Africa that total government employment fell both relative to population and in real terms.

cization of employment. In the former communist countries of Eastern Europe, by contrast, there is a need to build up a central civil service that historically has been relatively small, while at the same time making overdue reforms to the public enterprise sector that will almost certainly have the effect of reducing employment considerably. Finally, while there has been a trend towards decentralization in Latin America and the Caribbean, it is uncertain whether this has had a real impact on services below the elite level, especially where the smaller countries in the region are concerned. There are also considerable differences between countries.

Thus there are substantial differences between regions. Differences between individual countries are even greater. The number of employees dropped by 44 per cent in Uganda, but rose by 59 per cent in Sri Lanka. In Uganda again, across-the-board pay rises of 43, 85 and 37 per cent in 1991/92, 1992/93 and 1993/94 respectively (Government of Uganda, 1994), financed partly by the drop in numbers, did much to restore pay to previous levels. However, in Tanzania, Uganda's East African neighbour, pay continued to stagnate. It follows that attention should be given to countries that have purposefully made dramatic changes in the size and cost of their public payrolls, as well as to those where there has been a deterioration in the position.

The 'correct' size?

It is perhaps only by adopting an *a priori* position on the role of the state that one can generalize about the size and cost of the public payroll. Those who adopt the minimalist view with which the World Bank and IMF have sometimes appeared willing to identify themselves will be satisfied only by a state that confines itself to basic law and order functions (not less: minimalists are not anarchists). Since the opposite, 'maximalist' view is not presently espoused by any government or expert, others – including some within the Bretton Woods institutions (for example, Schiavo-Campo et al., 1997) – are likely to feel that the 'correct' size and cost of the government payroll will be contingent on the functions of the state in particular countries, and the economic, political and social context in which the state operates. This still leaves plenty of room for arguments that the payroll should be smaller in particular cases (or larger, for that matter: see Reddy and Pereira, 1998), but perhaps not for the sweeping generalizations advanced in the 1980s and early 1990s.

Pay and employment reform: how it has happened

Reform instruments

This section considers the techniques that governments have used to reform pay and employment. I begin by reviewing some issues to do with the process of reform, before going on to address the content of reform.

The reform process

Process issues, including the need for prior analysis, phasing, sequencing and so on, are not unique to pay and employment reform, but they have endangered reform when left unattended. One reason for this is that an exclusively content-driven approach tends to reduce the ownership and commitment of key stakeholders, thus reducing the size of the reform constituency.

Diagnosis

Stevens (1994b) describes how baseline data on the size and cost of the civil service and the payment of civil servants were obtained at the beginning of the reform programme in Tanzania. The analysis shows how an increase in the number of civil servants far out stripped the capacity of government to pay for them, as GDP rose only sluggishly, with the inevitable result that the increase in the number of jobs was at the expense of individual civil servants' wages.

Other, more qualitative diagnostic data have also had a bearing on the design of reform. In Zambia, a review of legal provisions showed that implementing a proposed retrenchment package, under which retirement benefits would have been paid only on reaching the normal retirement age rather than on the date of retrenchment, would have required a change in legislation (Coopers and Lybrand, 1995). In Nepal, a consultation exercise conducted with internal clients of the Public Service Commission (PSC) revealed a strong preference for a centralized model of staff management: clients had greater confidence in the integrity of the PSC than in that of their own departments and agencies (McCourt, 1998c). Such data have included some knowledge of recent reform history. In Uganda, for instance, natural sensitivity to retrenchment was heightened by the painful memory of the first round of retrenchments in the early 1990s, when staff were dismissed without compensation on the basis of nothing more than a poor rating in an annual confidential report (Langseth and Mugaju, 1994).

Design of reform

Phasing, sequencing and co-ordination had a bearing on the effectiveness of reform. A particular problem was co-ordination between ministries of finance and public service (or their equivalents). In some African countries (Ghana is an example) the latter has been accused by the former of being a 'Trojan horse' inside government, a kind of informal trade union representing the interests of senior civil servants (Corkery and Land, 1996).

Uganda is a good example of this. When the National Resistance Movement under Yoweri Museveni took power in 1986, it found a public administration reduced to penury through lawlessness, corruption and mismanagement. Its primary reform mechanism was the Public Service Review and Reorganization Commission, which submitted a report that included

255 recommendations. Implementation of the report was devolved to the Implementation and Monitoring Board – which took operational decisions about rightsizing – and monitoring was provided by the Civil Service Reform Co-ordination Committee, made up of directors-general of departments. Despite this attention to the machinery of reform, it was still possible to have a retrenchment team in the Ministry of Public Service working towards job reductions while their colleagues on the other side of the building were carrying out a rolling programme of restructuring reviews whose net result was to recommend a staff increase (Government of Uganda, 1994).

Reform by numbers

Many reforming countries set numerical targets at the beginning of reform: Ghana's projected annual reductions of 12,000 staff are typical in this respect. There is a well-established methodology for this approach, which is outlined by Nunberg (1994), who presents it as a series of steps in ascending order of political difficulty. They are set out in the list below, with a few additional measures not covered by Nunberg, and are followed by a brief selective commentary.

Measures to avoid redundancy:

- human resource planning
- job flexibility
- retraining
- redundancy procedures
- *ad hoc* measures
- remove ghosts
- book transfers
- delete empty posts
- enforce retirement ages
- introduce part-time and flexible work schedules
- appoint new staff on temporary contracts
- natural wastage/recruitment freezes
- suspend automatic advancement
- redeployment
- voluntary redundancy
- privatization/contracting out
- freeze salaries[1]
- compulsory redundancy

Measures to avoid redundancy

Systematic approaches to avoiding redundancy, a mainstay of personnel practice in industrialized countries (McCourt, 1998a), have not been widely used. In developing countries, the human resource planning function is often weak, making an orderly reduction in jobs difficult to achieve. Governments also took some *ad hoc* measures in order to forestall redundancies, especially in Eastern Europe. Five million workers in Russia had their hours cut in 1994 and an additional 7.4 million were placed on involuntary leave. In fact, in that year only 40 per cent of Russian workers were paid in full and on time (Klugman and Braithwaite, 1998).

Remove ghost workers

This has been a major preoccupation of African governments – one official involved in a 'ghost-hunting' expedition in Malawi even reported finding an entire 'ghost school' with an impressively complete complement of head teacher, teachers and other staff and lacking only a basis in reality. The scale of the problem can be substantial. Ghana eliminated 11,000 ghosts in 1987/88; by 1997 Uganda had identified no fewer than 40,000 (McCourt, 1998a).

Book transfers

These have also accounted for some ostensible reductions. For example, a significant proportion of the reductions in Uganda were achieved through transfers, such as setting up the Uganda Revenue Authority, which removed a large number of staff from the books of the traditional public service.

Delete empty posts

This has had the effect of removing posts that may have been vacant for some time but are still listed in the staffing 'establishment'.

Enforcing retirement ages

This has also made a contribution to numbers reduction. In Tanzania, attempts by local government officers to claim that they were below the official retirement age were so widespread that government felt obliged to ban officers from producing affidavits for that purpose.

Voluntary redundancy

This has been perhaps the most widely used – but also the most unsatisfactory – job reduction method. Although in theory voluntary redundancy should be targeted at staff whose jobs or skills are redundant, in practice the staff opting to leave are often the most needed, as in Sri Lanka (Hilderbrand and Grindle, 1995). Voluntary (and compulsory) redundancy has also been the largest factor in the cost of reform, which is discussed below.

Compulsory redundancy

Although there is reliable evidence for only certain countries, it appears that compulsory redundancy (CR) has accounted for only a modest proportion of job reductions in many countries, contrary to the popular image. In Uganda, only 14,000 of 160,000 job reductions came through CR. Even several years after the fall of the Berlin Wall, in the transition economies of Eastern Europe, public employers were still tending to take a soft line on redundancy, although overall unemployment had definitely increased.

One difficulty in this context was that governments did not always distinguish correctly between CR and disciplinary dismissal. In Ghana, Tanzania and Uganda, many job losses fell into the latter category, as governments removed people identified as incompetent or sometimes, more colourfully, as 'drunkards'. Senior officials in Uganda admitted that the quality of information on which these dismissals were based was weak, leading to unfairness. Staff dismissed in this way are likely to be stigmatized as 'lemons', casting a blight on their re-employment prospects. There is evidence that individuals in industrialized countries have needed up to five years to eradicate such a reputation (Turnbull and Wass, 1997).

Privatization and contracting out

Privatization and contracting in this context offer the politician the best of both worlds: a substantial reduction in the number of public jobs is achieved while the service remains intact. Privatization accounted for the lion's share of job reductions in the UK in the 1980s; contracting out was the largest single factor in job reduction there in the 1990s (HMSO, 1996). However, there are also political difficulties: privatization and contracting out will almost certainly be opposed by the staff of the public agencies affected, who may mobilize opposition through trade unions. Such measures may also be opposed by the public at large, who fear that they will result in cuts in services, lower quality services or (higher) charges for the same services.

There are sometimes legal restrictions affecting the transfer of activities from the public to the private sector. In the member countries of the European Union, regulations often require a private sector contractor who has won the contract to supply a service previously provided by a public agency to employ the agency's staff on their existing terms and conditions of employment. In the European Union, Zimbabwe's contracting out of rubbish collection would almost certainly be covered by those restrictions. Countries of Central and Eastern Europe that have been admitted into the European Union have become subject to them.

Reforming pay

Governments have identified five principal problems with pay, which they have tackled in different ways. They are listed in Table 6.3.

Table 6.3   Pay problems and solutions

Problem	How the problem has been tackled
Inadequate pay across the board	Across-the-board pay rises
Opaque remuneration systems	Consolidation of remuneration
Unclear link between pay and responsibilities	Job evaluation
Unclear link between pay and performance	Performance-related pay
Insufficient pay to retain employees with scarce skills	Pay decompression and pay differentials

Across-the-board pay rises

With evidence of a link between low pay on one hand and the incidence of corruption (World Bank, 1997) and 'moonlighting' (van der Gaag et al., 1989) on the other, many governments have set the objective of increasing the pay of their public servants. Their success in doing so, however, has been uneven. As shown earlier, pay fell somewhat as a proportion of GDP per capita in developing countries as a whole. Real wages fell over the reform period in nine of the 18 developing countries studied by Abed et al. (1998) on behalf of the IMF, although there were significant rises in a few countries, notably Bolivia and Uganda. Among transition countries in Eastern Europe, there have been numerous problems with both the value and the payment of wages. Wage freezes have sometimes been used to avert redundancies, as in the Czech Republic's coal mining industry (Pavlinek, 1998). Budgetary difficulties have also led to wage arrears, which in 1997 were estimated to be running at an average of 122 per cent of the monthly pay bill in four industrial sectors in Russia (Clarke, 1998). Thus the aspiration of governments to improve the pay of their employees have not been realized in any consistent way.

Consolidation of remuneration

Especially in developing countries, housing, transport and other benefits have sometimes been worth as much as the nominal wage. The pay compression ratio between the highest- and the lowest-paid staff of 1:6.8 in Uganda changed to 1:100 after non-monetary allowances and benefits were included (Government of Uganda, 1994). The opaqueness of remuneration in such countries is exacerbated by the difficulty of calculating some of its elements, notably the provision of free housing. There has thus been a move to consolidate and monetize the remuneration package in some countries, replacing non-monetary benefits such as housing with a single, somewhat increased wage.

Linking pay and responsibilities

Some governments have taken steps to put the grading and relative pay of their staff on a more 'rational' footing. This has often been done through the technique of job evaluation, defined as 'the determination of the relative worth of jobs as a basis for the payment of differential wages and salaries' (Smith 1983: 69).

In many countries pay is based largely on qualifications and seniority, rather than on responsibility. Job evaluation aims to correct this imbalance, giving a more justifiable basis for pay differentials. Job evaluation can also help avoid gender discrimination in pay. Job evaluation has been used in countries like Lesotho, South Africa and Tanzania, normally with donor-funded consultancy support. The technical nature of job evaluation can cause problems: a review of one such scheme in South Africa found that while it was effective in its own terms, the technical nature of the scheme created problems of sustainability once the consultants had withdrawn.

Linking pay and performance

Among developing countries, Malaysia has probably gone furthest in linking pay to performance. Performance-related pay (PRP) was introduced in Malaysia in 1991 – as a major feature of the New Remuneration System – in an attempt to achieve a 'shift in the work culture' of civil servants. The government had launched a national development policy that aimed to distribute wealth through economic growth, and had identified a number of strategic needs for the civil service in terms of responsiveness, flexibility, innovation and ethical behaviour. PRP was supposed to support the necessary changes in behaviour.

The new approach had strong political backing: Prime Minister Mahathir Mohammad chaired the committee that produced the system. PRP awards are made following the annual performance appraisal interview, and are based on a manager's assessment of performance against objectives (called 'work targets' in the Malaysian system) set jointly by manager and employee, in the context of overall departmental objectives.

Larger pay increases are given to employees that receive high performance ratings. Each department has a quota for how many employees can enjoy accelerated salary progression: a manager's rating of an employee as outstanding may not be endorsed if the department's quota has been exceeded (Government of Malaysia, 1991; Hamid, 1995).

But relatively few countries outside Malaysia have made the link between pay and performance, though rather more have floated the idea. This is because of problems of capacity and fairness. PRP decisions are only as good as the judgements of staff performance ratings (normally deriving from some form of performance appraisal system) on which they are based, and such ratings are often inaccurate or biased, especially in countries where nepotism prevails. It is notoriously difficult to quantify the performance of public servants in the way that such a system requires; even the World Bank as an employer seems to find it hard (Reid, 1997). In Malaysia, the civil servants' union is predictably hostile, but privately so too are some senior officials (McCourt, 1998a).

Decompressing and differentiating pay

Public sector pay policies in many developing countries followed a common trajectory after independence. Adopting an egalitarian ethos, many took steps to reduce the differential between the highest paid (who, in the colonial period, were usually expatriates) and lowest paid. Zambia is a typical example: the 'decompression ratio' there decreased from 17:1 to 3.7:1 between 1971 and 1986 (Lindauer, 1994). From the early 1980s onwards, some governments acted to reverse that trend. Thus in Ghana the decompression ratio rose from 2.2:1 in 1984 to 10:1 in 1991 (Burton et al., 1993), and in 1993 the government of Tanzania set the target of raising its compression ratio from 5.74:1 to 12:1 (Stevens, 1994b).

Transition countries in Eastern Europe have experienced 'one of the biggest and fastest increases in inequality ever recorded' (Milanovic, 1998). However, here it is the external comparison between public and private wages rather than the internal compression ratio between the highest and the lowest wages paid within the public sector that is significant.

Clearly setting the 'right' compression ratio is a subjective judgement. Information about wage movements in the external labour market would make it less arbitrary, but such information is not often available in developing countries. The extent of wage compression is, in any case, hard to determine, since the allowances, which tend to be paid disproportionately to senior officials, qualify the picture, as already shown.

Another form of pay separation is paying more to staff – not necessarily the most senior – who have scarce skills, such as doctors and accountants. It is possible to use job evaluation (see above) to bring this about, or to do it through pay decentralization. Pay decentralization has not been widely attempted in developing countries, partly because of the heavy load that it places on fragile administrative capacity (Nunberg, 1995). Moreover, and despite all the above, public opinion in at least some countries stubbornly continues to favour narrowing rather than widening the earnings gap between senior and other staff (Fosh, 1978; Robinson, 1990).

The cost of reform

Reform has usually had the simple aim of saving money – albeit this has often been one aim among others. Thus it is ironic that reform has sometimes proved to be very expensive. An employer who opts for voluntary redundancy (VR) as a way of reducing jobs must offer a large enough compensation package to persuade staff to volunteer. As a result, payment of redundancy benefits took up no less than 2 per cent of government expenditure in the first five years of the VR scheme in Ghana (Younger, 1996). (This problem is not confined to developing countries: the United

Kingdom spent roughly $12.8 billion between 1979 and 1992 on making coal miners redundant; Wass, 1996.)

Personnel substitution

Moreover, additional expenditure has sometimes been incurred even after VR, in other ways. The first of these is the return of staff who have 'taken the package' as consultants or in some other guise. This has been observed in Malaysia, South Africa, Sri Lanka (McCourt, 1998e) and also in the United Kingdom, where Treasury officials have labelled it 'manpower substitution'. Solving this problem requires a drastic simplification of departmental budgets, thus removing the incentive to move spending on staffing from one budget head to another. However, since the relationship between this problem and the structure of the budget is not widely appreciated in developing countries, such a simplification appears not to have been widely attempted.

Other cost problems

There are two other reasons why job reduction has not always gone hand-in-hand with cost reduction. First, governments have sometimes continued to recruit even while they have been laying off staff. This can be a problem of co-ordination between central government departments; it can also be because many appointments, including temporary and part-time appointments, are delegated to lower levels and evade central controls. Second, an ostensible reduction in the number of civil servants has sometimes disguised the fact that they are merely staff who have been restructured out of the central civil service into some other agency, as in the case of the suddenly ubiquitous, freestanding Revenue Authorities of sub-Saharan Africa (Mozambique and Zambia among others).

Pay reform has made its own contribution to the cost of reform. While some pay increases have been financed from savings generated by job cuts, pay rises have often come, partly or wholly, from general government expenditure, as in Malaysia, where the government recognized explicitly that pay reform would add substantially to the pay bill (Government of Malaysia, 1991). It is unclear whether such rises are to be praised – as the reward for enduring the pain of difficult macroeconomic reform – or criticized for frustrating the cost reduction goal of employment reform.

Social safety mechanisms

We turn, finally, to the effect of reform on workers and their dependants. Not everyone agrees that government has an obligation to provide a safety mechanism for displaced workers. The authors of one study of retrenched civil servants in Guinea argued that the latter's salaries represented a 'rent' that they had done little to earn, so they should not expect much in the way of compensation when they were retrenched (Mills and Sahn, 1996).

There is also evidence from Ghana that the hardship caused by displacement was less severe than feared (Younger, 1996). In a more populist vein, President Museveni of Uganda made a series of speeches after coming to power in which he criticized the shortcomings of the country's civil servants. Not by coincidence, in the first round of retrenchment those staff were simply dismissed without compensation.

None the less, governments have increasingly recognized the need to make provision for staff who are retrenched. They have done so either because they feel a responsibility for their welfare or because they want to minimize political damage. In the past, donors have taken the view that severance packages should be the responsibility of the government itself (the World Bank's own rules prohibit it from contributing), but more recently donors have been prepared to make a contribution to their cost, or even to underwrite the entire cost.

Worker participation in reform

References to the participation of workers in the design and conduct of reform are conspicuous by their absence from the reform literature, which has an exclusively 'unitarist' orientation (Fox, 1974), that is, an orientation to the needs of managers rather than workers. Perhaps the only information on the actual practice of governments comes from my research that touched on the involvement of worker representatives in reform in Ghana, Malaysia, South Africa, Sri Lanka and Uganda (McCourt, 1997, 1998a).

Ghana's experience is especially instructive. It was one of the first countries to undergo structural adjustment, following a period from the late 1970s to 1981 when the economy was in disarray and real incomes dropped substantially. An economic development programme was launched in 1983 with employment reform as a major component. Between 1970 and 1982, civil service numbers had grown by 14 per cent, five times the annual rate of economic growth.

Civil servants in Ghana are represented by the Civil Service Association (CSA). This is not a union in the strictest sense of the word, and in fact is not a member of the Ghanaian Trades Union Congress. However, the CSA was involved in decisions about rightsizing from the beginning, through its membership on the key steering committee, the Redeployment Management Committee (RMC). Far from putting spokes in the wheel, the CSA consented to decisions that might be seen as having an adverse impact on its members. However, membership in the RMC enabled the CSA to argue for a package of measures to alleviate the hardship caused by retrenchment (McCourt, 1997, 1998a).

Trade unions were also involved in decisions about reform in Malaysia and South Africa. In Sri Lanka and Uganda, unions had no involvement, despite their lobbying – and in Sri Lanka there was even some hostility in official circles to the idea that they might be. It is striking that Ghana, where there was participation, did manage to implement a package of measures for retrenchees while Uganda, where there was no participation, failed to do so.

Severance packages: the amount

In order to mitigate financial hardship, employers often offer a severance package. This can take one of several forms:

- a minimum, if there is one, which the country's law requires;
- a package previously agreed between the government as employer and its staff (and which may, as in Zambia, have the force of law); or
- an enhanced package designed to offset hardship or to make voluntary redundancy attractive.

Packages have varied in generosity. Below are some examples (taken from Nunberg, 1994; McCourt, 1998b):

- Argentina: (on average) 75 per cent of basic salary for six months service-related; severance payment (averaging $3,000), paid in six instalments.
- Ghana: severance payment of four months' salary; end-of-service payment of two months' salary for each year of uninterrupted service; pension entitlement frozen until normal retirement date (no 'extra years' given).
- Laos: one year's salary.
- Uganda: standard 'safety net' figure of $1,000; three months' salary for each year of service up to a maximum of 20 years; workers over 45 years of age who had served at least ten years received their pension immediately; 'repatriation' allowance to help 'retrenchees' move back to their home region.

Severance packages: the style

There is clear evidence that it is preferable to include a substantial lump sum in the package. Studies of investment behaviour show that people tend to invest lump sums, contrary to popular belief, but that they regard staggered monthly payments as an extension of their salaries. Fewer retrenched civil servants in Guinea, where the package was staggered, invested their severance payments than in Ghana, where there was a substantial lump sum element (Mills and Sahn, 1996; Younger, 1996).

Winners and losers

The details of the package determine who the winners and losers will be. Uganda paid a 'repatriation' package to its retrenchees, ostensibly to cover the cost of moving back to their home areas, though few actually did so. This had the effect of favouring retrenchees whose original homes were in distant areas, such as Karamoja in northern Uganda. According to a Ugandan trade union representative, this was a very lucrative component of the package.

It may also be desirable to have at least a 'flat rate' element in the package (as Uganda did) in order to reduce the problem of the socially regressive impact of retrenchment. The bulk of severance payment spending often goes on a relatively small number of senior civil servants who are more likely to have alternative earning opportunities outside government.

Other forms of assistance

It has been argued that while financial severance packages, preferably with a lump sum payment as a major element, have been effective, other forms of assistance such as retraining and business start-up help have not. However, it is possible that local factors have affected the latter. Ghana's provision of retraining and business start-up help (Government of Ghana, 1987) started a year late, at a point when sensible retrenchees would have already made their own arrangements; Uganda's never started at all, foundering on the mistaken assumption that banks and the Ministry of Labour would be willing to participate (McCourt, 1998a).

Psychological hardship

Moreover, the hardship caused by redundancy is psychological as well as financial. The Ugandan Civil Service Union has fielded many complaints from retrenched staff whose marriages have broken up, who have lost status in their villages and so on as a result of retrenchment (McCourt, 1998a). This, though anecdotal, is in line with industrialized country studies of the effects of unemployment, which show the unemployed having poorer physical and mental health (Argyle, 1989). Thus there is room to argue that more skilful measures would have contributed to the welfare of retrenchees. To give one example, communication with employees was clearly necessary to alleviate anxiety about the threat of retrenchment. Uganda's first retrenchment exercise, said one official, was 'shrouded in secrecy, and the news that they were to be retrenched came as a shock to most retrenchees'. Thus this section reviews some of the non-financial social safety mechanisms governments have adopted, focusing on the experience of Ghana, which had the relatively elaborate social safety net Programme to Mitigate the Social Cost of Adjustment, for which retrenchees, among others, were eligible.

Information about retrenchment

The government of Ghana obtained funding from UNDP to mount an information campaign in which mass media were used to inform potential retrenchees. This was partly a reaction to problems experienced in an earlier round of retrenchment, when many retrenchees believed that their severance was only temporary, and that they would be re-employed once government finances were in better shape. It was also an attempt to reassure civil servants that retrenchment would not be used to victimize supporters of the former government.

Counselling and guidance

In Ghana, again, the need to provide guidance to retrenchees was recognized by providing counselling and guidance training to 103 Labour Department staff who would be involved in the exercise. In Tanzania, similar training was part of the programme provided for local authority personnel specialists who would be responsible for retrenchment in Tanzanian councils.

Retraining

In the United Kingdom many employers provide an 'outplacement' service, where staff made redundant are placed with other employers to gain work experience. In Ghana, training programmes in such areas as blacksmithing and entrepreneurship were mounted.

Business start-up help

Ghana subsidized the purchase of business equipment, such as hairdryers for hairdressers and photographic equipment for photographers. The cost of the programme was modest.

Conclusion: cosmetic gestures?

It is in providing assistance to 'retrenchees' that there has been the greatest gap between aspirations and reality in the conduct of reform. Retraining and business start-up programmes have been criticized as ineffective. In Ghana and Uganda, as has been shown, and also to some extent in the United Kingdom, that was for the simple reason that they either never actually happened, or happened too late to be of any use. Governments will need to take concerted action if they are to avoid the accusation that their programmes of assistance have been merely a cosmetic exercise aimed at reassuring public opinion rather than at genuinely mitigating hardship. They will also need to bear in mind that programmes should address psychological as well as financial hardship.

Reform as an anti-poverty strategy

It is important to take account of the effect of pay and employment reform initiatives on poverty. Early employment reform policies, in common with the first generation of structural adjustment policies, took little account of their potential for causing hardship. But more recently some governments have addressed that possibility.

Building a poverty element into reform design can be done in two ways:

- by bolting measures designed to prevent or mitigate hardship onto conventional reform policies; or
- by making poverty elimination a central thrust of reform.

In practice, the first of these, which I have discussed above, has been the usual approach. Is it possible to make poverty elimination a central thrust of reform? I have already mentioned that alleviating poverty has not been a central objective of pay and employment reform. But there have been some individual actions, and there are also analogies from reform in other areas on which I can draw in order to speculate on how poverty alleviation might be integrated into the design of reform. There are perhaps three ways in which this might happen:

- by earmarking savings from reform for capital or personnel expenditure on priority services;
- by reallocating staff to areas of greater need; or
- by improving the living conditions of civil servants.

Earmarking savings

It is theoretically possible to earmark the savings from employment reform for spending on services that will benefit the poor. The government of Uganda claims to have used savings from retrenchment to increase the pay of primary school teachers in the context of a government commitment, made in 1997, to provide universal free primary education – and primary education is a central plank in an anti-poverty strategy. However, this attractive approach may not be very realistic, at least in the short term, when the costs of reform are likely to be greater than the savings, as shown earlier. Only when reliable actuarial calculations of the costs of reform have been made, and the payback period for reform has been calculated, can such a strategy be considered.

Reallocating staff

A second way that reform can assist poverty alleviation is by the reallocation of staff. At the time of writing, the government of Tanzania had embarked, with donor assistance, on a scheme to reallocate teachers to areas where the pupil–teacher ratio was relatively high. There is nothing new about such programmes. Developing countries have been using human resource planning techniques for many years to achieve an even distribution of, for instance, doctors between rural and urban areas (Ojo, 1989). It must be admitted, however, that staff allocation initiatives in developing countries have not always been successful and one cannot be sanguine about the likelihood of them succeeding in future.

Improving conditions for civil servants

The third way that reform might contribute to poverty alleviation is by raising the income of public servants living in poverty. The new government that took power in Ethiopia inherited a civil service where pay levels had been static for a quarter of a century, so that there was a monthly pay range of $8 to $250 against a household absolute poverty line of $60. The government has raised pay to a range of $16 to $400, with a minimum entry-level salary for front-line basic service providers of about $35 per month (Adedeji et al., 1995). Among industrialized countries, a large job evaluation exercise in UK local authorities in the late 1980s had the same intention.

But as shown earlier, the thrust of pay reform in developing countries in recent years has been to 'decompress' pay, with the effect of reducing the salary of low-paid staff relative to their senior colleagues. Although salaries in Cameroon are lower now than in 1985, the lowest civil service salary is still three times the official poverty line, below which 50 per cent of the population lives. In short, although greater pay equality remains popular among the public in at least some developing countries, its justification as part of an anti-poverty strategy must be assessed on a case-by-case basis.

Conclusion

Our admittedly speculative discussion of the link between reform and poverty elimination obliges us to draw a positive and a negative conclusion. The positive conclusion is that measures can be taken to reduce hardship caused by reform (they are discussed in an earlier section of this chapter). The negative conclusion is that broader measures may not succeed. The likelihood of generating savings from reform that can be spent on priority services is not great; the history of reallocating staff into areas of greater need has been poor; and increasing pay for low-paid civil servants needs a case-by-case justification. However, this is the area in which there are fewest examples of successful practice, and it is possible that governments may be able to devise innovative and imaginative strategies that will harness reform to the goal of poverty alleviation.

The outcomes of reform

As has been shown, the outcomes of reform have been mixed. Job reduction has been dramatic in some countries, non-existent in others; promised pay increases have materialized in some countries, but pay has stagnated or even fallen in real terms in others. As Schiavo-Campo et al. (1997) have pointed out, a country-by-country analysis is necessary. But a few generalizations are possible.

The 'big picture'

Overall, it is clear that the curve of civil service numbers that rose steeply up to the early 1980s in developing countries has flattened, if not dipped downward. The vertiginous increases of the 1960s and 1970s are, temporarily at least, a thing of the past. Thus the bleak assessment of failure advanced by some observers (Nunberg, 1997; Abed et al., 1998) may be a little overstated. Elsewhere, while civil service employment did not rise steeply in Eastern Europe – numbers actually fell somewhat in Poland in the latter half of the martial law period – public enterprise reforms are taking or are likely to take large numbers out of the public sector.

But even where the number of jobs is declining, job reduction, as has been shown, is not always synonymous with cost reduction. The costs of redundancy, together with the effects of personnel substitution and other factors previously discussed, mean that the short-term fiscal benefits that common sense might have predicted have often not materialized. In the short term, reform has been successful mainly in stopping the situation from getting any worse. Actual fiscal benefits are most likely to be experienced in the medium to long term at best.

Delinking pay reform

It is not difficult to argue that pay increases are desirable in many countries. The value of pay has declined dramatically, and low pay has been associated with corruption and low morale. Yet for many governments the state of public finances means that pay increases on the scale necessary to restore the previous value of pay are simply not possible, even after downsizing has reduced the number of employees. Certainly, governments need to work towards restoring the value of pay, but it is advisable to pursue pay reform and other employment reforms separately. Delinking them will avoid the danger of the credibility, or even the viability, of other employment reforms being damaged by failure to make progress on pay reform.

Reform and effectiveness

Reforms have tended to improve the efficiency of government, if only because there are fewer people doing the same work. But whether they have improved its effectiveness, in terms of doing work better, is open to question. Since reforms, especially when sponsored by the Bretton Woods institutions, have often been fiscally- rather than performance-driven, they have tended to apply to productive and unproductive jobs alike. However, one study that considered this (McCourt, 1998a) found that public agencies in Ghana, Uganda and the United Kingdom – three countries with particularly lengthy experiences of reform – did not feel that they had lost scarce skills. On the contrary, they saw reform as a way of 'cutting out dead wood'. However, the return as consultants of many staff who have taken

VR in countries like South Africa and Sri Lanka suggests that that has not always been the case.

Reform and hardship

Unlike in other areas of government reform, such as the removal of food subsidies, hardship caused by pay and employment reform has been serious though not catastrophic. This has been because compulsory redundancies have been on a lower scale than feared. In developing countries, job reductions have been possible without large-scale redundancies through eliminating ghost workers and other measures. In transition countries, however, they have yet to be implemented – even ten years after the fall of the Berlin Wall – held at bay by pay delays, reductions in working hours and the like. As Russia's former Deputy Prime Minister Boris Fyodorov commented in 1999, '[u]nemployment is artificially low. People go to the factories, there is no work for them to do and they don't get paid. We are still sitting on the same industrial dinosaurs we had ten years ago' (*Observer*, 1999).

Another reason is that governments have in fact taken steps to cushion the blow through the provision of severance and other benefits. The impact on women or other disadvantaged groups has not been disproportionate, but is still a cause for concern. Since job reduction has probably not bottomed out in most countries, there is a need to remain vigilant to the danger of hardship in the future.

Strategic reform

What direction should reform take in the future? Many have argued for a 'second generation' of reform in developing countries, which have been undertaking reform for 15 years or more. Sometimes the second generation turns out to be the same as the first, only more so (Lienert and Modi, 1997; Nunberg, 1997). Sometimes, though, there are arguments for a more strategic approach, in which pay and employment reform form part of a package of HRM reforms – which would include such elements as more professional recruitment and the introduction of performance management – all in the context of the strategic management of the public service (Hilderbrand and Grindle, 1995; OECD, 1996; Schiavo-Campo et al., 1997; McCourt, 1998e). I have referred to some of the elements of the package in this chapter, but activity in relation to them has been overshadowed by job reduction programmes with which (as has been shown) reform as a whole has often been synonymous.

It is the strategic approach that offers the best hope of lasting improvement. What does strategy mean in this context? It means starting from a view about the fundamental tasks of the public service, one covering the extent and nature of the state's involvement in economic activities and delivery of services. In the light of that view, a review is carried out of the alignment of the existing structure of government with strategic priorities. Review at the level of an individual department or service is a further stage, and the final stage is review at the level of the individual job or family of jobs. Thus pay and employment reform, along with other HRM reforms, derives from this strategic process. Thus also job reduction 'falls out' of the strategic process – or job increase: strategy is neutral on this score. It follows from the experience of employment reform, and the need that I have emphasized for case-by-case analysis, that all of this should be done incrementally. This is in keeping with the strategic tradition that derives from Lindblom (1959) and Mintzberg (1989), which emphasizes the importance of just such an incremental, 'emergent' approach. (See McCourt, 1998e for an expansion of this 'strategic model' of reform.)

Implementing reform

A factor militating against the somewhat sophisticated approach just outlined is the administrative capacity of governments. One reason why many governments have preferred to set simple numerical targets for reduction in the size of the public workforce is that such targets are relatively easy to manage. Even a relatively sophisticated government like South Africa's made a deliberate decision not to manage reform through devolving budgets to departments, believing that this would overstrain capacity. There is inevitably a trade-off to be made between a comprehensive, but complex, approach to reform on one hand and a crude, but practicable approach on the other. However, this picture is changing rapidly in some countries, as experience of reform leads to the development of expertise.

In conclusion

Pay and employment reform is not an autonomous phenomenon, but a reflection of political priorities, particularly concerning the role of the state. There was perhaps less outright hostility towards the existence of a strong state in the year 2000 than there was ten years earlier. Changes in political control in influential countries such as Germany, the United Kingdom and the United States play a part here, as do analyses of the importance of *dirigiste* approaches to economic development in East Asia (such as Wade, 1990). It is very unlikely, however, that the clock will be turned back. Even those emphasizing the importance of primary services like health and education are canvassing the possibility of alternative modes of service provision through the private sector and civil society agencies. The pressure on civil service numbers is unlikely to relax in the foreseeable future, and the impact of reform on poverty will need to be monitored closely in the years ahead.

Note

1. Strictly speaking, 'suspend automatic advancement' and 'freeze salaries' are pay rather than employment reform measures. They are included to complete the list of steps that governments can take to reduce staffing costs.

References

Abed, G. et al. (1998) *Fiscal Reforms in Low Income Countries: Experience under IMF-Supported Programs*, Occasional Paper No. 160, Washington, DC: International Monetary Fund.

Adedeji, A., R. Green and A. Janha (1995) *Pay, Productivity and Public Service: Priorities for Recovery in Sub-Saharan Africa*, New York: UNICEF.

Alderman, H., S. Canagarajah and S. Younger (1994) 'Consequences of Permanent Layoff from the Civil Service: Results from a Survey of Retrenched Workers in Ghana', in D. Lindauer and B. Nunberg (eds.), *Rehabilitating Government: Pay and Employment Reform in Africa*, Washington, DC: World Bank, pp. 211–37.

Ardagh, J. (1996) *Germany and the Germans* Harmondsworth: Penguin.

Argyle, M. (1989) *The Psychology of Work* Harmondsworth: Penguin.

Bangura, Y. (2000) *Public Sector Restructuring: The Institutional and Social Effects of Fiscal, Managerial and Capacity Building Reforms*, Occasional Paper 4, Geneva: The Next Step in Social Development, UNRISD.

Bennet, A. (1991) 'Downsizing Doesn't Necessarily Bring an Upswing in Corporate Profitability', *Wall Street Journal*, (6 June), B1 and B4.

Brydon, L. and K. Legge (1996) *Adjusting Society: The World Bank, the IMF and Ghana*, London: Tauris.

Burton, J., C. Joubert, J. Harrison and C. Athayde (1993) *Evaluation of ODA Project in Support of Ghana Civil Service Reform Programme*: Volumes I and II, London: ODA Evaluation Department.

Cameron, K. (1994) 'Strategies for Successful Organizational Downsizing', *Human Resource Management*, Vol. 33: 189–211.

Clarke, S. (1998) 'Trade Unions and Non-payment of Wages in Russia', *International Journal of Manpower*, 1, 2: 68–94.

Coopers and Lybrand (1995) *ODA: Zambia Civil Service Retrenchment Consultancy: Draft Final Report*, London: Coopers and Lybrand.

Corkery, J. and A. Land (1996) *Civil Service Reform in the Context of Structural Adjustment*, Maastricht: European Centre for Development Policy Management.

Davis, J. (1991) 'Institutional Impediments to Workforce Retrenchment and Restructuring in Ghana's State Enterprises', *World Development*, Vol. 19: 987–1005.

De Meuse, K., P. Vanderheiden and T. Bergmann (1994) 'Announced Layoffs: Their Effect on Corporate Financial Performance', *Human Resource Management*, Vol. 33: 509–30.

Dunleavy, A. and C. Hood (1994) 'From Old Public Administration to New Public Management', *Public Money and Management*, (July–September): 9–16.

Economist (1998) 'The Zhu Takes on the Red-tape Army' (14 March): 45 (UK 83).

European Community (1996) *Employment Observatory: Eastern and Central Europe*, Brussels: European Community.

Fosh, P. (1978) 'Attitudes of East African White-collar Workers to Income Inequalities', *International Labour Review*, Vol. 117, No. 1.

Fox, A. (1974) *Beyond Contract: Work, Power and Trust Relations*, London: Faber and Faber.

Government of Ghana (1987) *Programme of Actions to Mitigate the Social Costs of Adjustment*, Accra: Government of Ghana.

Government of Malaysia (1991) *Report of the Special Committee of the Cabinet on Salaries for the Public Sector*, Kuala Lumpur: National Printing Department.

Government of Uganda (1994) *Management of Change: Context, Vision, Objectives, Strategy and Plan*, Kampala: Ministry of Public Service.

Griffin, K. (1975) *Political Economy of Agrarian Change*. London: Macmillan.

Hamid, T. (1995) *The Civil Service of Malaysia: A Paradigm Shift*, Kuala Lumpur: Perceketan Nasional Malaysia Berhad.

Heller, P. and A. Tait (1983) *Government Employment and Pay: Some International Comparisons*, Occasional Paper No. 24, Washington, DC: International Monetary Fund.

Henkoff, R. (1990) 'Cost Cutting: How To Do it Right', *Fortune*, Vol. 9 (April): 26–33.

Her Majesty's Stationery Office (1996) *Civil Service Statistics: 1996*, Norwich: HMSO.

Hilderbrand, M. and M. Grindle (1995) 'Building Sustainable Capacity in the Public Sector: What Can Be Done?', *Public Administration and Development*, Vol. 15: 441–63.

Johnson, S. (1995) 'Employment and Unemployment', in E. Lazear (ed.), *Economic Transition in Eastern Europe and Russia: Realities of Reform*, Stanford, CA: Hoover Institute, pp. 391–418.

Klugman, J. and J. Braithwaite (1998) 'Poverty in Russia during the Transition: An Overview', *World Bank Research Observer*, Vol. 13, No. 1: 37–58.

Langseth, P. and J. Mugaju (eds.) (1994) *Post-Conflict Uganda: Towards an Effective Civil Service*, Kampala: Fountain.

Lienert, I. and J. Modi (1997) *A Decade of Civil Service Reform in Sub-Saharan Africa*, Working Paper, Washington, DC: International Monetary Fund.

Lindauer, M. (1994) 'Government Pay and Employment Policies and Economic Performance', in D. Lindauer and D. and B. Nunberg (eds.), *Rehabilitating Government: Pay and Employment Reform in Africa*, Washington, DC: World Bank, pp. 17–32.

Lindblom, C. (1959) 'The Science of Muddling Through', *Public Administration Review*, Vol. 19: 78–88.

Lipton, M. (1997) *Why Poor People Stay Poor: Urban Bias in World Development*, London: Temple Smith.

McCourt, W. (1997) *The Experience of 'Rightsizing' and Retrenchment in Ghana, Uganda and the United Kingdom*, Department of Public Service and Administration, Pretoria: Government of South Africa.

McCourt, W. (1998) *Report on the Evaluation of a DFID Project to Support the Transformation of the Public Service in the Republic of South Africa*, Pretoria: Department for International Development.

McCourt, W. (1998a) 'Civil Service Reform Equals Retrenchment? The Experience of Staff Retrenchment in Ghana, Uganda and the United Kingdom', in M. Minogue, C. Polidano and D. Hulme (eds.), *Beyond New Public Management: Changing Ideas and Practices in Governance*, Cheltenham: Edward Elgar.

McCourt, W. (1998b) *Employment and Pay Reform: A Guide to Assistance*, London: Department for International Development.

McCourt, W. (1998c) *The Bloody Horse: Indigenous and Donor Prescriptions for Civil Service Reform in Sri Lanka*, IDPM Discussion Paper No. 54, Institute for Development Policy and Management, University of Manchester.

McCourt, W. (1998d) *The New Public Selection? Competing Prescriptions for the Development of the Public Service Commission of Nepal*, Institute for Development Policy and Management, Public Policy and Management Working Paper No. 8, Manchester.

McCourt, W. (1998e) *Towards a Strategic Model of Employment and Pay Reform: Explaining and Remedying Experience to Date*, Institute for Development Policy and Management, Public Policy and Management Working Paper No. 10, Manchester.

McCourt, W. (2001) 'Towards a Strategic Model of Employment Reform: Explaining and Remedying Experience to Date', *International Journal of Human Resource Management*, Vol. 12: 56–75.

Milanovic, B. (1998) *Explaining the Increase in Inequality during the Transition*, Working Paper Series No. 1935, Washington, DC: World Bank.

Mills, B. and D. Sahn (1996) 'Life after Public Sector Job Loss in Guinea', in D. Sahn (ed.), *Economic Reform and the Poor in Africa*, Oxford: Clarendon Press, pp. 203–30.

Mintzberg, H. (1989) 'Crafting Strategy', in H. Mintzberg, *Mintzberg on Management*, New York: Free Press, pp. 25–42.

Mosley, P., J. Harrigan and J. Toye (1991) *Aid and Power: The World Bank and Policy-Based Lending*, London: Routledge.

Nelson, J. (ed.) (1990) *Economic Crisis and Policy Choice*, Princeton, NJ: Princeton University Press.

Nunberg, B. (1994) 'Experience with Civil Service Pay and Employment Reform: An Overview', in D. Lindauer and B. Nunberg (eds.), Rehabilitating Government: Pay and Employment Reform in Africa, Washington, DC: World Bank, pp. 119–59.

Nunberg, B. (1995) *Managing the Civil Service: Reform Lessons from Advanced Industrialized Countries*, Washington, DC: World Bank.

Nunberg, B. (1997) *Re-thinking Civil Service Reform: An Agenda for Smart Government*, Washington, DC: World Bank.

Observer (1999) 'The Russian Reforms Were "Complete Failure"', (21 March): 9.

Organization for Economic Co-operation and Development (1994) *Public Management Developments*, Paris: OECD.

Nunberg, B. (1996) *Integrating People Management into Public Service Reform*, Paris: OECD.

Ojo, K. (1989) 'Health, Manpower and Development in Nigeria', *International Journal of Manpower*, Vol. 10, No. 6: 3–12.

Pavlinek, P. (1998) 'Privatisation of Coal Mining in the Czech Republic', in J. Pickles and A. Smith (eds.), *Theorizing the Transition: The Political Economy of Post-Communist Transformations*, London: Routledge, pp. 218–39.

Peak, M. (1996) 'An Era of Wrenching Corporate Change', *Management Review*, Vol. 85, No. 7: 45–9.

Pretoria News (1998) Untitled article, May.

Pronk, J. (1996) 'Preface', in P. de Haan and Y. Hees (eds.), *Civil Service Reform in Sub-Saharan Africa*, The Hague: Ministry of Foreign Affairs, p. 7.

Reddy, S. and A. Pereira (1998) *The Role and Reform of the State*, Working Paper No. 8, New York: United Nations Development Programme, Office of Development Studies.

Reid, G. (1997) *Making Evaluations Useful*, Washington, DC: World Bank.

Robinson, D. (1990) 'Public-sector Pay: The Case of Sudan', in J. Pickett and H. Singer (eds.), *Towards Economic Recovery in Sub-Saharan Africa*, London: Routledge, pp. 92–105.

Schiavo-Campo, S., G. de Tommaso and A. Mukherjee (1997) *An International Statistical Survey of Government Employment and Wages*, Policy Research Working Paper No. 1806, Washington, DC: World Bank.

Smith, I. (1983) *The Management of Remuneration: Paying for Effectiveness*, London: Institute of Personnel Management.

Standing, G. (1994) 'The Changing Position of Women in Russian Industry: Prospects of Marginalisation', *World Development*, Vol. 22: 271–83.

Stevens, M. (1994a) 'Preparing for Civil Service Pay and Employment Reform: A Primer', in D. Lindauer and B. Nunberg (eds.), *Rehabilitating Government: Pay and Employment Reform in Africa*, Washington, DC: World Bank, pp. 103–15.

Stevens, M. (1994b) 'Public Expenditure and Civil Service Reform in Tanzania', in D. Lindauer and B. Nunberg (eds.), *Rehabilitating Government: Pay and Employment Reform in Africa*, Washington, DC: World Bank, pp. 62–81.

Turnbull, P. and V. Wass (1997) 'Job Insecurity and Labour Market Lemons: The (Mis)management of Redundancy in Steel Making, Coal Mining and Port Transport', *Journal of Management Studies*, Vol. 34: 27–51.

van der Gaag, J., M. Stelcner and W. Vijverberg (1989) 'Wage Differentials and Moonlighting by Civil Servants: Evidence from Côte d'Ivoire and Peru', *World Bank Economic Review*, Vol. 3, No. 1: 67–95.

Wade, R. (1990) *Governing the Market: Economic Theory and the Role of Government in East Asia*, Princeton, NJ: Princeton University Press.

Wass, V. (1996) 'Who Controls Selection under "Voluntary" Redundancy? The Case of the Redundant Mineworkers' Payments Scheme', *British Journal of Industrial Relations*, Vol. 34: 249–65.

World Bank (1981) *Accelerated Development in Sub-Saharan Africa: An Agenda for Action* (the Berg Report), World Bank: Washington, DC.

World Bank (1996) *From Plan to Market: World Development Report 1996*, Washington, DC: World Bank.

World Bank (1997) *The Changing Role of the State: World Development Report*, Oxford: Clarendon Press.

World Bank (1998) *The Public Expenditure Handbook*, Washington, DC: World Bank Poverty and Social Policy Department.

Younger, S. (1996) 'Labour Market Consequences of Retrenchment for Civil Servants in Ghana', in D. Sahn (ed.), *Economic Reform and the Poor in Africa*, Oxford: Clarendon Press, pp. 185–202.

Part III

Decentralization Reform

7
Fiscal Decentralization Policy in Developing Countries: Bridging Theory and Reality

Paul Smoke

Introduction

During the 1990s, fiscal decentralization and local government reform became among the most widespread trends in development (World Bank, 2000: chapter 5). Many of these extensive and often costly efforts, however, have made only modest progress towards meeting their stated goals, and some have even created problems.[1] Given this uneven performance, there has been considerable debate about the desirability of fiscal decentralization and how to approach it.

This chapter examines the origins, conceptual foundations and practice of fiscal decentralization in developing countries. Several issues are covered. First, I briefly consider why historically fiscal centralization has been prominent in developing countries, and why the trend has been reversing. Second, I summarize conventional fiscal decentralization theory and consider its relevance for developing countries. Third, I review some popular claims made for and against fiscal decentralization and consider the available empirical evidence. Fourth, I outline major elements of fiscal decentralization and summarize key issues with each. Finally, I make some concluding observations on how to think about designing more effective fiscal decentralization in developing countries.

The historical basis of fiscal centralization

Although fiscal decentralization has emerged as a focus of public sector reform in many less-developed nations, the substantial body of theory and research on public finance in developing countries includes limited substantive work on the fiscal role of local government. Relatively few attempts to conceptualize the issues broadly and/or to compare fiscal decentralization across a group of countries have been made.[2] Much of this body of work is region- or discipline-specific, and little of it involves detailed, formal comparative research. Although the literature is helpful, it is not sufficiently comprehensive or synthetic to deeply inform theory or practice.

The limitations of the literature reflect the small fiscal role that local government has traditionally played in most developing countries. In the 1980s, just prior to the emerging fiscal decentralization trend, local governments in the Organization for Economic Co-operation and Development (OECD) countries accounted for, on average, 11 per cent of total public employment, and in some countries as much as 25 per cent. In contrast, local governments in developing countries accounted for an average of 4.5 per cent of public employment, ranging from 2.5 per cent in Africa to 8 per cent in Asia (Cochrane, 1983). Public expenditure data from the late 1980s and early 1990s indicate that the local government share of total government spending averaged around 32 per cent in the industrialized countries versus 15 per cent in the developing world (Bahl and Linn, 1992: chapter 1). The most recent available figures for industrialized and developing countries show that the gap is narrowing, but is still substantial.

In evaluating the suitability of fiscal decentralization, it is important to consider the historical basis for centralization and the factors underlying change. Traditional systems in certain areas, such as Asia and the Middle East, have been highly centralized for centuries. Local governments in some countries were introduced through colonization and/or development assistance, often taking a form that neither met their intended purpose nor gained local acceptance.[3] Post-independence leaders inherited an institutional framework that was not consistent with their culture and needs, and they commonly used local governments for administrative and control purposes rather than to promote self-determination, democratization and economic development.

Early development economists also discouraged local government by advising developing countries that they could maximize growth by centralizing control over the economy.[4] In many developing countries, a general lack of managerial and technical expertise has precluded – or been used as an excuse to avoid – decentralization.[5] Perhaps the most important reason for the neglect of local governments in developing countries is that central governments have often opposed decentralization,[6] sometimes for legitimate reasons, such as the need for nation-building in ethnically fragmented societies and central macro-economic control in fragile economies. Equally important, however, is the reality that the governing elite, who may be dominated by one ethnic group or political party, fear the loss of power and resources inherent in meaningful decentralization.

An emerging fiscal decentralization trend

Although many developing countries are likely to remain fairly centralized in the near term, a few evolving realities have generated a growing interest in developing or reviving local government (World Bank, 2000: chapter 5). First, centralized planning has not been successful in promoting adequate development. Although there have been periods of strong economic performance in the developing world during the past few decades, particularly in Asia, many countries have faced a variety of economic problems that central governments have been unable to cope with.

Second, changing international economic conditions and structural adjustment programmes designed to improve public sector performance created serious fiscal difficulties for developing countries. Growing service demands and under-performing economies resulted in large budget deficits, which were financed primarily by external borrowing. Over time, interest payments claimed an increasing share of public resources, and a vicious cycle of borrowing and overspending ensued. In response, some central governments began to reduce their role and to rely more on local governments, which are often under-utilized and may have untapped revenue potential.

Third, changing political climates also encourage the development of local governments in developing countries. As people become more educated, better informed through improved communications and more aware of the problems of central bureaucracies, they desire to bring the control of government functions closer to themselves. In numerous developing countries, there has been movement toward greater democracy as military regimes and dictatorships are forced to relinquish power and institute political reforms.[7] This sets an example for other countries and emboldens people to push for further changes, including efforts to decentralize.

The new focus on a greater fiscal role for local government has been increasingly supported by international development agencies. Both the United Nations Development Program and the World Bank, for example, place considerable emphasis on decentralization, and many other donors are increasingly assisting efforts to decentralize and strengthen local governments.[8]

Fiscal decentralization theory

Mainstream economists consider a suitable role for local government in the industrialized countries using the basic theory known as fiscal federalism.[9] Drawing on the standard model of public sector responsibility for stabilization, distribution and allocation (Musgrave, 1959), the decentralization theory provides direction for sharing functions among levels of government.

Stabilization

Primary responsibility for stabilization has been assigned traditionally to the central government. It is not tenable for local governments to control individual monetary policies, and the effects of local fiscal policy are expected to dissipate into other areas because local economies are highly open. In addition, deficit finance policies at the local level are considered undesirable because of concern that repayment would involve substantial real income transfers to creditors external to debtor jurisdictions. On the revenue side, the types of revenues considered most appropriate for local governments tend to be income-inelastic, constraining the ability of local governments to pursue appropriate fiscal policy. Of course, the international macro-economic environment has changed considerably since this theory was developed, but there is still general agreement that macroeconomic stabilization is primarily a central function.[10]

Distribution

Fiscal federalism also places principal responsibility for distribution with the central government because only the centre can redistribute resources from wealthier to poorer jurisdictions. In addition, differential local redistribution programmes would be expected to create problems if factors of production were mobile. Wealthy residents and businesses might move out of a jurisdiction practising redistribution, while poor individuals eligible for benefits would try to move in, thereby undermining the redistributive base. Although there have been challenges to the conventional recommendation that distribution be centralized, it is still generally accepted that decentralized governments are typically more constrained than the central government in altering the distribution of income, and they clearly cannot control what happens across jurisdictions.[11]

Allocation

The prescribed role of decentralized levels of government in the allocation function is substantial where demand for public services is not uniform across space. Welfare gains would be enhanced through decentralization because residents in each jurisdiction could choose the mix of public goods and revenues that best conforms to their preferences. In addition, expenditure decisions are tied more closely to real resource costs in smaller jurisdictions, and greater service delivery innovation is likely when there are many local governments. The logic of preference variation also suggests that in a system where there are opportunities for mobility, people will move to an area where a local government provides their preferred mix of public services.[12] There are important exceptions to the general rule of decentralizing to maximize allocative efficiency. Services that exhibit economies of scale or inter-jurisdictional externalities should be provided at a higher level.

Defining an efficient decentralized structure is a complex process because the optimal service area may vary greatly for different public goods and may in few or no cases correspond exactly to the boundaries of existing political jurisdictions. The welfare gains from establishing new levels with efficient boundaries for providing a particular public good must be weighed against transaction costs involved in having more jurisdictions. It is often more practical to pursue alternative policies that have the same overall effect, such as the formation of co-operative agreements among existing decentralized jurisdictions; or provision, subsidy, or regulation of services by a higher level.

On the revenue side, basic principles of efficiency, equity and administrative ease are important, but additional considerations are relevant. First, the spatial dimension of local government action requires that interdependence and competition across jurisdictions be explicitly considered and that mobile tax bases be avoided. Second, central governments have national goals regarding public service provision and interjurisdictional equity that justify intergovernmental transfers and service standards. Third, the optimal criteria for assigning revenue sources to local authorities will generally differ from the perspectives of central and local governments.[13] These differences in perspective and their potential effects must be recognized when designing local revenue systems.

Relevance for developing countries

Theories by definition involve simplification and generalization. This can be problematic when considering fiscal decentralization in developing countries because of highly diverse cross-country circumstances. Context should never be ignored in public policy analysis, but there are some relatively established practices and standard institutions that must be considered in assessing macroeconomic structure and performance, international trade management, etc. The rules of the game for considering fiscal decentralization in complex and varied contexts are much less clearly defined, and there is much less 'good practice' to draw on.

It is not, however, difficult to justify stabilization as a primarily central function in developing countries. First, macro-economic fluctuations can be particularly severe, especially in agricultural countries subject to unpredictable climate variations and/or heavily dependent externally for basic inputs, manufactured goods and credit. Under such conditions, stabilization policies must be planned and co-ordinated centrally. Second, as noted above, local governments in developing countries often play only a minor fiscal role and are subject to heavy central control.[14] The impact of their fiscal behaviour is, therefore, limited. Finally, the local revenue situation in developing countries is particularly problematic. In some cases, local governments are more dependent on taxes related to economic activity (agricultural, business and market) than on more stable wealth-based taxes (land and property) and user charges.[15] These dominant taxes are often structured such that they are inelastic during growth, but the fragility of the local economy can result in dramatic yield reductions during contractions, undermining local ability to behave counter-cyclically.

With respect to distribution, domestic mobility of the rich may be less significant in developing countries than in the industrialized countries because there are few cities that provide high levels of public services and wealth-responsive amenities. Thus, constraints on intra-jurisdictional redistribution may not be particularly problematic in developing countries. Even if this were true, there is no strong case to be made for substantially devolving distribution. Local resource bases and expenditure roles are often limited, as is local capacity to administer major redistributional programmes. In addition, prominent local residents with substantial influence might undermine redistributional policies.

Although the case for centralization of the stabilization and distribution functions in developing countries is relatively straightforward, the issues surrounding assignment of responsibility for both the expenditure and revenue dimensions of the allocation function in developing countries are more complex.[16] First, a number of explicit and implicit assumptions underlying public finance theory in general, and fiscal federalism in particular, may be violated in some developing countries. Among the potential concerns are: the relevance of individual preferences as the principal basis for defining demand in cultures with more imbedded group-oriented allegiances than in industrialized countries; constraints on mobility that may reduce its role in generating an efficient spatial pattern of service provision; the limited applicability of conventional models of public choice where democratic mechanisms are weak; and the lack of an adequate legal basis for an effective intergovernmental system. To the extent that certain key mechanisms and assumptions are not valid, some standard policy prescriptions of the theory may have to be discarded or adapted.

Second, even if basic principles are essentially valid, local conditions that are fairly common in developing countries can substantially affect the way they should be interpreted. Widespread poverty, for example, may make preferences for public services more homogeneous across local jurisdictions, justifying greater centralization of some functions. This could be offset, however, by substantial spatial diversity in local environments and economic bases, and/or by the existence of widely dispersed and poorly linked settlements, both of which might suggest a positive role for decentralization. In addition, a wide variety of cultural, political and institutional conditions can also influence the need and prospects for fiscal decentralization. Since these factors can vary across countries and can move the system in different directions, their relative importance must be understood in a specific case.

The greatest challenge for analysts is that the structure and characteristics of decentralized institutions are so diverse across countries. The overwhelming majority of developing countries are unitary states in which local governments are the creation of the centre. True federal states exist by virtue of a voluntary union of decentralized units, which agree to surrender certain powers to the central government.[17] Most of the few developing countries with semi-autonomous state governments, such as Argentina, Brazil, Mexico and Nigeria, are really quasi-federal in that the state structure was at least partially imposed from above.

Unitary governments display a wide variety of decentralization practices. Some have no true local governments, although there may be decentralized administrative units of the central government. In the field of local administration system, local governments operate as extensions of the state bureaucracy with few autonomous powers, as in former French colonies. In extreme cases, the higher levels of government may appoint at least some members of local councils rather than permit full election by popular vote. In contrast, a system of semi-autonomous local government was established in some developing countries, such as those colonized by the British. Local authorities under this system are legal entities, which can sue and be sued as well as enter into independent contracts. Non-trivial central control is often retained, but local authorities are usually governed with some degree of independence by locally elected councils.

Either federal or unitary systems can vary along several dimensions.[18] First, systems differ in the number of levels of government that exist and the constitutionally and legislatively mandated relationships among them. Second, local authorities differ in their degree of political decentralization and grassroots legitimacy. Some have significant political power and are popularly elected, while others are at least partially appointed councils that follow the directives of a more centralized level of government. Third, local authorities differ in their degree of revenue-raising and expenditure autonomy. Some have significant autonomy in both, others in one area, and still others have little genuine autonomy of any sort. Fourth, local authority systems differ in the average degree of fiscal capacity relative to service responsibilities. In some developing countries they can more or less finance their designated services, while in others they raise only a small percentage of the resources they spend. In some cases, the central government steps in with a reasonable level of financial assistance, while in others it does not. Thus, there are enormous differences in the way public sectors are structured and the way they share functions and resources across levels of government.

These significant variations in the way dimensions of decentralization – administrative, fiscal, and political – are defined complicates cross-country comparisons of the decentralization experience.[19] Such comparisons are further hindered by the lack of adequate data, particularly for smaller and least-developed countries and crisis states.[20] There are considerable differences across countries in the way fiscal data are classified and aggregated, so that even if data were available, it would be difficult to standardize the data for comparative purposes.[21]

Even with good definitions and good data, no single framework could take full account of the highly complex issues involved in assessing an appropriate fiscal role for local governments. Great variations in the context of developing countries along many dimensions can significantly influence the 'optimal' assignment of responsibilities and revenue-generating powers among levels of government, as well as the reforms required to alleviate existing deficiencies. Traditional economic concerns must, therefore, be balanced with careful consideration of the unique economic, cultural, institutional and political environment in a particular case and an understanding of how this affects the desirability of and possibilities for meeting the normative prescriptions of public finance theory.

Empirical effects of decentralization

Having briefly reviewed the broad relevance of conventional fiscal decentralization theory for developing countries, I now turn to whether there is clear empirical justification for avoiding or pursuing it. Unfortunately, evidence is scant, mixed and difficult to compare. This section briefly considers what is known about several potential effects of decentralization.

Economic development

Some analysts have long maintained that the more pronounced role of decentralized governments in industrialized countries suggests that decentralization may stimulate development and that local authorities have an important role to play in public sector management. Some recent empirical evidence suggests a negative effect of fiscal decentralization on growth, although other studies contradict this finding.[22] These studies typically use econometric analysis that relates income levels or growth rates to fiscal decentralization. In addition to the static nature and limited time-frame of some of these models, there is a problem with the key independent variable: fiscal decentralization is typically defined as the sub-national share of total government expenditure.

At one level, this is an obvious choice of variable, but it problematically abstracts from political and institutional context, the importance of which was discussed above. In particular, without knowing how much autonomy local governments have and whether there are accountability channels to improve responsiveness to local constituents, we cannot be sure that local governments are truly decentralized. Thus, local governments accounting for high percentages of public spending may simply be following central dictates. Without more sophisticated analyses that control for sub-national autonomy and accountability levels across countries, definitive generalizations cannot be made on this issue.

There is also a small literature that examines the impact of public infrastructure provision on local economic development. Most of this literature, which focuses on industrialized countries, suggests a positive and significant effect, including when infrastructure is a local responsibility. The topic, however, has not been widely studied in developing countries.[23]

Fiscal effects

A number of analysts suggest specific ways in which fiscal decentralization may harm fiscal stability.[24] The list of alleged problems is long, but several are particularly prominent and tend to recur. First, local governments in many countries tend to run deficits, and they draw on the national budget to cover their shortfalls. Second, strictly defined arrangements for sharing resources with local governments undermine central control over how to use public resources. Third, local governments fail to repay loans channelled through the centre, again hurting the central budget. Fourth, local governments extract resources from the centre because they have political power over it. Fifth, local governments tend to be more corrupt than central governments, leading to misuse of public resources. Sixth, decentralized units of government compete with the centre for tax bases, or compete with each other by undertaking policies that may affect business costs and free domestic trade. Collectively, these effects of decentralization are said to undermine national fiscal stability.

Most people with applied public finance experience would agree that at least some of these problems exist in many developing countries. They, are, however, somewhat misrepresented and misinterpreted. First, empirical evidence on the fiscal dangers of fiscal decentralization is mostly anecdotal. Many highly publicized stories about dramatic negative effects have occurred in a few countries where decentralized entities have unusually significant fiscal roles and are substantially autonomous. As noted above, local governments in many developing countries, even post-decentralization, remain relatively modest fiscal players. Few countries decentralize or allow uncontrolled access to capital markets to the extent that occurred in Argentine, Brazil and Russia during their fiscal crises in the 1990s.[25] Although there are a few cases – such as Ethiopia, Indonesia and Uganda – in which fiscal or political crisis led to plans for extensive fiscal decentralization, there were 'natural' constraints on the situation getting out of hand. In Ethiopia the planned level of decentralization did not materialize due to capacity constraints, in Indonesia a substantial volume of shared resources was used to fund employees transferred from the central to local governments, and in Uganda the government has backtracked in response to weak local performance.[26]

There are also cases in which exactly the opposite conditions of those alleged by the anti-decentralization camp are said to prevail.[27] For example, several analysts see corruption as a much greater problem at the central level, particularly in countries where adequate accountability has been established through the development of local democracy.[28] Similarly, many knowledgeable analysts of decentralization would argue that the centre typically has more control over local governments than the local governments have over the centre, although the influence of local governments has been an issue in some Latin American countries.[29] This includes the power of the central government to quickly stop local attempts to compete in a serious way with the central tax base.

Second, the effects of some of the potentially more widespread pitfalls of decentralization may be greatly overstated. Consider, for example, the debate about whether local governments can compete with each other in detrimental ways.[30] There may, of course, be some interjurisdictional tax competition among local governments in fiscally decentralized countries, but it is generally unlikely to be a major problem. The absolute levels of most local taxes in many developing countries are fairly low, and they are of little significance compared to national taxes that all firms must pay.[31] In addition, research in industrialized countries indicates that local tax differentials often have only a marginal influence on behaviour – other relevant considerations, particularly access to inputs and amenities, tend to be more significant in business and household location decisions.[32] There is little research in developing countries, but the effects are likely to be similar or even less important than in industrialized countries.

Third, decentralization critics focus on immediate negative macro effects of fiscal decentralization. Even if some exist, it is important to consider potential micro-economic gains. There is virtually no serious attention in the literature to the critical question of whether early negative fiscal effects might eventually be offset by potential micro-economic gains of decentralization. In addition, a few specific dimensions of the micro–macro 'trade-off' require special attention. For example, guaranteeing local governments a fixed share of central revenues does undermine central budgetary flexibility, but it also provides local governments with predictable revenues that may allow them to undertake and sustain activities that support local economic growth. More empirical evidence is needed to understand the dynamic relationship between micro and macro impacts of decentralization.

Finally, even to the extent that problematic results of fiscal decentralization are real, *they are not inherent flaws of fiscal decentralization; rather, they are empirical problems that ought to be the target of sensible fiscal decentralization programmes.* For example, local governments in some countries do impose taxes that might impede free economic activity, such as the infamous *octroi*, on inter-jurisdictional trade prominent in South Asia. Economists berate such taxes, but they often remain in force because they are so productive for local governments with few other reliable sources. The existence of such problematic taxes is a weak argument against decentralization; rather, the policy conclusion should be that the intergovernmental fiscal system ought to be structured in a way that both prohibits such potentially growth-constraining local taxation and provides local governments with viable revenue alternatives. More generally, many 'problems' of fiscal decentralization, particularly those related to local governments' large and pervasive budget deficits and their failure to repay debts, exist not because local governments are naturally irresponsible; rather, they are a function of poorly designed intergovernmental fiscal institutions and rules and a lack of capacity and incentives at both the local and central level to make the system work properly.

In summary, there can be no argument with analysts who point to *potential* macro-fiscal dangers and growth-retarding effects of fiscal decentralization. Most of the evidence, however, is anecdotal, relevant only under particular uncommon circumstances or focused on correctable rather than inherent problems. The appropriate degree and structure of fiscal decentralization will vary with the context of particular countries, and some steps can be taken in most cases to neutralize potential macroeconomic dangers. Simply decentralizing is not going to bring fiscal stability or development, and failing to decentralize is not necessarily going to undermine them. The challenge is to devise an appropriately structured system that enforces incentives for responsible local government fiscal behaviour and enables the creation of a climate conducive to private investment. It is also critical to develop the skills of local government employees to meet the requirements of the system and the abilities of central government officials to assist local governments in the process of their evolution to greater autonomy.[33] This issue is part of the broader problem of decentralization strategy – what to decentralize and when and how to do it – to which I return later.

Distribution and poverty reduction

The impact of decentralization on distribution is not well studied in developing countries. As discussed above, interregional redistribution cannot be effected in a highly decentralized system with substantial disparities in fiscal capacity across local governments. The burden for such redistribution should always be placed on the central government, which could effect the desired results through appropriate national tax, transfer and expenditure policies. There is some evidence that appropriately designed transfers can effect meaningful interregional redistribution, but there is limited empirical research on this topic, and some of it shows that redistributional transfers can be offset by other types of transfers and government activities.[34] Some evidence suggests that decentralized federal countries (of which there are few), such as Brazil, have been more successful at redistribution than more centralized federations, such as Mexico, India and Pakistan.[35] Decentralization can, however, worsen interregional disparities, a problem in some East Asian countries that have recently begun to decentralize.[36]

How decentralization would affect the interpersonal and inter-area inequalities *within* local government jurisdictions is particularly unclear. Although a major redistributive role for local governments in developing countries is not likely, they can be reasonably progressive internally in the way they finance and deliver services.[37] In some countries, for example, most local taxes are raised from relatively well-off local businessmen in the form of property taxes, licence fees and service charges. This revenue may be used to help provide general services, some of which may benefit the urban poor and rural peasants, who pay little to no local tax. If such a system were standardized throughout the country, there would be limited opportunity for avoiding local taxes by moving to another location. Thus, some redistribution can take place at the local level without necessarily inducing undesirable spatial efficiency effects, but this has not been well studied.

Somewhat more attention has been paid to poverty alleviation (pro-poor expenditures) than to redistribution. Whether the poor are better targeted seems to depend primarily on the types and level of development of governance conditions. Improved governance can potentially reduce the common problem of elite capture and lead to a more equitable distribution of public services, but this is far from automatic and it may take considerable time to develop. Without careful system design and implementation, the often highlighted pro-poor benefits of decentralization may not be realized, and the situation for marginalized citizens can even worsen.[38] Much more research is needed on this topic, however, before definitive statements and recommendations can be made.

Service delivery and revenue generation

Many alleged benefits of decentralization are claimed in the literature, most of which relate to improvements in the level and quality of local services and revenue sources, better matching of local services to the preferences of local constituencies, and greater accountability.[39] The evidence on service delivery is extremely limited and mixed. A number of studies, some of which are anecdotal or informally documented, suggest that spending levels, and in some cases, service expansions, have taken place to some extent under decentralization.[40] On the revenue side, the evidence is mixed, but generally less positive than on the service delivery side, with little or no improvement – and sometimes worsening – of weak subnational revenue performance under decentralization.[41] A lack of balance between the revenue sources (including transfers) allowed to local governments and the increases in service functions assigned to them can be a great constraint on service improvements under decentralization.[42] Governance matters discussed below are, of course, also important.

Data on whether decentralization improves the quality of services are even more scant.[43] Comparative studies are rare, or focus on overall quality of government/governance (see below) rather than specifically on services. These studies often use very different methods that complicate consistent interpretation of the results. A few country studies showing mixed results are available. A study of Kenya found that public water infrastructure services provided by local authorities are more accessible and reliable than those provided by the centre (Lewis, 1998). A survey of education decentralization in Chile found that devolution did not result in improved education quality (Parry, 1997). A study of the Philippines suggests that the success of service decentralization depends on prior local administrative capacity and locally responsive officials (Bird and Rodriguez, 1999). In Indonesia, there is some evidence that decentralization has improved the perceived quality of at least some services, although there remain areas of concern (Kaiser, Pattinassarany and Schulze, forthcoming).

Two key points emerge from available information. First, whether decentralization has positive effects on service delivery is likely to be a somewhat country- and sector-specific issue. Local-impact, low capital-intensive services are more likely to be efficiently decentralized, but variations in available technologies, institutional structures and local capacities will influence the desirability and performance of decentralization of a specific function in a particular country. Second, there is obviously a need for much more research – in terms of quantity, breadth and level of sophistication – on the impact of fiscal decentralization on local service delivery and revenue generation.

Governance

The evidence on the extent to which decentralization improves governance is very mixed. The literature on this topic, however, is extremely diverse and difficult to compare because decentralization and governance are measured in different ways, sometimes in simple quantitative measures that abstract from complex dynamics on the ground, and sometimes more qualitatively focusing on these dynamics in specific cases without much guidance on broader relevance. There is some evidence that participation, in terms of elections and interaction between the electorate and local officials, can be substantially enhanced by decentralization.[44] The quality and inclusiveness of participation, however, varies, and it does not always result in improved accountability of local government to their constituents. There is also modest evidence, both quantitative and qualitative, that decentralization can, under certain circumstances, improve governance (defined in diverse ways), although some studies show or suggest negative effects.[45] Several issues seem to matter here.

First, the extent of genuine autonomy is a critical concern. Local governments, fuelled by local participation, might make decisions that represent constituents' interests. If there is insufficient local autonomy, central authorities could overturn such decisions, angering local residents who might blame the local government. This is not to say that some degree of central control is inappropriate; on the contrary, in developing decentralized systems, there are some national priorities that should take precedence, and some types of supply-side standards may be appropriate for certain services and activities. Even so, it is critical that decision rules and standards are clearly specified and adhered to.

Second, it is well known that local elites can dominate local decision-making processes in developing countries.[46] Corruption can also be a problem under decentralization, but, as indicated earlier, it need not be.[47] Where elite capture and corruption are problems, other local people may become alienated from the local government and withdraw from participatory opportunities. Such a situation reduces the local government to an institution that is accountable and particularly beneficial only to a small, powerful group, reinforcing some of the concerns noted above about the impact of decentralization on the poorest and most marginalized elements of a community.

Third, the quality of participation may vary with the development of local experience with social decision-making.[48] In some cases, there may be considerable experience with local decision-making, such that residents are able to articulate their demands clearly and forcefully to local governments after decentralization. In other cases, local people do not clearly understand the choices they have or the basic rights and responsibilities of citizenship. They may automatically elect the person who would have been chosen as the local leader according to traditional rules, even if they do not believe that person will fairly represent their interests in making decisions. The presumed benefits of decentralization become available to local populations only when empowered local actors are downwardly accountable, and this inevitably requires mechanisms beyond elections.[49]

Fourth, it must be recognized that the development of genuine local participation and accountability is a process. Local governments themselves are often quite used to heavy subsidization from central governments, and they may not be accustomed to feeling accountable to anyone. Local government constituents may not be accustomed to paying for services or to expecting responsive local governments.[50] The mind-sets and patterns of behaviour that have developed over time will require years to change. In some cases, higher levels of government can help to build the awareness of people about the types of demands they can legitimately place on their local governments.[51]

Finally, it is important to keep in mind that there is a difference between responsiveness in terms of process and responsiveness in terms of outcomes. Residents may be genuinely satisfied with the mechanism that local governments develop to consult them about decisions. For many people, simply being consulted will seem like such an achievement that they may, at least initially, focus more on the process than the actual results.

Ultimately, however, accountability requires that local governments both develop processes that make residents feel their opinion is being solicited, and provide outcomes that make residents feel that their public service needs are being met. Little is understood about the relationship between decentralization process and decentralization outcome and how they evolve together over time.

Thus, decentralization guarantees neither local participation nor accountability of local governments to their residents, and neither of these things comes about automatically as a result of decentralization. This is a critical point for two reasons. First, some of the alleged benefits of decentralization can be realized only if local governments are able to develop a genuine accountability to their constituents. Second, bringing about accountability should not be expected to occur rapidly – the process of building trust between local government officials and their constituents takes time.

The elements of a good fiscal decentralization programme

Having considered whether the broad benefits and disadvantages commonly attributed to fiscal decentralization can be genuine, I now turn to a consideration of the key elements that should generally be included in a good fiscal decentralization programme.

Creating an adequate enabling environment

An enabling environment for fiscal decentralization can begin with constitutional or legal mandates for some minimum level of autonomy, rights and responsibilities for local governments. Such mandates also need to provide for basic institutional structures and operating procedures that help to ensure transparency, accountability, and financial discipline (hard budget constraint). These provisions create a foundation on which to build decentralization, but they do not guarantee successful fiscal decentralization. Many countries with constitutional clauses and laws on sub-national government have not managed to decentralize successfully.[52]

A number of elements are often considered critical in establishing a sustainable enabling environment for fiscal decentralization. The first is adequate political will. International or central budgetary pressures have sometimes fuelled decentralization programmes in the absence of genuine commitment. Although some degree of political will – which may come from the central government or be forced on it by the people if pressures for democratization are great – is important for decentralization to succeed, it is clearly not sufficient by itself. The second is a set of robust and well-defined constitutional and/or legal provisions to support decentralization and stronger sub-national levels of government. Again, such provisions are important, but they have to be effectively implemented and enforced. The third is an appropriately empowered mechanism for coordinating the complex activities typically associated with decentralization, without which competing and reluctant central agencies that have a role or stake in sub-national service delivery can work against each other. In the final analysis, a framework needs to be supported by a strategy to implement it, as discussed below.

Assigning appropriate functions

The principles for assignment of services to local governments as developed in the fiscal federalism literature summarized above are fairly clear, and there is no need to elaborate on them here. Many countries do follow these principles broadly.[53] The problems with fiscal decentralization on the expenditure side appear to be related more to a lack of attention to implementation than to decentralizing inappropriate services. Three aspects are particularly worth noting.

First, no matter what a constitution or law says, central agencies rarely have a desire to decentralize services, particularly when this involves a loss of prestige and resources and they perceive each other as competitors. Thus, they almost invariably try to slow the process. Second, most enabling frameworks define functions broadly, so that there is always almost a need for extensive follow-up legislation and regulations, and this is often a sector-specific exercise.[54] Third, if too many sectors are decentralized too rapidly and local governments do not have the capacity to handle new responsibilities, they will perform poorly. If this happens, central agencies hostile to decentralization can use poor local performance as an excuse for keeping functions centralized.[55] If the local government sector is large and the problems widespread, some of the adverse macro-effects discussed above may materialize.

Assigning appropriate revenues

The fiscal federalism principles for assignment of revenues to local governments, like the service assignment principles discussed above, are well defined and generally appropriate. Many developing countries basically follow these principles, with a few prominent exceptions, such as the infamous South Asian *octroi* noted above (Bahl and Linn, 1992; Shah, 1994). Thus, central governments generally attempt to assign to local governments revenue bases that are relatively immobile and should, therefore, not lead to serious spatial efficiency effects, which do not compete seriously with central tax bases, and so on.

Four particularly problematic concerns remain on the revenue side. First, assigned revenues are almost never adequate to meet local expenditure requirements. This means that intergovernmental transfer programmes are inevitably required. Second, local governments often use too many unproductive revenue sources that barely cover the costs of collecting them.

Third, the same lack of attention to implementation discussed above in relation to service decentralization also plagues the revenue side. Fourth, individual local revenue sources suffer from some serious design problems, such as static bases, overly complex structures and ineffective collection mechanisms.[56]

One of the most critical international lessons of local tax reform is that local governments should focus on a few local sources of revenue that can provide substantial yields and pay less attention to the many minor taxes that they typically have access to. This often includes property taxes,[57] user charges[58] and various types of fees and licences. A second critical lesson is that rapid implementation of any or a multiple of these revenues, particularly without service delivery improvements, can be politically problematic. Thus, care is required in developing them, and exactly how to start the reform process is a somewhat country-specific exercise.

Designing appropriate intergovernmental transfers

Virtually all countries have intergovernmental transfer programmes, which include both shared (often on an origin basis) national taxes and pooled resources that are distributed to sub-national governments on the basis of certain criteria. Transfers serve multiple purposes. First, they help to supplement inadequate local own-source revenues. Second, they can meet national redistributional objectives by reducing interjurisdictional fiscal disparities. Third, they can encourage local expenditures on goods and services that exhibit positive externalities or are considered to be basic needs. Most transfer systems are intended, at least officially, to meet such objectives.[59]

Several issues and problems are typically involved in designing transfer programmes. First, macro-economic problems can be created if too large a percentage of central resources are guaranteed to local governments each year. The potential dangers, however, must be weighed against the value of providing local governments stable revenues. Second, different types of transfers are appropriate for different purposes. Unconditional transfers are best for redistribution, while conditional transfers better encourage priority expenditures. Third, transfers have often been highly fragmented and nontransparently implemented. Reforms are often needed to consolidate programmes to the extent possible and to allocate resources through objective formulae. Fourth, it is often politically and/or technically difficult to define and measure the formula allocation criteria for transfers. This may mean settling for criteria that can be agreed on and measured, even if they may not fully meet expressed policy goals. Finally, transfer programmes may have conflicting objectives or unintended results. For example, equalizing grants may be offset by categorical grants to wealthier areas, and transfers may substitute for local tax effort. Careful research prior to transfer design and monitoring during implementation can help policy-makers to understand and, as appropriate, adjust such effects.

It is difficult to make generalized prescriptions for the appropriate structure of an intergovernmental transfer system, which should be expected to vary across countries depending on national objectives, the extent of service and revenue devolution, local fiscal capacity and the extent of inter-jurisdictional inequalities. In an emerging system, such as Cambodia, local governments are being given only modest resources to provide local services considered important by the community rather than mandatory functions (Smoke, forthcoming). This approach can make local people better off and help to improve governance and capacity. Because local governments are responsible for such a small portion of public expenditures, they pose no threat to macro-economic stability. In advanced systems where local governments have significant service responsibilities and generally inadequate revenues, such as South Africa, a more substantial and sophisticated system of transfers is being developed. In this case, local revenue capacity and autonomy are being enhanced as transfers are being reformed (Bahl and Smoke, 2003). Under such conditions, the national Treasury is justified in keeping watch over the size of the local fiscal system.

Developing adequate access to investment capital

Sub-national governments in many developing countries get much of their capital budget from intergovernmental transfers, but some decentralized governments, typically states, provinces and large cities, are able to borrow in certain countries. Where local borrowing occurs, often through a municipal credit institution, loans may be allocated by political criteria, interest rates may be subsidized and loan repayment is often inadequate. Recent economic and fiscal changes, however, as well as increasing evidence that subsidization does not primarily benefit those in need, have stimulated reforms, mostly through creating more market-oriented mechanisms.[60]

A good fiscal decentralization programme requires the development of an appropriate spectrum of options to finance capital investment, from grants and subsidized loans for poorer sub-national governments and non-self-financing projects, to various types of loans and bonds for fiscally sound sub-national governments and self-financing projects. In cases where decentralized governments are relatively strong, efforts to develop direct access to capital markets make sense, but the centre must regulate borrowing and enforce a hard budget constraint. In more typical developing countries, where sub-national governments have few functions and are fiscally weak, special credit institutions may be appropriate. Initial public management of these institutions gives the centre considerable control over sub-national borrowing, although this must be structured to minimize abuse. Such institutions can be increasingly privatized as sub-national governments develop creditworthiness. Serious impacts of sub-national debt on the broader economy can generally be avoided if municipal credit markets are properly structured, managed and developed over time (G. Peterson, 2000).

Perhaps the most critical challenge in more advanced fiscal decentralization is how to 'graduate' sub-national governments from extreme dependence on grants and subsidized loans to greater use of credit markets. This requires coordinated development of both grant and loan options. It is critical to ensure that wealthy municipalities cannot use grants for self-financing projects, thereby diverting scarce resources from projects with weak revenue potential and from poorer local governments unable to borrow.[61] At the same time, grants and subsidized lending mechanisms must create incentives for weaker sub-national governments to improve fiscal discipline and begin to borrow. A multifaceted system that incorporates these critical elements could help to prevent the type of debt crisis feared by those suspicious of fiscal decentralization.

Few developing countries have made major progress in developing sub-national government access to credit. In some cases, such as Argentina, Brazil and Russia, irresponsible over-borrowing by sub-national governments nearly precipitated major fiscal crises and created pressure for developing and enforcing a stronger borrowing framework. More typically, in countries where sub-national governments often have fewer borrowing powers and modest borrowing capacity, there has been a tendency to rely on state mechanisms. More successful countries have been ones that have been able to increasingly involve the private sector in lending to sub-national governments, such as Colombia and a number of Eastern European countries (G. Peterson, 2000).

A note on the role of donors and international agencies

Donors and international agencies, as noted above, often play a key role in driving and/or supporting fiscal decentralization programmes. In spite of current international rhetoric, however, the donors do not always behave in ways that genuinely support strategic decentralization, institution-building and sectoral co-ordination.[62] Such efforts are time-consuming and difficult and, therefore, may cause substantial delays in moving funds. Given common pressures on programme officers to keep to expenditure schedules, particularly in large lending institutions, substantial funds continue to flow for investment, even if it is clear that recipient governments lack the capacity to ensure that funds will be well spent and that funded projects will be maintained.

Donors often try to get round the difficult problem of sectoral co-ordination by carving out their own project territory in terms of particular sectors, specific regions or particular local units. Since donors tend to impose preferred systems and procedures on the various areas they are working in, and central governments rarely exercise much control over such donor-sharing schemes, the process of building a consistent fiscal decentralization system may be greatly hindered. Moreover, because individual donors often develop client relationships with particular ministries or local governments, they may exacerbate interagency competition for control of the decentralization process. Thus, the behaviour of the donors supporting fiscal decentralization initiatives may sometimes contribute to the failure of these programmes in meeting their ambitious objectives.

Moving forward

This chapter covers considerable territory related to fiscal decentralization, offering a variety of ideas, but often limited evidence about its desirability and the shape it might take. Perhaps the single most relevant lesson is that decentralization is not a neatly generalizable exercise because the economic, political, fiscal and institutional context in which it must function varies so much across developing countries. It is, however, possible to summarize a few key issues that are likely to be critical in crafting an appropriate fiscal decentralization programme.

Fundamentals

Fiscal decentralization is appropriate from an economic perspective when there are variations in demand for public services across local jurisdictions, and the benefits of decentralized service provision are not offset by scale economies or inter-jurisdictional externalities. Such factors are not easy to measure precisely and to balance empirically, but careful analysis can set some basic boundaries for the appropriate functions of different levels of government. In addition, gains to local governments from fiscal decentralization must be balanced against the start-up costs of decentralizing and the possible negative macro-economic consequences discussed earlier. It is also important to recognize that decentralization of fiscal functions gives primary functional responsibility to local governments, but they may contract with private providers to deliver these functions.

Assuming macro-economic concerns are not serious or can be controlled through appropriate mechanisms, three important 'prerequisites' must be in place to maximize the potential long-term benefits of fiscal decentralization. First, there must be a viable local political mechanism to determine local preferences and to hold the local governments accountable to their constituents. Second, local governments must have the institutional, technical and managerial capacity to deliver the services demanded by their constituents. Third, local governments must have access to the financial resources required to meet their responsibilities. Almost by definition, these prerequisites do not exist in developing countries. Thus, even if analysts are able to use the economic, spatial and demographic characteristics of a country to determine an 'ideal' degree of fiscal decentralization and an 'ideal' structure of local government jurisdictions, such a system is not going to appear smoothly and rapidly. A process and strategy are required to define and implement it.

Process

Normative fiscal principles are unlikely to be the starting point for many of the actors involved in fiscal decentralization. Different institutions will typically have different perspectives on how far to push decentralization and what form it should take. There will often be political and bureaucratic resistance to even the most carefully defined programme of fiscal decentralization. As discussed earlier, competing central government agencies that would lose power and resources under a fiscal decentralization programme may try to undermine progress. In some cases, local governments may also resist decentralization if they are comfortable being managed and financed by the centre. When such conditions exist, there is a need to develop a political negotiation process for defining the fiscal decentralization goals and strategy. Getting consensus from key institutional actors on how to define fiscal decentralization may be more critical, at least initially, than the specific initial form the intergovernmental system takes. If the process is reasonably fair, there is a greater likelihood that it will result in a system with at least some basic checks and balances among various organizations and individual employees in key institutions, so that none are too powerful in the process of defining what fiscal decentralization means or controlling its implementation.

Entry point

Decentralization must generally be seen as a lengthy process in which the attitudes of key actors at all levels must be changed and capacity at all levels must be built. Thus, an effective fiscal decentralization programme requires a strategic implementation approach in which reforms are pragmatically phased in, even if there is a strong political will and an enabling framework is rapidly introduced. Initial steps could be undertaken in sectors and functions for which rapid success is likely. This requires prioritizing reforms, focusing on simple tasks that don't immediately threaten the central power base or overwhelm local capacity. However, even if initial reforms are defined modestly, they should be based on a broader conception of the desired system.

A second component of the entry point is the treatment of local governments. Decentralization programmes tend to treat all local governments (or classes – large urban, small urban, rural, and so on) by default, as if they were very similar in capacity and staffing. In fact, there are great differences among local governments in most countries, even among those of a particular type. It will generally be more effective, even if sometimes politically and administratively difficult, to decentralize asymmetrically. Treating local governments with weak capacity as if they can handle responsibility invites failure. Unduly controlling and providing technical assistance to capable local governments wastes resources.

Implementation strategy

A fiscal decentralization implementation strategy would ideally build strategically on the starting point discussed above. There are two key concerns in this regard. First, the individual elements of fiscal decentralization programmes should be closely linked, even for the most modest first steps. Local sources of revenue should be matched as closely as possible to local expenditure responsibilities. Intergovernmental transfer systems should target local expenditure needs and local fiscal capacity differences. Local government lending mechanisms cannot be defined independently of local fiscal capacity and transfer programmes. Fiscal mechanisms cannot be expected to work if there is not an adequate degree of local political development and accountability. The historical tendency in many countries of dealing with these various elements as separate aspects of intergovernmental reform has resulted in imbalances between expenditure responsibilities and sources of revenues, transfer programmes that undermine incentives to collect local own-source revenues, unnecessary grant financing of local governments that can afford to tap capital markets, the awarding of loans to local governments without adequate managerial and fiscal capacity to repay them, and a general lack of connection among the administrative, fiscal and political dimensions of decentralization.

Second, the various elements of fiscal decentralization reforms should also be linked to central government efforts to build capacity (broadly defined) and performance progressively. These reforms can be implemented in a way that makes it clear to local governments exactly what they must do before they will be assigned additional responsibility or resources. Specific steps could be designed in a way that helps to build local political and institutional capacity, such that what I labelled 'prerequisites' above should more accurately be considered key elements or building blocks of a strategic fiscal decentralization programme. The central government normally has considerable leverage, and it can strategically use access to grants, loans and technical assistance to encourage the development of political mechanisms, the adoption of new procedures and other key reforms.

Concluding statement

Fiscal decentralization will typically be a slow, painful and uneven process because common constraints on developing it are often serious, and they are not going to disappear suddenly. In addition, some standard tools for analysing decentralization may have limited applicability or need to be used with particular care. Available conceptual frameworks are useful, but they are not designed to deal with some of the most important factors affecting the prospects for effective fiscal decentralization. Moreover, implementation is complex and requires careful attention.[63]

The type of gradual, strategic, integrated approach broadly outlined above would require a different and slower path to fiscal decentralization than the conventional technocratic approach, which focuses on establishing normatively desirable frameworks, structures and incentives. This more developmental approach may well be the best course to take, particularly in countries with weak capacity and/or uncertain political commitment. It is almost certainly preferable to embed political compromises in a fiscal decentralization process from the beginning than to risk having powerful forces sabotage it before it begins or in mid-course, perhaps effectively removing fiscal decentralization from the policy agenda. Such an approach also raises the prospects for initial success, creating a limited base on which to build additional reforms. Finally, by slowing fiscal decentralization and building capacity in a strategic way, this approach reduces the likelihood that the negative macroeconomic effects often attributed to fiscal decentralization will arise. In some cases the political momentum for reform (or perceived reform) will be so great that a developmental approach will be difficult to adopt, but it should generally be possible in most cases to incorporate at least some strategic features in fiscal decentralization policy.

The most critical problem fiscal decentralization analysts face is a dearth of good comparative information on the extent to and conditions under which the alleged benefits and disadvantages of fiscal decentralization have been realized. Anecdotal evidence and case studies can provide certain insights on how to structure and sequence decentralization. Clearly, however, additional policy experimentation and more systematic research is needed to help us understand more broadly the realities of and prospects for fiscal decentralization in developing countries. This knowledge, in turn, can lead the way to better conceptual development and more effective public policy.

Notes

1. Olowu and Smoke (1992: 1–17); Smoke (1993: 901–23); Kim (1993); Dillinger (1995); Tendler (1997); Rondinelli (1997); Bird and Vaillancourt (1998); Litvack, Ahmad and Bird (1998); Manor (1998); Burki, Perry and Dillinger (1999); Cohen and Peterson (1999); Blair (2000: 21–40); World Bank (2001); Ahmad and Tanzi (2002); World Bank (2005); Smoke, Gomez and Peterson (forthcoming).
2. Dillinger (1995); Bird and Vaillancourt (1998); Litvack et al. (1998); Manor (1998); Burki, et al. (1999); Cohen and Peterson (1999); World Bank (2001); Ahmad and Tanzi (2002); Smoke (2003); Wunsch and Olowu (2003); World Bank (2005); Smoke, Gomez and Peterson (forthcoming).
3. For a more detailed discussion of this issue, see Mawhood (1987: 10–22).
4. See, for example, Brenner (1966).
5. Rondinelli (1981); Cochrane (1983); Rondinelli and Nellis (1986: 3–23); Litvack, et al. (1998).

6. Rondinelli et al. (1989: 57–87); Rondinelli (1990); Wunsch and Olowu (1990); Olowu and Smoke (1992); Litvack et al. (1998); Manor (1998); and Wunsch and Olowu (2003).

7. Huntington (1991); Diamond (1997); Litvack et al. (1998); Manor (1998); World Bank (2000).

8. World Bank (1991 1996, 2000) and UNDP (1992, 1997 and 2004).

9. Fiscal federalism is detailed in Oates (1972) and further discussed in Oates (1999).

10. The case for centralizing the stabilization function is laid out in Oates (1972). The standard arguments are partially challenged in Gramlich (1987); Roy (1995); Shah (1997a); and Spahn (1998).

11. The case for centralization of distribution in Oates (1972) has been partially challenged on both theoretical and empirical grounds. Pauly (1973: 33–58) suggests that local income redistribution may increase the utility of higher income people, who want to alleviate poverty where it most directly affects them. Crane (1992: 84–98) demonstrates that the effects of local redistribution policies on social welfare are not as unambiguous as conventional wisdom holds. Sewell (1995) argues that the regulatory powers of subnational governments, such as land use, rent controls, and user charges, have profound distributional implications.

12. This theory was proposed by Tiebout (1956: 416–424).

13. Bahl and Linn (1992) argue that central priorities are to: (a) limit local competition for key national tax bases; (b) limit local taxes whose burden is exportable to residents of other jurisdictions; (c) provide buoyant local revenues to limit demands on the centre; (d) minimize local regressive taxes; (e) encourage taxes that can be easily administered locally; and (f) encourage taxes that closely reflect the costs, including congestion. Local governments are likely to agree with criteria (c) through (f), but would oppose (a) and (b), preferring a share of productive national tax bases and exportable taxes.

14. See, for example, Cochrane (1983); Bahl and Linn (1992); Litvack et al. (1998).

15. The impact of such a revenue structure on local tax stability is illustrated in Smoke (1994).

16. Smoke (1989 and 1994); Bahl and Linn (1992); Prud'homme (1995: 201–220 and 2003); Tanzi (1995: 295–316); Bird and Vaillancourt (1998); Ter-Minassian (1997); and Litvack et al. (1998).

17. For a good discussion of these systems, see Smith (1985) and Cohen and Peterson (1999).

18. See Smoke (1994); Cohen and Peterson (1999); and Ebel and Yilmaz (2002).

19. See Ebel and Yilmaz (2002); Treisman (2002a); Schneider (2003); and Smoke (2003).

20. The IMF uses uniform data classifications, but data for decentralized levels of government are not as fully collected and standardized as central government data.

21. See, for example, Ebel and Yilmaz (2002); Treisman (2002a); Schneider (2003).

22. Reviews of the studies on fiscal decentralization and economic growth are provided in Spahn (1998); Smoke (2001a); Ebel and Yilmaz (2002); and Martinez-Vazquez and McNab (2003).

23. See Lewis (1998), who reviews the broader literature and develops a model that finds a positive impact of roads and water infrastructure on municipal economic development in Kenya.

24. Tanzi (1995); Prud'homme (1995 and 2003); Ter-Minassian (1997); and Brueckner (2000).

25. Shah (1997a); Manor (1998); and Spahn (1998).
26. These cases are respectively discussed in World Bank (1999); Alm, Martinez and Indrawati (2004); and Smoke (2001b).
27. See, for example, Walsh (1992); Sewell (1995); Shah (1997a); and Huther and Shah (1998).
28. See, for example, evidence and reviews in Shah (1997a) Manor (1998); and Martinez-Vazquez and McNab (forthcoming).
29. See Smoke, Gomez and Peterson (forthcoming).
30. For a discussion of the conceptual issues involved, see Bucovetsky (1991: 167–181).
31. For example, see Bahl and Linn (1992); Ebel and Yilmaz (2002); World Bank (2005).
32. For example, see Carrol and Wasylenko (1994). For a literature review, see Gilbert (1995).
33. Requirements for decentralized fiscal systems are discussed in Shah (1994 and 1997b); Roy (1995); Ter-Minassian (1997); Bird and Vaillancourt (1998); Spahn (1998); and Bahl (2000).
34. Shah (1994); Bahl (2000); Bird and Smart (2002); and Schroeder and Smoke (2002).
35. Shah (1997b) reviews the evidence on this point.
36. World Bank (2005: chapter 4).
37. See, for example, Crane (1992); Smoke (1994); and Sewell (1995).
38. These issues are discussed and some mixed evidence is reviewed, for example, in Santos (1998); Bardhan and Mookherjee (2000a, 2000b, 2000c); Belshaw (2000); Galasso and Ravillion (2000); Grote and von Braun (2000); Grindle (2002); Crook (2003); and Schneider (2003).
39. There is substantial literature on the potential benefits of decentralization. See summary reviews in Litvack et al. (1998), Bardhan and Mookherjee (1998), Azfar et al. (2001); World Bank (2000) and Smoke (2003).
40. Studies or reviews of evidence are provided in Estache and Sinha (1995); Burki, Perry and Dillinger (1999); World Bank (2001 and 2005), and Lewis (forthcoming).
41. See, for example, Schneider (2003), Lewis (2003); and World Bank (2005: chapter 6).
42. Indonesia is an interesting exception. See Lewis (2003) and Lewis (forthcoming).
43. In one study on quality, Humplick and Estache (1995) develop a set of indicators for roads, electricity and water in a large sample (minimum of 75 countries per sector) of developing countries. Negative impacts were rare. Increases were more common, but often decentralization had no statistically perceptible impact. In some cases, there was evidence of a functional split, such that facilities are better provided centrally, but decentralized operation is less expensive and more effective when decentralized.
44. See, for example, Crook and Manor (1994), Manor (1998); Blair (2000); Crook (2003); Ribot (2003).
45. See, for example, Brillantes (1994: 576–86); Crook and Manor (1998); Panganiban (1994); Slater (1994); Souza (1994); de los Reyes and Jopillo (1995); World Bank (1995); Rajas and Verdesoto (1997); Shah (1997a); Manor (1998); Porter and Onyach-Olaa (1999); UNCDF (1999); Andrews and Shah (2000); Blair (2000); Azfar, Kahkonen and Meagher (2001); de Mello and Barenstein (2001); Bardhan (2002); Treisman (2002b); Crook (2003); Olowu (2003); Ziblatt and O'Dwyer (2003); and Martinez-Vazquez and McNab (forthcoming).

46. For a review of some of this literature, see Cernea (1985); Chambers (1986); Moser (1989); Tendler (1997); Bardhan and Mookherejee (1998); Cook and Kothari (2001); World Bank (2005: chapters 11 and 12).
47. For example, a cross-country study by Fisman and Gatti (2002) finds a significant negative correlation between the subnational share of public spending and corruption. Kaiser, Pattinassarany and Schulze (2005) found some evidence of corruption but not of local elite capture in Indonesia.
48. This argument draws on Putnam's (1993) analysis of Italy.
49. Manor (1998); Agrawal and Ribot (1999); Allen (1999); Blair (2000); Olowu (2003); Wunsch and Olowu (2003).
50. In a study of South Africa, Taylor and Mattes (1998) found that citizens considered local governments to be the least responsive level of government and did not want to pay for local services, even if improved.
51. See, for example, the case analysed in Tendler (1997).
52. Indonesia, for example, became more centralized after a major decentralization law was passed in 1974 (Smoke and Lewis, 1996). More recent decentralization legislation is being implemented, but in a somewhat problematic way (Alm, Martinez and Indrawati, 2005). Another interesting case is Thailand, which has developed an elaborate framework, but only modestly implemented it (World Bank, 2005: chapter 2).
53. Bahl and Linn (1992); Shah (1994); World Bank (2005: chapter 5).
54. Andrews and Schroeder (2003); World Bank (2005: chapter 5).
55. Smoke and Lewis (1996); Litvack et al. (1998); and Smoke (2000).
56. Bahl and Linn (1992); Shah, 1994; Bird (1999); Bahl (2000); World Bank (2005: chapter 6).
57. Useful discussions of property taxes may be found in Bahl (1979); Bahl and Linn (1992); Dillinger (1992); Kelly (1993); Netzer (2001).
58. Useful discussions of user charges and willingness to pay are found in Gertler (1987: 67–88); Anderson (1989: 525–42); Gertler and van der Gaag (1990); Jimenez (1990); Bahl and Linn (1992); Whittington et al. (1991: 179–98); Crane (1994); and Beede and Bloom (1995: 113–50).
59. Much of the literature on transfers is reviewed in Bahl and Linn (1992); Shah (1994); Bird and Smart (2002); and Schroeder and Smoke (2002).
60. Examples of the literature on developing local government credit markets include: Davey (1988); Ferguson (1993); Smoke (1999); G. Peterson (2000); and Peterson and Crihfield (2000).
61. See Smoke (1999) for a discussion of grant–loan linkages.
62. See, for example, Smoke (2000) and Romeo (2003). See Easterly (2003) for a more general critique of donor behaviour.
63. Recent considerations of the design and implementation of fiscal decentralization programmes include Bahl (2000: 94–100) and Smoke (2000: 101–9).

References

Agrawal, A. and J. Ribot (1999) 'Accountability in Decentralization: A Framework with South Asian and West African Cases', *Journal of Developing Areas*, Vol. 33, No. 3: 473–502.

Ahmad, E. and V. Tanzi (2002) *Managing Fiscal Decentralization* London: Routledge.

Alatas, V., L. Pritchett and A. Wetterberg (2002) 'Voice Lessons: Local Government Organizations, Social Organizations, and the Quality of Governance', *Policy Research Working Paper 2981*, Washington, DC: World Bank.

Allen, H. (1999) 'Changing Conceptions of Local Governance in Public Administration and Development and its Predecessors', *Public Administration and Development*, Vol. 19, No. 5: 439–53.

Alm, J., J. Martinez-Vazquez and S. Indrawati (eds.) (2004) *Reforming Intergovernmental Fiscal Relations and the Rebuilding of Indonesia*. Cheltenham and Northampton, MA: Edward Elgar.

Anderson, D. (1989) 'Infrastructure Pricing Policies and the Public Revenue in African Countries', *World Development*, Vol. 17, No. 4: 525–42.

Andrews, M. and A. Shah (2000) 'Voice and Local Governance in the Developing World: What is Done, to What Effect, and Why?' Background paper for the Conference of Governance and Accountability of Social Sector Decentralization, Washington, DC: World Bank.

Andrews, M. and L. Schroeder (2003) 'Sectoral Decentralization and Intergovernmental Arrangements in Africa', *Public Administration and Development*, Vol. 23: 29–40.

Azfar, O., S. Kahkonen and P. Meagher (2001) '*Conditions for Effective Decentralized Governance: A Synthesis of Research Findings*', College Park, MD: Institutional Reform and the Informal Sector Center, University of Maryland.

Bahl, R. W. (ed.) (1979) *The Taxation of Urban Property in Less-Developed Countries*, Madison, WI: University of Wisconsin Press.

Bahl, R. W. (2000) 'How to Design a Fiscal Decentralization Program', in W. Yusuf et al., *Local Dynamics in an Era of Globalization*, Oxford: Oxford University Press.

Bahl, R. W. and J. Linn (1983) 'The Assignment of Local Government Revenues in Developing Countries', in C. E. McClure (ed.), *Tax Assignment in Federal Countries*, Canberra: Australian National University.

Bahl, R. W. and J. Linn (1992) *Urban Public Finance in Developing Countries*, New York, Oxford University Press.

Bahl, R. W. and P. Smoke (eds.) (2003) *Restructuring Local Government Finance in Developing Countries: Lessons from South Africa*. Cheltenham and Northampton, MA: Edward Elgar.

Bardhan, P. (2002) 'Decentralization of Governance and Development', *Journal of Economic Perspectives*, Vol. 16, No. 4: 185–205.

Bardhan, P. and D. Mookherejee (1998) 'Expenditure Decentralization and the Delivery of Public Services in Developing Countries', *IED Discussion Paper*, Boston University.

Bardhan, P. and D. Mookherejee (2000a) 'Capture and Governance at Local and National Levels', *American Economic Review* (May).

Bardhan, P. and D. Mookherejee (2000b) 'Corruption and Decentralization of Infrastructure Delivery in Developing Countries', Working paper, Department of Economics, Boston University.

Bardhan, P. and D. Mookherejee (2005) 'Decentralizing Anti-Poverty Program Delivery in Developing Countries', *Journal of Public Finance*, 675–704.

Beede, D. and D. Bloom (1995) 'The Economics of Municipal Solid Waste', *World Bank Research Observer*, Vol. 10, No. 2: 113–50.

Belshaw, D. (2000) 'Decentralised Governance and Poverty Reduction: Relevant Experience in Africa and Asia', in P. Collins (ed.), *Applying Public Administration in Development: Guideposts to the Future*, Chichester: John Wiley and Sons.

Bird, R. M. (1999) *Rethinking Tax Assignment: The Need for Better Sub-National Taxes*, Washington, DC: The World Bank.

Bird, R. and E. Rodriguez (1999) 'Decentralization and Poverty Alleviation: International Experience and the Case of the Philippines', *Public Administration and Development*, Vol. 19: 299–319.

Bird, R. and M. Smart (2002) 'Intergovernmental Fiscal Transfers: International Lessons for Developing Countries', *World Development*, Vol. 30, No. 6: 899–912.

Bird, R. and F. Vaillancourt (eds.) (1998) *Fiscal Decentralization in Developing Countries*, Cambridge: Cambridge University Press.

Blair, H. (2000) 'Participation and Power at the Periphery: Democratic Local Governance in Six Countries', *World Development*, Vol. 28, No. 1: 21–39.

Brenner, Y. S. (1966) *Theories of Economic Development and Growth*, New York: Praeger.

Brillantes, A. (1994) 'Redemocratisation and Decentralization in the Philippines: The Increasing Leadership Role of NGOs', *International Review of Administrative Sciences*, Vol. 60, No. 4: 575–86.

Brueckner, J. (2000) 'Fiscal Decentralization in LDCs: The Effects of Local Corruption and Tax Evasion', *Annals of Economics and Finance*, Vol. 1: 1–18.

Bucovetsky, S. (1991) 'Asymmetric Tax Competition', *Journal of Urban Economics*, Vol. 30: 161–81.

Burki, S., G. Perry and W. Dillinger (1999) *Beyond the Centre: Decentralizing the State*. Washington, DC: The World Bank.

Carrol, R. and M. Wasylenko (1994) 'Do State Business Climates Still Matter? Evidence of a Structural Change', *National Tax Journal*, Vol. 47, No. 1: 19–37.

Cernea, M. Putting (1985) *People First: Sociological Variables in Rural Development*, Oxford: Oxford University Press.

Chambers, R. (1986) *Managing Rural Development: Ideas and Experience from East Africa*, West Hartford, CT: Kumarian Press.

Cochrane, G. (1983) 'Policies for Strengthening Local Government in Developing Countries', *World Bank Staff Working Paper No. 582*, Washington, DC: World Bank.

Cohen, J. and S. Peterson (1999) *Administrative Decentralization: Strategies for Developing Countries*, West Hartford, CT: Kumarian Press.

Cook, B. and U. Kothari (eds.) (2001) *Participation: The New Tyranny*, London: Zed Books.

Crane, R. (1992) 'Voluntary Income Redistribution with Migration', *Journal of Urban Economics*, Vol. 31: 84–98.

Crane, R. (1994) 'Water Markets, Market Reform and the Urban Poor: Results from Jakarta, Indonesia', *World Development*, Vol. 22: 71–83.

Crook, R. (2003) 'Decentralization and Poverty Reduction in Africa: The Politics of Local–Central Relations', *Public Administration and Development*, Vol. 23, No. 1: 77–88.

Crook, R. and J. Manor (1998) *Democracy and Decentralization in South Asia and West Africa*, Cambridge: Cambridge University Press.

Davey, K. (1988) Municipal Development Funds and Intermediaries, Policy, Planning and Research Paper No. 32, Washington, DC: World Bank.

de los Reyes, R. and S. Jopillo (1995) *Responding to Local Government Council Demands and Challenges*, Quezon City: Institute of Philippine Culture, Ateneo de Manila University.

de Mello, L. and L. Barenstein (2001) 'Fiscal Decentralization and Governance: A Cross-Country Analysis', *IMF Working Paper WP/01/71*, Washington, DC: International Monetary Fund.

Diamond, P. (1997) *Consolidating the Third Wave Democracies*, Baltimore, MD and London: Johns Hopkins University Press.

Dillinger, W. (1992) *Urban Property Tax Reform: Guidelines and Recommendations*, Washington, DC: World Bank.

Dillinger, W. (1995) *Better Urban Services: Finding the Right Incentives*, Washington, DC: World Bank.

Easterly, W. (2003) 'The Cartel of Good Intentions: The Problem of Bureaucracy in Foreign Aid', *Journal of Policy Reform*, pp. 1–28.

Ebel, R. and Yilmaz, S. (2002) *Concept of Fiscal Decentralization and World Wide Overview*, Washington, DC: World Bank Institute.

Estache, A. and S. Sinha (1995) 'Does Decentralization Increase Public Infrastructure Expenditure?', in A. Estache, *Decentralizing Infrastructure: Advantages and Limitations*, Discussion Paper No. 290, Washington, DC: World Bank.

Ferguson, B. (1993) 'The Design of Municipal Development Funds', *Review of Urban and Regional Development Studies*, Vol. 5: 154–73.

Fisman, R. and R. Gatti (2002) 'Decentralization and Corruption: Evidence across Countries', *Journal of Public Economics*, Vol. 83, No. 3: 325–45.

Galasso, E. and M. Ravallion (2000) 'Distributional Outcomes of a Decentralized Welfare Program', *Working Paper No. 2316*, Washington, DC: The World Bank.

Gertler, P. (1987) 'Are User Fees Regressive? The Welfare Implications of Health Care Financing Proposals in Peru', *Journal of Econometrics*, Vol. 36.

Gertler, P. and J. van der Gaag (1990) *The Willingness to Pay for Medical Care: Evidence from Two Developing Countries*, Baltimore, MD: Johns Hopkins University Press.

Gilbert, J. (1995) 'Accountability Mechanisms: Smart Bombs in the Bidding Wars or False Sense of Security', Master's thesis, Cambridge, MA: Department of Urban Studies and Planning, Massachusetts Institute of Technology.

Gramlich, E. M. (1987) 'Federalism and Federal Deficit Reductions', *National Tax Journal*, Vol. 40, No. 3: 299–313.

Grindle, M. (2002) *Good Enough Governance: Poverty Reduction and Reform in Developing Countries*, Prepared for the Poverty Reduction and Economic Management Unit, Washington, DC: World Bank.

Grote, U. and J. von Braun (2000) *Does Decentralization Serve the Poor?* Bonn: Centre for Development Research, University of Bonn.

Humplick, F. and A. Estache (1995) 'Does Decentralization Improve Infrastructure Performance?' in A. Estache (ed.), *Decentralizing Infrastructure: Advantages and Limitations*, Discussion Papers 290, Washington, DC: World Bank.

Huntington, S. (1991) *The Third Wave: Democratisation in the Late Twentieth Century*, Norman, OK: University of Oklahoma Press.

Huther, J. and A. Shah (1998) *Applying a Simple Measure of Good Governance to the Debate on Fiscal Decentralization*, Washington, DC: World Bank.

Jimenez, E. (1990) 'Social Sector Pricing Policy Revisited: A Survey of Some Recent Controversies', *Proceedings of the World Bank Annual Conference on Development Economics*, Washington, DC: World Bank.

Kaiser, K., D. Pattinasarany and G. Schulze (forthcoming) 'Decentralization, Governance and Public Services in Indonesia', in P. Smoke et al. (eds.), *Decentralization in Asia and Latin America: A Comparative Interdisciplinary Perspective*, Cheltenham and Northampton, MA: Edward Elgar.

Kelly, R. (1993) 'Implementing Property Tax Reform in Developing Countries: Lessons from the Property Tax in Indonesia', *Review of Urban and Regional Development Studies*, No. 4.

Kim, K. (1993) *Urban Finances in Selected Eastern and Southern African Countries*, Nairobi: Urban Management Programme, United Nations Centre for Human Settlements.

Lewis, B. (1998) 'The Impact of Public Infrastructure on Municipal Economic Development: Empirical Results from Kenya', *Review of Urban and Regional Development Studies*, Vol. 10, No. 2: 142–56.

Lewis, B. (2003) 'Tax and Charge Creation by Regional Governments under Fiscal Decentralization: Estimates and Explanations', *Bulletin of Indonesian Economic Studies*, Vol. 39, No. 2: 177–92.

Lewis, B. (forthcoming) 'Indonesian Local Government Spending, Taxing and Saving: An Explanation of Pre- and Post-Decentralization Fiscal Outcomes', *Asian Economic Journal*.

Litvack, J., J. Ahmad and R. Bird (1998) *Rethinking Decentralization at the World Bank*, Discussion Paper, Washington, DC: World Bank.

Manor, J. (1998) *The Political Economy of Democratic Decentralization*, Washington, DC: World Bank.

Martinez-Vazquez, J. and R. McNab (forthcoming) 'The Interaction of Fiscal Decentralization and Democratic Governance', in P. Smoke et al. (eds.), *Decentralization in Asia and Latin America: A Comparative Interdisciplinary Perspective*, Cheltenham and Northampton, MA: Edward Elgar.

Martinez-Vazquez, J. and R. McNab (2003) 'Fiscal Decentralization and Economic Growth', *World Development*, Vol. 31, No. 9: 1597–616.

Mawhood, P. (1983) *Local Government in the Third World: The Experience of Tropical Africa*. Chichester: John Wiley and Sons.

Mawhood, P. (1987) 'Decentralization in the Third World in the 1980s', *Planning and Administration*, Vol. 14, No. 1: 10–23.

Moser, C. (1998) *Approaches to Community Participation in Urban Development Programs in Third World Countries*, Washington, DC: Economic Development Institute, World Bank.

Musgrave, R. (1959) *The Theory of Public Finance*, New York: McGraw-Hill.

Netzer, D. (2001) 'Local Property Taxation in Theory and Practice: Some Reflections', in W. Oates (ed.), *Property Taxation and Local Government Finance*, Cambridge, MA: Lincoln Institute of Land Policy.

Oates, W. (1972) *Fiscal Federalism*, New York: Harcourt, Brace, Jovanovich.

Oates, W. (1999) 'An Essay on Fiscal Federalism', *Journal of Economic Literature*, Vol. 37: 1120–49.

Olowu, D. (2003) 'Local Institutional and Political Structures and Processes: Recent Experience in Africa', *Public Administration and Development*, Vol. 23, No. 1: 41–52.

Olowu, D. and P. Smoke (1992) 'Determinants of Successful Local Government in Africa', *Public Administration and Development*, Vol. 12, No. 1: 1–17.

Panganiban, E. (1994) 'Democratic Decentralization in Contemporary Times: The New Local Government Code of the Philippines', Conference paper, London: Institute of Commonwealth Studies, University of London.

Parry, T. (1997) 'Achieving Balance in Decentralization: A Case Study of Education Decentralization in Chile', *World Development*, Vol. 25, No. 2: 211–25.

Pauly, M. (1973) 'Income Redistribution as a Local Public Good', *Journal of Public Economics*, Vol. 2: 35–58.

Peterson, G. (2000) *Building Local Credit Systems*, Urban and Local Government Background Series, No. 3, Washington, DC: World Bank.

Peterson, J. and J. Crihfield (2000) *Linkages between Local Governments and Financial Markets: A Tool Kit for Developing Sub-sovereign Credit Markets in Emerging Economies*, Urban and Local Government Background Series, No. 1, Washington, DC: World Bank.

Porter, D. and M. Onyach-Olaa (1999) 'Inclusive Planning and Allocation for Rural Services', *Development in Practice*, Vol. 9, No. 1–2: 56–67.

Prud'homme, R. (1995) 'The Dangers of Decentralization', *World Bank Research Observer*, Vol. 10, No. 2.

Prud'homme, R. (2003) 'Fiscal Decentralization in Africa', *Public Administration and Development*, Vol. 23, No. 1: 17–27.

Putnam, R. (1993) *Making Democracy Work: Civic Traditions in Modern Italy*, Princeton, NJ: Princeton University Press.

Rajas, G. and L. Verdesoto (1997) *La participacion como reforma de la politica: Evidencias de una cultura democratica Boliviana*, La Paz: Ministerio de Desarrollo Humano.

Ribot, J. (2003) 'Democratic Decentralization of Natural Resources in Sub-Saharan Africa', *Public Administration and Development*, Vol. 23, No. 1: 53–65.

Romeo, L. (2003) 'The Role of External Assistance in Supporting Decentralization Reform', *Public Administration and Development*, Vol. 23, No. 1: 89–96.

Rondinelli, D. (1981) 'Government Decentralization in Comparative Perspective: Theory and Practice in Developing Countries', *International Review of Administrative Sciences*, Vol. 47, No. 2: 133–45.

Rondinelli, D. (1990) *Decentralizing Urban Development Programs: A Framework for Analysing Policy, Office of Housing and Urban Programs*, Washington, DC: USAID.

Rondinelli, D., J. McCullough and R. Johnson (1989) 'Analysing Decentralization Policies in Developing Countries: A Political Economy Framework', *Development and Change*, Vol. 20: 57–87.

Rondinelli, D. and J. R. Nellis (1986) 'Assessing Decentralization Policies in Developing Countries: The Case for Cautious Optimism", *Development Policy Review*, Vol. 4: 3–23.

Roy, J. (ed.) (1995) *Macroeconomic Management and Fiscal Decentralization*, Washington, DC: World Bank.

Santos, B. (1998) 'Participatory Budgeting in Porto Allegre: Towards a Redistributive Democracy', *Politics and Society*, Vol. 26, No. 4: 32–56.

Schneider, A. (1999) 'Participatory Governance for Poverty Reduction', *Journal of International Development*, Vol. 11, No. 4: 521–34.

Schneider, A. (2003) 'Who Gets What from Whom? The Impact of Decentralization on Tax Capacity and Pro-poor Policy', Working Paper, Institute of Development Studies, University of Sussex.

Schneider, A. (2003) 'Decentralization: Conceptualisation and Measurement', *Studies in Comparative International Development*, Vol. 38, No. 3: 32–56.

Schroeder, L. and P. Smoke (2002) 'Intergovernmental Transfers in Developing Countries: Concepts, International Practices and Policy Issues', P. Smoke and Y. H. Kim, *Intergovernmental Transfers in Asia: Current Practice and Challenges for the Future*, Manila: Asian Development Bank.

Sewell, D. (1995) 'The Dangers of Decentralization according to Prud'homme: Some Further Aspects', *World Bank Research Observer*, Vol. 11, No. 1.

Shah, A. (1994) *The Reform of Intergovernmental Fiscal Relations in Developing and Emerging Market Economies*, Policy and Research Series No. 23, Washington, DC: World Bank.

Shah, A. (1997a) *Fiscal Federalism and Economic Governance: For Better or For Worse?* Washington, DC: World Bank.

Shah, A. (1997b) *Fostering Responsive and Accountable Governance: Lessons from Decentralization Experience*, Washington, DC: World Bank.

Slater, R. (1994) 'Strengthening Local Government in Sri Lanka', Conference paper, London: Institute of Commonwealth Studies, University of London.

Smith, B. (1985) *Decentralization: The Territorial Dimension of the State*, London: George Allen and Unwin.

Smoke, P. (1989) 'Is Local Public Finance Theory Relevant for Developing Countries?', *Development Discussion Paper No. 316*, Cambridge, MA: Harvard Institute for International Development, Harvard University.

Smoke, P. (1993) 'Local Government Fiscal Reform in Developing Countries: Lessons from Kenya', *World Development*, Vol. 21, No. 6.

Smoke, P. (1994) *Local Government Finance in Developing Countries: The Case of Kenya*, Nairobi: Oxford University Press.

Smoke, P. (1999) 'Improving Infrastructure Finance in Developing Countries through Grant–Loan Linkages", *International Journal of Public Administration*, Vol. 22, No. 12: 1561–85.

Smoke, P. (2000) 'Strategic Fiscal Decentralization in Developing Countries: Learning from Recent Innovations', in W. L. Yusuf et al., *Local Dynamics in an Era of Globalization*, Oxford: Oxford University Press.

Smoke, P. (2001a) *Fiscal Decentralization in Developing Countries: A Review of Current Concepts and Practice*, Geneva: UNRISD. DGHR Paper No. 2.

Smoke, P. (2001b) 'Fiscal Decentralization in East and Southern Africa: A Selective Review of Experience and Thoughts on Making Progress', Prepared for the International Monetary Fund, Washington, DC.

Smoke, P. (2003) 'Decentralization in Africa: Goals, Dimensions, Myths and Challenges', *Public Administration and Development*, Vol. 23, No. 1: 7–16.

Smoke, P. (forthcoming) 'Cambodia's Nascent Decentralization: From Donor Experiment to Sustainable Government System?' in P. Smoke et al. (eds.), *Decentralization in Asia and Latin America: A Comparative Interdisciplinary Perspective*, Cheltenham and Northampton, MA: Edward Elgar.

Smoke, P., E. Gomez and G. Peterson (eds.) (forthcoming) *Decentralization in Asia and Latin America: A Comparative Interdisciplinary Perspective*, Cheltenham and Northampton, MA: Edward Elgar.

Smoke, P. and Y. H. Kim (eds.) (2002) *Intergovernmental Transfers in Asia: Current Practice and Challenges for the Future*, Manila: Asian Development Bank.

Smoke, P. and B. Lewis (1996) 'Fiscal Decentralization in Indonesia: A New Approach to an Old Idea', *World Development*, Vol. 24, No. 8: 1281–99.

Souza, C. (1994) 'Political and Financial Decentralization in Democratic Brazil', *Local Government Studies* (Winter).

Spahn, P. B. (1998) *Intergovernmental Relations, Macroeconomic Stability, and Economic Growth*. Frankfurt am Main: Goethe University.

Tanzi, V. (1995) *Fiscal Federalism and Decentralization: A Review of Some Efficiency and Macroeconomics Aspects*, Proceedings of the World Bank Annual Conference on Development Economics.

Taylor, H. and R. Mattes (1998) *Public Evaluations of and Demands on Local Government*, Cape Town: Public Opinion Centre.

Tendler, J. (1997) *Good Government in the Tropics*, Baltimore, MD: Johns Hopkins University Press.

Ter-Minassian, T. (ed.) (1997) *Fiscal Federalism: Theory and Practice*, Washington, DC: IMF.

Tiebout, C. (1956) 'A Pure Theory of Local Expenditure', *Journal of Political Economy*, Vol. 64, No. 5: 416–24.

Treisman, D. (2002a) *Defining and Measuring Decentralization: A Global Perspective*, Department of Political Science University of California at Los Angeles.

Treisman, D. (2002b) *Decentralization and the Quality of Government*, Department of Political Science, University of California at Los Angeles.

United Nations Capital Development Fund (1999) *Taking Risks*, New York: UNCDF.

United Nations Development Programme (UNDP) (1992) *The Urban Environment in Developing Countries*, New York: UNDP.

United Nations Development Programme (UNDP) (1997) *Global Program on Decentralization*, Management Governance and Development Division, New York: UNDP.

United Nations Development Programme (UNDP) (2000) *The Impact of Participation in Local Governance: A Synthesis of Nine Case Studies*, Management Development and Governance Division, New York: UNDP.

United Nations Development Programme (UNDP) (2004) *Decentralized Governance for Development: A Combined Practice Note on Decentralization, Local Governance and Urban/Rural Development*, New York: United Nations.

Walsh, C. (1992) *Fiscal Federalism: An Overview of Issues and a Discussion of their Relevance to the European Community*, Federalism Research Centre Discussion Paper No. 12, Canberra: Australian National University.

Whittington, D. et al. (1991) 'A Study of Water Vending and Willingness to Pay for Water in Nigeria', *World Development*, Vol. 19: 179–98.

World Bank (1991) *Urban Policy and Economic Development: An Agenda for the 1990s*, Washington, DC: World Bank.

World Bank (1995) *Colombia Local Government Capacity: Beyond Technical Assistance*, Report No. 14085-C, Washington, DC: World Bank.

World Bank (1996) *Urban Sector Policy Paper*, Washington, DC: World Bank.

World Bank (1999) *Regionalisation in Ethiopia*, Washington, DC: World Bank.

World Bank (2000) *World Development Report 1999/2000: Entering the 21st Century*, Washington, DC: World Bank.

World Bank (2001) *Decentralization in the Transition Economies: Challenges and the Road Ahead*, Washington, DC: World Bank.

World Bank (2005) *Decentralization in East Asia and the Pacific*, Washington, DC: World Bank.

Wunsch, J. and D. Olowu (1990) *The Failure of the Centralized State: Institutions and Self-Governance in Africa*, Boulder, CO: Westview Press.

Wunsch, J. and D. Olowu (eds.) (2003) *Local Governance in Africa: The Challenges of Democratic Decentralization*, Boulder, CO: Lynne Reinner Publishers.

Yusuf, W., W. Wu and S. Evenett (2000) *Local Dynamics in an Era of Globalization*, Oxford: Oxford University Press.

Ziblatt, D. and C. O'Dwyer (2003) 'Does Decentralization Make Government More Efficient and Effective?' Paper prepared for the American Political Science Association Conference, Philadelphia, PA.

Zhang, T. and H. Zou (1998) 'Fiscal Decentralization, Public Spending and Economic Growth in China', *Journal of Public Economics*, Vol. 67.

8

Decentralization Policies and Practices under Structural Adjustment and Democratization in Africa

Dele Olowu

Introduction and overview

For a variety of reasons – historical, political and economic – developing countries are generally more centralized than industrialized countries. In the 1990s, however, a number of factors led to renewed interest by national governments and international development agencies in local government in developing countries (LDCs). These factors included globalization, economic crisis, structural adjustment and democratization, as well as local and domestic forces, such as rapid urbanization and strengthened ethnic identities (see McCarney, 1996).

This chapter reviews African decentralization experiences generally, but with special attention to developments in the 1980s and 1990s and beyond. This period coincides with major political and economic changes and reforms in the region. The relationship between adjustment/democratization and the institutionalization of local government in Latin America and the former Eastern European countries has been the subject of much more systematic research and analysis (Regulska, 1993; Campbell, 1997; Fukasaku and Hausmann, 1998). Compared to other developing countries, decentralization policies have remained poorly analysed and developed in African countries.

For instance, a review of World Bank decentralization programmes in developing countries notes that, even though Africa has the highest proportion of such programmes, the continent has the least formal analytical work on decentralization or intergovernmental relations (Litvack et al., 1997: 35). Decentralization policies and programmes in Africa are designed more often on the basis of ideological arguments (which extol the supremacy of party, state or market) than on an analysis of the empirical reality of what exists on the ground. This is further aggravated by the paucity of information on local political economy issues. This may also explain why evaluations of decentralization programmes in African countries have generally tended to be negative and normative, with a few, very limited exceptions (compare Rondinelli, 1981; Mawhood, 1983; Olowu, 1988; Crook and Manor, 1994; with Olowu, 1989; Olowu and Smoke, 1992).

This chapter approaches decentralization as a complex, relative, multidimensional process and seeks to highlight the motivations and dilemmas of recent decentralization policies and provide an overview of African decentralization policies and practices since 1945 with special focus on the last two phases – the period of structural adjustment and liberalization, i.e. the 1980s and 1990s. Finally, we propose a framework for analysing decentralization policies and programmes in developing countries, on the basis of which suggestions are proffered for the improved design and implementation of decentralization policies in African states.

Decentralization: conceptual clarification and classification

Decentralization – the deliberate and planned transfer of resources away from the central state institutions to peripheral institutions – has acquired considerable popularity especially in developing countries, partly because the state is a highly centralized institution in these countries. But this popularity in the scholarly and policy circles has not always been for the best: it has made the term 'become slippery' (Bird, 1995), such that it can mean all things to all people (Conyers, 1985).

Decentralization takes many forms – e.g. the administrative delegation of responsibility and authority to field units of the same department or level of government – referred to as *deconcentration* or the political *devolution* of authority to lay persons or special-purpose authorities. Other forms include *privatization* and *deregulation* (Rondinelli, 1981), but there are also references to *territorial* and *functional* decentralization (United Nations, 1965; Rondinelli, 1981; Smith, 1985). Variants in the decentralization family have also been suggested: *hybrid or partial decentralization* – whereby responsibilities and personnel are decentralized but not financing (as in the Decentralization Act of 1982 in Nepal) (Silverman, 1992: 15). Another is *market decentralization* – referring to decentralization from governments to market, quasi-market and non-governmental organizations, as distinct from most of the forms mentioned earlier, which are referred to as *intergovernmental decentralization* (Bennett, 1994: 11). Decentralization is thus a comprehensive term that incorporates all of the diverse forms identified above.

Decentralization is a relative, complex and multidimensional process. It is relative in that it describes the distribution of state resources (responsibility, finance, personnel or discretionary authority) between various institutional actors within the state and/or society against some normative mode in space or time. It is a complex process in that it incorporates and is impacted upon by political, economic, institutional and cultural factors. Moreover, programmes of decentralization are a mixture of centralization, privatization, deconcentration and, in some cases, devolution. Finally, decentralization is a multidimensional process that defines the distribution of power and resources between state and society, the executive and other branches of the government, at micro-level between central and local governments, central government and their field administrations, central/local governments and non-governmental entities, as well as at higher levels between governmental units within a federal or international system.

Three aspects of decentralization are the focus of this chapter – *devolution, deconcentration* and *federations* – for two reasons. First, they are closely related to one another conceptually: they belong to the generic form of decentralization that can be referred to as intergovernmental or intragovernmental decentralization. While market decentralization or privatization may be related in some sense to efforts to decentralize, they raise several other issues relating to the management of national economies that are beyond the scope of this discussion. Second, and more importantly, these three concepts are usually referred to in government policy documents on decentralization in LDCs and especially in African countries.

Through devolution, the central government confers self-governing capacities on local communities. Critical attributes of local self-government include locality, representativeness, governmental character or responsibilities and institutional autonomy (see Mawhood, 1983; Olowu, 1988; Anderson, 1995). Any programme of devolutionary decentralization (DD) will thus involve the transfer of legislative, political, administrative and financial authority to plan, make decisions and manage public functions and services, from the central government to local authorities.

Deconcentration or field administration is just as important as devolution. There are, however, three fundamental differences between the two. First, one involves the *intra-organizational* transfer of *responsibilities* (deconcentration), whereas the other is *inter-organizational* delegation of *responsibilities* and *discretionary authority*. Second, the primary objective of deconcentration is the efficiency and effectiveness of the central administrative system, whereas the primary consideration of devolution is political participation and empowerment. Field administrations could be organized along functional or prefectoral lines (fully or partially integrated).

Federations are different from the first two concepts of decentralization in two important respects. First, a federation relates to the delimitation of responsibilities between two separate political entities – one of which operates at the national level while the other operates at the meso- or regional level. On the other hand, local governments and field administrations are based primarily at the micro- or community level. Second, and more importantly, federations utilize the principle of *constitutional non-centralization* rather than decentralization. The idea is to create a system of governance, which at the same time provides opportunities for collaboration over a number of strategic areas while the federating units keep their relative independence in respect of other domestic matters. The federal principle is also being utilized at the supranational (e.g. the European Union) and metropolitan (e.g. Abidjan municipality comprising ten city districts) levels (Elazar, 1987).

Until the 1980s, African decentralization policies were either explicitly or implicitly confined to deconcentration even though the language of devolution was used. Even federal systems in the few countries that utilized them on the continent were operated as unitary systems. By the end of the 1990s, however, structural adjustment and political liberalization policies had compelled many states in the region to adopt devolutionary decentralization and, in a few but growing number of cases, even federalism. It is thus possible at the present time to classify African countries in terms of those with progressive policies on decentralization and those that have stuck with the old forms of deconcentration. In yet another category are those that have gone further, to experiment with federal arrangements. A sample of countries in the different groups is provided in Table 8.1.

In the next section, we provide the background to the present state of affairs – decentralization policies and practices since the end of the Second World War, when many of these mostly poor countries started to become self-governing.[1]

Four phases of decentralization in Africa

Like other LDCs, African states can be described as both highly centralized and decentralized. In terms of broad state–society relations, African countries are decentralized. Most economic activities remain uncaptured by the state, a fact regarded as an illustration of state weakness (Hyden, 1983). Yet they are also highly centralized, having been forged out of colonial conquest. Colonized peoples were regarded as possessing neither the intellectual nor cultural capacity for local self-governance. Beginning in India and

Table 8.1   Forms of decentralization in the 1990s with national examples

Type	National examples
Deconcentration with nominal devolution	Cameroon, Ghana, Kenya, Malawi, Zambia
Devolution	Côte d'Ivoire, Mali, Mauritius, Nigeria, Senegal, Sierra Leone, Tanzania, Uganda
Partial devolution (urban areas only)	Botswana, Mozambique, Namibia
Federations	Ethiopia, Nigeria, Republic of South Africa and Tanzania

spreading later to Africa, the predominant form of government was 'indirect rule'. This meant rule by a few colonial officials with the aid of the most compliant traditional rulers. Where no such rulers existed, they were created – as in eastern Nigeria and parts of eastern and southern Africa. The objective was to provide the minimal conditions for law and order, taxation and justice for the colonial order. Local administration comprised a native court system, a local tax and a treasury.

While this system succeeded in guaranteeing the conquered territory for its new masters, it could not serve as the vehicle for economic and social development of the colonies. Most importantly, it failed to provide avenues for political participation and empowerment for the growing number of educated elites that the colonial system itself produced. Opposition to traditional rulers also grew as many of them remained illiterate, extremely conservative and corrupt. Countries such as Tanzania abolished the institution of indirect rule altogether.

Phase 1: 1945–early 1960s

After the Second World War, decolonization came to top the agenda in international relations for a variety of reasons: as a reward for the colonized peoples' participation in the war; agitation by the growing number of educated elites from the colonies, and the ascendancy of social liberal parties in the colonizing countries: Britain and France. Evidence of this was the colonial despatch of the British Secretary of State for the Colonies in 1947, in which he argued that the 'development of an efficient and democratic system of local government' was a key to success in African administration (cited in Hicks, 1961: 4).

Largely as a result of this policy shift, important changes were made in local government throughout British, and later Francophone, Africa. During the late colonial period, the outlines of the system of local government were thus already fully established in British Africa, and to some extent in the French municipalities. It had the following key attributes:

- a tradition of elected councils;
- a well-defined local tax system (ranging from per capita flat rates in most places to graduated personal rates in eastern Africa, and the beginning of a property/land tax in the major urban centres);
- involvement of local governments in a range of minimal infrastructure services: especially in education, health and sanitation, rural roads and water supply, agricultural extension services and natural resource management – all of these with carefully articulated grant systems from the central government;
- involvement of local/municipal governments in major capital investment activities and of rural ones in co-operatives and community development activities (Mawhood and Davey, 1980; Stren, 1989).

This period has been described as the golden age of local government in Africa, and the experience was not peculiar to that continent (Hicks, 1961; Olowu, 1989). Reform efforts since that time have tried to place local government on the same pedestal it was on during this period.

Phase 2: early 1960s–late 1970s

Instead of building on the gains of this period, Africa's post-independence leaders sought to dismantle this legacy. There were two major rationales for this. First, on the economic front, Africa's new crop of indigenous political leaders believed that the only way to demonstrate their own worth was through rapid development achievements. They subscribed to a programme of central planning and in many places to a socialist ideology to promote development. Ghana's Kwame Nkrumah argued that political independence was the springboard for economic and social development. They had to 'deliver', and saw democratic local governments as irritants at best, if not obstacles to their ambition to build powerful economic states.

Second, the consolidation of the nation state via a single party mechanism was also high on the agenda. A new wave of decentralization reforms ensued that tried to forge local administrations that were essentially instruments of control within the framework of the one-party or military state. Local governments – read local administrations – were designed primarily for the maintenance of law and order and only secondarily for the implementation of centrally determined development plans. They also had political objectives such as participation, but these were to be carried out mainly through consultative assemblies, which had no real powers over the government officials in charge of the local governments.

Philip Mawhood best captured the state of affairs:

> In the 1960s, [there followed] for most countries a swing away from local autonomy in favour of central planning and greater control over public resources. A deconcentrated administration was left in charge of the locality, similar to but weaker than the colonial one. It was aided by committees that hardly had a role beyond discussing development plans and giving help in their implementation. (1983: 8)

Other reviews confirmed that most of these decentralization policies (in Africa as well as in other LDCs) 'were merely attempts at window dressing increasing centralization' (Olowu, 1988: 40). Legislation was passed, institutions were established, but the will to ensure that the power to act was actually transferred to local authorities to grapple with real problems was usually withheld. Essentially, these reforms sought to convert the fledgling local government systems into field administrations, even though they continued to be referred to as 'local governments'.

There were, no doubt, good grounds for placing severe limits on decentralization – the fragile nature of the nation state; the desire for rapid economic growth; and the command, highly centralized economies, etc. (see Olowu, 1990). On the other hand, it is not difficult to demonstrate that this tendency towards centralization via decentralization was, together with other dimensions of centralization, an important explanation for the economic and governance crisis that engulfed African countries in the late 1970s (World Bank, 1989; Wunsch and Olowu, 1995). Indeed, many of the main actors involved in the process regretted it afterward. For instance, former Tanzanian President Julius Nyerere recanted:

> There are certain things I would not do if I were to start again. One of them is the abolition of local governments and the other was the disbanding of co-operatives. We were impatient and ignorant ... We had these two useful instruments of participation and we got rid of them. It is true that local governments were afraid of taking decisions but instead of helping them we abolished them. Those were two major mistakes ... (1984:828)

Phase 3: late 1970s–late 1980s

When economic crisis struck in the late 1970s, most countries responded, usually at the prompting of international financial institutions, by adopting structural adjustment programmes (SAPs), which approached decentralization to local governments as another possible means of cutting back central government expenditures. The usual pattern was to devolve responsibilities, but not the financial or human resources to local units. Also, these early experiments did not pay much attention to the particular characteristics of the local institutions that were being created. All sub-national structures were regarded as local administrations or local government administrations. In reality, decentralized structures everywhere were extensions of the central government into the field and were dependent on the centre for budgets, personnel and ideas. In many cases, their management committees were selected by the central governments.

How did the SAPs impact on decentralization, and what forms of decentralization did they promote? Even before SAPs, many governments in Africa had sought to hive off their responsibilities to private corporations largely as a response to declining resources. Decentralization of responsibilities for services – not only to state-created structures, such as local governments/administrations, but also to community groups and to religious and philanthropic organizations such as churches – was sought in a number of countries (see Hyden, 1983). The Kenyan government, for instance, relaunched its commitment to *harambee* – a programme whereby communities provided the basic resources for building specific social infrastructure with the central government complementing these efforts. Similar efforts have been noted in other parts of Africa (see policies on hometown associations and *tontines* in West Africa: Barkan et al., 1991; Trager, 1995; Olowu, 1999a).

With SAPs, such initiatives became formalized into policies. World Bank lending portfolios emphasized the need for its borrowers to utilize opportunities provided by parallel or informal economies and institutions as alternative instruments for the delivery of services. The reasoning here was that these institutions could help to promote competition in the public sector in the production of goods and services (see Silverman, 1992; Litvack et al., 1997).

A second reason for embracing local governments was that they offered opportunities to develop the local public and private sector economies – an idea premised on the possibility of *separating provision from production* of services. Provision deals with such questions as what public goods and services ought to be provided in what quantity and quality, how to finance the production of such goods and services, and how to monitor and regulate the production of such goods and services. On the other hand, production is the technical transformation of resources into the delivery of these goods and services. Since many of the justifications for decentralization relate to the provision function and most of the criticisms relate to the production function – i.e. the lack of capacity to perform the production of these services – the separation of these two functions reduces the need for attempting to create large technical capacities in local government. Unfortunately, many decentralization programmes gave local governments the production responsibilities while the central government kept the provision responsibilities. Furthermore, since the state was in most cases in financial crisis, funding for these decentralized services was sought not from the traditional tax sources or government transfers but from user fees – for basic services like health and education – and also from private sector and non-governmental organizations, including community groups (Barkan et al., 1991; Corkery et al., 1995; Leighton, 1996).

Economic restructuring programmes (ERPs) suggest that local governments should have the power to make the decisions relating to location-specific investments, subject to national guidelines. They should have the right to contract for these services with other agents of production, especially private sector organizations. Besides ensuring a more efficient allocation of responsibilities between central and local governments, this pattern of responsibility allocation would assist the development of an indigenous, small-scale private sector. In a document he produced for the World Bank, Silverman (1992: 11–12) submits that 'demand by local governments for private sector production of public goods and services should result, eventually, in the decentralization of much of the private sector itself'. This has made it possible in many countries for the public sector to train managers of private sector enterprises who have contracts for the delivery of roads and construction activities to the local governments (e.g. Burundi, Central African Republic, Ghana, Kenya, Sierra Leone, Tanzania, Uganda and the Democratic Republic of the Congo). Madagascar and Tanzania have opened their training schools to private sector contractors as well.

The expectations are that this arrangement will result in:

- substantial reduction in the functions and size of all governments, including local governments;
- possibility of improved capacity of local governments to perform the more limited range of economic management activities;
- reduction of local government expenditures – on both investments and staffing;
- reduction of local government and public sector deficits with possible positive results for increasing finance available to the private sector;
- competitive production of public services that would improve the quantity and delivery of services, and also enhance competition and the development of the private sector.

Considerable effort and resources actually went into the implementation of these programmes of decentralization in many African countries. The central idea was to seek opportunities to reduce central and local government expenditures and size. In many countries it gave new life to decentralization initiatives. A number of countries (notably Ghana, Malawi and Zambia) adopted new decentralization policies. In most cases, these led to the creation of new structures of local government referred to as district development agencies or funds (DDFs), which were patterned after the Kenyan 'district focus'.

These structures, which were often dominated by appointed officials of the central government, but had some locally elected people as well, would make the plans for their respective communities or districts with field agencies of the main central line ministries operating in that district. Moreover, in a country like Zambia, for instance, health and education services were actually taken away from local governments and given to separate, central organs to administer. This was also the logic that was followed by many Anglophone countries, which tried to adopt the British model of the health care service. The hallmark of these organs was a strong connection to central ministries for effective delivery of services with significant downplaying of their political aspects.

The attraction of all these models for many national governments in Africa is that they leave these agencies primarily under their control. And this was important for governments that were not very secure politically. This was the case with decentralization reforms in Cameroon and the earlier phases of Côte d'Ivoire reforms. Similarly, in Ghana, local assemblies' executive committees were chaired by centrally appointed officials –

the district chief executive (DCE). A review of the Malawi DDF noted that district development committees (DDCs) promoted effective intersectoral co-ordination among field agencies of the government. On the other hand, they had no legal mandate or financial and human resources of their own. They were concerned only with 'development' and not governance or the recurrent costs of development. In any case, these organs received considerable amount of financial resources mainly from donors who were interested in assisting programmes of decentralization in these countries. For instance, the Malawi DDFs received 80 per cent of their funding from donors. The original expectation that these would lead to major breakthroughs in improved delivery of services, economic performance or participation has not been realized. If anything, DDCs have become obstacles to the development of effective local government institutions as articulated in the relevant constitutions or statutes of these countries.

In sum, the fundamental weakness of the decentralization reforms of the 1980s associated with SAPs and ERPs was their lack of attention to the nature and type of decentralized structures they were promoting. No clear distinction was made between deconcentrated and devolved organs. Yet, all the analysis pointed to the fact that the key problem faced by these countries was one of governance: the manner in which power was being used and wielded by those who held it – who, in the case of Africa, were all located in the centre. There was no real commitment to shifting the power base from the centre to the localities. That had to wait for the 1990s.

Phase 4: 1990s–present

In Africa, the onset of democratization in the 1990s brought to the fore a fourth wave of decentralization reforms. It is both a continuation of the past approaches to decentralization and a search for local institutions that are genuinely participatory and responsible to local communities. In the following section there is a detailed discussion of some of the factors that have motivated these fundamental reforms and the dilemmas that these countries confront in designing decentralization policies and programmes that enhance democratic participation and improve services.

Motivations and dilemmas of democratic decentralization

At the beginning of the 1980s, the state remained largely formally centralized in most of these countries. Available figures indicate that, whereas personnel of local governments in OECD countries constituted 42 per cent of all government employees, they made up only 21 per cent in Asia, 29 per cent in Latin America and 10 per cent in Africa (Heller and Tait, 1983). More recent figures (Schiavo-Campo, 1998) show that financial decentralization follows the same pattern. Data from UNDP's (1993: 69) *Human*

Development Report 1993 reveal that in industrialized countries, local governments normally account for 20–35 per cent of total government expenditure – decentralization expenditure ratios are even higher in countries like Denmark (45 per cent) and Finland (41 per cent). In developing countries, however, the ratio is usually below 15 per cent and is not substantially higher even when defence and debt servicing are excluded.

The case for centralized governance has dominated the policy and academic literature in African decentralization (see Wunsch and Olowu, 1995; Hulme and Turner, 1997). Nevertheless, in the 1990s, the following factors led to renewed interest in programmes and policies on decentralization in Africa:

- The failure of centralized public sector management evidenced by economic, fiscal and political crises (Wunsch and Olowu, 1995). The resulting decline in state resources increased pressure for economic, institutional (public sector) and political reforms (World Bank, 1981; 1989; Cornea and Helleiner, 1994) as part of the search for new paradigms of governance.
- The above-mentioned failures have stimulated pressures for political reforms by domestic actors outside the state, many of whom became more visible, politically, and more sophisticated in their critique of and protest against state policies as the economic crisis bit harder. Most of these actors sought to bridge the gulf between the state and the citizen by demanding greater involvement of citizens in the policy processes and the synchronization of informal local realities with the highly centralized structures and operations of the (formal) state system. The most dominant form of politics in Africa is local politics, but the state has always been organized in a manner that is oblivious of this reality. This is a phenomenon that some have argued is responsible for the persistence long after the colonial period of both the formal public, which is amoral, and the informal public, which is the real public realm to which most citizens hold moral allegiance (Ekeh, 1975; Joseph, 1987; Hyden, 1999).
- Pressure from external donors – an important consideration given the fact that many African states are heavily dependent on donor funds for development expenditures – some for more than a half of total expenditures (Doe, 1998). Democratic decentralization is regarded as one of the key elements of good governance (GG) programmes. The others are transparency, accountability, rule of law, electoral reforms and conflict mitigation. GG programmes are regarded as central to poverty alleviation, to which most bilateral and multilateral donors committed themselves in the 1990s (OECD, 1997; UNDP, 1997). The European Union and several European bilateral donors have initiated programmes of 'decentralized co-operation' that look beyond the traditional central

government organs in the recipient countries to incorporate private, non-governmental and local government organs (see Hertog, 1998; Materu et al., 2000).

• Growing urbanization and metropolitanization in most countries. Urbanization is variable in Africa, but it is marked everywhere by high rates of growth.[2] This phenomenon is itself only a symptom of fundamental changes to the modes of economic production on the continent. Structural adjustment stimulated economic diversification in most countries. In agriculture, many producers have moved away from cash to arable farming and agro-based industrialization. There has also been a greater movement of people towards the service industries. Retrenchment in the public and private sectors has led to the growth of the informal/service sectors, which are based mainly in cities. Other forces in addition to the traditional push–pull factors have also stimulated great flows of urban migration. One of these is the increased number of women with secondary education and another the massive movement of people in conflict-prone societies to the safety of the major cities. Whereas primary education has fallen compared to 1980, secondary education has actually more than doubled (from 10 per cent to 22 per cent of the age group between 1980 and 1993 for females, and from 20 per cent to 27 per cent for males (World Bank, 1997: 22). Many metropolitan cities in Africa especially have swollen – the more so if they are in countries that have experienced massive conflict in recent times (see Rakodi, 1997). The urban population has increased from 23 per cent in 1980 to 31 per cent in 1995 (projected to rise to 54 per cent by 2020), but in addition, the proportion of the total population living in cities of over 1 million population has gone up from only 5 per cent in 1980 to 8 per cent in 1995 (UNHCS 1996; World Bank, 1997: 231). In the past, the infrastructure of the few major urban centres was financed from central state coffers via central government parastatals, which were created to deliver important services. Economic restructuring has led to a situation in which many of these parastatals have been dissolved and their responsibilities transferred to local authorities or the private sector. Urban municipalities on the continent represent strong voices of the opposition wherever there have been free party political competition (IDEA, 2004).

• The conscious use of decentralization as a political mechanism by ruling groups to neutralize, contain or seek compromises with regional or local elites (Crook and Manor, 1994; Boone, 1998). Decentralization has proved to be a crucial mechanism in national and international efforts to resolve conflicts in many parts of the continent. It played a role, for instance, in the resolution of the long conflicts in Ethiopia, Mozambique and South Africa, and looks promising in the resolution of raging conflicts in Angola, the Republic of the Congo and the

Democratic Republic of the Congo (former Zaire), Morocco, Senegal and the Sudan, among others.

In general, devolutionary decentralization and federal systems are sought by state and society actors for their potential to empower the people by giving them greater opportunities for 'voice', and to promote self-governance and resource mobilization. In African countries in particular, they are sought to remedy the three most serious institutional weaknesses of their governmental systems – *weak accountability, poor integration between formal and informal structures of governance,* and *poor outputs in terms of the quantity and quality of basic service delivery.* Accountability is weak in most public sector organizations because public service norms and enforcement mechanisms are weak. Formal state-based structures are also separated from the informal, community-based structures. Finally, weak and ineffective tax instruments, together with the first two problems, result in poor and un-sustainable delivery of basic services in most communities (Ekeh, 1975; Dia, 1996; Joseph, 1999).

But the implementation of democratic decentralization confronts formi-dable obstacles.

Problems and dilemmas of democratic decentralization

Democratic decentralization confronts theoretical and practical problems in all countries, but especially in poor African countries.

First, with respect to theory, some scholars have wondered whether local government and democracy are indeed compatible, even in industrial soci-eties. One extols the principle of equality whereas the other celebrates the principle of differentiation (Langrod, 1953). While this has been vigorously contested, serious doubts have been cast on the idea of local democracy in developing countries where the preconditions for popular democracy – high levels of literacy, communication and education; an established and secure middle class; a vibrant civil society; relatively limited forms of mate-rial and social inequality and a broadly secular public ideology – are for the most part not yet present. All of these are the product of the industrial or capitalist revolution, which is yet to take place in most countries of the developing world (Huntington, 1968; Hyden, 1983; Leftwich, 1993).

Second, it has also been argued that local autonomy is only feasible at high levels of economic development. Fred Riggs (1964) spoke of the 'law' of circular causation in poor countries. Democratic decentralization would only promote the decentralization of poverty (see also Bennett, 1994; Prud'homme, 1995). According to this view, local governments may make contributions to the *allocative functions* of government, but they are unable to contribute to *distributive* and *stabilization* functions. In a developing country context, local governments are impaired by a variety of factors –

absence of a democratic culture, difficult inter-local mobility by persons and, most importantly, rampant corruption at the local level – from promoting allocative efficiency goals (Prud'homme, 1995).

These views have been challenged in recent years. Smoke (1994) demonstrates how local governments in all countries – rich and poor – actually enhance allocative and distributive goals, the latter especially through intra-local equity, and other researchers have reported similar observations in studies in Latin America, Africa and Asia (Bossert and Beauvais, 2001; Bossert et al., 2003). There is also evidence that local people possess substantial knowledge of their own environments and societies, enabling them to contribute to solving their own problems locally (Esman and Uphoff, 1984; Richards, 1985; Ostrom, 1990; Olowu et al., 1991). Appropriate institutional and policy design can help ensure that local governments impact positively on efficiency, equity and macro-economic stability (Ostrom et al., 1993; Litvack et al., 1997; Silverman, 1997).

The feasibility of effective local governments in African states thus seems to turn on the practical problems confronting decentralization. These can be categorized into three types of dilemmas – *political, economic* and *managerial*.

Political dilemmas

Devolutionary decentralization confronts two major political problems. The first is the unwillingness of political and administrative leaders to share monopoly power, inherited from colonial times. This is due in part to objectively held fears that devolutionary decentralization might undermine national cohesion and fan the embers of secession, which is usually a real consideration in societies in which ethnic and community loyalties are quite strong relative to national cohesion. Politics is always defined in local terms. There is also the fear, however, that devolution might compromise the integrity of nationally delivered services. In many instances, these rational fears are often a cloak for the fear of loosening their grip on political power, which in many countries is monopolized by the ruling elites at the centre. Another way national elites view devolutionary decentralization is through the lens of a zero-sum power game, in which local actors gain at the expense of the centre, rather than through that of a positive-sum power game in which all players, both local and central, gain over time.

A second political dilemma is the problem of local elite capture. In many instances, it is local elites rather than the most vulnerable that capture decentralized power, which is then utilized to repress the local minorities, women and foreigners in the various communities. Many traditional rulers in different parts of Africa have used decentralized power to obstruct development by diverting decentralized resources to personal uses; such rulers may thus be opposed to basic modern education, health services, sanitation and water supplies because of their fear that these may break their hold on local power. When this situation exists, it confirms the reality of the weakness of social movements and pressures for reshaping patterns of resource allocation.

Several countries have come up with pragmatic responses to these problems. With respect to the first problem, several countries (Philippines, India, Nigeria, Uganda, South Africa, Bolivia) have sought for constitutional protection for local governments, a major innovation from the point of view of western jurisprudence that regards local governments as creatures of the state. But it also means that the process of decentralization needs to be carefully thought through, allowing capacity to be transferred to local governments and in some cases devolving responsibilities to other institutional actors, such as user groups (e.g. parents' teachers associations) or communities instead of multi-purpose local governments (see Fass and Desloovere, 2004; Geshberg and Winkler, 2004). This is also a part of the response to the second problem: construction of effective accountability mechanisms, both upward and downward.

Economic dilemmas

Decentralization in poor countries confronts three major economic dilemmas. The first is the fear that devolution may complicate the tasks of economic stabilization, as central actors may not be able effectively to control local spending. Many also believe that local governments are not very good at addressing redistribution questions, although this is the case only when the focus is on interjurisdictional rather than intra-jurisdictional inequalities as already discussed.

A second real economic problem is the absence of wider institutional, political and economic reforms. Centralized infrastructure investment decisions by public and private agencies make it difficult to implement decentralization. Nzokenu (1994) suggested the need for land reforms in many parts of Africa if decentralization is to be advanced in the rural areas where land is presently held by local elites or governments – ostensibly in trust for the people, but in reality accessible only to the rich and powerful. But land reform must also be accompanied by the reform of the banking system, as most banks are at present concentrated in the urban centres. A number of experiments with community banking and micro finance have shown the great possibilities that exist for mobilizing idle savings in the rural areas for economic development purposes (CGAP, 2004). Clearly, the development of a favourable local economic system will provide the enabling environment for the development of critical economic *and* social infrastructure, which are both crucial for economic development. Similarly, effective and accessible judicial organs are crucial to the enhancement of decentralized governance. Instead of the present cumbersome and expensive dispute resolution process in local communities among individuals through formal courts systems, informal and local judicial organs have been particularly helpful in many countries in the continent (e.g. Uganda) when they operate within the purview of formal law. The same argument goes for policing (see Wunsch and Ottemoeller, 2004). Similarly, effective local legislatures can act as more effective checks on local executives than the central government in many instances.

A third economic dilemma arising from all of the above-mentioned considerations is that decentralization involves more, not less, costs – the costs of new institutions, staffing, procedures and training for all concerned (WHO, 1997). In the short run, resources must be mobilized to underwrite these costs. Unfortunately, many countries have a very weak fiscal resource base and cannot, therefore, finance these costs. Indeed, the fiscal crisis was, as noted earlier, one of the foremost reasons why some of the countries embarked on political and economic reforms, including decentralization.

Management dilemmas

These include the issue of appropriate institutional designs that respond adequately to the above-mentioned problems and the question of how to sustain a programme of decentralization once it is initiated. The problem is compounded by the absence of reliable data on governmental performance and also by weak capacity at central and local levels, and particularly so for local governing organs.

This third set of problems is usually the most difficult to resolve. Some of the most difficult design and management issues include the following: whether to make decentralization policies applicable to all parts of a country, given their different levels of development, or to adopt a phased approach; and how to transform the zero-sum game perception of decentralization into a positive-sum game in which all sides gain. Other critical design issues include how to ensure that decentralization helps national integration rather than secessionist bids; and how to mobilize the necessary resources to finance the heavy cost of decentralization reforms, which are often designed in the first instance to reduce costs. Yet other issues include allocation of responsibilities between central and local governments and between different tiers of local authorities; the balance between financial powers and/or resources and allocated responsibilities; the treatment of regions as distinct from local community structures, and of rural and urban areas. Another difficult design issue is how to integrate the informal structures of community governance with the formal structures of the state without undermining the integrity of either. Failure in any of these areas has often sounded the death knell of local government reforms in many African countries.

These problems have remained pervasive in most countries, almost negating all efforts at democratic decentralization until the 1980s and 1990s, when the combined impulse of structural adjustment, liberalization and democratization started some countries down the path of genuine democratic decentralization. We evaluate these developments next.

Evaluation of African democratic decentralization policies and programmes of the 1990s

As noted above, a new type of decentralization programme is discernible in countries such as Côte d'Ivoire, Ethiopia, Mali, South Africa and Uganda. What constitutes the main elements of this new form of decentralization? Conventionally, evaluations of decentralization programmes tend to focus on institutions or processes. An attempt is usually made to measure the extent to which decentralization policies or processes increase the autonomy of decentralized agencies (see, for instance, Rondinelli, 1981; Vengroff and Umeh, 1997). Philip Selznick (1949) suggested the following four criteria:

discretion: the power to determine what to do;
personnel: the power to hire and fire;
finance: the power to raise and commit resources;
co-operation: the power to establish harmonious relationships between the organization and its environment.

Building on these earlier efforts, we propose that, since decentralization is a means not an end in itself, it is necessary to establish the *goals* that are sought by decentralization policies and to distinguish these from the *means* or *mechanisms* for realizing such goals. In developing an analytical framework, three intermediate goals are identified for DD in Africa. These are *accountable use of resources, institutional synergy between formal and informal sectors* and *effective delivery of services*. They are intermediate to the goals of *self-governance, democratic participation, institutional diversity and differentiation* and *economic growth*, which are mentioned either explicitly or implicitly in many decentralization policy statements (Adamolekun, 1999; Wunsch, 1991; Dia, 1996; Ostrom, 1996; Smith, 1996; Kickert et al., 1997; OECD, 1997; Gershberg, 1998; Olowu, 1999b).

The analysis that follows takes four sample cases from the more progressive forms of devolutionary decentralization and federal forms and contrasts them with one case of the conventional type (Ghana). As was pointed out earlier, deconcentration could be a legitimate policy goal. However, its objective is essentially to decongest the central government and possibly increase central government control on the localities. To the extent that incentives are created for effective performance of central functions, it has value in increasing policy implementation effectiveness. Devolution and federalism, on the other hand, seek to create incentives for local (governance) actors to make and implement decisions in respect of crucial, locally-based services, thus forcing them to mobilize resources and strategize their use in a responsible way.

Seven major mechanisms are used to implement DD and can also be seen to evaluate the extent of decentralization in any country (see Table 8.1

above p. 231). The analysis starts with the *allocation of responsibilities for services* between central and local level governments. In a completely centralized polity, all services – no matter how local – are delivered by central government. In contrast, the principle of subsidiarity suggests that the smallest possible beneficiary local area should provide possible local responsibilities. As already indicated, many LDCs do decentralize responsibilities, but not the means of financing the programme of decentralization. A second mechanism in decentralization is therefore the *decentralization of financing arrangements*. This could be in the form of granting local governments their own revenue sources (with responsibilities to set the base and rate), cost recovery (nominal, full or partial), transfers from higher governments and borrowing powers. The third mechanism is the *decentralization of decision-making powers*. Many central governments would give financial powers to local communities, but not the authority to approve budgets or laws. Such decisions continue to be made by the central governments – often defeating the very essence of decentralization. For instance, there is documented evidence that central governments cause delays in approving local government budgets in Kenya and Nigeria, and that this is one of the chief reasons for programme implementation failures. In the latter country it led to radical reforms of local government in the 1980s (Olowu, 1990; Oyugi, 1990). But this is a responsibility that could and should be undertaken by local governments that are responsible to their constituents.

The fourth mechanism is *the management of the personnel of decentralized services*, whether by central or local entities. For various reasons this often takes a longer time to delegate fully to local governments. The unified approach is a midway house between the extremes of integrated and separate personnel arrangements, but unified services in many African countries have ended up functioning as integrated personnel systems. Furthermore, many professionals are reluctant to work in local governments, fearing reduction in their status or job security. Different approaches have been used to resolve this problem in many countries (see Tendler's (1997) analysis of health sector reform in Brazil in 1987–92, and Olowu and Wunsch's (1995) analysis of the same phenomenon in Nigeria).

The fifth mechanism – often a very difficult one – relates to *the enforcement of local government accountability*. Should national government bureaucracies or local assemblies enforce accountability? Both are problematic in developing country circumstances. Contrary to conventional thinking, accountability is actually weak even in national governments because there are no strong institutions to canvass for or enforce accountability at this level. Many central agencies are limited to post-audit financial reports, and even this is in arrears of five to ten years in some countries. On the other hand, citizens at the local level are not able to use either voice or exit options because of the high transaction costs involved – e.g. moving from one locality to another without credit, reliable information or access to land, etc. The best solution is a mixture of both, but each circumstance will need to ensure the right mix appropriate to that environment.

The sixth mechanism is *the involvement of other institutional actors outside the state in the delivery of services*. There are two possibilities here – to involve private organizations and NGOs or communities as agents, or to privatize the services to them. In the former 'co-production' arrangement, they help to produce the service while the responsibility for provision rests with the local authority. In the latter, these organizations are responsible for providing and producing the service, under some form of local authority regulatory framework.

Finally, there is the *extent of political competition that is allowed at the local level*. Some countries legally disallow party competition at the local level, even though they may permit it at the national level, as is the case in Ghana. In other countries, party competition is barred at the national and local levels, as in Uganda, but citizens are allowed to make reasoned choices among several candidates that are in effect sponsored by different local political forces. In yet others, the state may officially allow multiple parties, but effectively ensure the neutralization of political forces at the local level, and at times even at the national level as well (e.g. Ethiopia).

This framework does not assume that any form of decentralization is either good or bad. Rather, evaluation is made contingent on the three objective goals of decentralization: *accountable use of resources, institutional synergy* and *service delivery*; and on the seven suggested mechanisms that are used to measure the maturity or success of any programme/policy of decentralization. Besides, overall judgement of whether the programme of decentralization is deconcentrated or devolved is the outcome of the analysis rather than accepting official labels, which can be very confusing. Finally, the framework analyses decentralization from the viewpoint of polycentric or complex networks in which each of the institutional actors (central authority, local government, private and non-governmental organizations) is an essential player. For instance, it is a paradoxical but significant fact that effective decentralization requires the deliberate strengthening of central institutions and agencies to enable them to support the effectiveness of decentralized agencies (Ostrom, 1996; Tendler, 1997; Gershberg, 1998; Adamolekun, 1999). These issues have been further developed in Olowu and Wunsch (2004).

Case studies of five African decentralization programmes are analysed using this framework, with their summary ratings provided in Table 8.2. (For details of the basis for the ratings, see Olowu 2001.)

Conclusion

In concluding this chapter, it is helpful to make the point that two broad patterns of decentralization are discernible in African countries at the

Table 8.2 Framework for analysing decentralization in developing countries:
African applications (potential and actual scores)*

	Côte d'Ivoire	Ethiopia	Ghana	Nigeria	Uganda
1. Transfer of responsibilities (10) Major (10)/minor basic services (5)	10	10	10	10	10
2. Transfer of financial resources (10) Major tax sources (5) User fees (nominal/partial/full cost recovery) (3) Central transfers adequacy/ equity/responsiveness) (2)	5	6	6	8	6
3. Decision-making powers (10) Budget making/approval (6) Budget implementation (4)	7	10	5	10	10
4. Personnel management (15) Separate (10) Unified (5) Integrated (0)	7	6	4	8	10
5. Accountability mechanisms (10) Central (monitoring and evaluation) (3) Local citizens (5) Central/local citizens (10)	5	5	4	4	8
6. Involvement of other institutional actors (10) Privatization and local regulation (5) Co-production (10)	3	2	2	3	3
7. Local political competition (10) Full (10) Partial (5) None (0)	5	3	0	5	3
TOTAL (70)	42	42	31	48	50

*All main elements have a score of 10. Numbers assigned to sub-elements are indicative of their relative weights and do not necessarily add up to the total for the main element. Scores based on data obtained from literature on country decentralization experiences as of 2000.

present time. There is decentralization as a conscious choice and policy.
But there is also decentralization by default – a situation in which citizens
and non-governmental actors move into fields where state institutions were
no longer active. For countries that pursue deliberate polices of decentral-

ization, what comes across strongly is that even though there are some fundamentally new orientations, serious problems persist. They include the following:

- The preoccupation of decentralization policies with vertical transfers of authority and resources from central to local governments at a time when central governments are experiencing severe resource shortages. In contrast, much less attention is devoted to inter-local governmental relations (e.g. among the five tiers of local government in Uganda, or among urban and rural areas in Ethiopia)[3] and between local governments and non-governmental (for-profit and not-for profit) organizations.
- The uneven and unequal development of infrastructural and institutional capacities between regions and communities belies the commitment to overall decentralization. This strengthens the case for asymmetric decentralization – starting with the most able regions – a strategy that may increase such inequalities. Some countries have already adopted this approach (e.g. Namibia, Tanzania).
- Few countries have been able to allow party political competition and democratic decentralization. Many countries seem interested in democratic decentralization within the context of a de facto one-party state (e.g. Ethiopia, Ghana, Uganda).
- Most of the decentralization plans have incorporated large intergovernmental transfers to the new localities. Less attention has been focused on developing alternative revenue sources. In some cases, large infusions of grants to regional/local governments undermine incentives for the development of local revenue-generating efforts (e.g. Ghana, Nigeria). There is a need to strengthen classical accountability mechanisms of representation with additional participatory forms such as recall, referendum, local ombudsmen, service delivery surveys and participatory budgeting. There are a number of new initiatives to encourage more active civic participation in the budgetary processes patterned after some Latin American experiences (e.g. those sponsored by the Municipal Development Programme in Harare).

The resolution of these problems will take time, as well as the determination and imagination of those involved in managing these processes in these countries. A few crucial issues of strategy could help.

First, democratic decentralization should be approached as a process not an event. As a process, it may need to be phased beginning from the urban and fast-growing metropolitan areas. A second and related policy issue is the need for African states to move beyond the confines of the institutional resources of the public and private sectors for the development of local government. In particular NGOs, such as religious and community-based organs that are at present largely sidelined in the process of democratic decentralization, could become critical players (as they were in the colonial period). Many donors are also helping to encourage this process further through their programmes of governance assistance, although there is a need to harmonize such activities.

Second, local governments can help alleviate poverty, because they are particularly well placed to help target small-scale industries, agricultural support and needy members of the community, provided the capacity exists to deliver such programmes.

Third, there is need to enhance the capacity of central governments to undertake policy development, as well as the monitoring of decentralization policy implementation.

Finally, resources for decentralized governance should be mobilized through property taxes, user charges and investment portfolios, particularly in urban centres, where this has not been the case (e.g. in western, central and some parts of eastern Africa).

Notes

1. Although African socio-economic conditions improved somewhat in the second half of the 1990s, poverty is an important reality in the continent. Africa is home to the largest numbers of least developed countries. Over a half of the countries in the continent have per capita incomes below the poverty line.
2. The level of urbanization in Africa is low by world standards (40 per cent compared to the world average of 51 per cent). However, the rate of growth for the region is high. The southern part is the fastest growing region followed by the west, the east, and the north (see United Nations, 1991).
3. The Ethiopian national and regional constitutions make no reference to municipal councils. A few states are beginning to consider draft statutes that give legal recognition to municipal councils in this rapidly urbanizing country.

References

Adamolekun, L. (1999) 'Decentralization, Sub-national Governments and Intergovernmental Relations', in L. Adamolekun (ed.), *Public Administration in Africa*, Boulder, CO: Westview Press, pp. 49–67.

Anderson, M. (1995) *Case Study: Malawi Development Fund*, New York: United Nations Capital Development Fund.

Ayee, J. A. (1996) 'The Measurement of Decentralization: The Ghanaian Experience, 1988–92', *African Affairs*, Vol. 97, No. 378: 31–50.

Ayee, J. A. (1997) 'Local Government Reform and Bureaucratic Accountability in Ghana', *Regional Development Dialogue*, Vol. 18, No. 2: 86–104.

Ayenew, M. (1998) 'Some Preliminary Observations on Institutional and Administrative Gaps in Ethiopia's Decentralization Process', Working Paper No. 1, *Regional and Local Development Studies*.

Barkan, J. D., M. McNulty and M. Ayeni (1991) 'Hometown Voluntary Associations and the Emergence of Civil Society in Western Nigeria', *Journal of Modern African Studies*, Vol. 29, No. 3: 457–80.

Bennett, R. (1994) *Local Government and Market Decentralization: Experiences in Industrialised, Developing, and Former Eastern Bloc Countries*, Tokyo: United Nations University Press.

Bird, R. (1995) *Financing Local Services: Patterns, Problems and Possibilities*, Report No. 31, Toronto: Centre for Urban and Community Studies.

Boone, C. (1998) 'State Building in the African Countryside: Structure and Politics at the Grassroots', *Journal of Development Studies*, Vol. 34, No. 4: 1–31.

Bossert, T. and Larrañaga O., Giedion U., Arbelaez J. and Bowser D. (2003) 'Decentralization and Equity of Resource Allocation: Evidence from Colombia and Chile', *Bulletin of World Health Organization*, Vol. 81, No. 2: 95–100.

Bossert T. and J. Beauvais (2001) 'Decentralization of Health Systems in Ghana, Zambia, Uganda and the Philippines: A Comparative Analysis of Decision Space', in *Health Policy and Planning* (December).

Campbell, T. (1997) 'Innovations and Risk-Taking: The Engine of Reform in Local Government in Latin America and the Caribbean', *Discussion Paper No. 367*, Washington, DC: World Bank.

CGAP (Consultative Group to Assist the Poor) (2004) *Building Inclusive Financial Systems: Donor Guidelines on Good Practice in Micro-Finance*, Washington, DC.

Conyers, D. (1985) 'Decentralization: A Framework for Discussion', in H. Hye (ed.), *Decentralization, Local Government and Resource Mobilization*, Comilla: Bangladesh Academy for Rural Development, pp. 22–42.

Corkery, J., A. Land and J. Bossuyt (1995) *The Process of Policy Formulation: Institutional Path or Institutional Maze*, Maastricht: European Centre for Policy Development and Management.

Cornea, G. A. and G. K. Helleiner (eds.) (1994) *From Adjustment to Development in Africa*, New York: St. Martin's Press.

Crook, R. C. (1994) 'Four Years of the Ghana District Assemblies in Operation: Decentralization, Democratization and Administrative Performance', *Public Administration and Performance*, No. 3: 339–64.

Crook, R. C. (1996) 'Democracy, Participation and Responsiveness: A Case Study of Relations between the Ivorian Communes and Their Citizens', *Public Administration*, Vol. 74, No. 4: 695–720.

Crook, R. C. and J. Manor (1994) *Enhancing Participation and Institutional Performance: Democratic Decentralization in South Asia and West Africa*, London: Overseas Development Administration.

Dia, M. (1996) *Africa's Management in the 1990s and Beyond: Reconciling Indigenous and Transplanted Institutions*, Washington, DC: World Bank.

Doe, L. (1998) 'Civil Service Reform in the countries of the West African Monetary Union', *International Social Science Journal*, No. 155: 125–44.

Ekeh, P. (1975) 'Colonialism and the Two Publics in Africa: A Theoretical Statement', *Comparative Studies in Society and History*, Vol. 17, No. 1: 91–112.

Elazar, D. (1987) *Exploring Federalism*, Tuscaloosa: University of Alabama Press.

Enemuo, F. (2000) 'Problems and Prospects of Local Governance', in G. Hyden, D. Olowu and W. Okoth-Ogendo (eds.), *African Perspectives on Governance*, Trenton: African World Press, pp. 181–204.

Esman, M. J. and N. T. Uphoff (1984) *Local Organizations: Intermediaries in Rural Development*, Ithaca, NY: Cornell University Press.

Fass, S. M and G. M. Desloovere (2004) 'Chad: Governance by the Grassroots', in D. Olowu and J. Wunsch, *Local Governance in Africa*, Boulder, CO: Lynne Rienner, pp. 155–80.

Fukasaku, K. and R. Hausmann (eds.) (1998) *Democracy, Decentralization and Deficits in Latin America*, Paris: Organisation for Economic Co-operation and Development.

Gboyega, A. (1998) 'Decentralization and Local Autonomy in Nigeria's Federal System: Crossing the Stream while Searching for Pebbles', in J. Barkan (ed.), *Decentralization and Democratisation in Sub-Saharan Africa*, Occasional Paper No. 49, University of Iowa, Iowa.

Gershberg, A. I. (1998) 'Decentralization, Recentralization and Performance of Accountability: Building an Operationally Useful Framework', *Development Policy Review*, Vol. 16: 405–31.

Geshberg, A. I. and D. R. Winkler (2004) 'Education Decentralization in Africa: A Review of Recent Policy and Practice', in *Building State Capacity in Africa: New Approaches, Emerging Lessons* Washington DC: World Bank Institute Development Studies, pp. 323–56.

Government of Ethiopia (1994) *The Constitution of the Federal Republic of Ethiopia* (unofficial English translation), Addis Ababa: Ministry of Justice.

Heller, P. and A. Tait (1983) *Government Employees and Pay: Some International Comparisons*, Washington, DC: International Monetary Fund.

Hertog, E. (1998) 'What Role for Local Government in Decentralised Cooperation?' *Discussion Paper No. 8*, Maastricht: European Centre for Policy Development and Management.

Hicks, U. K. (1961) *Development from Below: Local Government and Finance in Developing Countries of the Commonwealth*, Oxford: Clarendon Press.

Hulme, M. and D. Turner (1997) *Governance, Administration and Development: Making the State Work*, London: Macmillan.

Huntington, P. S. (1968) *Political Order in Changing Societies*, New Haven, CT: Yale University Press.

Hyden, G. (1983) *No Shortcuts to Progress: African Development Management in Perspective*, Berkeley: University of California Press.

Hyden, G. (1999) 'Governance and the Reconstitution of Political Order', in Richard A. Joseph (ed.), *State, Conflict, and Democracy in Africa*, Boulder, CO: Lynne Rienner, pp. 179–96.

IDEA (2004) *Democracy at the Local Level*, Internation Institute for Democracy and Election Assistance Hand Book Series No. 4, Stockholm.

Joseph, R. (1997) *Democracy and Prebendal Politics in Nigeria: The Rise and Fall of the Second Republic*, Boulder, CO: Lynne Rienner.

Joseph, R. (1999) *State, Conflict and Democracy in Africa*, Boulder, CO: Lynne Rienner.

Kickert, J. M., E. Klijn and J. F. M. Koppenjan (eds.) (1997) *Managing Complex Networks: Strategies for the Public Sector*, London: Sage.

Langrod, G. (1953) 'Local Government and Democracy', *Public Administration*, Vol. 31: 25–33.

Leftwich, A. (1993) 'Governance, Democracy and Development in the Third World', *Third World Quarterly*, Vol. 14, No. 3: 605–24.

Leighton, C. (1996) 'Strategies for Achieving Health Financing Reform in Africa', *World Development*, Vol. 24, No. 9: 1511–25.

Litvack, J., J. Ahmad and R. Bird (1997) *Rethinking Decentralization in Developing Countries, Poverty Reduction and Economic Management*, Washington, DC: World Bank.

Lubanga, F. (1995) 'Decentralization in Uganda: A country experience in reforming local government', in P. Langseth, S. Nogxina, D. Prinsloo and R. Sullivan (eds.), *Civil Service Reform in Anglophone Africa*, Washington, DC: Economic Development Institute/Overseas Development Administration, pp. 133–44.

Materu, J., T. Land, V. Hauck and J. Knight (2000) *Decentralised Cooperation and Joint Action*, Maastricht: European Centre for Development Policy Management.

Mawhood, P. (ed.) (1983) *Local Government in the Third World*, Chichester: Wiley.

Mawhood, P. and K. Davey (1980) 'Anglophone Africa', in D. C. Rowat (ed.), *International Handbook on Local Government Reorganization: Contemporary Developments*, Westport, CT: Greenwood Press, pp. 404–14.

McCarney, P. L. (1996) 'Reviving Local Government: The Neglected Tier in Development', in P. McCarney (ed.), *The Changing Nature of Local Governments in Developing Countries*, Toronto: Centre for Urban and Community Studies, pp. 3–32.

Nyerere, J. (1984) 'Interview', *Third World Quarterly*, Vol. 6, No. 4: 815–38.

Nzokenu, J. M. (1994) 'Decentralization and Democracy in Africa', *International Review of Administrative Sciences*, Vol. 60: pp. 213–27.

OECD (1997) *Evaluation of Programs of Promoting Participatory Development and Good Governance*, Synthesis report, Paris: Organization for Economic Co-operation and Development.

Olowu, D. (1988) *African Local Governments as Instruments of Economic and Social Development*, No. 1415, The Hague: International Union of Local Authorities.

Olowu, D. (1989) 'Local institutes and African Development', *Canadian Journal of African Studies*, Vol. 23, No. 2: pp. 201–31.

Olowu, D. (1990) 'Achievements and Problems of Federal and State Transfers to Local Governments in Nigeria since Independence', in L. Adamolekun, R. Robert and M. Laleye (eds.), *Decentralization Policies and Socio-Economic Development in Sub-Saharan Africa*, Washington, DC: Economic Development Institute, pp. 116–56.

Olowu, D. (1996) 'Decentralization in Africa: Appraising the Local Government Revitalization Strategy in Nigeria', in G. Nzongola-Ntalaja and M. C. Lee (eds.), *The State and Democracy in Africa*, Harare: SAPES Books, pp. 164–89.

Olowu, D. (1999a) 'Local Governance, Democracy and Development', in R. A. Joseph, *State, Conflict, and Democracy in Africa*, Boulder, CO: Lynne Rienner, pp. 285–98.

Olowu, D. (1999b) 'Building Strong Local Government through Networks between State and Non-governmental (Religious) Institutions in Africa', *Public Administration and Development*, Vol. 19, No. 4: 409–12.

Olowu, D. (2001) *Decentralization Policies and Practices under Structural Adjustment and Democratisation in Africa*, Geneva: United Nations Research Institute for Social Development.

Olowu, D., S. Ayo and B. Akande (1991) *Local Institutions and National Development in Nigeria*, Ile-Ife: Obafemi Awolowo University Press.

Olowu, D. and P. Smoke (1992) 'Determinants of Success in African Local Governments: An Overview', *Public Administration and Development*, Vol. 12, No. 1: 1–17.

Olowu, D. and J. S. Wunsch (1995) 'Decentralization, Local Government and Primary Health Care in Nigeria: An Analytical Study', *Journal of African Policy Studies*, Vol. 1, No. 3: 1–22.

Olowu, D. and J. S. Wunsch (eds.) (2004) *Local Governance in Africa: The Challenges of Democratic Decentralization* Boulder, CO: Lynne Rienner.

Ostrom, E. (1990) *Governing the Commons: The Evolution of Institutions of Collective Action* Cambridge: Cambridge University Press.

Ostrom, E. (1996) 'Crossing the Great Divide: Co-production, Synergy and Development', *World Development*, Vol. 24, No. 6: 1073–87.

Ostrom, E., L. Schroeder and S. Wynne (1993) *Institutional Incentives and Sustainable Development*, Boulder, CO: Westview Press.

Oyugi, W. O. (1990) 'Decentralised Development Planning and Management in Kenya: An Assessment', in L. Adamolekun, R. Robert and M. Laleye (eds.), *Decentralization Policies and Socio-Economic Development in Sub-Saharan Africa*, Washington, DC: Economic Development Institute, pp. 157–91.

Prud'homme, R. (1995) 'The Dangers of Decentralization', *World Bank Research Observer*, Vol. 2, No. 10: 201–10.

Rakodi, C. (ed.) (1997) *The Urban Challenge in Africa: Growth and Management of Large Cities*, Tokyo: United Nations University Press.

Regulska, J. (1993) 'Local Government Reform in Central and Eastern Europe', in R. J. Bennett (ed.), *Local Government in the New Europe*, London: Bellhaven Press, pp. 183–96.

Richards, P. (1985) *Indigenous Agricultural Revolution*, London: Hutchinson.

Riggs, F. W. (1964) *Administration in Developing Countries: The Theory of Prismatic Society*, Boston: Houghton Mifflin.

Rondinelli, D. (1981) 'Government Decentralization in Comparative Perspective', *International Review of Administrative Sciences*, Vol. 47, No. 2: 133–45.

Schiavo-Campo, S. (1998) 'Government and Pay: The Global and Regional Evidence', *Public Administration and Development*, Vol. 18, No. 5: 457–78.

Selznick, P. (1949) *T.V.A. and the Grassroots*, Berkeley: University of California Press.

Silverman, J. M. (1992) Public Sector Decentralization: Economic Policy and Sector Investment Programs, *Technical Paper No. 186*, Washington, DC: World Bank.

Silverman, J. M. (1997) 'Analysing the Role of the Public Sector in Africa: Implications for CSR Policies', in D. W. Brinkerhoff (ed.), *Policy Studies and Developing Nations*, Vol. 5: 159–86.

Smith, B. C. (1985) *Decentralization: The Territorial Dimension of the State*, London: Allen and Unwin.

Smith, B. (1996) 'Sustainable Local Democracy', *Public Administration and Development*, Vol. 16, No. 2: 163–78.

Smoke, P. (1994) *Local Government Finance in Developing Countries: The Case of Kenya*, Oxford: Oxford University Press.

Stren, R. E. (1989) 'Urban Local Government in Africa', in R. Stren and R. White (eds.), *African Cities in Crisis: Managing Rapid Urban Growth*, Boulder, CO: Westview Press, pp. 37–68.

Tendler, J. (1997) *Good Government in the Tropics*, Baltimore, MD: Johns Hopkins University Press.

Tibaigaina, M. R. (1998) *Regional Report on Decentralization: The Case of Uganda*, Municipal Development Programme, Mimeo, Harare.

Trager, L. (1995) 'Women Migrants and Rural–Urban Linkages in South-western Nigeria', in J. Baker and T. Aina (eds.), *The Migration Experience in Africa*, Uppsala: Nordiska Afrikainstitutet, pp. 269–88.

UNDP (1993) *Human Development Report 1993*, New York: Oxford University Press.

UNDP (1997) *Reconceptualising Governance*, Discussion Paper 2, New York: United Nations Development Programme.

United Nations (1965) *Decentralization for National and Local Development*, New York: United Nations.

United Nations (1991) *World Urbanization Prospects*, New York.

United Nations Centre for Human Settlements (1996) *An Urbanizing World: Global Report on Human Settlements* United Nations: Nairobi.

Vengroff, R. and O. J. Umeh (1997) 'A Comparative Approach to the Assessment of Decentralization Policy in Developing Countries', in D. W. Brinkerhoff (eds.), *Policy Analysis Methods in Developing Nations*, Greenwich, CT: JAI Press.

WHO (1997) *The Role of Local Government in Health: Comparative Experiences and Major Issues*, Division of Strategic Support to Countries in Greatest Need, Geneva: World Health Organization.

World Bank (1981) *Accelerated Development in Sub-Saharan Africa*, Washington, DC: World Bank.

World Bank (1989) *Sub-Saharan Africa: From Crisis to Sustainable Growth—A Long Term Perspective Study*, Washington, DC: World Bank.

World Development Report 1997, (1997) New York: Oxford University Press.

Wunsch, J. S. (1991) 'Sustaining Third World Infrastructure Investments', *Public Administration and Development*, Vol. 11, No. 1: 5–24.

Wunsch, J. S. and D. Olowu (eds.) (1995) *The Failure of the Centralized State: Institutions and Self-Governance in Africa*, second edition, San Francisco: Institute for Contemporary Studies.

Wunsch, J. S. and D. Ottemoeller (2004) 'Uganda: Multiple Levels of Local Governance', in D. Olowu and J. S. Wunsch (eds.), *Local Governance in Africa: The Challenges of Democratic Decentralization* Boulder, CO: Lynne Rienner, pp. 181–210.

9

Pubic-Private Partnerships and Pro-Poor Development: The Experience of the Córdoba Water Concession in Argentina

Andrew Nickson

Introduction

There has been a rapid growth in public–private partnerships in Argentina over the decade following the introduction of pioneering legislation in 1989. In the case of water supply and sanitation, contracts have been signed with the private sector in the capital city, Buenos Aires, as well as other major cities, including Córdoba, Formosa, Corrientes, Santa Fe, Mendoza and Tucumán. The Córdoba experience is unusual in two respects. First, it represents a rare example in which the municipality is not the legal representative of the public sector in the partnership arrangement with the private sector in the delivery of water supply within its own jurisdiction. Second, the ambitious nature of the long-term concession contract stands in contrast to the more limited nature of service contracts developed elsewhere in Latin America.

This chapter focuses on the extent and manner in which the concessionaire has addressed the needs of the urban poor in Córdoba and the implications for capacity-building within the municipality of Córdoba.[1] The broad political, administrative, economic and participatory context within which private sector participation has evolved in Argentina is examined first, followed by a review of the emergence of a favourable environment for public–private partnerships. This is followed by a description of the unusual institutional arrangement for the delivery of water and sanitation services in Córdoba, an outline of the content of the concession contract and a review of performance by the concessionaire. Next, the water needs of the urban poor are identified. Key issues that affect the poor are then highlighted, followed by a number of areas where capacity-building is needed in order to improve the role of the municipality in support of pro-poor activities in the water sector. The chapter concludes by identifying lessons for other municipalities from the Córdoba experience.

The context of private sector participation in Argentina

Several contextual factors have moulded the current environment for private sector participation in basic service provision in Argentina in general, and Córdoba in particular. The most important of these are: a long history of political centralization; a partially institutionalized system of local public administration; a deteriorating economic situation and growing poverty; and the limited development of citizen participation.

A long history of political centralization

Argentina is a federal nation with three levels of government: national, provincial and municipal. In addition to the federal government, there are 23 provincial governments and 1,719 municipal authorities. The 1853 Federal Constitution, still in force today, did not include any municipal legislation and made no reference to municipal autonomy. Instead, it empowered each province to approve its own constitution and to establish norms for the municipalities within its own jurisdiction. For over a century thereafter, provincial constitutions reflected the prevailing view that municipalities were mere administrative appendages of provincial government. During the military governments of 1966–73 and 1976–83 local government elections were abolished. Provincial governors and municipal mayors were appointed by the federal government. With the return to civilian rule in 1983, there was a new impetus towards municipal autonomy, as was reflected in the reform of provincial constitutions in Córdoba, La Rioja and Salta where municipalities now enjoy a significant degree of political autonomy. In some provinces, comprehensive municipal laws are sanctioned by the provincial legislature only, while in others, notably Córdoba, individual municipal charters may be drafted by a local citizens' convention, a procedure that is unique to Latin America (Nickson, 1995). In 1995 a local constituent assembly enacted a new such municipal code for the municipality of Córdoba.

The municipality of Córdoba, the capital of the province of Córdoba, has one of the largest areas of any major city in Latin America. On the map, it appears as an enormous 24 km square, measuring 576 sq. km. In demographic terms it is the second largest municipality in the country, with a population in 1999 of 1,339,164 and a budget of US$420million, giving a per capita expenditure of $314. The municipality is governed by a directly elected mayor *(alcalde)*, and a legislature comprising 31 councillors *(concejales)*. The mayor and councillors are elected concurrently for a four-year term of office. The deputy mayor presides over the municipal council without voting rights and the mayor may not seek immediate re-election.

Together with Porto Alegre (Brazil) and Montevideo (Uruguay), the municipality is a pioneer within Latin America in bringing local government closer to its citizens, with a network of nine neighbourhood offices, *Centros de Participación Comunal* (CPCs), located around the city.

A partially institutionalized system of local public administration

Local government in Argentina tends to have an unprofessional and over-staffed bureaucracy. This is a product of the political culture of clientelism that subordinates both provincial and local government to short-term party interests. Job tenure is limited, appointment procedures are non-transparent, professional merit is not the main factor in promotion, and staff turnover is rapid at election time. Following the return to democracy, municipal employment rose rapidly during the 1980s. This was primarily as a welfare mechanism to offset the increase in unemployment brought about by the impact of IMF structural adjustment policies. Given that the share of local government in gross domestic product did not rise during the period, employment growth was made possible only by a significant decline in the real income of municipal employees. In turn, this led to declining skill levels and higher rates of absenteeism. Gross overstaffing continues to be a major feature of local government in much of the country. As a result, personnel costs absorb the lion's share of recurrent expenditure, thereby greatly constraining the growth of capital expenditure.

In marked contrast to this prevailing situation, the municipality of Córdoba has a public administration system that is far more institutionalized. Although, as elsewhere in the country, there is no formal career system, the turnover of professional staff in response to changes in political leadership is far less pronounced. To some extent, this is the result of an unusual sixteen-year period of political stability (1985–99), during which two mayors from the same party each served two non-consecutive four-year terms of office. Nevertheless, when a different political party took office in 1999, the municipal administration was not subjected to the wholesale turnover of staff that is still the norm in many parts of Argentina. A contributory factor is the job stability for public sector employees enshrined in the provincial constitution (art. 23, para. 13).

A deteriorating economic situation and growing urban poverty

During the 1990s, under President Carlos Menem, Argentina underwent one the most rapid and deep-rooted processes of economic liberalization in the world. As a result of a mix of extensive tariff cutting and widespread privatization, the country was transformed from a highly protected economy to one of the most liberalized countries in the world. But the process was not without its social cost. From the mid-1990s Argentina has experienced a marked increase in income disparities and, more recently, the country has suffered a prolonged economic recession.

Córdoba is the major industrial centre of the country outside of the capital city of Buenos Aires. The twin effects of liberalization and economic recession have hit its industrial base hard. Nevertheless, the city has adapted more effectively than many parts of the country to the rapid process of liberalization and has sought to restructure its economic base in order to compete more effectively on the global market. The urban area of the city grew rapidly during the 1990s as residents moved out from the central area in search of their own homes and as its relative prosperity attracted an inflow of migrants in search of work from other more depressed parts of the country.

The limited development of citizen participation

On the surface at least, the city of Córdoba has a long history of citizen participation in local government. The territorial base for this tradition of participation is the neighbourhood, or *barrio*, with which citizens have developed a strong identification. Those *barrios* that are formally recognized by the municipality possess elected neighbourhood committees, known as *Comisiones Vecinales* (CVs). They were banned and repressed by the military government in the 1970s, but re-emerged with the return to civilian rule in 1983. The provincial constitution of Córdoba provides mechanisms that facilitate citizen involvement in municipal affairs. Among these are referendums, citizen initiatives that oblige the council to consider any issue of interest to them, and a system of popular recall under which an elected mayor may be removed from office before the expiry of his/her term of office.

However, the prevailing political clientelism in local government in Córdoba, as in most large cities in Argentina, has had a negative effect on citizen participation. The majority of the *Comisiones Vecinales*, rather than representing the local citizenry as a whole, have become closely identified with one or other political party. As such, they exert influence through personal contacts with leading municipal authorities rather than through the formal institutions of local government.[2] Under this political culture of clientelism, municipal councillors play a key role as brokers, negotiating 'patron–client' deals between the mayor and party supporters at the neighbourhood level. In mid-2000 there were around 300 legally recognized CVs in the municipality of Córdoba, of which 250 were actually functioning.

The emergence of a favourable environment for private sector participation

The privatization programme

Prompted by the severe fiscal crisis and hyper-inflation, in December 1989 the incoming Peronist government of President Carlos Menem initiated a major structural adjustment programme designed to reduce the public sector borrowing requirement radically. This consisted of economic liberalization (tariff and non-tariff reduction), financial and economic deregulation (transport, ports and postal service), a currency convertibility plan establishing parity between the Argentine peso and the US dollar, and reform of the state, involving the wholesale privatization of state companies. By the mid-1990s the effects of the privatization programme had been far-reaching. Some 20 per cent of the foreign debt outstanding in 1989 had been written off by debt-for-equity swaps. Total employment in thirteen previously state-owned companies had fallen from 260,000 in 1990, to 60,000 by 1993, with most of the reduction achieved through voluntary redundancies.

Although the major impact by far has been the transfer of federally-owned companies to the private sector, local government was also encouraged to extend the practice of contracting out service provision to the private sector. In December 1991 the incoming administration in the municipality of Córdoba for the period 1992–96 prepared a strategy document that included provision for private sector participation in basic service provision in the form of concession contracts (Marianacci, 1992). A study of the municipality of Córdoba, where virtually all basic urban services (street cleaning, solid waste collection, traffic lights, car parks, parks and gardens, and public lighting) were contracted out, has highlighted the lack of impact evaluation of municipal investment projects, the absence of any structure to monitor contract compliance by private contractors, and the absence of any overall sectoral co-ordination of municipal activities (Herzer, 1992).

The decentralization process

In 1987 a new provincial constitution was promulgated in Córdoba which gave municipalities a high degree of political, administrative and economic autonomy. It granted local government a wide range of responsibilities, most of which are held concurrently with the provincial government. Uniquely in Latin America, it enabled individual municipalities to draw up their own municipal code. The decentralization strategy pursued since 1989 in the province of Córdoba was based on the gradual transfer of responsibilities to local government by means of agreements or *convenios*, signed by the province and individual municipalities. Between 1989 and 1993, 2,450 such *convenios* were signed, covering the construction and maintenance of school buildings, the maintenance of paved roads and the operations of drinking water systems (Furlan, 1995). Interestingly, when responsibility for sewerage was transferred from the provincial government to the municipality in 1991, the agreement contemplated a similar transfer of responsibility for water supply within six months. This would have enabled far better co-ordination for urban planning because the latter already held responsibility for sanitation. It has been argued that the decision by the provincial government instead to retain ownership of the water assets and privatize service delivery by a concession contract was driven by fiscal considerations. By so doing, the province was assured of a sizeable revenue increase in the form of royalty payments, amounting to US$13million in 1999.

The regulatory environment

By the end of the millennium there was widespread dissatisfaction in Argentina at the laxity of regulation during the decade of privatization carried out by the Peronist government of President Menem (1989–99). In several cases, regulatory bodies were established after the key privatization decisions had been taken. High price rises and poor service quality were major sources of complaint. This criticism reached a high point during the power failure that blacked out large parts of Buenos Aires for ten days in February 1999. At that time regulatory agencies in general were strongly criticized in the media for their weakness.

At the federal level, in 2000 the incoming Partido Radical government sought to encourage greater competition among privatized utilities by clamping down on what are seen as abuses of privilege by private companies that have benefited from monopoly conditions under weak regulation for nearly a decade. This tighter regulatory stance by the federal government was mirrored by the incoming provincial government of Córdoba in May 2000, headed by the new Peronist Governor, José Manuel de la Sota. The regulatory framework for public utilities, including urban water supply, was radically altered by the creation of a new Secretariat for Control and Management of Contracts, *Secretaría de Control y Gestión de Concesiones*. Hitherto water regulation in the province had been the responsibility of the Water and Sanitation Department, *Departamento de Aguas y Saneamiento* (DAS), of the provincial government.

In addition, the new provincial government created a novel multi-sectoral regulatory agency, known as the *Ente Regulador de Servicios Publicos* (ERSEP), which will regulate a diverse range of privatized public services. The mixed bag of responsibilities of the new agency reflects the complex mosaic of public sector ownership under Argentina's federal system of government. For example, although Aguas Cordobesas supplies water only within the jurisdiction of the Municipality of Cordoba, the assets belong to the provincial government and not to the municipal government.

The new regulatory agency is collegiate in nature. Its six-member board comprises three members appointed by the governing party in the provincial assembly, two members from the opposition parties and one member representing consumers. This direct representation of consumer interests on a regulatory body is a unique case in the world, and reflects the widespread dissatisfaction among consumers over the Argentine privatization programme. But the direct inclusion of consumer interests in ERSEP has come in for criticism because of the danger of their 'regulatory capture' by the other political interests represented on the board. ERSEP will be financed through a 1.5 per cent levy on the tariffs of the privatized utilities, as well as any fines that it imposes. This levy has been criticized as excessively high.

In the particular case of urban water supply for the city of Córdoba, ERSEP contracts out responsibility for monitoring water quality to a state-owned laboratory that examines 600 samples per month. ERSEP also monitors implementation of the investment programme of the concessionaire, Aguas Cordobesas. The company submits daily, monthly and annual reports to ERSEP. It is still unclear whether the newly established ERSEP will play the role of a regulatory body, *ente regulador*, balancing the interests of consumers and of the private concessionaire, or whether it will play the role of contract enforcement, *orgáno de control*, on behalf of the provincial government. The confusion is enhanced by the fact that ERSEP is not an autonomous body, but does not report directly to the provincial governor either. Instead, it comes under the remit of the Ministry of Public Works of the provincial government.

The Córdoba partnership

The split in institutional responsibility for water and sanitation

Water supply in the city of Córdoba is a provincial responsibility, while sanitation is the responsibility of the municipality. This unusual division of responsibility for water and sanitation has an historical explanation. According to the 1923 constitution, water supply throughout Argentina was a municipal service but over time this responsibility was transferred to a federal entity, Obras Sanitarias de la Nación (OSN). In 1975, the federal government devolved responsibility for both water and sanitation from OSN to the provincial level. In the case of the province of Córdoba, this took the form of a newly created Empresa Provincial de Obras Sanitarias (EPOS) of the provincial government. This decision formed part of a national policy of decentralization. Next, in 1990 the provincial government transferred responsibility for sanitation to the municipality of Córdoba, while retaining responsibility for water supply. In 1997 it signed a concession contract with Aguas Cordobesas for water supply for the city of Córdoba. The municipality of Córdoba took no part in these negotiations, even though the area of the water concession was confined exclusively to the jurisdiction of the municipality.

The current institutional arrangement means that, although it is solely responsible for sanitation, the municipality of Córdoba has no formal involvement in urban water supply within its own jurisdiction. Nor is it involved with the regulation of Aguas Cordobesas and the monitoring of contract compliance by the concessionaire, both of which remain the sole preserve of the provincial government. The institutional split in responsibility for water and sanitation in the city of Córdoba makes the regulatory task of ERSEP more difficult because it does not report to the municipal government itself, even though the latter's jurisdiction is the same as the geographical area of the concession.

The content of the concession contract

On 21 April 1997 the provincial government of Córdoba signed a 30-year concession contract with Aguas Cordobesas for the operations of water supply and sanitation within the 24 sq. km jurisdiction of the municipality of Córdoba. The contract came into force in May 1997. Aguas Cordobesas has a paid-up capital of $30 million and is owned by a consortium of Argentina and foreign companies, in which the French utility multinational, Suez-Lyonnaise des Eaux is the largest shareholder. In turn, Suez-Lyonnaise des Eaux is the technical operator of Aguas Cordobesas.

The concession contract imposed the following stipulations on the concessionaire:

- Operate and maintain the 2,766-km pipe network.
- Achieve the following water coverage targets:
  Year 2 (1998)   75%
  Year 10 (2006)   82%
  Year 20 (2016)   96%
  Year 30 (2026)   97%
- Make an annual payment of $9,922,000 to the provincial government for exercising the concession.
- Pay a canon for water abstraction ($0.019/$m^3$) and for water transportation ($0.077/$m^3$).
- Reduce the average tariff by 8.2 per cent at the start of the concession.
- Carry out an investment programme of $150 million in the first two years.

Performance in contract implementation

The overall performance of the concessionaire to date is generally perceived as satisfactory by citizens and the provincial government. In the two years to March 1999 the number of inhabitants covered by the network increased from 1,000,000 to 1,140,000. The number of connections rose from 208,526 in 1997 to 223,462 in 1999. By mid-2000 service coverage for water had reached 87 per cent, compared with only 40 per cent for sewerage. Annual gross income in 1999 was $65million. Net profit was $5million, representing an 11 per cent rise over 1998. In the same year Aguas Cordobesas paid $9,922,000 for exercising the concession and $3,149,668 for water abstraction and transportation, amounting to a total royalty payment of $13,071,668. Staff numbers fell from around 1,300 before the concession was awarded to 436 in 1999, giving an acceptable ratio of 1.95 staff per 1,000 connections. Aguas Cordobesas had provided three direct benefits to consumers since the contract was signed in 1997: the 8 per cent price reduction in average tariffs, an end to water cut-offs and improved water quality, leading to a sharp drop in sales of bottled water. There is a further indirect benefit in the form of the annual $13 million royalty payment to the provincial government.

Despite this favourable performance to date, two issues could have a potentially negative effect of this perception in the future. First, there is the question of policy towards supply cut-offs. To date Aguas Cordobesas has not cut supply to customers who have defaulted on their water bills. However, in February 2000, the company began legal proceedings in order to obtain debts totalling $2 million from 2,500 customers, equivalent to 1.1 per cent of the total number of customers, who have refused to pay their bills ever since the company was awarded the concession in 1997. There is little evidence that these debts are linked to problems of ability to pay among low-income residents. Rather, they are the consequence of a long-standing and widespread practice of non-payment of utility bills across the social spectrum.

Second, there is the question of the sequencing of the investment pro-gramme. Under the terms of the contract, Aguas Cordobesas must achieve 97 per cent coverage by 2026 (year 30). The total investment required to meet this target has been estimated at around $460 million. In contrast to the concession contract for Buenos Aires, the Córdoba contract specifies ten-yearly coverage targets, and not five-yearly targets, within the frame-work of the total period of the overall concession. For this reason, there is some risk of 'backloading', whereby the concessionaire postpones major investment towards the end of the concession period. In this eventuality, citizens of low-income neighbourhoods would be the main stakeholders to suffer from delays in connection to the network.

Water and the urban poor in Córdoba

By mid-2000, some 196,000 citizens of Córdoba, equivalent to 14 per cent of the municipal population of 1.4 million, were still not connected to the piped network operated by Aguas Cordobesas on behalf of the provincial government. The fact that so many residents are not connected to the water network is largely the outcome of poor municipal management prac-tices in the past. First, it was common for real estate developers to contra-vene municipal regulations by selling plots without providing basic services (water and electricity), a practice which has now been outlawed. Second, local politicians often encouraged residents to make illegal connections as a conscious strategy to put pressure on the former provincial water utility, EPOS, to invest in extension of the network. Unfortunately, in most cases, EPOS was either unwilling or unable to respond to these pressures.

Table 9.1   Córdoba: population not connected to piped network in 2000

Situation	Form of provision	Population	Share
Independent private providers	Autonomous	84,000	6%
Neighbourhood villas without land titles	Illegal /vendors	70,000	5%
Neighbourhood barrios with land titles	Vendors/municipal tankers	42,000	3%
Total		196,000	14%

Source: Author's own estimates.

Those households not connected to the piped network (Table 9.1) may be classified into three different situations, as follows:

- Neighbourhoods served by independent private providers, *prestadores particulares*, that account for 6 per cent of the city population. These are often supplied from local wells and the water quality is poor. The pipework is poor, of narrow diameter and encrusted with lime. As a result, it cannot withstand high pressure and needs replacing for connection to the piped network.
- Neighbourhoods occupying private or state-owned land without titles. There are an estimated 40 such sites, which are known as *villas*. Together, they accounted for 54,000 people in 1998, but their population is estimated to have risen to 70,000 by mid-2000, equivalent to 5 per cent of the city population. They are often located adjacent to railway lines, main roads or occupy enclaves close to the city centre. They are usually served by illegal connections. Given the lack of titling and the desirability of relocation in the longer-term, the solution is to supply standpipes rather than individual house connections.
- Neighbourhoods with land titles but without any formal connection to the network, that account for 3 per cent of the city population. Some 30 such neighbourhoods, *barrios*, are not connected to the piped network. These are served either by precarious clandestine connections or by private and municipal water tankers, or by a mix of both. In most cases the illegal connections did not follow the technical norms of the water utility, EPOS, resulting in a narrow diameter pipe that causes problems of bursts and low pressure. Again, the solution is to replace an existing connection or to install a new connection to the piped network.

Although not having any formal responsibility for urban water supply within its jurisdiction, the municipality of Córdoba has collaborated since 1998 on several pilot projects aimed at connecting poor communities much earlier than envisaged under the long-term plan for extending the piped network. Two funding sources have been crucial in order to implement these projects. First, the municipality has contributed an investment grant from a special local development fund, the *Fondo de Acción Solidaria* (FAS). Second, the municipality has accessed a federal job-creation scheme, the *Plan Trabajar*, under which long-term unemployed men are identified by CVs and paid $200 per month (one third of the minimum wage) for a five-hour daily shift as unskilled labourers. The pilot projects are carried out as a tripartite arrangement between the municipality, which contributes finance, Aguas Cordobesas, which contributes technical assistance, and the community, which contributes voluntary unskilled labour. The results have varied considerably, as shown by a review of four small-scale pilot projects to connect poor neighbourhoods to the piped network (Table 9.2). Two were relatively successful (Barrio Quebracho and Estación Flores), while two experienced delays caused by conflicts over the control of funds (San Ignacio and Parque Liceo-3ra Vía). Interestingly, the successful projects were in neighbourhoods that were both previously supplied by private vendors and in which the community participated in the project by supplying voluntary labour. The success of the two pilot projects in Barrio Quebracho and Estación Flores was linked to three factors: transparency of the leadership in the management of grant aid; a non-political approach that encouraged the participation of community members in the project; and a centralized leadership that was willing to castigate members who were unwilling to make their own contribution to the communal effort.

Table 9.2   Features of pro-poor pilot projects

Feature	Quebracho	Estación Flores	San Ignacio	Parque Liceo- 3ra Vía
Population	2,600	3,800	2,000	5,400
Size of FAS grant	$100,000	$48,000	$70,000	$150,000
Plan Trabajar programme	Yes	No	Yes	No
Voluntary community labour	Yes	Yes	No	No
Work carried out directly by Aguas Cordobesas	No	No	No	Yes
Previous form of supply	Private vendors	Private vendors and some illegal connections	Illegal connections	Illegal connections
Meters installed	No	No	No	No
Project completed	Yes	Yes	No	Yes

Key issues

The situation that has developed in Córdoba during the implementation of the concession contract since 1997 is complex and involves several uncommon practices. Yet despite their lack of formal involvement, the mayor and most councillors seem satisfied with the performance of the concessionaire to date and the municipal council is broadly in favour of further private sector initiatives in service delivery. A number of the key issues affecting the municipality are discussed further in this section.

The water tariff structure and the urban poor

The current water tariff structure in Córdoba is both complex and inequitable. A mix of factors – both volumetric charging and property-based charging – determines the tariff. All householders pay the same standing charge that entitles them to a minimum volume, one that is directly related to the size of property. In practice this has two negative effects on equity. First, the property-based standing charge is extremely regressive with regard to the size of property. The larger the property size, the greater the minimum volume permitted under the standing charge. In practice, for higher-income families living in larger properties, the minimum volume entitlement incorporated within the standing charge is extremely high. Consequently, very few high-income consumers end up paying the mildly progressive tariff rates incorporated in the step tariff. Second, even for those consuming in excess of the volume permitted under the standing charge, the actual step tariff applied is only mildly progressive. This is because properties are not individually classified but are grouped into broad band geographical zones. High-value properties in lower band zones benefit from this arrangement, while low-value properties in high band zones suffer.

The concession contract signed in 1997 stated that metering would be gradually introduced and that new domestic connections would have meters installed. Aguas Cordobesas did install 50,000 new water meters from 1997 to 2000. Yet no meters have been installed in the four pilot projects for low-income communities that were examined in this research. At the time of writing, ERSEP was negotiating with Aguas Cordobesas for the introduction of a so-called 'social tariff' for low-income families. In the meantime, the company was not even charging for water in the above-mentioned pilot projects.

The linkage between land titling and coverage targets

The absence of a land titling programme poses a major obstacle to the development of pro-poor private sector participation in Córdoba. The poorest 5 per cent of the city's population live in the so-called '*villas*'. These are a patchwork of densely populated squatter settlements, often not far from the city centre, where landless families have constructed rudimentary housing on private or public land. Because residents do not have land titles, there is no legal requirement on the concessionaire to extend the piped network into these communities. Although the contract between the provincial government and Aguas Cordobesas requires the latter to achieve 97 per cent water coverage by its expiry date, it remains unclear whether this target includes that part of the city population living in the *villas*. According to the managing director of Aguas Cordobesas, no mention was made of the specific problem of connection and payment for residents of the *villas* when the company submitted its bid for the 1997 contract.

The provision of water tankers to the *villas*

At present, it is the municipality (and not Aguas Cordobesas) that supplies water to those citizens (mainly living in *villas*) who are not connected to the piped network. Aguas Cordobesas provides the water, for which no charge is apparently made, to the municipality. Demand for water is increasing as a result of population growth within the *villas*. Residents here are increasingly dependent on water supplied from municipal water tankers.

The takeover of small-scale private suppliers

At present, some 50,000 residents of Córdoba are supplied by small private water companies, *prestadores particulares*, and water co-operatives. Many of these operators supply water at a higher cost and of lower quality than Aguas Cordobesas. There is a generally agreed policy gradually to reduce the number of such private operators and to absorb these systems within the piped network operated by the concessionaire. However, it seems that the 1997 contract did not spell out specific time-linked targets for Aguas Cordobesas with regard to absorbing the operations of these private water companies. In 1997, 44 such private systems were in operation, and by mid-2000 eleven had been transferred to Aguas Cordobesas. The new provincial regulatory body, ERSEP, is actively involved in such negotiations. Most of these systems operate under contracts signed originally with the provincial government, although some were signed with the municipality. In practice most of the contracts have expired. Consequently, there is no legal requirement for compensation when supply is transferred to Aguas Cordobesas.

The division of responsibility for bearing the cost of connection

According to the tender documents for the 1997 concession contract, the responsibility of Aguas Cordobesas is only to construct the primary pipeline in extending the network. Responsibility for the secondary pipeline (defined as less than 160 mm diameter) and residential connections are the responsibility of the municipality and/or individual households. Many residents in low-income neighbourhoods contest this view. They believe that the concessionaire alone should bear the cost of secondary pipeline. In any case, whatever is the distribution of the overall cost, co-operation between Aguas Cordobesas and the municipality is essential in order to resolve this issue on a case-by-case basis. This is because of their common interest to achieve the coverage targets, even though the municipality is not a signatory to the contract itself.

The lack of integration of the water sector within strategic planning of the city

Despite the approval over the years of several master plans, *plan director*, with geographical zonification, in practice these have not been used as the basis for guiding the growth of the city. Instead, powerful real estate companies have decided the direction and pace of city growth. Typically, the municipality has granted approval to real estate companies for new residential developments without any prior consideration of the cost implications for basic service provision. Hence there has been minimal co-ordination with the long-term investment programme of Aguas Cordobesas for extending the piped network. In practice, this often means that the water investment programme has to be adjusted at short notice to accommodate such demands.

Building municipal capacity in support of a pro-poor PPP

Although the municipality of Córdoba has no legal involvement in the public–private partnership for urban water supply in the city, capacity building at the local level is crucial to the success of pro-poor public–private initiatives carried out within the context of the concession contract. This section examines the extent to which the municipality has developed a range of such core and poverty-related competencies.

Basic understanding of the operating context for service partnerships

Although the municipality has a detailed understanding of the extent and nature of poverty within its own jurisdiction, the provincial government paid little attention to the water needs of the urban poor during negotiation of the concession. For example, the contract stipulates that domestic connections and new secondary network (defined as less than 160 mm diameter pipe) are the responsibility of residents, and not the concessionaire. Although new residential developments typically incorporate this work within the house sale price, this stipulation discriminates against low-income residents in long-established neighbourhoods that are not yet connected to the network. Through its growing involvement in the poverty alleviation programme of the federal government, notably the *Plan Trabajar* work programme, the municipality has developed a much deeper understanding of the poverty context.

Strategic understanding of opportunities and constraints of public–private partnerships in urban management

Both the provincial government and the municipality display a limited awareness of the potential value of private sector participation in the context of poverty reduction strategies. In part, this is because until recently Argentine municipalities have only had a rhetorical competence for poverty reduction activities. In practice, they have played a minimal role in such activities, confining their explicit 'contribution' to overstaffing with low-paid workers. For this reason, although the municipality views the experience of private sector participation in water supply as broadly favourable, this is basically because of its major contribution to improved service delivery in general, rather than for any explicit contribution that it makes to poverty reduction.

Project preparation

When negotiating the joint venture in 1996–97, the provincial government was able to build on the prior national experience of the water and sanitation concession for Buenos Aires to Aguas Argentinas. However, the provincial government did not display any ability to initiate and prepare project documents. Instead, it reacted to a standard proposal put forward by the eventual private sector concessionaire. There is little evidence that the provincial government displayed ability during the contract negotiations to incorporate the particular needs of the urban poor. The municipality was not formally involved in these negotiations. But there does not appear to have been any lobbying by poor neighbourhoods on the provincial government, either directly or mediated through the municipality, to ensure that their needs would be taken into consideration during these negotiations. Consequently, there was no sense, from the outset, of a four-partner arrangement between the province, the private sector, the municipality and local communities. Instead, it was perceived exclusively as a contractual arrangement between the provincial government and the private concessionaire.

Understanding of and ability to engage with civil society

There is growing awareness in the municipality of the need to encourage and strengthen genuine community involvement in basic service provision in general, and in the water and sanitation sector in particular. The problem faced by the municipality is that past practices of clientelism have left a legacy of weak civil society organizations that have often lost credibility because of their manipulation by politicians. In the negotiation and implementation of pilot projects, the municipality lacks skills in acting as a 'broker' between the local community and the private company. At present it is by far the weakest link in the triangular arrangement. As a result, the concessionaire usually deals directly with the community without any effective participation by the municipality. There is growing recognition within the municipality that in order for pro-poor urban water supply projects to succeed, they must have a more active presence in the neighbourhoods, *barrios*, themselves in order to engage in a confidence-building dialogue with residents.

Basic knowledge of financing arrangements

During the negotiation of the contract, the provincial government displayed limited understanding of the special financing needs affecting the urban poor. With regard to the cost of connection to the network, the question of who would bear the cost of the secondary network and meter installation remained unclear in the contract. This is still the subject of some controversy, with communities arguing that the concessionaire should bear the cost, while the latter argues that the cost should be borne by individual households. It seems also that the questions of affordability and willingness to pay were not explicitly addressed when the contract was negotiated despite the fact that it established performance indicators in the form of extending coverage to 97 per cent of the target population by the end of the concession period. In practice, the municipality rather than the provincial government has subsequently acted as intermediary in response to concerns expressed by poor communities over connection charges and affordability.

Understanding of capacity-building

The provincial government displays a keen understanding of the importance of capacity building with regard to regulatory matters and contract compliance, but less so with regard to pro-poor policy-making. Although it has no formal involvement in the concession contract for water supply, the municipality has the advantage of a technical team specializing in the closely related area of sanitation. The municipality is addressing this problem by taking a very pro-active role in the training of a 'new generation' of community leaders in the management of community development projects, who, it is hoped, will be more representative of their communities. In this way it is hoped to break down the deep-rooted practice of political clientelism, under which corrupt politicians have for long manipulated community organisations and their leadership. To this end, in May 2000, the municipality established a training school for community leaders.

Strategic management and supervision of contract

The strategic management capacity of the municipality – to monitor and evaluate whether the service is being delivered efficiently and effectively, to manage non-compliance of contract obligations and to revise arrangements in response to impact assessment – is extremely limited because of the legal ownership of the assets by the provincial government, which signed the contract. In practice, the municipality can only exercise this strategic management capacity through informal pressure on the provincial government. The effectiveness of this pressure, not easy at the best of times, is called into question at times when the provincial and municipal tiers of government are controlled by opposing political parties, such has occurred since 1999. At present, the absence of serious city-wide strategic planning by the municipality means that ERSEP, the regulatory body of the provincial government, cannot monitor the activities of Aguas Cordobesas within the framework of a wider concern for the balanced and sustainable growth and development of the city as a whole.

Conclusions: lessons for other municipalities

The Córdoba case study demonstrates that, even where it is has no formal involvement in the institutional arrangement of the water sector, the municipality still has an important role to play in promoting the water needs of the urban poor. It also highlights the importance of the municipality in promoting capacity-building among community leaders in order to defend the interests of the urban poor. While several aspects of the Córdoba case are unusual and unlikely to be widely replicated, it nevertheless provides important lessons for other municipalities engaged in public–private partnerships.

The separation of responsibility for water and sanitation weakens the regulatory role of the public sector

The force of the regulatory role that the public sector undertakes in PPPs is jeopardized by the separation of responsibility for water and sanitation between different tiers of government. The lack of symmetry between the provincial ambit of the asset-owner and the municipal jurisdiction of the concession contract dulls the overall regulatory role of the public sector, at the same time enhancing the bargaining strength of the private concessionaire.

The absence of a career service within the public sector calls into question the sustainability of private sector participation in UWS

The lack of job security and constant rotation of senior and middle-ranking staff within the provincial government and its regulatory body produces a structural imbalance between the public sector owner and the private concessionaire. The institutional memory of the concession arrangement becomes embodied in the private concessionaire. This superior knowledge soon translates into a power imbalance between the two parties.

The representation of consumer interests within regulatory bodies is questionable

The direct representation of the interests of water users on a multi-person and multi-sectoral regulatory body, such as ERSEP, is questionable for two reasons. First, where traditions of political clientelism are strong, there is the strong risk of their capture by political interests. This is especially the case where the other members of the ERSEP board are direct political nominees. Second, in the case of such multi-sectoral agencies, the specific concerns of water users are subsumed with a general concern for consumer interests.

Leadership training for citizen participation should be carried out independently of the municipality

Where traditions of political clientelism are strong, municipal efforts to train a new generation of more representative community leaders should be contracted out to independent bodies, such as universities or NGOs. They should not be carried out 'in-house' for fear of manipulation by the very forces that the training is designed to eradicate.

A structured approach to pro-poor initiatives is advisable, with legally binding written agreements between stakeholders

Pro-poor initiatives for UWS are often complex, and require the active involvement of many different stakeholders in order to succeed. The Córdoba experience suggests that such initiatives may grind to a halt because of disputes over 'who does what'. In order to avoid this, a more structured approach is required, with legally binding written agreements from the outset that spell out the respective responsibilities of different stakeholders.

Local champions are important in explaining why some pro-poor initiatives are more successful than others

The Córdoba experience suggests that the degree of charisma and selflessness of community leaders are important elements in explaining the differential impact of pro-poor initiatives in UWS. A transparent and non-political leadership style, as well as a willingness to castigate members who are unwilling to make their own personal contribution to the communal effort are key factors necessary in order to sustain the active participation of community members to successful project completion.

Notes

1. The study was carried out as part of the DFID-funded Building Municipal Capacity for Private Sector Participation research project led by GHK International, in March 2000.
2. Although evidence from the municipalities of Resistencia and Neuquén points to the emergence of more independent citizen associations which suggests a gradual rejection of the clientelist relationship with local government authorities (Pírez, 1991: 121–46; Herzer and Pírez, 1992: 95–121).

References

Artana, D., Navajas, F. and Urbiztondo, S. (1996) *Regulación, organización e incenntivos: la economía política de los servicios de agua potable – el caso argentino*, Buenos Aires: Fundación de Investigaciones Económicas Latinoamericanas.

FIEL (1999) *La regulación de la competencia y de los servicios públicos: teoría y experiencia argentina reciente*, Buenos Aires: Fundación de Investigaciones Económicas Latinoamericanas.

Furlan, J. L. (1995) *Descentralización y desarrollo municipal*, Córdoba: Instituto para el Desarrollo Municipal. Ch. 3: Como descentralizar? La experiencia de la Provincia de Córdoba.

GHK (2000) *Research Framework for Building Municipal Capacity for Private Sector Participation*, DFID Research project R7398.

Herzer, H. (1992) *Gestión urbana en ciudades medianas seleccionadas de América Latina: el caso de la ciudad de Córdoba, Argentina*, Buenos Aires: CENTRO.

Herzer, H. and Pírez, P. (eds.) (1988) *Gobierno de la ciudad y crisis en la Argentina*, Buenos Aires: IIED.

Marianacci, G. (1992) *Gestión urbana en Córdoba, Argentina: la perspectiva del municipio*, Santiago: Economic Commission for Latin America.

Municipalidad de Córdoba (1995) *Carta Orgánica de la Ciudad de Córdoba*.

Municipalidad de Córdoba (1998) *Código Electoral Municipal* (Ordenanza No. 9846).

Nickson, R. A. (1995) *Local government in Latin America*, Boulder, CO: Lynne Rienner, Chapter 10: Argentina.

Nickson, R. A. (1997) 'The Public–Private mix in urban water supply', *International Review of Administrative Sciences*, Vol. 63, No. 2: 165–86.

Pírez, P. (1991) *Municipio, necesidades sociales y política local*, Buenos Aires: IIED.

Tecco, C. (1994) 'Los municipios y la gestión del desarrollo local y regional', *Administración Pública y Sociedad* (IIFAP, Universidad Nacional de Córdoba), Vol. 6, No. 9 (December): 93–104.

Conclusion

Public Sector Reform – What are the Lessons from Experience?

George A. Larbi and Yusuf Bangura

Public sector reform is a live issue in developing countries. This will continue to be so as long as governments continue to seek ways of modernizing their public administration systems in order to improve service delivery, respond to domestic and external pressures and meet the challenges of globalization. The contributors to this volume have examined various aspects of public sector reforms drawing on examples from a variety of developing countries. A common thread that runs through all the chapters is that reforms are driven by a combination of factors, notably fiscal and economic crises, the influence of international financial institutions and donor agencies, and domestic pressures. Some factors are more relevant to some contexts than others. For example, fiscal crisis and external donor influence seem to be more prominent drivers of reforms in poor and aid dependent countries in Africa than elsewhere in the developing world. Thus, as Therkildsen (Chapter 2) concludes, the reform agenda in countries do not just reflect national and local concerns but also international priorities, approaches and pressures.

Whilst the new public management (NPM) has had a significant influence on the design of reforms, the actual implementation is rather thin on the ground and the outcomes are uncertain. At the same time there are significant non-NPM public sector reforms such as decentralization and pay and employment reforms. This concluding chapter draws together lessons from the experiences of reforms and suggests ways forward.

Perspectives on recent reform experience

A recent workshop on pubic service reforms in five African countries (Ghana, Kenya, Tanzania, Uganda and Zambia) highlighted the following lessons captured by Kiragu (2002):

- public service reforms are more crucial to developing countries because of the need for fiscal stability and strategic management of available resources to prioritise service delivery improvement and the need to meet the challenges of globalization;

- there has been significant public service reform gains (e.g. streamlining of government structures and improved organizational capacity) but limited impact on service delivery;
- major problems and constraints persist because of difficulty of sustaining support at all levels, weak implementation capacity, resources constraints and poor incentives;
- there are dangers of reversals and inertia; some of the gains in cost-containment measures such as downsizing have been reversed in some countries (e.g. Ghana and Kenya);
- early progress is crucial to achieve and sustain the broad support of the public and politicians;
- there is a need for new impetus to focus on service delivery improvements;
- there is a need to strengthen the link between public service reform programmes and sector-wide programmes (SWPs);
- institutional pluralism is imperative for sustainable service delivery improvements: promoting non-state providers' participation in the delivery of basic services and decentralization of service delivery to local levels and communities; and
- donor and other external assistance could be more effectively channelled, for example by making less use of expensive external technical assistance and support local expertise, and by gradually shifting from project-oriented approaches to sector-wide approaches (SWAPs) in public service reform programmes.

The World Bank has provided significant support to the public service (particularly civil service) reform programmes in a number of developing countries – about 169 operations in 80 countries between 1987 and 1998 (World Bank, 1999). A review of these reforms provide further lessons, including:

- lack of performance measures for assessing civil service reform progress, leading to lack of accountability;
- limited attention and role given to strategic management and cultural change;
- absence of coordination arrangements and checks and balances; and
- failure to appreciate labour market institutional constraints.

Overall, reforms have not generated sustained improvement in government performance, especially in service delivery. Learning from these lessons, the Bank (and some bilateral donors) are adopting a much broader approach to reforms that include shifting from project to programmes and linking civil service reforms with other institutional reforms. The rest of this chapter will expand on some of the lessons learned, whilst drawing on the contributions to this volume.

NPM – the potential for developing countries

There has been a lot of debate about the applicability of the NPM model to different cultural contexts (cf. Schick, 1998; Batley, 1999; Batley and Larbi, 2004, and this volume). As the contributors to this volume suggest, some developing countries have introduced elements of NPM, though not in a systemic or comprehensive way. There have been some successes. For example, contracting out has delivered efficiency gains in some cases by reducing the cost of certain services (e.g. road maintenance in some African countries and port management in Malaysia). However, in the social sectors, such as health and education, one has to be more cautious. It is also clear that the executive agency model seems to be working in some contexts (e.g. Jamaica's Registrar-General). However, implementation of NPM-type reforms remains patchy and elusive as Therkildsen (Chapter 2) and Nickson (Chapter 3) argue. Consequently, reform outcomes and impacts have been limited. This is also the case for non-NPM reforms such as decentralization, fiscal decentralization and pay and employment reforms (see Olowu, Smoke and McCourt respectively, this volume).

Thus traditional hierarchical bureaucracies in developing countries have not been substantially replaced by decentralized and contractual relationships. Most public services functions continue to be performed in hierarchical and large bureaucracies (Manning, 2001; Batley and Larbi, 2004). Overall, whether or not NPM is appropriate to developing countries depends on the context, timing and necessary preconditions. NPM presents a menu of ideas for reforms in the public sector and developing countries do not have to adopt the whole package in one comprehensive reform programme. As we elaborate later in this concluding chapter, selectivity, incrementalism and sequencing to match implementation capacity and context may be more effective approaches to public sector reforms in developing countries than comprehensive and often overlapping reforms. The experience of public sector reforms in the 1980s and 1990s suggests that the comprehensive approach, trying to undertake several reforms simultaneously, tend to overtax the capacity of already weak reforming organizations.

The importance of institutional context

Following from the previous section, it is also apparent that reforms have to be sensitive to local context and conditions and tailored to regional and countries' circumstances. In South Africa, it is apparent that reforms have been significantly shaped by the experience of history and less externally driven compared to other countries in the sub-region. (Therkildsen, Chapter 2). Nickson (Chapter 3) also notes that the dominance of administrative law and the absence of a traditional Weberian bureaucracy and a professional civil service in most Latin American countries have meant the lack of a solid foundation for NPM-type reforms such as executive agencies. Creating semi-autonomous agencies will require changes in legal and institutional frameworks. This is consistent with variations in NPM-driven public sector reform experiences in Europe and elsewhere (Ridley, 1996; Christensen and Lægreid, 2002). Different countries have different legal, political and administrative systems rooted in their historical and cultural traditions, which influence the content and path of reform processes. Even in the same country (e.g. the UK) the same reform ideas, such as autonomization/agencification and 'contractualization', have worked differently in different sectors (cf. Boyne et al., 2003). For example, in examining the decentralization of the British civil service, Rhodes et al. (2003) found that reforms have 'created more territorially differentiated and institutionally federated civil service than previously existed' in England and Wales, Scotland and Northern Ireland (ibid.: 2). Part of the explanation for the differentiation in public management reforms lies in the history of the evolution of the administrative systems in the different nations. Thus, as Pollitt (2002: 277) notes, 'path-dependent explanations fit public management rather well'. Similar reform pressures and ideas tend to work differently in different countries and contexts. Thus the process and outcome of reforms may be different from the 'home countries' of the reform idea.

Taking account of politics and process issues in introducing reforms

Some of the failures and weakness of the public sector reform in developing countries may be traced to the lack of attention to politics and process issues in the design, introduction, implementation and management of reform. Reforms in the 1980s and 1990s focused more on issues of *what to do* and less on issues of *how to do it*. Politics were often downplayed or ignored. One would agree with Therkildsen that reform implementation is highly political because it redefines the power relationships between state and society, between politicians and bureaucrats, between service providers and users, and between different government organizations (see also Caiden, 1991; Bekke et al., cited in Therkildsen, this volume). It is therefore vital to understand who the key actors in the reform process are and what their incentives and interests in reforms are. In the context of developing countries, the key actors in reforms include state elites (bureaucrats and politicians), interests groups (e.g. trade unions and other civil society groups) and donors (multilateral and bilateral). Some reforms may increase the influence of one group at the expense of the others. For example, executive agencies tend to increase the autonomy and authority of public managers at the expense of politicians and parent ministries who may oppose or seek to sabotage such reforms. Decentralization tends to increase the authority and resources available to local governments at the expense of central government and its agencies.

It is also worth noting that reforms with a strong emphasis on fiscal stability and use of budgetary instruments tend to increase the power of the Ministry of Finance and/or economic planning/development. This was noticeable in the 1980s and 1990s in most developing countries that undertook structural adjustment programmes where the Ministry of Finance also played a leading role in pushing through reforms (e.g. in Ghana, Malawi, Tanzania and Uganda). The current shift among some donors from project-based funding to general budget support (GBS) has potentially strengthened the power of the Ministry of Finance *vis-à-vis* sector ministries. Under GBS, donors contribute directly to partner governments' overall budget account. This potentially changes the power dynamics and gives finance (and perhaps planning ministries) a greater pivotal role and more control over resource allocation to sector ministries and other public organizations. Understanding the change in power dynamics and how these could be used to leverage change in the public sector are issues for further research.

Understanding the political dynamics of reforms also requires appreciation of interest group politics and public opinion, which could raise the political stakes in certain types of reforms (e.g. pay and employment reforms, user fees) (Batley and Larbi, this volume). The political feasibility of reforms may partly depend either on the ability of these groups to mobilize for or against specific reforms, or to wield influence over reform decisions. This is evident in the case of South Africa, where the Congress of South African Trade Unions uses its close association with the government of the African National Congress to have a strong voice in and influence over the design of reforms (Therkildsen, this volume).

Therkildsen also points out how the unexpected pay rise for teachers in Tanzania in 1997 was influenced by the Teachers Union. There also have been cases where reforms were either stymied or the rules of fiscal discipline suspended close to elections, as happened in Ghana before the 1992 and 1996 elections; Malawi in the period of transition to democracy; and Tanzania in the period leading to the 2000 presidential, national and local elections. In all these cases there were significant increases in public sector pay close to elections. In the case of Ghana, this led to the suspension of World Bank loans. Thus pay reforms can be manipulated for political gains. The vulnerability of public sector reforms to politics is also illustrated by Nickson's example of how political changes and setbacks during the second term of President Cardozo of Brazil effectively shelved previous plans for administrative reforms and reversed a programme to create executive agencies. This was partly blamed on resistance from trade unions and on patrimonial politicians who feared losing opportunities for patronage.

Another political dimension of public sector reforms is the wave of democratization reforms in most developing countries since the late 1980s through the 1990s. As Bangura (this volume) notes, most countries undergoing public sector reforms are also grappling with complex and sometimes fragile democratization and consolidation processes. We know little about the relationship between public sector reforms and the democratization processes in developing countries; the subject has not received much attention in research and academic writing. However, it is reasonable to hypothesize that democratization (particularly competitive politics) redefines the environment for public sector reforms and raises the political stakes in reforms. It creates the political space and opportunity for citizens to demand reforms or for some groups to voice concerns and/or oppose certain aspects of reforms. The examples of public sector pay awards (cited above) in the period leading to elections and the tendency for elected governments to delay or even withdraw support for certain types of reforms, provide anecdotal evidence of the potential influence of the democratization process on public sector reforms.

Recent work by Grindle (2004) on education reform in Latin America also demonstrates the importance of politics and process issues in public sector reform and reinforces the need for political economy approaches to reform. She argues that it matters how policy changes are introduced, approved and implemented and how reformers manage these processes as they evolve over time. Using a political economy approach, she demonstrates how the process of reform affects the chances for successful outcomes. She identifies a number of process issues that significantly affected the outcome of reform initiatives in some Latin American countries. These include:

- *Finding the reasons for reform*, i.e. a 'burning platform' for change: This involves accumulating evidence about the severity of a problem and communicating the vision and need for change, including the potential benefits of change.
- *Leadership for change*: In all the cases she found that 'reform-mongering' by key politicians such as presidents and ministers was important in increasing the salience of education as a policy issue. Where reforms were relatively successful, leaders sought to control the timing of reform initiatives and sometimes used their powers of appointment to bolster the capacity to lead policy change and to stay ahead of the game in relation to reform opponents.
- *Designing policy and building alliances for change*: It was evident from the cases of Bolivia, Ecuador and Mexico that the composition of the design teams, as well as their ability to work effectively as a team, their credibility, their interactions with political and bureaucratic hierarchies and their ability to enlist the support of domestic and international supporters were all critical to the acceptance and pursuit of reform.

Thus successful reforms require, *inter alia*, not only understanding the political context, but also managing the processes of designing, introducing and implementing reforms with local ownership and leadership.

Changing approaches to PSR?

In recognition of the importance of politics and other institutional factors in reforms, some external donors (e.g. the UK Department for International Development and the World Bank) are adopting political economy approaches to reforms (see World Bank 2004a, b). An example of this approach is 'Drivers of Change' (DoC), which seeks to understand the processes of economic, social and political change that impact on development outcomes and link them to an agenda for action. Among other things, it encourages an understanding of how different political systems and institutions change and acknowledges the need to adopt long-term perspectives for reform interventions and support in developing countries (Duncan, 2003). DoC analysis suggests that the feasibility of structural changes in developing countries is often weaker than perceived. Moreover, power tends to depend heavily on patronage systems, which limit the freedom of political leaders to engage in structural reforms.

In the past the World Bank and donors supporting reforms in developing countries paid little attention to political dynamics in the design of reforms. However, more recently the Bank has argued that successful public sector reforms require understanding and addressing political realities as reforms pose both political and technical challenges. Reforms 'may be relatively easy to achieve technically, but very tough to implement politically' (World Bank, 2004a). Thus there is a shift (in principle) from technocratic to political economy approaches to public sector reform. It is too early to assess the extent to which the Bank and donor agencies will actually embed the new political economy approaches in the design and implementation of interventions in developing countries in practice.

Public sector reform and improvement in service delivery

Ultimately, public sector reforms should deliver improvement in public services. However, service delivery improvement has only recently been a major focus of public sector reform programmes in most developing countries and the evidence of improvement in service delivery is rather elusive. It is difficult to make a direct link between reform and improvement in service delivery. Evaluation of some of the early reform programmes (e.g. Ghana and Tanzania) shows that reforms have not succeeded in improving service delivery, though there has been marginal improvement in the capacity of the civil service (Kiragu, 2002; Adei and Boachie-Danquah, 2003).

Having said this, there are some promising examples of success in improving service delivery. To illustrate, Tanzania's 'quick wins' service improvement programme resulted in significant reduction in the time it takes to process passports, work permits, licences, land titles and other services. A similar re-engineering exercise in the judiciary sector has speeded up access to courts in Uganda; the number of cases disposed of tripled in the first year of the project (Kiragu, 2002). The 'quick wins' approach to reform was borne out of the experience that there was little political and public support for reforms because there were no clear benefits in terms of tangible improvements in public service delivery (Rugumyamheto, 2004) despite the cost and pain of earlier phases of reform.

There also have been improved funding and access to basic education and health in the past decade in a number of African countries (e.g. Kenya, Tanzania and Uganda) partly due to the removal of user fees. Nickson (this volume) also cites the cases of tax authorities in Peru and Brazil in the 1990s as examples where performance improved. In the case of Brazil's SRT (Secretaria da Receita Federal), innovations in the use of the internet for tax declaration reduced the average processing time from 4.5 months to 45 days and at the same time improved efficiency by halving the unit cost of processing tax forms. In Zambia, the restructuring of the Ministry of Works and Supply in the mid-1990s to allow for the participation of the private sector resulted in improvement in road surface and drainage from 20 per cent in 1995 to 40 per cent by the year 2000. The improved road condition has facilitated trade and commerce within and among provinces (Kiragu, 2002).

Initiatives to make public services more accountable and responsive to users by introducing service charters, user surveys, client complaints mechanisms and other opportunities to increase user voice are underway in several countries (e.g. Uganda, Tanzania, Ghana). Although the impact may be too early to judge, evidence from elsewhere suggests that these initiatives can yield good results if properly designed and implemented. These include the use of report cards in Bangalore (see Ravinda, 2004) and in the Philippines.

Despite some successes, there is a need to strengthen linkage between public sector reforms and improvement in service delivery, for example by strengthening the link with sector-wide approaches. Kiragu (2002) points out that the major gains in delivery of primary health care in Uganda from the mid-1990s, for example, is attributed to an effective sector-wide approach to sector development. Reforms need to target sectors and organizations that have the potential to improve service delivery, especially to the poor.

Public sector reforms and capacity

The contributors to this volume have all raised the issue of capacity as a significant issue in public sector reforms (see especially Batley and Larbi, this volume). The limited results of reforms, relative to the comprehensive nature of their design, raise questions about capacity, especially the capacity to implement reforms. For example, performance management initiatives in a number of countries have been hampered by weak information management systems, the unpredictability of resources and the absence of other preconditions for effective implementation. Capacity building is therefore a key issue that requires significant attention in public sector reforms. Pre-reform diagnostic measures can help to test for readiness of organizations and systems for reforms and point to possible capacity weaknesses to be addressed earlier in reforms or as part of reforms. There may be a need to sequence and phase in reforms to meet existing capacity for implementation or to reduce reform ambitions. Given the weak capacities, the approach to reforming public sector may be to take small incremental steps, starting with the reform of basic incentives that strengthen accountability and improve performance (World Bank, 2003). As administrative capacity develops and 'incentives become better aligned and internalized, more advanced reforms can be introduced to support deeper institutional change and scaling up' (ibid.). However, technical capacity needs to be complemented by the political capacity to implement reform.

Linked to capacity is the issue of a competent state. Critiques of the state in the 1980s as large, over-bloated, centralized and inefficient now acknowledge that the state has important roles to play, especially with the current global concerns with poverty reduction and realizing the Millennium Development Goals (MDGs). But the state must continue to reform and redefine its role whilst building the institutional capacity of government to manage reforms that deliver benefits to citizens and provide enabling environment for non-state actors (Rondinelli and Cheema, 2003).

Developing and maintaining a constituency and momentum for change

Experience in introducing and implementing public sector reforms around the world suggests that it is crucial to get the support of key stakeholders and the public. Reform champions and advisers can encourage and support coalitions around common issues of interest to key stakeholders in reforms and use the momentum generated to initiate change (Larbi and Sandy, 2004). Batley and Larbi (2004: 223) note that in Sri Lanka and Ghana earlier liberalization and privatization of state enterprises and deregulation of industries in the 1980s and 1990s created a new set of incentives for entrepreneurs and created support for further liberalization to encourage foreign investment and employment. Similarly, in Kenya officials who had initially resisted the removal of the state monopoly in maize marketing eventually came to support it after seeing its positive effects. Again, the millers and traders who began to deal in imported maize and rice in Kenya and Sri Lanka became a constituency for further reform. 'Thus some reforms sow the seeds for further change through an emerging constituency of support' (Batley and Larbi, 2004: 224). However, building coalitions and maintaining the momentum for change will require reformers to understand political constraints and opportunities (Grindle, 2004). Building such coalitions for reforms may be slow and more difficult in some contexts than others, especially where authority is more diffused, as was the first post-apartheid government in South Africa in the mid-1990s, and in Sri Lanka where coalition governments were in power and included trade unions.

Unlike the earlier 'stroke-of-the-pen', first-generation reforms in the late 1980s and early 1990s, the more recent reforms in public services present more difficult reform tasks as they embody more institutional elements, which require changing or redefining the rules of the game. 'They have less clear-cut goals, offer uncertain benefits, involve multiple actors, challenge existing provider groups, and require long-term commitment on the part of government and donors' (Batley and Larbi, 2004: 224). All these mean that one has to be better informed about the social, political and institutional context of reforms in order to design and implement more realistic reforms.

Conclusion

Public sector reform is a recurrent agenda in developing countries and will continue to preoccupy governments and their international development partners. Although most developing countries have had substantial reform initiatives, the actual implementation and outputs have been limited. In particular, the impact on improving service delivery has been generally elusive, though there are isolated examples of success in some countries and sectors.

The NPM model is an influential factor in determining the content and nature of reform efforts in developing countries. Its applicability to developing countries remains a subject of discussion and debate, but its potential should not be underestimated as the preconditions for application of some of its elements improves. However, non-NPM reforms such as devolution, fiscal decentralization, and pay and employment reform will also remain significant for improving governance in the public sector. NPM and non-NPM reforms need to complement and not contradict each other.

Overall, the reform experiences so far provide a number of useful lessons, including the importance of local context and conditions, the need to take account of politics in the design and implementation of reform, and building momentum and consensus for reforms. A key issue that will preoccupy governments in the next decade will be improvement in service delivery, especially basic services for the poor. Making public sector reform deliver improvement in service delivery will be the challenge ahead as the year 2015, the target date for the realization of the Millennium Development Goals, approaches.

References

Adei, S. and Y. Boachie-Danquah (2003) 'The Civil Service Performance Improvement Programme (CSPIP) in Ghana: Lessons of Experience', *African Journal of Public Administration Management*, Vol. XIV, Nos. 1 and 2: 10–23.

Batley, R. A. and G. A. Larbi (2004) *The Changing Role of Government: The Reform of Public Services in Developing Countries*, Basingstoke: Palgrave Macmillan.

Batley, R. A. (1999) 'The New Public Management in Developing Countries: Implications for Policy and Organizational Reform', *Journal of International Development*, Vol. 11: 761–5.

Boyne, G. A., C. Farrel, J. Law, M. Powell and M. R. Walker (2003) *Evaluating Public Management Reforms*, Buckingham: Open University Press.

Christensen, T. and P. Lægreid (2002) 'Introduction', in T. Christensen, and P. Lægreid (eds.), *New Public Management: the Transformation of Ideas and Practice*, Aldershot: Ashgate.

Duncan, A. (2003) 'Drivers of Change: Reflections on Experience to Date', *Discussion Note*, Oxford Policy Management.

Grindle, M. S. (2004) *Despite the Odds: Contentious Politics and Education Reform*, Princeton, NJ: Princeton University Press.

Kiragu, K. (2002) 'Improving Service Delivery through Public Service Reform: Lessons of Experience from Selected Sub-Saharan African Countries', Discussion paper presented at the Second Meeting of the DAC Network on Good Governance and Capacity Development, Paris: OECD Headquarters, 14–15 February.

Larbi, G. A. and Sandy, J. (2004) *Public Sector Reform and Service Delivery*, Paper prepared for the Policy Division, Department for International Department (DFID), London.

Manning, N. (2001) 'The Legacy of New Public Management in Developing Countries', *International Review of Administrative Sciences*, Vol. 62, No. 2: 297–312.

Pollitt, C. (2002) 'New Public Management in International Perspective: An Analysis of Impacts and Effects', in K. McLauglin, P. Osborne and E. Ferlie, *New Public Management: Current Trends and Future Prospects*, London: Routledge, pp. 274–92.

Ravinda, A. (2004) '*Citizen Report Cards on the Performance of Agencies*', *ECD Working Paper Series 12*, Washington DC: World Bank.

Rhodes, R. A. W., J. M. Carmichael, and A. Massey (2003) *Decentralizing the Civil Service: From Unitary State to Differentiated Polity in the United Kingdom*, Buckingham, Open University Press.

Ridley, F. (1996) 'The New Public Management in Europe: Comparative Perspectives', *Public Policy and Administration*, Vol. 11, No. 1: 16–29.

Rondinelli, D. A. and S. Cheema (2003) *Reinventing Government for the 21st Century: State Capacity in the Globalizing Society*, Bloomfield, CT: Kumarian Press.

Rugumyamheto, J. A. (2004) 'Innovative Approaches to Reforming Public Services in Tanzania', *Public Administration and Development*, Vol. 24, No. 5: 437–446.

Schick, A. (1998) 'Why Developing Countries Should not Try the New Zealand Reforms', *World Bank Research Observer*, Vol. 13, No. 1: 123–31.

World Bank (1999) 'Rethinking Civil Service Reform, *PREM Notes* (Public Sector), No. 31 (October).

World Bank (2003) *World Development Report 2004: Making Services Work for the Poor*, Oxford: Oxford University Press.

World Bank (2004a) 'Public Sector Governance Reform Cycle: Available Diagnostic Tools', *PREM Notes* (Public Sector), No. 88 (July).

World Bank (2004b) 'Operationalising Political Analysis: The Expected Utility Stakeholder Model and Governance Reforms', *PREM Notes* (Public Sector), No. 95 (November).

Index